VIETNAM

A VISUAL ENCYCLOPEDIA

VIETNAM

A VISUAL ENCYCLOPEDIA

PHILIP GUTZMAN

PRC

PREFACE

First published 2002 by
PRC Publishing Ltd,
64 Brewery Road, London N7 9NT

A member of **Chrysalis** Books plc

This edition published 2002
Distributed in the U.S. and Canada by:
Sterling Publishing Co., Inc.
387 Park Avenue South
New York, NY 10016

ISBN 1 85648 639-7

Printed and bound in China

Picture credits for the Cover

Military Archive and Research Services
for the pictures on the front and back
covers.

The war in Vietnam was America's longest and most divisive. Politically it was never fully explained to the American people in terms they could understand, and the goals established for it were neither fully developed nor clearly articulated. This book provides the reader with an A-Z reference of many of the common topics, key people and events of the time. It is a comprehensive source answering many questions on one of the most controversial conflicts of all time.

While America's involvement in Vietnam had begun in World War II, and expanded in the late 1950s, President John F Kennedy took the initial decisions that placed American combat forces in the war. Following his assassination, under the Johnson administration it escalated into a full blown war. In many ways it was treated as a political distraction that diverted attention from the Great Society programs that were the real goal of the Johnson administration, and many came to believe that America had blundered into the war serendipitously. Others believe that it was nearly inevitable that America would get involved.

At the end of World War II communist ideology was expanding throughout the world and there was no one nation with the power to oppose it except the United States. The other major industrial nations of the West had been devastated by that war and were either in the process of rebuilding or fully engaged elsewhere. Attempts were made to try to "contain" communism through the creation of a series of treaties with nations on the communist states peripheries. NATO was created in Europe, CENTO in the Middle East, and SEATO in Southeast Asia, but these essentially failed.

In 1945 Poland, Hungary, Latvia, Lithuania, Estonia, Romania, and Bulgaria became communist. East Prussia disappeared forever from the maps of the world, and both Korea and Germany were divided between communism and democracy. Russia was attempting to occupy northern Iran, and in Vietnam the French had returned to reclaim a colonial outpost and were opposed by a broad nationalist coalition. This broad based coalition of nationalists, however, was rapidly subverted and communized by Ho Chi Minh and the Viet Minh.

In 1948/49 Czechoslovakia voted itself communist, and Mao Tse Tung succeeded in forcing the Kuomintang out of China and converted it to a communist state. The Hukbalapap communist insurgency was expanding in the Philippines, Tito forcibly combined Slovakia, Bosnia, Montenegro, Croatia and Serbia into a communist Yugoslavia, and Greece was engaged in a guerrilla war with communist insurgents on its northern border.

In the 1950s, France began to falter in Vietnam and withdrew, forcing a division at the 17th parallel, only to become bogged down in a guerrilla war in Algeria. Britain was trying to withdraw from east of the Suez, and was engaged with communist terrorists in Malaya. The communist Chinese routinely shelled the Nationalist Chinese islands of Quemoy and Matsu, and communist and Nationalist Chinese fighter planes frequently fought each other over the straits of Taiwan. The Hukbalapaps threatened Manila, communists were on the rise in Indonesia, and the North Koreans invaded South Korea. Russia crushed democratic uprisings in Hungary and East Germany, one state of newly emergent India voted itself communist, and Castro communized Cuba. In Laos, the Pathet Lao initiated a communist guerrilla war against the Royal Government, and the Viet Cong became active in South Vietnam. The Russian Premier announced to the world that the Soviet Union would support "wars of national liberation" wherever they occurred and the Russians began to airlift arms and ammunition into Lao.

As the 1960s opened, China invaded northern India and, as American decision makers looked at the world and the numbers of formerly free nations that had become communist states, it became clear to them that the communist expansion had to be opposed somewhere. It had also been proven repeatedly that the communists considered diplomacy simply as a tool to shield their actions until too late. They first looked at intervention in Laos, but the nature of the terrain and the lack of transport access made that an undesirable choice, though they did send a limited number of Special Forces there to see how the emerging doctrine of counterinsurgency might really be employed.

The Bay of Pigs fiasco in Cuba convinced President Kennedy and his advisors that only US military power would work, and they chose Vietnam as the locale to attempt to curb communist expansion. The first step for President Kennedy was to dispatch Air Force and Army combat units to Vietnam, as well as fighter and bomber squadrons under the Farmgate Program, helicopters with their associated gunners to provide mobility to the ARVN, and the Special Forces units to activate the CIDG among the Montagnards and train the South Vietnamese. President Johnson, fearful that his administration would be accused of "losing Vietnam" to communism added conventional combat battalions with the deployment of the Marines.

Simultaneously attempts were made to expand the number of nations that were contributing to the anticommunist crusade in South Vietnam, and a number of nations, notably Australia, New Zealand, South Korea, Thailand, and the Philippines sent troops.

The American military that existed at the outset of the Vietnam War was ill-prepared to undertake the kind of a conflict that the North Vietnamese had unleashed in the south. The senior leadership looked to the things that had contributed to their success in World War II and failed to grasp the essentials of this new battlefield until it was far too late. A first result of this lack of understanding was the almost immediate push to supplant the Vietnamese as the primary combatants in the field and relegate them to a

secondary role. General Westmoreland continually looked for the big set-piece battle where he could crush the North Vietnamese military, the "bomber generals" of the Air Force continually pressed for authority to unleash an unrestricted assault against North Vietnam, and almost the entire hierarchy pressed at one time or another for an invasion of the north.

At the same time, the US did not unify the command in Vietnam and headquarters as far away as Honolulu were in charge of many of the activities in-country. With the addition of the B-52 bomber to the war, even the Strategic Air Command in Omaha, Nebraska had a say in combat operations. On top of this, the Secretary of Defense and the President, distrustful of the senior military leadership, retained tactical control of many of the decisions, even minor ones, in Washington DC.

The American units were heavily dependent on mechanized support and, though very powerful in any engagement, had no real training in counterinsurgency or counter-guerrilla operations. Even though the new Air Assault Division appeared to hold some promise, the traditional military opposed its assignment to Vietnam, jockeying instead for the deployment of their former or favored organizations instead. Internally, the various military forces fought each other for both control of operations and budgetary authority to expand their roles.

In a similar fashion, the US State Department was convinced that any large-scale commitment of American power would trigger a communist Chinese intervention and result in a massive land war in Asia . Even when it became clear that such a turn of events was extremely unlikely, they insisted that they could negotiate a settlement of the conflict, and frequently pointed to the agreement on the neutralization of Laos as a model.

Against this, the North Vietnamese waged a total war for the unification of the two halves of Vietnam under their aegis. Building from their study of how Mao Tse Tung had succeeded in China, and their own success against the French, they mobilized their entire population to fight and began the task of creating a similar fervor in the rural areas of South

Vietnam. Simultaneously they promoted themselves as oppressed nationalists struggling to be free from the Americans and antiwar movements grew in both Europe and America.

Internally at war with itself over the effort in Vietnam, America fought on, looking for some way to extricate its forces without simply surrendering, and eventually hit on the idea of "Vietnamization," where combat responsibility would be transferred to the ARVN and the US would provide backup firepower and air support only. This process was carried out, and eventually accelerated. Unfortunately, however, the ARVN did not have the indepth logistical support organizations, air mobility assets, and the overwhelming firepower that American units had.

As Vietnamization progressed the North Vietnamese planned and organized to take advantage of the withdrawal of American power and unleashed the Easter Offensive in 1972, a major conventional attack on South Vietnam. Unfortunately, they had underestimated the extent and fury of the American reaction and their units were savagely mauled by American air and naval forces and the South Vietnamese turned out to be a much more tenacious opponent than they had anticipated. However, they did succeed in occupying a significant amount of outlying territory along the borders.

The last American combat unit departed Vietnam in August 1972, and the last unit, other than the Marine Corps Embassy Guard Detachment, was gone by April 1973. During this period of final disengagement, the Watergate Scandal forced President Nixon from office, and the new Ford administration was determined to put the war behind them. At the same time, Congress drastically cut back the amount of aid available to South Vietnam and limited the President's authority to employ forces.

Two years later, when America did not react to a series of offensive operations in early 1975, the North Vietnamese again launched an all-out attack on the south, throwing 24 divisions into the fray and, due in part to inept military leadership on the part of the South Vietnamese, within a matter of weeks Saigon fell.

GLOSSARY

AAA Anti-Aircraft Artillery
AATTV Australian Army Training Team—Vietnam
ACAV Armored Cavalry Assault Vehicle
ACTOV Accelerated Turnover to Vietnam
AFCV Association of Foreign Correspondents in Vietnam
AFL—CIO American Federation of Labor—Congress of Industrial Organizations
ANZAC Australia—New Zealand Army Corps
AID Agency for International Development
AO Area of Operations
ARA Aerial Rocket Artillery
ARVN Army of the Republic of Vietnam
AFCV Association of Foreign Correspondents in Vietnam
AWOL Absent Without Official Leave
CALCAV Clergy and Laymen Concerned About Vietnam
CAP Combined Action Program
CAS Continental Air Services
CBU Cluster Bomb Unit
CBS Columbia Broadcasting System
CCC Command and Control, Central
CCN Command and Control, North
CCS Command and Control, South
CHECO Contemporary Historical Evaluation of Combat Operations
CIA Central Intelligence Agency
CIDG Civilian Irregular Defense Group
CINCPAC Commander-In-Chief Pacific
CLC Central Logistics Command
CMH Congressional Medal of Honor
CO Conscientious Objector; Commanding Officer
CORDS Civil Operations and Revolutionary Development Support
COSVN Central Office for South Vietnam
COWIN Conduct of the War in Vietnam
DEROS Date of Estimated Return from Overseas
DHLF Dega Highlands Liberation Front
DMZ Demilitarized Zone
DRV Democratic Republic of Vietnam
EDS Electronic Data Systems
ELINT Electronic Intelligence
EW Electronic Warfare
FAC Forward Air Controller
FANK Forces Armees National Khmer
FBI Federal Bureau of Investigation
FOR Fellowship of Reconciliation
FSB Fire Support Base
FULRO Le Front Unifie de Lutte des Races Opprimees (The United Front for the Liberation of Oppressed Races)
FWA Free World Assistance Program
H & I Harassment and Interdiction
HAWK Homing All the Way Killer
HE High Explosive
HEAT High Explosive Anti-Tank
HES Hamlet Evaluation System
HNC High National Council
I&I Intoxication and Intercourse

ICC International Control Commission
ICCS International Commission for Control and Supervision
ICEX Intelligence Coordination and Exploitation
ICP Indo-Chinese Communist Party
ICSC International Commission for Supervision and Control
IRC International Rescue Committee
JCS Joint Chiefs of Staff
JGS Joint General Staff
JPRC Joint Personnel Recovery Center
JUSPAO Joint United States Public Affairs Office
KIA Killed in Action
L&L Liquor and Lovin'
LAW Light Antitank Weapon
LBJ Long Binh Jail; Lyndon Baines Johnson
LCM Landing Craft, Mechanized
LLDB Luc Luong Dac Biet (Vietnamese Special Forces)
LOH Light Observation Helicopter
LRRP Long Range Reconnaissance Patrol
LVTH-6 Landing Vehicle, Tracked, Howitzer,—Model 6
LST Landing Ship, Tank
LVTP-5 Landing Vehicle, Tracked, Personnel, - Model 5
LZ Landing Zone
MAAG—V Military Assistance Advisory Group—Vietnam
MAC Military Airlift Command
MACV Military Assistance Command
MAF Marine Amphibious Force
MEB Marine Expeditionary Brigade
MEDCAP Medical Civic Action Program
MGF Mobile Guerrilla Force
MIA Missing in Action
MOS Military Occupational Specialty
MR Military Region
MEB Marine Expeditionary Brigade
MRB Mobile River Base
MRC Military Revolutionary Council
MRF Mobile Riverine Force
MSC Military Sealift Command
MSTS Military Sea Transport Service
MSU Michigan State University
NCC National Coordinating Committee (To End The War In Vietnam)
NCNRC National Council of National Reconciliation and Concord
NCO Non-Commissioned Officer
NFLSV National Front for the Liberation of South Vietnam
NSA National Security Agency
NSC National Security Council
NVA North Vietnamese Army
OSS Office of Strategic Services
PACV Patrol Air Cushion Vehicle
PARU Police Aerial Reinforcement Unit
PAVN People's Army of Vietnam
PBR Patrol Boat, River
PEO Programs Evaluation Office
PF Popular Forces

PIRAZ Positive Identification and Radar Advisory Zone
PLAF People's Liberation Armed Forces
PSDF People's Self Defense Force
POW Prisoner of War
PRC People's Republic of China
PRG People's Revolutionary Government
PRU Provincial Reconnaissance Unit
PSDF People's Self Defense Force
PSYOPS Psychological Operations
PTSD Post-Traumatic Stress Disorder
R&R Rest & Rehabilitation
RAND Research and Development (Corporation)
RF Regional Forces
RF/PF Regional Forces/Popular Forces
RIO Radar Intercept Officer
RHAWS Radar Homing and Warning System
ROE Rules of Engagement
RP Route Package
RPG Rocket Propelled Grenade
RRU Radio Research unit
RVN Republic of Viet Nam
RVNAF Republic of Viet Nam Air Force; Republic of Vietnam Armed Forces
RWT Road Watch Team
SAC Strategic Air Command
SAM Surface to Air Missile
SAR Search and Rescue
SDS Students for a Democratic Society
SEALORDS Southeast Asia Lake, Ocean, River, Delta Strategy
SEATO Southeast Asia Treaty Organization
SEAL Sea, Air, Land
SLAM Search, Locate, Annihilate, Monitor
SLF Special Landing Force
SMM Saigon Military Mission
SOG Studies and Observations Group
SPAT Self-Propelled Anti-Tank
SRAO Supplemental Recreation Activities Overseas
TAOR Tactical Area of Responsibility
TOW Tube-Launched, Optically-tracked, Wire-guided (Missile)
USARV United States Army - Vietnam
USIA United States Information Agency
USO Uniformed Services Organization
USSR Union of Soviet Socialist Republics
VC Viet Cong
VCI Viet Cong Infrastructure
VNA Vietnam National Army
VNAF Vietnamese Air Force
VNMC Vietnamese Marine Corps
VNN Vietnamese navy
VVAW Vietnam Veterans Against the War
WAC Women's Army Corps
WAF Women in the Air Force
WAPM Wide Area Anti-Personnel Munition
WAVES Women Accepted for Voluntary Emergency Service
WP White Phosphorous
WSAG Washington Special Action Groups

CHRONOLOGY

VIETNAM: A VISUAL ENCYCLOPEDIA

1954

[Text highlighted in bold is explained in more detail in later sections of the book.]

25 January–18 February	The foreign ministers of the "big four"—the United States, **Britain**, **France**, and the **USSR**—meet in Berlin. They agree to hold a conference on **Korea** and Indochina in **Geneva** in April.
13 March	**Vo Nguyen Giap** launches an assault on Dien Bien Phu.
20 March	Admiral Radford, Chairman of the **Joint Chiefs of Staff**, recommends a nuclear strike to aid the French at Dien Bien Phu. Settles for one massive air strike.
25 March	**National Security Council** approves the Radford Plan. The US tentatively decides to fight in Indochina.
7 April	**President Eisenhower** advances the **Domino Theory** at a news conference.
24 April	Radford and Dulles meet with British Foreign Secretary **Anthony Eden** to solicit British support in Indochina. **Eden** takes the proposal to the Prime Minister.
25 April	Prime Minister Winston Churchill rejects the US plan.
26 April	The Far Eastern Conference opens in **Geneva**. **Giap**, convinced he can win a significant political as well as military victory, tightens the siege at Dien Bien Phu.
7 May	Dien Bien Phu falls to the **Viet Minh**.
8 May	The nine delegations assemble in **Geneva** to negotiate the end of the war in Indochina as part of a larger settlement in the region.
1 June	Colonel Edward Lansdale arrives in **Saigon** as head of the **Saigon Military Mission (SMM)** and begins setting up paramilitary and psychological operations in opposition to the **Viet Minh**.
16 June	China's **Chou En-Lai (Zhou Enlai)** becomes the head negotiator for the communists; suggests that the communists withdraw from **Laos** and **Cambodia**. Along with the **USSR**'s Molotov, he pressures the **Viet Minh** to accept a partition of **Vietnam**. Vietnamese later claim they were sold out by the Russians and Chinese.
18 June	**Bao Dai** appoints **Ngo Dinh Diem** Prime Minister of the State of **Vietnam**.
20–21 July	An "Agreement on the Cessation of Hostilities in Viet Nam" is signed by General Ta Quang Buu for the **Viet Minh** and General Henri Delteil for **France**. A second agreement, the "Final Declaration of the Geneva Conference" is prepared, but never signed. It states that: (1) **Vietnam** is provisionally partitioned at the 17th parallel into North and South **Vietnam**, pending reunification through nationwide **elections**; (2) for a period of 300 days all persons may pass freely from one zone to the other; (3) limits are imposed on foreign military bases North and South, on personnel movements, and rearmament; (4) nationwide **elections** are scheduled for July 20, 1956; (5) an International Control Commission made up of representatives of India, **Canada,** and **Poland** is established to supervise the implementation of the agreements. The US rejects the final declaration and does not support it. **Bao Dai**'s government of the State of Vietnam denounces all agreements.
August	Armistice is declared. **Vietnam** is partitioned at the 17th parallel. **Laos** and **Cambodia** are granted full independence from **France**. Almost 1,000,000 **refugees**, the bulk of them **catholics** led by priests, stream into South **Vietnam**.
8 September	The Manila Treaty, which establishes the **South East Asia Treaty Organization (SEATO)**, is signed by the United States, **Britain**, **France**, **Australia**, **New Zealand**, the **Philippines**, **Thailand**, and Pakistan. A separate protocol designates **Laos**, **Cambodia**, and "the free territory under the jurisdiction of the State of **Vietnam** [South Vietnam]" as territories subject to the provisions of the treaty. It later serves as the justification for US support of anticommunist regimes in Southeast Asia.
19 September	The Chief of Staff, General Hinh, the leader of the **Binh Xuyen**, and the leaders of the **Cao Dai** and **Hoa Hao** religious sects organize a coup against **Diem**.

20–24 September	The Cabinet resigns. Colonel Edward Lansdale buys off the religious sects. **Diem** forms a coalition government with the **Cao Dai** and **Hoa Hao**.
11 October	The French leave **Hanoi** and **Ho Chi Minh** takes over.
13 October	The Vietnamese Marine Corps is formed.
24 October	**President Eisenhower** sends a letter to **Diem** offering US support and military aid. **President Johnson** later cites this letter as the beginning of the US commitment to South **Vietnam**.
November	**President Eisenhower** sends **General J Lawton Collins** to **Saigon** and gives him the rank of Ambassador.
December	**Hanoi** signs an aid agreement with the **People's Republic of China**.

1955

January	**US Military Assistance Advisory Group—Indochina (MAAG)** ordered to assist the South Vietnamese in training their army.
3 February	**Diem** implements a **land reform** program. Net result is that land previously distributed to the peasants by the **Viet Minh** is returned to the original landlords. Communists capitalize on peasant unrest, particularly in the **Mekong Delta**.
28 March	**Diem** attacks **Binh Xuyen** in **Saigon**. **Cao Dai** and **Hoa Hao** forces support the **Binh Xuyen**.
April	**Diem**'s troops clear the **Binh Xuyen** and religious sect forces from **Saigon**, they retreat to the Delta.
June	**Diem** crushes the remaining **Binh Xuyen**. **Cao Dai** and **Hoa Hao** forces near the Cambodian border are overrun and the sects sue for peace.
July	**Diem** declares that South **Vietnam** is not bound by the **Geneva Agreements** because they were never signed. **Britain**, **France**, and the United States urge him to respect the agreements.
10 August	**Diem** declares that, since South **Vietnam** devolved from the State of **Vietnam**, which existed prior to the **Geneva Accords** of 1954, it is "the only legal state" and rejects talks with North **Vietnam** on reunification.
18 October	**Bao Dai** attempts to dismiss **Diem**, but **Diem** intercepts the decree and it is never disseminated.
23 October	**Diem** holds a referendum between himself and **Bao Dai**. He receives over 98 percent of the vote. Opponents charge that the election was rigged; the **CIA**'s Edward Lansdale plays a prominent part.
26 October	**Diem** announces the creation of the Republic of **Vietnam** with himself as the President, Prime Minister, Defense Minister, and Supreme Commander of the Armed Forces. The United States, **France**, **Britain**, **Australia**, **New Zealand**, Italy, **Thailand**, South **Korea** and **Japan** immediately recognize it.
12 December	The United States closes its consulate in **Hanoi**.
19 December	The US Senate formally ratifies the **SEATO** Treaty with its protocol concerning **Laos**, **Cambodia**, and **Vietnam**.

1956

11 January	**Diem** promulgates Ordnance No. 6, which allows the internment of people "considered as dangerous to national defense and common security." He uses it to round up former **Viet Minh**, and by the end of the year dismembers nearly 90 percent of the communist cells in the south.
20 July	The date for **elections** under the **Geneva Accords** is ignored. The remaining **Viet Minh** initiate a scattered low-grade insurgency.
8 November	**Hanoi** formally abolishes the Peoples Agricultural Reform Tribunals. It is estimated that between 10,000–15,000 landowners were killed and between 50,000–100,000 imprisoned or deported under the program.
11–20 November	The 325th Division is used to suppress a revolt against Hanoi's **land reform** program in **Ho Chi Minh**'s native Nghe An province. Approximately 1,000 peasants die as a result.

1957

3 January	The International Control Commission reports that neither North nor South **Vietnam** is complying with the **Geneva Agreements**.
8 May	**President Eisenhower**, during **Ngo Dinh Diem's** visit to the United States, hails the South Vietnamese President as the "Miracle Man of Asia" and pledges to support his regime.
24 June	A US Army **Special Forces** team begins training South Vietnamese Commandos at **Nha Trang**.
22 October	Thirteen Americans are wounded when the communists bomb three American installations in **Saigon**
31 October	The communists organize 37 main force combat companies in the **Mekong Delta**.

1958

7 March	**Pham Van Dong** sends a letter to **Ngo Dinh Diem** recommending that North and South Vietnamese delegations meet.
26 April	**Diem** rejects **Pham Van Dong's** offer, calling it a propaganda ploy.
December	The **CIA** intercepts a directive from **Hanoi** to its Headquarters for the **central highlands** stating that the Party Central Committee has decided to "open a new stage of the struggle" and launch an overt insurgency in South **Vietnam**.

1959

January	The **CIA** intercepts an order from **Hanoi** directing the establishment of two guerrilla operational bases, one in the western **central highlands** and one in Tay Ninh province astride the Cambodian border.
April	The **Transportation Group 559** is formed under the Lao Dong Central Committee. It is to open and improve a route, and oversee all land infiltration into the south.
May	**US Army** advisors are assigned down to the regimental level in the South Vietnamese armed forces.
May	At the 15th Plenum of the Central Committee, **Hanoi** decides to take direct control of the insurgency in the south, and to begin large-scale infiltration.
June	4,000 **NVA** troops are sent to the south.
July	Group 579 is organized by **Hanoi** to oversee seaborne infiltration.
8 July	Major Dale Buis and Master Sergeant Chester Ovnand are killed in a communist raid on **Bien Hoa**, becoming the first American casualties of the war.
24 July	Twelve US Army **Special Forces** training teams and a control team of 11 men arrive in Laos under **Project Hotfoot**.
30 August	General **elections** in South **Vietnam** result in an overwhelming victory for the government. Only government supporters are permitted to take part.

1960

17 January	A popular uprising against the **Agroville** Program in **Ben Tre** is taken over by the communists and an **Army of the Republic of Vietnam (ARVN)** counterattack is beaten off.
26 January	In the first large scale insurgent military operation of the war, 200 guerrillas overrun an **ARVN** Regimental Headquarters at **Trang Sup** in Tay Ninh province, capturing a large amount of weapons and ammunition.
9 August	Paratroop Captain **Kong Le** seizes control of Laos.
5 September	The 3rd Congress of the **Lao Dong Party** addresses the need to overthrow the **Diem** regime militarily.
8 November	**John F Kennedy** is elected President of the United States.
11–12 November	Paratroop battalions and a Marine unit surround the Presidential Palace and demand that **Diem** institute reforms. He stalls until loyal forces put down the revolt.
4 December	**Ambassador Elbridge Durbrow** tells Washington that it may be necessary to consider alternatives to **Diem**. The **USSR** begins airlifting weapons and equipment to the **Pathet Lao** in Laos.
16 December	**General Phoumi Nosavan**, with US **CIA** and Thai support, recaptures **Vientiane**

	20 December	from **Kong Le**, who retreats to the **Plain of Jars**. **Hanoi** announces the formation of the **National Liberation Front of South Vietnam**. **Diem** derisively refers to them as the **Viet Cong**, a pejorative term for Vietnamese communists.
1961	6 January	Premier Nikita Khrushchev declares that the **USSR** will back all "wars of national liberation" wherever they occur around the globe. This concerns **Kennedy**.
	13 January	The **CIA** begins to recruit and arm the **Hmong** in **Laos** under **Project Momentum**.
	15 January	The **North Vietnamese Army (NVA)** 925th Independent Battalion joins the **Pathet Lao** fighting on the **Plain of Jars**. **NVA** Senior General **Chu Huy Man** is assigned as the liaison to the **Pathet Lao** and arrives at the headquarters in Khang Khay on the **Plain of Jars**.
	9 March	**President Kennedy** authorizes **Operation Mill Pond**, the use of **B-26 bombers** against the **Pathet Lao** on the **Plain of Jars**.
	23 March	**Pathet Lao**/North Vietnamese antiaircraft guns shoot down an SC-47 enroute from **Vientiane** to **Saigon** over the **Plain of Jars** in Laos.
	1 April	Two major **Viet Cong** attacks, in Kien Hoa province and at Ben Cat north of **Saigon**, are repulsed by **Army of the Republic of Vietnam (ARVN)** troops. The **Viet Cong** lose over 100 men.
	4 May	At a press conference **Secretary of State Dean Rusk** says **Viet Cong** forces number over 12,000 and the US will provide **Saigon** with "all possible help." He declines to say whether US troops will be sent to **Vietnam**.
	5 May	**President Kennedy** tells a press conference that the use of American troops "is under consideration."
	11 May	**President Kennedy** dispatches 400 **Special Forces** troops and 100 other advisors to **Vietnam**. He orders clandestine strikes against North **Vietnam**.
	16 May	A 14-nation conference on the neutralization of **Laos** convenes in **Geneva**.
	9 June	**Diem** request US assistance in expanding the **ARVN**.
	1 October	**SEATO** meets in Bangkok to discuss the escalating war in **Vietnam**. The US considers sending troops.
	11 October	US Air Force pilots and trainers deploy to **Vietnam** under **Operation Farm Gate**.
	18 October	**RF-101 Voodoo** reconnaissance jets are sent to **Saigon** and begin flying over the Delta replacing the **Lockheed RT-33A**.
	November	US **Special Forces** personnel in **II Corps** begin the development of the **Civilian Irregular Defense Group (CIDG)** Program among the **Montagnards**.
	11 December	The USS *Core*, a ferry-carrier, delivers the first US **helicopter** units to **Vietnam**.
	14 December	In a public exchange of letters, **Kennedy** and **Diem** announce the American troop build-up. **Kennedy** writes, "We will promptly increase our assistance to your defense effort."
	16 December	**Operation Farm Gate** pilots are authorized to fly combat missions if they have a Vietnamese National aboard.
1962	January	The US installs a tactical air control system in **Vietnam**.
	12 January	**Operation Ranch Hand**, the **defoliation** of broad areas of South **Vietnam**, begins.
	15 January	Asked at a Washington news conference if the US was fighting in **Vietnam**, **Kennedy** says "No."
	15 January	The People's Revolutionary Party is organized in South **Vietnam**.
	February	The first regular US ground forces, the 39th Signal Battalion, arrives in **Vietnam** and the first **Civilian Irregular Defense Group (CIDG)** camps are activated.
	4 February	The first US helicopter is shot down.
	8 February	President Kennedy authorizes the establishment of the **Military Assistance Command—Vietnam (MACV)** in **Saigon**.

11 February	The first of the **Operation Farm Gate** crew is killed when an SC-47 is lost 70 miles north of **Saigon**.
27 February	Two South Vietnamese Skyraider pilots bomb and strafe the Presidential Palace.
22 March	**Operation Sunrise** starts the program to resettle the rural peasant population into **Strategic Hamlets**.
15 April	The first Marine helicopter unit arrives in Soc Trang in the Delta as part of **Operation Shufly**.
May	The **Viet Cong** begin forming battalion size units in the **central highlands**. **Australia** dispatches advisors to **Vietnam**.
25 May	The International Control Commission charges North Vietnam with subversion and aggression and the United States with violating the **Geneva Accords** stricture against the introduction of foreign military forces.
23 July	The Declaration and Protocol on the Neutralization of **Laos** is signed.
August	**Special Forces** establishes a **Civilian Irregular Defense Group (CIDG)** Camp at **Khe Sahn** to monitor infiltration across the **Demilitarized Zone (DMZ)**.
October	The Cuban Missile Crisis plays out.
December	US troop strength approaches 11,000. There have been 109 killed or wounded.

1963

2 January	At the Battle of **Ap Bac** 300 guerrillas inflict heavy casualties on 2,500 **ARVN** and escape. Senior US officials claim it was a victory.
26 February	US helicopters and advisors are authorized to "shoot first."
17 April	**Ngo Dinh Diem** initiates the **Chieu Hoi (Open Arms) Program**.
8 May	The catholic Deputy Province Chief fires on **buddhists** celebrating Buddha's birthday in **Hue**. **Diem** refuses to take action against him and blames the **Viet Cong**.
11 June	**Thich Quang Duc** immolates himself in front of the press in **Saigon** to protest against **Diem**'s government.
4 July	**General Tran Van Don** informs the **CIA** that the generals are planning a coup.
21 August	**Special Forces** Troops loyal to **Diem**, disguised as regular soldiers, attack **buddhist** temples and sanctuaries in **Hue**, **Danang**, **Saigon** and other cities.
5 October	**Ambassador Henry Cabot Lodge** reports to **President Kennedy** that the coup against **Diem** is imminent.
1–2 November	The Generals overthrow and execute **Diem**.
19 November	**Prince Sihanouk** charges the **CIA** with attempting to remove him from power.
22 November	**President Kennedy** is assassinated.
24 November	**President Johnson** confirms the US intention to continue military and economic support to South **Vietnam**.

1964

January	**President Johnson** approves **OPLAN 34A**; covert actions against North **Vietnam** are begun.
13–15 April	At the **SEATO** meeting in **Manila** the French Foreign Minister argues for the "neutralization" of **Vietnam**, much the same as had happened in **Laos**. It is rejected.
14 April	The **Military Assistance Advisory Group—Vietnam (MAAG—V)** is absorbed into **Military Assistance Command—Vietnam (MACV)**.
20 June	**General William Westmoreland** assumes command of **MACV**.
July	**New Zealand** sends troops to **Vietnam**
2–4 August	North Vietnamese Torpedo Boats attack US Destroyers in the **Gulf of Tonkin**
5 August	US Navy aircraft from the carriers *Constellation* and *Ticonderoga* strike North **Vietnam**, two are shot down and **Lieutenant Everett Alvarez** becomes the first American **Prisoner of War**.
7 August	US Congress overwhelmingly passes the **Gulf of Tonkin Resolution**, granting **President Johnson** authority to use unlimited military force against North **Vietnam**.

	1 November	The **Viet Cong** attack the **Bien Hoa** Air Base. Five Americans die and 26 planes are destroyed as a result.
	3 November	**President Johnson** is re-elected in a landslide victory.
	December	The lead regiment of the North Vietnamese 325th Division arrives in the **Central highlands**. The other two are in transit. The character of the war changes. **Operation Barrel Roll**, the bombing of the **Ho Chi Minh Trail in Laos**, begins.

1965

	4 January	At a press conference the National Liberation Front announces a major **ARVN** defeat at the **Battle of Binh Gia**, 40 miles southeast of **Saigon**.
	11–27 January	Buddhist strikes and demonstrations disrupt all of the major cities of **Vietnam**. A buddhist nun in Nha Trang immolates herself, the first self-immolation since 1963.
	7 February	The **Viet Cong** attack the American helicopter base and barracks in Pleiku. Eight Americans die and 126 are wounded. **President Johnson** orders **Operation Flaming Dart**, which involves retaliatory air strikes against North **Vietnam**.
	8 February	US dependents are ordered out of **Vietnam**.
	26 February	Korean troops arrive in **Vietnam**.
	2 March	**Operation Rolling Thunder**, the sustained air campaign against the north, begins.
	8 March	US Marines land in **Danang**. American ground combat troops are now in **Vietnam**.
	11 March	**Operation Market Time**, naval interdiction of coastal infiltration, begins.
	24 March	The first **Teach-In** against the war is called at the University of Michigan.
	1 April	The heads of state of 17 non-aligned nations call for peace through negotiations in **Vietnam**.
	3–12 May	The 173rd Airborne Brigade, the first **US Army** combat unit, arrives in **Vietnam**.
	22 May	US intelligence confirms that the **USSR** is building antiaircraft emplacements around **Hanoi** and **Haiphong**.
	17 June	Operation **Arc Light** begins, **B-52 bombers** from Guam strike **Viet Cong** positions outside **Saigon**.
	28–30 June	The 173rd Airborne Brigade and the **ARVN** launch the first major US ground operation in **War Zone D**. There is no contact with the enemy and it is called off after three days.
	18–24 August	In the first major ground operation of the war conducted only by US forces, **Operation Starlight** reflects a change in mission to active combat operations from the defense of an **enclave**.
	October	The **Viet Cong** and **NVA** attack the Plei Me **Special Forces** Camp in **II Corps**.
	3 November	To protest against the war, Norman Morrison, a 32-year-old Quaker, immolates himself in front of the Pentagon.
	14–17 November	The **Battle of the Ia Drang** is the first engagement between US forces and the regular North Vietnamese Army. Both sides suffer heavy losses.
	18–19 December	**Montagnard** tribesmen in the **central highlands** revolt against the South Vietnamese government, demanding autonomy.

1966

	January	**President Johnson** announces his "Fourteen Points."
	24 January	**Operation Masher/White Wing**, the first major **search and destroy** operation, begins in northern Binh Dinh province.
	6–9 February	**President Johnson** and Premier Ky meet at the **Honolulu Conference**.
	9–11 March	The **NVA** overrun the A Shau **Special Forces** Camp
	21 April	Six American pacifists try to organize antiwar demonstrations in **Saigon**. The embassy intervenes to get them expelled rather than executed.
	18 August	The Battle of Long Tan, the largest Australian engagement of the war, begins.
	1 September	French President Charles DeGaulle condemns US intervention in **Vietnam** and calls for a US withdrawal.
	14 September	**Operation Attleboro** begins. The **Viet Cong** fight for their base areas.
	5 December	The destroyer USS *Ingersoll* is damaged by fire from a North Vietnamese shore battery.

	23 December	North Korean pilots are confirmed to be in North **Vietnam** training the Vietnamese to fly the **MiG-21**.
	25–26 December	**Harrison Salisbury** of *The New York Times* reports from **Hanoi** that the US is bombing civilian areas and killing innocent people. Relations between the military and the **media** worsen.
1967	2 January	**Operation Bolo** results in the largest air-to-air engagement of the war. US pilots down seven **MiG**s.
	8–26 January	**Operation Cedar Falls** begins in the **Iron Triangle**.
	16 February	Communist ground fire downs 13 US helicopters, a one-day record for the war.
	22 February	**Operation Junction City**, the largest ground operation of the war begins.
	13 March	**General Earle Wheeler**, the Chairman of the **Joint Chiefs of Staff**, tells the House Appropriations Committee that the North Vietnamese "don't expect to win a military victory in South **Vietnam**, but expect to win victory in the war right here in Washington DC"
	4 April	For the first time, **Martin Luther King** links the civil rights movement with the antiwar movement.
	7 April	**Secretary of Defense Robert McNamara** initiates the construction of a ground barrier against infiltration south of the **Demilitarized Zone**, the **McNamara Line**.
	15 April	Massive antiwar demonstrations are held in New York and San Francisco.
	24 April	Fighting begins for control of the hills (the **Battle of Hills 881 North and South**) around **Khe Sahn**.
	2 May	An **International War Crimes Tribunal** opens in Stockholm.
	29 July	Fire breaks out of the carrier USS *Forrestal* in the **Gulf of Tonkin**, killing 134 crewmen and destroying 21 planes. The worst naval disaster since World War II.
	September	The first Thai troops arrive in **Vietnam**.
	1 September	The **Battle of Con Thien** begins.
	3 September	**Thieu** and Ky are re-elected in **Saigon** with 35 percent of the vote. The remainder is divided among ten other candidates.
	21 October	The **March on the Pentagon** draws 50,000 antiwar protesters.
	3–22 November	The **Battle of Dak To**, one of the bloodiest in the highlands, takes place.
	30 November	Senator **Eugene McCarthy** enters the US Presidential election.
	December	The **NVA** commit the 316th Infantry Division and 335th Independent Regiment to stop the **Hmong** drive against Route 19 southwest of Dien Bien Phu in **Laos**.
1968	4 January	**Cambodia** announces that it is accepting aid from the **People's Republic of China** because it is threatened by the United States.
	12 January	Two North Vietnamese planes bomb Site 85 in **Laos**. One is shot down with an **AK-47** by a **CIA** helicopter crew chief.
	13 January	A joint **NVA** and **Pathet Lao** force takes Nam Bac, a Laotian town 60 miles north of the Royal Capitol of Luang Prabang.
	20 January	The siege of **Khe Sahn** begins.
	30–31 January	The North Vietnamese and **Viet Cong** launch the **Tet Offensive**.
	31 January	**Viet Cong Sappers** penetrate the US Embassy grounds. The battle for **Hue** begins.
	1 February	US troops drive the **Viet Cong/NVA** attackers away from **Tan Son Nhut** Air Base.
	7 February	Spearheaded by tanks, the North Vietnamese overrun the Lang Vei **Special Forces** Camp west of **Khe Sahn**.
	10 February	Except for **Hue**, and some fighting in the **Saigon** suburb of **Cholon**, the **Tet Offensive** has been repelled and the **Viet Cong** crushed, while the **NVA** suffer enormous losses.
	24 February	The Imperial Palace and Citadel Fortress in **Hue** are recaptured.
	1 March	**Clark Clifford** replaces **Robert McNamara** as Secretary of Defense.
	2 March	The Battle for **Hue** ends.
	7 March	The Battle for **Saigon** ends.

10 March	Site 85 in **Laos** is overrun by **NVA Sappers**.
12 March	Eugene McCarthy wins 42 percent of the vote in the New Hampshire Democratic primary election.
14 March	For the first time in the war, North Vietnamese troops are encountered in the Delta.
16 March	C Company, 1st Battalion 20th Infantry, **American Division** slaughters several hundred unarmed civilian men, women, and children in **My Lai**.
31 March	**President Johnson** suspends the bombing of North **Vietnam** above the 20th parallel and announces his decision not to run for re-election.
1 April	**Operation Pegasus** to relieve the siege of **Khe Sahn** begins.
8 April	The siege of **Khe Sahn** ends.
16 April	The Pentagon announces the policy of **Vietnamization**.
12 May	The **Kham Duc Special Forces** Camp near the Laotian border is evacuated under heavy fire.
13 May	Peace talks are initiated in **Paris**.
1 July	President **Nguyen Van Thieu** approves the **Phoenix (Phung Huong) Program**.
3 July	**General Creighton Abrams** replaces **General William Westmoreland** as Commander of **MACV**.
8 July	**Cambodia** lodges a formal complaint with the **United Nations** that US forces killed a group of farmers near the border.
26–29 August	The Democratic Convention is held in Chicago. Antiwar demonstrations trigger what was characterized as a "police riot" and violence escalates dramatically.
26 September	**U Thant** tells the UN General Assembly that the war in **Vietnam** is a "nationalist struggle" and that the major powers should keep out of it.
8 October	**Operation SEALORDS** begins.
31 October	**President Johnson** orders a halt to all bombing raids over North **Vietnam**.
8 November	**Richard Nixon** is elected president of the United States.
29 November	**Hanoi** radio calls for the destruction of the Phoenix Organization units.
December	The delegations to the **Paris** negotiations squabble about the shape of the negotiating table.

1969

15 January	**President Johnson**'s final budget reflects a $3.5 billion dollar reduction in war related expenditures. The first reduction since America entered the war.
25 January	The first plenary session of the **Paris** peace talks is held.
March	A series of letters from Ronald Ridenhour trigger the investigation of the **My Lai** massacre.
18 March	**Operation Menu**, secret **B-52** raids in **Cambodia**, begins.
28 March	One of a number of mass graves containing the bodies of civilians executed by the communists in **Hue** is discovered.
16 April	**President Nixon** writes to Prince Sihanouk that the US respects the **neutrality** and territorial integrity of **Cambodia**. Sihanouk expresses an interest in restoring diplomatic relations.
8 May	At the **Paris** peace talks the **National Liberation Front of South Vietnam** presents a ten-point program for ending the war.
10–20 May	The Battle of **Ap Bia** Mountain (**Hamburger Hill**) takes place in **I Corps**.
22 May	Responding to criticism over the heavy casualties at **Hamburger Hill**, the Commanding General of the 101st Airborne Division says that his orders were to "destroy enemy forces" in the **A Shau**, not to reduce casualties by avoiding battle.
5 June	**Lieutenant Calley** is returned to the US to face murder charges in connection with the massacre at **My Lai**.
8 June	**Presidents Nixon** and **Thieu** meet at the **Midway Island Conference**. **Nixon** announces that 25,000 troops will be withdrawn.
10 June	The **National Liberation Front of South Vietnam** announces the formation of a **Provisional Revolutionary Government** to rule **Vietnam**.
12–15 June	Bulgaria, **Cambodia**, the **People's Republic of China**, Cuba, Czechoslovakia, East **Germany**, Hungary, Mongolia, **North Korea**, North **Vietnam**, **Poland**, Rumania,

	Syria, the **USSR**, and Yugoslavia recognize the **Provisional Revolutionary Government of South Vietnam**.
7 July	A battalion of the US 9th Infantry Division is the first contingent of US combat troops to be withdrawn.
15 July	**President Nixon** forwards a secret letter to **Ho Chi Minh** expressing his desire to work for peace. Jean Sainteny, a retired French diplomat, forwards a US proposal for secret negotiations to **Xuan Thuy**, the chief North Vietnamese representative. **Hanoi** agrees.
August	The Cambodian port of Sihanoukville is closed to communist shipping. Greater reliance has to be placed on the **Ho Chi Minh Trail**.
3 September	**Ho Chi Minh** dies.
5 September	**Lieutenant Calley** is formally charged with the murder of 109 people at **My Lai**.
15 November	More than 250,000 protesters gather in Washington DC in the largest antiwar protest in the nation's history.
24 November	The Secretary of the Army appoints **Lieutenant General William Peers** to investigate charges that army commanders covered up the commission of war crimes in conjunction with **My Lai**.
5 December	**Lieutenant Calley** refuses to testify.
12–20 December	The **Philippines** withdraws its forces from South **Vietnam**.

1970

30 January	**President Nixon** tells a news conference that the policy of **Vietnamization** is irreversible, even without progress at the **Paris** peace talks.
1 February	**Le Duan** warns the North Vietnamese people that they "must be prepared to fight for many more years" to force the US out of South **Vietnam**.
21 February	Presidential Assistant **Henry Kissinger** and **Le Duc Tho** hold the first secret meeting in **Paris**.
9 March	The US Army **XXIV Corps** assumes command of US forces in **I Corps** from 3rd Marine Amphibious Force as the marines withdraw.
18 March	**Lon Nol** deposes **Prince Sihanouk** and takes charge of the Cambodian government.
27–28 March	In consultation with the new Cambodian government, South Vietnamese troops launch a major operation into **Cambodia**'s Kandal province.
30 April	**President Nixon** orders the Cambodian Incursion to disrupt **Viet Cong/NVA** logistical centers and bases.
4 May	Ohio National Guardsmen kill four students at **Kent State University** during an antiwar protest.
24 June	The US Senate repeals the **Gulf of Tonkin Resolution**.
30 June	US troops withdraw from **Cambodia**. The Senate passes the **Cooper–Church Amendment** that bars the use of US funds to support operations in **Cambodia**. It is dropped in negotiations with the White House on July 9.
19 August	The US signs an agreement to provide military assistance to the new Cambodian government.
21 September	The revised **Hamlet Evaluation System** used by the US to measure progress in **pacification** indicates that 92.8 percent of the population is under government control. Troops in the field find this number difficult to believe.
7 October	In a televised speech **President Nixon** calls on North **Vietnam** and the **Viet Cong** for a "cease fire in place" and an agreement to attend a conference on Indochina to negotiate an end to the war.
14 October	North **Vietnam** releases a statement rejecting **President Nixon**'s October 7 offer.
9 November	The **Supreme Court** refuses to hear a case brought by the state of Massachusetts challenging the legality of the **Vietnam War**.
20 November	**Lieutenant Colonel Arthur "Bull" Simons** leads a 50-man **Special Forces** team in a raid of the **Son Tay** Prisoner of War Camp near **Hanoi**. Though the raid is a surprise attack, no prisoners are rescued because they were previously removed.
22 December	A revised version of the **Cooper–Church Amendment** that bars the use of US troops in **Laos** is passed.

1971

2–25 January	Cambodian and South Vietnamese forces try to reopen Cambodian Route 4 from **Phnom Penh** to the port of Kompong Som. They fail because of damage to the road and bridges and Phnom Penh must rely on convoys up the Mekong River for critical supplies.
6 January	In recognition of a spreading problem, **General Creighton Abrams** announces a widespread program to curb drug use.
22 January	The **Khmer Rouge** attack Phnom Penh for the first time.
8 February	South Vietnamese forces invade **Laos** in **Operation Lam Son 719**. Their objective is to seize **Tchepone**, a critical **NVA** logistics center on the **Ho Chi Minh Trail**.
1 March	The Weather Underground an extremist antiwar group, detonates a bomb in the Capitol building.
6 March	South Vietnamese troops take **Tchepone**.
17 March	**New Zealand** begins withdrawing its troops.
24 March	Withdrawing under a heavy North Vietnamese counterattack, South Vietnamese troops complete their evacuation of Laos.
29 March	**Lieutenant Calley** is found guilty of the murder of 22 civilians at **My Lai**.
1 April	**President Nixon** orders **Lieutenant Calley's** release pending appeal.
6 April	**Operation Lam Son 719** ends.
13 May	The **Paris** peace talks enter their fourth year still in deadlock.
13 June	*The New York Times* begins publication of the **Pentagon Papers**.
July	The last **Marine** combat units are withdrawn.
13 July	**Hmong** Guerrillas successfully re-occupy the strategic **Plain of Jars** in **Laos**.
2 August	The Nixon Administration formally acknowledges that the **CIA** is conducting a secret war in **Laos** using **Hmong** tribesmen as the backbone of their army.
15–16 September	The Royal Lao forces, in a bitter battle, recapture the strategic Bolevens Plateau town of Paksong in southern **Laos**.
3 October	**President Nguyen Van Thieu** is re-elected in a controversial one-man race.
20 December	Two **NVA** Divisions support **Pathet Lao** forces in overrunning the 6,000 **Hmong** defenders and retake the **Plain of Jars** in Laos.

1972

1 January	Heavy North Vietnamese artillery fire forces the **Hmong** to evacuate their headquarters at **Long Tieng** and rally in the mountains around it.
18 January	A US Navy pilot downs a **MiG** over North **Vietnam** while protecting a reconnaissance aircraft. The first **MiG** shot down in 22 months.
4 February	The last Thai soldiers depart **Vietnam**.
21 February	**President Nixon** arrives in Peking. **Chou En-Lai's (Zhou Enlai)** call for an early peace in **Vietnam** stokes North Vietnamese fears of a sell-out.
11 March	6,000 North Vietnamese overrun Sam Thong in **Laos**, driving 4,000 Thai defenders back toward Long Tieng, seven miles away.
23 March	US negotiator **William J. Porter** announces an indefinite suspension of the **Paris** peace talks.
30 March	Twelve reinforced **NVA** divisions, approximately 150,000 men, preceded by major artillery and rocket bombardments, and led by over 500 tanks storm south. The **Easter Offensive** begins.
2–4 April	The South Vietnamese 3rd Infantry Division begins to crack as the **NVA** offensive closes in on **Quang Tri** city. Thousands of **refugees** fill the roads south toward **Hue**.
3 April	The carrier *Kitty Hawk* is ordered to **Vietnam** from the **Philippines**. 7th Fleet is ordered to support the Vietnamese.
4 April	A massive US air campaign is authorized.
5 April	The **NVA** open the second prong of their offensive, driving out of **Cambodia** toward **An Loc** and **Saigon**, cutting the roads to the battlefield. The 56th **ARVN** Regiment at **Khe Sanh** surrenders en masse.
6 April	Clear weather allows **Operation Linebacker I**, a massive series of air raids on North Vietnamese targets, to begin.
12 April	The **NVA** open the third prong of their offensive with an attack on Kontum in the

	central highlands. Fifty US infantrymen from the 196th Infantry Brigade refuse to go on patrol around **Phu Bai**.
13 April	An **NVA** tank-infantry task force attacks **An Loc**, the capitol of Binh Long province, and takes half the city with hand-to-hand combat.
16 April	**B-52 bombers** attack **Hanoi** and Haiphong for the first time in the war.
19 April	Patrol boats and **MiGs** attack 7th Fleet units bombarding the coast. The destroyer USS *Higbee* is heavily damaged during an attack by a **MiG-17** fighter-bomber. Several North Vietnamese patrol boats are sunk, aircraft are shot down, and shore batteries destroyed in the heaviest sea battle of the war.
27 April	The **Paris** peace talks resume. **NVA** armored spearheads shatter the **ARVN** 3rd Division, which flees south, and close in on Quang Tri City.
28 April–2 May	**An Loc**, Kontum, are under siege. Quang Tri falls. Only a brigade of Vietnamese Marines stands between the **NVA** and **Hue**.
2 May	Secret meetings between **Henry Kissinger**, **Le Duc Tho**, and **Xuan Thuy** resume.
8 May	**President Nixon** announces the mining of all North Vietnamese harbors. Foreign ships are given three days to get clear.
13 May	The Vietnamese Marines counterattack toward Quang Tri. **NVA** tanks and troops assault Kontum.
15 May	A seventh aircraft carrier arrives on **Yankee Station**. Two **Marine** A-4 squadrons begin flying close support missions from **Tan Son Nhut** and six more destroyers join the gun-line and open fire on targets along the coast.
23 May	**President Nixon** removes most restrictions on air strikes in North **Vietnam**.
25–30 May	The **NVA** launches a frontal assault on Kontum. It fails.
7 June	At the UN Conference on the Environment in Stockholm, Sweden characterizes the US use of defoliants in **Vietnam** as "ecocide."
17 June	Five men are arrested for breaking into the Democratic National Committee headquarters in the **Watergate** Hotel in Washington DC.
11 July	The siege of **An Loc** is broken and the **NVA** retreat into **Cambodia**.
11 August	The last American combat unit, the 2nd Battalion 21st Infantry, departs **Vietnam**.
8 September	The destroyer USS *Warrington*, damaged by a mine, is declared beyond repair.
16 September	Quang Tri is recaptured from the **NVA**.
17 October	The **Pathet Lao** and the Royal Laotian Government open peace talks.
22 October	**Operation Linebacker I** ends.
26 October	North **Vietnam** releases the text of a draft agreement with the US to end the war.
1 November	**President Thieu** blasts the Kissinger–Le Duc Tho agreement as "surrender."
14 November	**President Nixon** tells **President Thieu** that the US will "take swift and severe retaliatory action" if North **Vietnam** violates the pending ceasefire.
13 December	The **Paris** peace talks collapse again.
14 December	**President Nixon** warns the North Vietnamese that if they don't begin talking seriously, they must suffer the consequences.
18 December	**President Nixon** orders an all-out air campaign against North **Vietnam**. **Operation Linebacker II** begins. **Australia** withdraws its last 60 personnel from South **Vietnam**.
26 December	**Hanoi** says it is willing to resume negotiations if the US will stop the bombing above the 20th parallel. The US launches the most violent air attack of the war; **B-52s** pound **Hanoi** for nearly an hour.
30 December	**President Nixon** restricts bombing to below the 20th parallel when **Hanoi** agrees to return to the peace talks immediately.

1973

8 January	**Henry Kissinger** and **Le Duc Tho** resume negotiations in **Paris**.
15 January	Citing progress in the negotiations, **President Nixon** suspends all military action against North **Vietnam**. The cessation does not include South **Vietnam**.
27 January	The **Paris** Peace Agreement is signed. The last American serviceman to die in the war, Lieutenant Colonel William B Nolde, is killed by artillery at **An Loc**.
28 January	**Lon Nol** proposes a ceasefire in **Cambodia**.

	12–27 February	All but 67 US prisoners of war return home.
	21 February	The Laotian government and the **Pathet Lao** announce that they have reached a ceasefire agreement. US air strikes in **Laos** end.
	March	North **Vietnam** begins a massive logistical buildup in the south, and starts upgrading the remaining parts of the **Ho Chi Minh Trail** to an all-weather route.
	27 March	**President Nixon** announces that **B-52** raids will continue in **Cambodia** until there is a ceasefire between the **Khmer Rouge** and the **Lon Nol** government.
	29 March	The last US troops depart **Vietnam**, leaving only the Marine Embassy Guard and the Defense Attaché Office. **Hanoi** releases the last 67 prisoners that it acknowledges it is holding.
	19 June	The **Case–Church Amendment** bars any further US military action in Southeast Asia after 15 August.
	24 June	**Graham Martin** arrives as the Ambassador to South **Vietnam**.
	July	Navy **Task Force 78** completes **Operation End Sweep**, the clearing of **mines** from North **Vietnam**'s harbors and rivers.
	14 August	The last **B-52** raid is flown over **Cambodia**.
	22 August	**President Nixon** appoints **Henry Kissinger**, replacing William Rogers as Secretary of State.
	16 October	**Henry Kissinger** and **Le Duc Tho** are awarded the Nobel Peace Prize. **Le Duc Tho** declines to accept his, saying there is no peace.
	7 November	Congress overrides **Nixon**'s veto of the **War Powers Act**.
1974	19 January	**Secretary of Defense James Schlesinger** accuses Congress of reneging on the **Paris** Peace Agreements.
	22 February	The National Academy of Sciences reports that American defoliation operations have seriously damaged the ecology of **Vietnam** and that it may take a century for it to recover.
	4 April	The House of Representatives rejects a White House request for increased military aid to South **Vietnam**.
	5 April	A coalition government is set up in **Laos** with the communists holding a majority of the key positions.
	9 May	The House of Representatives Judiciary Committee opens impeachment hearings against **President Nixon**.
	22 May	The last Thai forces are withdrawn from **Laos**.
	30 July	The House votes to impeach **President Nixon** on three counts.
	5–11 August	Congress massively reduces military aid to South **Vietnam**. In 1973 it was $2.8 billion, in 1974 it was $700 million, and in 1975 it was reduced to only $300 million.
	9 August	**President Nixon** resigns and is replaced by **Vice President Gerald Ford**.
	19–26 September	The **Pathet Lao** release 215 Thai prisoners of war at Phongsavan on the **Plain of Jars**.
	October	**Le Duan** convinces the North Vietnamese Politburo that the end of the war is near and organizes for the last push.
	13 December	The North Vietnamese abrogate the **Paris Peace Agreements** with an attack on Phuoc Long in a test of American will to re-enter the war, or provide support to the South Vietnamese. There is no American reaction.
1975	6 January	Phuoc Long province falls. Lack of American reaction encourages **Le Duan** to order the preparation for a General Offensive by 1976.
	8 January	The North Vietnamese Politburo approves the General Staff plan for the final assault on **Saigon** in 1976.
	5 February	**General Van Tien Dung** goes to South Vietnam to assume command of the forces there.
	10–13 March	The North Vietnamese take **Ban Me Thout** in the **central highlands**.

14 March	**President Thieu** orders the abandonment of the **central highlands** and **I Corps**, except for **Danang**.
16 March–1 April	**ARVN** forces withdraw from **Pleiku** and Kontum. A civilian panic sets in and masses of **refugees** fill the route. The North Vietnamese attack the withdrawing columns, killing thousands.
17 March	**Refugees** begin fleeing **Hue** for **Danang**
19 March	**Quang Tri** city is captured by the **NVA**.
24 March	Tam Ky is overrun by the **NVA**.
24 March	Reacting to the speed and scale of their success, **Hanoi** Orders General Dung to complete the conquest of South **Vietnam** before the May rains. The final offensive is underway and it is named the **Ho Chi Minh Campaign**.
25 March	**Hue** is abandoned.
28 March	**NVA** attack the few **Marine** defenders of **Danang** north of the city.
28 March	**President Ford** orders Navy and contracted civilian vessels to assist in the evacuation of South Vietnamese forces and **refugees** form the coastal cities.
30 March	**Danang** falls.
31 March	The **NVA** reach Tuy Hoa.
4 April	**Operation Baby Lift** begins. A C-5 crashes on take-off, killing over 100 orphans.
7 April	**Le Duc Tho** arrives at **Loc Ninh** to oversee the final drive on **Saigon**.
8–21 April	The **ARVN** 18th Division, reinforced by an Airborne brigade and a regiment of the 5th Division, stop the attackers in their tracks at **Xuan Loc** and hold out for two weeks. Four reinforced **NVA** divisions finally swamp them.
12 April	The US Embassy is evacuated from **Cambodia**.
16 April	The **Lon Nol** government surrenders **Cambodia** to the **Khmer Rouge**.
21 April	President **Thieu** resigns, condemns the United States for denying South **Vietnam** the wherewithal to fight on.
23 April	President Ford tells a crowd at Tulane University, "The war is finished as far as America is concerned."
25 April	President **Thieu** flees **Vietnam**.
28 April	**Vice President Tran Van Huong** transfers authority as Chief of State to General **Duong Van Minh**.
29–30 April	After months of procrastination **Ambassador Graham Martin** orders the evacuation of the embassy. Over 400 are left behind inside the embassy walls when the marines are ordered by Washington DC to cease flights into **Saigon**.
30 April	The communists seize the Presidential Palace and **General Duong Van Minh** unconditionally surrenders. The Republic of **Vietnam** ceases to exist.
May	The coalition government in **Laos** collapses. The **Pathet Lao** and North Vietnamese resume military action.
12 May	The **Khmer Rouge** seize the US merchant ship *Mayaguez* in the Gulf of **Thailand**.
14 May	The Marines attack Tang Island and bomb Ream Air Base in an effort to get the *Mayaguez* back. The ship and crew are recovered.
16 May	Congress appropriates $405 million to fund a program for the resettlement of 140,000 Vietnamese and Cambodian **refugees** in America.
23 August	The **Pathet Lao** take **Vientiane**, the Administrative Capitol of **Laos**.
3 December	The **Pathet Lao** abolish the 600-year-old Laotian monarchy, sending the King and Royal Family to a "re-education camp" where they later die. The People's Democratic Republic of **Laos** is proclaimed.

Top: A soldier retrieves concertina wire from around the 1st Battalion, 5th Mechanized Division Command Post in the A Shau Valley.

Right: A rifleman from the 5th Mechanized Division looks out over the fog-shrouded A Shau Valley.

A Shau (Ashau) Valley

The A Shau Valley is located in Thua Thien province in the northern part of South Vietnam. Long and narrow, the A Shau is bordered on the west and south by Laos, and both flanks of the valley are rugged, mountainous jungle. During the war it was part of I Corps. It was a major terminus of the Ho Chi Minh Trail throughout the war. Route 548, a graveled road coming out of Laos, traversed most of it. In order to monitor infiltration, the American Special Forces established a camp in the valley in April 1963. In March 1966, the North Vietnamese/ Viet Cong overran the camp after a ferocious struggle. During this a US Air Force A-1 Skyraider pilot earned the Medal of Honor for landing on the damaged airstrip in the middle of the battle and rescuing his wingman, who had been shot down a short time before. The A Shau was the scene of some of the fiercest combat of the war, most notably the battle for Ap Bia mountain, later dubbed Hamburger Hill by the 101st Airborne Division, who fought there during Operation Apache Snow. Though the Americans and South Vietnamese repeatedly attacked the A Shau complex and cleaned out the enemy units there at the time, because the Allies never occupied terrain for any length of time, the NVA rapidly moved back into the valley. It remained in enemy hands and functioned as a major logistics area from the fall of the Special Forces Camp to the end of the war.

Abilene, Operation

Between March 30 and April 15, 1966, the 2nd and 3rd Brigades of the US 1st Infantry Division, reinforced by an Australian battalion and a New Zealand artillery battery, clashed with the D800 Viet Cong Main Force Battalion and elements of the 5th and 94th Viet Cong Regiments during a search and destroy operation in Long Khan and Phuoc Tuy provinces approximately 40 miles east of Saigon. The heaviest combat took place on 11 April, when C Company, 16th

Infantry, engaged a platoon of the D800 Battalion and then pursued them into a trap set by the remainder of the Viet Cong force. US casualties were so severe, 107 men killed or wounded out of a company strength of 134, that the US Army Chief of Staff told the 1st Division commander that people in the US would not support the war if such losses continued.

Abrams, Creighton W

As the Vice Chief of Staff of the US Army from 1964 to 1967, General Abrams was deeply involved in the American buildup for the war. Assigned as the Deputy Commander of MACV in 1967, within a short time he and General William Westmoreland were in disagreement concerning the strategy and tactics for pursuing the war. Abrams opposed the large unit search and destroy tactics and the Attrition Strategy and favored pacification. As the Tet Offensive raged, he was sent to I Corps to stabilize the situation and retake Hue. General Abrams formally assumed command of MACV

on July 3, 1968, and was charged with overseeing the drawdown of American forces and the "Vietnamization" of the war. He emphasized small unit

Above: A soldier of the 1st Infantry Division motions to a Vietnamese woman and her children to keep their heads down during a firefight during the Abilene Operation.

operations to keep the NVA and VC off balance. The Vietnamese assumed more responsibility for the war, but also controlled the Cambodian Incursion and the Vietnamese thrust into Laos on Operation Lam Son 719. He was promoted to Chief of Staff of the US Army in 1972 and died in office on September 4, 1974.

Accelerated Pacification Campaign

Begun on November 1, 1968, the Accelerated Pacification Campaign was essentially a "clear and hold" operation in which Regional Forces were inserted into contested hamlets in order to take advantage of the devastating losses the Viet Cong suffered during the Tet Offensive. Originally planned by CIA pacification specialist Robert Komer, it was carried out by his successor, William Colby. Though the weapons, equipment, and training of the Regional Forces were significantly upgraded as they went into the campaign, and over a million hectares of land was redistributed to the peasants, the outcome of the effort was a mixed bag at best. The Viet Cong infrastructure had been seriously damaged, but not destroyed, and the Regional

Left: General Creighton Abrams replaced General William Westmoreland as the Commander of the MAVC.

Forces, which devoted over 500,000 men to the pacification effort, were not capable of surviving the withdrawal of American support, because the Vietnamese Army support was inadequate to replace it.

Acheson, Dean

Dean Acheson was the US Secretary of State from 1949–1953. After leaving the State Department, Acheson became one of the advisors to Presidents Kennedy and Johnson known informally as the "wise men." His blunt assessment that the war was lost in 1968 influenced President Johnson's thrust to deescalate and end it.

Adams, Sam

A CIA analyst who believed that General Westmoreland was manipulating enemy troop strength numbers to make it appear that the US was doing better than they were. His revelations resulted in a documentary by CBS news and a lawsuit by Westmoreland. The result was that his contention was apparently vindicated.

Aderholt, Harry C "Heine"

Brigadier General Aderholt began his career dropping agents behind enemy lines in Korea. He commanded secret flights into Tibet in 1960 in support of anticommunist rebels, and supported

Above: This aerial rocket artillery gunship also carries a pair of SS-11 wire-guided antitank missiles to fire at bunkers.

other CIA clandestine projects worldwide. As the commander of the 1st Air Commando Wing, he established special operations capabilities in South Vietnam and Laos. In 1966 and 1967, using aged propeller-driven bombers, notably the B26K, his men led the Air Force in the destruction of trucks and traffic on the Ho Chi Minh Trail. His repeated clashes with 7th Air Force Commander General William Momeyer, who did not want any propeller-driven aircraft in the Air Force, over tactics for interdiction, revealed the schism between the regular Air Force

and its special operations elements that still exists today.

Aerial Rocket Artillery (ARA)

In order to support air mobile operations beyond the range of conventional artillery, the 1st Cavalry Division modified a number of UH1-B helicopters to carry up to 48 2.75in folding fin rockets. These provided fire support to ground units until regular artillery could be moved into range.

Agency for International Development (AID)

US government body that, from the mid-1950s, was responsible for administrating the economic assistance program to the Republic of Vietnam (sometimes known as USAID). AID provided assistance through numerous agricultural, education, public health, public safety, law enforcement, local government, public works, industrial development, land reform and refugee relocation projects. By providing vital economic support to the fledgling South Vietnamese government, the AID program did much to ensure its survival.

Agent Orange

To reduce the ability of guerrilla units to establish ambushes along roads or trails

Below: An Air Force doctor vaccinates a Vietnamese woman during the Accelerated Pacification Campaign.

and to hide their base camps in heavy jungle, the US Defense Department developed a strategy of defoliating key areas by spraying herbicides from the air. Agent Orange, named for the colored band around the shipping drums, was the most widely used. The defoliation effort lasted from 1962 to 1969 in Vietnam and until 1971 in Cambodia. During this time more than 46 percent of South Vietnam's forests, nearly five million acres, was sprayed at least once, along with 500,000 acres of cropland. Though considered non-toxic to animals and humans except in very large doses, epidemiological studies suggested a link between the dioxin in Agent Orange and many debilitating illnesses, rashes, tumors, and birth defects. By 1984, the Veterans Administration officially recognized disability claims by veterans related to Agent Orange, and the birth defect spina bifida in their children.

Agrovilles
The Agrovilles represented an effort by President Diem in 1959 to concentrate the peasants into fortified hamlets that could be more easily defended. The Agrovilles would also serve to separate the population from the insurgents. By 1961, the program was abandoned as it was plagued by corruption, and resisted by the peasants who wouldn't leave their ancestral homelands.

Right: An Air America Turbo-Porter takes off from the Quang Tri airfield for Laos.

Air America
Owned by the CIA, this conglomerate airline provided critical support to the Hmong guerrilla forces fighting the Pathet Lao and North Vietnamese in Laos, as well as supporting clandestine operations in Cambodia and Vietnam. Air America played a key role in the US evacuation in 1975, and was disestablished in 1976.

Air Cavalry
Recognizing the potential of the helicopter, during the Korean War the US Marine Corps began development of a tactic known as vertical envelopment. It envisaged landing combat forces from

Above: A Project Ranch Hand C-123 sprays Agent Orange along a tree line near An Loc.

transport helicopters and supporting them with armed variants. The US Army further developed this concept and organized a test unit at Fort Benning, Georgia, the 11th Air Assault Division, to determine if it was actually feasible in combat. Though opposed by the Army Staff and many senior generals in the traditional Army, the results of the test were encouraging, and President Kennedy's administration believed that it offered significant potential. When the decision was made to escalate the Vietnam War,

Above: A crew chief loads the mini-gun on his Loach, which sports the crossed sabers of the Air Cavalry.

Secretary of Defense Robert McNamara directed that the Air Assault Division be deployed to Vietnam. Reconstituted as the 1st Cavalry Division (Airmobile) the unit arrived in the central highlands in 1965. Because the tactics employed by the test unit had been built on existing armored cavalry operational and tactical doctrine, and because of the long-standing traditions of the 1st Cavalry Division, the term Air Cavalry came into widespread use. As a result of the Division's stellar combat performance, the US Army organized several more Air Cavalry units.

Air Cushion Vehicles, Patrol (PACV)

Developed from a British commercial craft, the Patrol Air Cushion Vehicle, (PACV), could hit 70mph and maneuver over shallow water or rice paddies. Noise, fuel consumption, and restricted visibility limited their use on the rivers and canals. However, they provided a serious challenge to Viet Cong units in

Right: 1st Cavalry Division UH-1D helicopters launch a combat assault north of Bong Son in II Corps.

the Plain of Reeds, where their ability to plow through the vegetation frequently disrupted enemy movements.

Air Defense (North Vietnamese)
With the assistance of Russian advisors, and using modern Soviet weapons, North Vietnam constructed the most elaborate air defense system in the world in the 1960s and 1970s. The defenses used a combination of guns, missiles, and fighter aircraft to insure that there were no altitudes or target areas that US planes could operate in with impunity. At the lowest altitudes, the militia fired at any aircraft they saw with rifles, and light and heavy machineguns. Late in the war the SA-7 shoulder launched antiaircraft missile was added to this low-level mix. Light flak guns of 23–37mm, firing from 80–240 rounds per minute up to 9,000ft, stiffened the lowest layer and engaged aircraft out of rifle/machinegun range. Large numbers of S-60 radar-directed 57mm guns attacked aircraft up to 15,000ft with up to 70 6lb shells per minute. They were, in turn, augmented by 85mm M1944 guns firing 20 20lb shells per minute up to 30,000ft. Between 30,000ft and 45,000ft, 100mm guns were engaged with 15 35lb shells per minute, and the 130mm guns hurled 12 74lb shells per minute to the same altitude. From the medium to the highest altitudes, the SA-2 surface-to-air missile

presented a serious threat. Leavened throughout all of the layers, MIG-17, 19, and 21 fighters flew ground controlled intercepts of American flights that appeared to be either vulnerable or approaching critical target areas. Though MiGs and SAMs were most frequently

Above: A US Navy Patrol Air Cushion Vehicle (PACV) glides along the shoreline near Hue.

Below: These North Vietnamese 57mm antiaircraft guns were too slow to catch the RF-101 Voodoo whose shadow streaks between them.

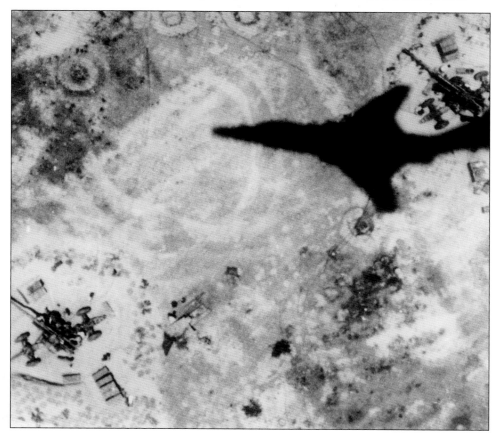

written about, over 70 percent of all aircraft shot down over North Vietnam were victims of small arms and antiaircraft guns. The US lost 1,034 fixed wing aircraft over North Vietnam, of which it was calculated that 758 fell to small arms fire and antiaircraft guns.

Air Mobility

One of the major tactical innovations of the Vietnam War, the airmobile doctrine entailed the integrated use of helicopters for reconnaissance, the simultaneous movement of artillery and transportation of troops to the battle area, immediate

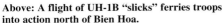

Above: A flight of UH-1B "slicks" ferries troops into action north of Bien Hoa.

fire support using gunships and aerial rocket artillery, medical evacuation of the wounded, and rapid reinforcement and logistical support. Airmobile units overcame the problems posed by the terrain as a major obstacle to movement. They were more flexible, agile, and had shorter reaction times. The troops arrived at the point of decision rested and ready, since they didn't have to walk or carry as much weight as normal units did.

Airborne Operations

In February 1967, part of the 173rd Airborne Brigade jumped during Operation Junction City. Though Special Forces and reconnaissance units routinely parachuted into operational areas, it was the only major US airborne operation. While the Vietnamese airborne sometimes jumped into combat, by 1966 the helicopter had proven a more efficient way to insert forces.

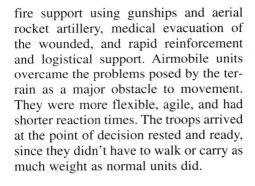

Left: A 57mm gun crew blasts away at bombers attacking the Dragon's Jaw Bridge at Than Hoa, North Vietnam.

Left: A group of female parachute riggers learn how to pack the T-10 parachute.

Below: An American Combat Control Team marks a drop zone for Vietnamese paratroopers in III Corps.

Aircraft

Attack Aircraft

The US Navy characterizes airplanes that have a primary mission of bombing targets and a secondary mission of air defense as attack aircraft. The US Air Force calls the same aircraft a fighter-bomber or a strike aircraft, essentially reversing the roles, though both ended up using the term attack aircraft in routine parlance. US Forces employed a number of attack aircraft in Vietnam. Above the Demilitarized Zone, the unsophisticated but highly reliable Douglas A-4 Skyhawk, a lightweight single engine, somewhat slow, carrier plane, bore the brunt of the Navy war over North Vietnam until the highly capable Vought A-7 Corsair II assumed the mission in 1968. Even then, it soldiered on throughout the war and was still in service aboard the USS *Hancock* when the war ended. More A-4s were shot down than any other carrier aircraft. The Republic F-105 Thunderchief, originally designed to be a long-range nuclear strike fighter, carried the Air Force war to Hanoi. Though it was scheduled to be replaced

Below: A pair of Skyraiders load up and prepare to escort a "Jolly Green" rescue helicopter.

Attack Aircraft

Designation	Crew	Armament	Ordnance	Speed	Range	Used
Douglas A-1 Skyraider	1	4–20mm	8,000lb External Stores	321kt	915mi	1960–75
McDonnell Douglas A-4 Skyhawk	1	2–20mm	8,200lb External Stores	670kt	340mi	1964–73
Grumman A-6 Intruder	2	N/A	18,000lb External Stores	644kt	1,010mi	1965–73
Vought A-7 Corsair II	1	1–20mm Vulcan 2- Sidewinder	15,000lb External Stores	693kt	490mi	1967–73
Cessna A-37 Dragonfly	1	1–7.62mm Mini-gun	5,680lb External Stores	507kt	460mi	1966–75
AT-28D Trojan	1	2–.50 Cal. MG	4,000lb External Stores	352kt	1,200mi	1962–75
F8F Bearcat	1	4–20mm	1,000lb	421kt	1,105mi	1955–62
North American F-100 Super Sabre	1	4–20mm	7,500lb External Stores	864kt	1,500mi	1964–71
Republic F-105 Thunderchief	1	1–20mm Vulcan	14,000lb	1,390kt	1,850mi	1964–73
General Dynamics F-111A Aardvark	2	1–20mm Vulcan	30,000lb	1,650kt	2,925mi	1968–73

by the more versatile McDonnell F-4 Phantom, from 1965–1970 it was the primary strike aircraft flown over North Vietnam by the Air Force and, up through 1967, accounted for more combat losses than any other type. One of the glaring shortcomings of American airpower early in the war was the inability to strike at night or in periods of bad weather. The Grumman A-6 Intruder rectified that and provided the first all-weather day or night strike capability available in Vietnam. In South Vietnam, almost without contradiction, if troops in contact had their choice they would prefer to have the Douglas A-1 Skyraider fly their close air support missions. This

Right: An armed F-105 Thunderchief waits to be armed before a raid.

Below: An F-100 drops a bomb south of Saigon. Not designed as a fighter-bomber, the F-100 flew more close air support strikes than any other aircraft in the war.

Above: A pair of A-4 Skyhawks return to the carrier after completing their mission.

Left: The A-6E Intruder was rated as the most effective and versatile attack aircraft of the war.

Above right: The A-7 Corsair II replaced the A-4 Skyhawk, and was also used by the Air Force.

Right: The A-37 Dragonfly gave the Vietnamese Air Force a jet ground attack plane to supplement their A-1s.

aged Korean War vintage propeller plane carried a heavy ordnance load, could loiter for extended periods of time, and was extremely accurate in its bombing and strafing attacks. Though it cannot be called one of the glamour aircraft of the war, and was actually designed as America's first supersonic fighter, in South Vietnam the North American F-100 Super Sabre flew far more strikes than any other type.

Above: This F-111 Aardvark sits on the flight line waiting for its crew.

Right: A B-66 Destroyer leads a group of F-105s on a radar-controlled strike against North Vietnam.

Bomber Aircraft

Designation	Crew	Armament	Ordnance	Speed	Range	Used
Douglas A-3B Sky Warrior	3	2–20mm	8,000lb	600kt	2,100mi	1965–66
Douglas B-26 Invader	2	12–.50 Cal. MG	8,000lb	324kt	550mi	1961–69
Boeing B-52 Stratofortress	10	4 –.50 Cal. MG	81,000lb	650kt	12,500mi	1965–73
Martin B-57 Canberra	2	4–20mm	6,000lb	541kt	805mi	1963–72
Hyushin *IL-28 Beagle	3	4–23mm	6,614lb	559kt	1,365mi	N/A

Though they had a number of II-28 "Beagle" light twinjet bombers, the North Vietnamese never used them.

Below: The B-57 Canberra was one of the first aircraft to deploy to Vietnam. Many were later modified for night reconnaissance over the Ho Chi Minh Trail.

Bottom: An A-3B Sky Warrior bomber reaches the end of its rollout while landing on the USS *Kitty Hawk* in 1966.

Bomber Aircraft

America employed four bombers in the Vietnam War. The first to arrive was the World War II vintage Douglas B-26 Invader. Powered by two 2,500hp radial piston engines, it carried a 5,000lb load of bombs and napalm and had eight .50 caliber machineguns mounted in the nose. Initially introduced under the Farmgate program in 1961, eventually its primary operational area became the Ho Chi Minh Trail where it proved to be exceptionally effective at killing trucks. It remained in service as a light bomber in this role until late 1969, with some fighting on until the end of the war. The next bomber to arrive on the scene was the Martin B-57 Canberra, a light twinjet that carried eight wing mounted .50 caliber machineguns and 6,000lb of stores. As other, more capable fighter-bombers came into service it was modified to the B-57G configuration for night operations over the Ho Chi Minh Trail, and later, under Project Patricia Lynn, to the B-57E. The B-57E was the most effective night reconnaissance aircraft flying over the Trail. In 1965, the Navy employed the A-3B Sky Warrior over both the north and the south, but its secondary capability, that of an airborne tanker, the KA-3B, caused it to be withdrawn by late 1966 and converted to that role. The most famous bomber of the war was the Boeing B-52D Stratofortress. This eight jet strategic bomber could carry a massive 60,000lb payload and devastated areas it struck. Largely confined to South Vietnam, Cambodia and Laos until the Linebacker raids of 1972/73 it was acknowledged after the war by the North Vietnamese as the most feared weapon in America's arsenal. If you were caught in a target box during a raid there was virtually no hope of survival.

Fighter Aircraft

Designation	Crew	Armament	Ordnance	Speed	Range	Used
McDonnell Douglas F-4 Phantom	2	4–Sparrow 4–Sidewinder	16,000lb External Stores	1,415kt	600mi	1964–73
McDonnell Douglas F-4E Phantom	2	1–20mm Vulcan 4–Sparrow	16,000lb External Stores	1,485kt	958mi	1968–73
Northrop F-5A Freedom Fighter	1	2–20mm 2–Sidewinder	6,200lb External Stores	977kt	1150mi	1965–75
Northrop F-5E Skoshi Tiger	1	2–20mm 2–Sidewinder	7,000lb External Stores	1,083kt	1,543mi	1974–75
Vought F-8 Crusader	1	4–20mm 4–Sidewinder	N/A	1,133kt	1,425mi	1964–73
Grumman TF-9J Cougar	2	2–20mm	2,000lb External Stores	705kt	600mi	1965–67
*Grumman F-14 Tomcat	2	1–20mm Vulcan 6–Phoenix	N/A	1,564kt	2,000mi	1975
Convair F-102 Delta Dagger	1	6–Falcon	N/A	825kt	670mi	1962–68
Lockheed F-104 Starfighter	1	1–20mm Vulcan	4,000lb External Stores	1,500kt	775mi	1965–67
** MiG-15 "Fagot"	1	1–23mm	N/A	630kt	590mi	1964–75
***MiG-17 "Fresco"	1	1–37mm, 2–23mm	N/A	711kt	915mi	1964–75
MiG-19S "Farmer A"	1	3–30mm 4–Alkali Radar Homing	N/A	901kt	870mi	1970–75
MiG-21 (PFS) "Fishbed E"	1	1–23mm twin 2– Atol IR	N/A	1,386kt	930mi	1966–75

*The F-14 flew air cover for the evacuation of Saigon from the USS *Enterprise*, but did not engage in combat.

**When the war began the North Vietnamese had a few MiG-15s. They kept them in China and used them as trainers. The Cambodian Air Force operated them in the mid-1960s.

***The NVA used the MiG-17 as a fighter-bomber to attack US destroyers in 1972. One severely damaged the USS *Higbee*. The Cambodian Air Force also operated MiG-17s.

Fighter Aircraft

Four American and three North Vietnamese fighter types clashed in the air above North Vietnam. In these clashes the premier American fighter was the Navy Vought F-8 Crusader, a small, agile, fast, pure fighter aircraft that was heavily armed. Sporting four 20mm cannons and four Sidewinder missiles it eventually picked up the nickname "MiG Master." Flying the Crusader, Navy and Marine pilots achieved a kill ratio of 6:1 against their North Vietnamese adversaries. The second most effective fighter was the Navy version of the F-4 Phantom. Though carrying a pure missile armament, which was extremely unreliable, Navy and Marine pilots achieved a 5.4:1 kill ratio with the Phantom. The Air Force also flew the fighter version of the Phantom, though their kill ratio was only 3:1. The Air Force flew one "pure" fighter against the North Vietnamese, the Convair F-102 Delta Dagger, a delta wing interceptor that had been optimized against Russian bombers in the late 1950s. The F-102 kill ratio was 0:1 in favor of the MiG-21. Similarly, after they dumped their bomb loads the Republic F-105 Thunderchief was classed as a fighter and frequently engaged the MiGs. Its kill ratio was a meager 1.4:1.

Early in the war the North Vietnamese flew older Mikoyan-Gurevich MiG-17s and MiG-19s, and the Americans achieved a fairly steady 2:1 kill ratio against them, undesirable from the North Vietnamese standpoint, but significantly

Right: An F-4B Phantom II is recovered aboard the USS *Enterprise* after a mission over North Vietnam.

Left: Two F-4 Phantoms bank and begin a slow turn as they enter the landing pattern.

Below, left: The F-8 Crusader achieved the highest kill ratio of the war. It became known as the "MiG Master."

below what American pilots had achieved in World War II or the Korean War. That changed dramatically with the introduction of the MiG-21. When the MiG-21 took to the air, encounters between Navy/Marine fighters and the MiG-21 resulted in a 1:1 kill ratio, and dogfights with the Air Force ran 1:3 in favor of the MiG-21. Fortunately for US forces, President Johnson's bombing halt in 1968 gave them time to analyze the problems, institute better air-air combat training, and resolve a number of the missile reliability problems that had surfaced. When the Americans went back over the north the Air Force MiG-21 kill ratios reversed, and the Navy/Marine numbers climbed.

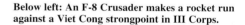

Below left: An F-8 Crusader makes a rocket run against a Viet Cong strongpoint in III Corps.

Below: 20mm shells from a F-105 rip into a North Vietnamese MiG and it bursts into flame.

Above: An F-5 Skoshi Tiger fighter unloads a pair of bombs on a target in South Vietnam.

Right: The Grumman F9F-8T Cougar trainer was pressed into service by the Marines as a FAC aircraft in 1965.

Below: The MiG-21 was the most dangerous adversary American pilots faced over North Vietnam.

Reconnaissance Aircraft

The Lockheed RT-33A was used for covert reconnaissance missions over Laos in 1961 as part of Project Field Goal. It had a maximum speed of 600kt and a 1,025-mile combat range, but within a year it was replaced by the far more capable McDonnell RF-101 Voodoo as the need for greater intelligence increased. The Voodoo's 1,012kt maximum speed and 2,045-mile combat range were required to provide coverage over North Vietnam. It was later supplemented by RF-4C Phantoms, and replaced by them in 1970. The Navy and Marines flew a number of variants of the RF-8 Crusader, as well as the North American RA-5C Vigilante, which was one of the fastest and heaviest aircraft ever used for carrier service.

The big twin-engine jet had a maximum speed of 1,385mph and a combat range of 2,650 miles. Specially configured Martin B-57 Canberra bombers prowled the Mekong Delta and the Ho Chi Minh Trail at night under Operations Tropic Moon and Patricia Lynn.

Maritime reconnaissance was carried out by the Lockheed P-2 Neptune, which had a hybrid power plant of two radial piston engines and two light turbojets. It carried up to 8,000lb of bombs, torpedoes, mines, depth charges, or rockets and was particularly valuable in patrolling the outer barrier of Operation Market Time. They were gradually replaced as the P-3 Orion, a four-engined turboprop, maritime, patrol aircraft that carried up to 19,250lb of ordnance, became available.

Above: An RB-57 pilot is given the signal to start his engines prior to a reconnaissance mission over the Ho Chi Minh Trail.

Left: The RF-8A Crusader was the workhorse of the Navy reconnaissance throughout most of the Vietnam War.

VIETNAM: A VISUAL ENCYCLOPEDIA

Transport Aircraft

Beginning in January 1962, the Fairchild C-123 Provider contributed a substantial share of the in-theater air transport. Powered by two 2,500hp radial piston engines, the C-123 could haul 60 troops or 15,000lb of cargo. The CIA, the Vietnamese Air Force, the Khmer Air Force, the Royal Lao Air Force, and the Royal Thai Air Force also operated it. Though very important for its transport role, it is best remembered as the spray plane in Operation Ranch Hand. It was also used in the NC-123K version for Black Spot night interdiction missions on the Ho Chi Minh Trail.

The Lockheed C-130 Hercules was the most important transport aircraft of the war. The big four-engine turboprop could carry 92 troops or 45,000lb of cargo and was used for intra-theater transport by all of the Allies. The US Air Force, Australia, and New Zealand also used it for strategic transport to supplement the older Douglas C-124 Globemaster and C-133 Cargomasters that carried the burden until sufficient C-141 Starlifters and C-5 Galaxys became available. The De Havilland of Canada C-7 Caribou was initially operated in Southeast Asia by the Army. It was used to provide airlift into Special Forces

Above: A C-130 transport makes an emergency landing at the Buon Blech Special Forces Camp.

Right: A Caribou Light Transport cruises above the clouds on the way to a Special Forces Camp in I Corps.

Below: A 1st Cavalry Division Caribou takes off after delivering ammunition to a Special Forces Camp in II Corps.

camps and small airfields that could not be used by the larger C-123 and C-130 transports. The Australians and the South Vietnamese Air Force also operated Caribous.

The North Vietnamese operated Il-12 "Coach" and Il-14 "Crate" transports. Though they were not used after American combat aircraft became common in North Vietnamese air space, early in the war the North Vietnamese used them to airlift men and equipment to their Pathet Lao allies on the Plain of Jars in Laos.

Utility Aircraft

There were over 25 types of utility aircraft used in the Vietnam War. Three require special mention. Undoubtedly the most famous was the Cessna O-1 Bird Dog. When the Republic of Vietnam was formed it acquired 20 of the high-wing Cessnas, known at that time as the L-19, from the French. Redesignated as the O-1 in 1962, this fragile piston-engined airplane was used for extensive service with the US Air Force, the Vietnamese Air Force, the US

Above: The OV-10 Bronco, originally called the LARA (Light Armed Reconnaissance Aircraft) was the first choice for FACs over the Ho Chi Minh Trail.

Right: A FAC getting used to the OV-10 Bronco in 1969.

Below: The ubiquitous Cessna L-19 Bird Dog, redesignated the O-1, was used everywhere but North Vietnam.

Army, the US Marines, and the Khmer Air Force as a reconnaissance and forward air control aircraft. The twin turboprop, North American OV-10 Bronco provided the FACs with a more powerful, rugged, and heavily armed aircraft for working in the extremely dangerous skies over the Ho Chi Minh Trail. The third, the Antonov AN-2 "Colt," was a rugged Soviet bi-plane with good short takeoff and landing characteristics. It was used by the North Vietnamese to resupply isolated outposts and Pathet Lao forces. It was the only aircraft that successfully carried out a bombing raid against US ground forces during the war when two of them struck Site 85, a ground control radar outpost in Laos. During the same engagement it also gained the ignominious distinction of being the only fixed wing combat aircraft ever shot down by a helicopter.

Aircraft Carriers

As part of the 7th Fleet's Task Force 77, American aircraft carriers operated off the coast of Vietnam from 1964 to 1975. Fully fledged carrier operations began in

Below: The Military Sea Transport Service ferry carrier, USNS *Core*, delivers a load of A-1 Skyraiders to Saigon.

1964 with reconnaissance flights over the Plain of Jars in Laos from "Yankee Station." Later that year, in response to the Gulf of Tonkin incident, they initiated combat strikes against targets in North Vietnam and continued attacking that country and the Ho Chi Minh Trail until the Paris Peace Agreement in 1973. They also flew ground support missions in South Vietnam from "Dixie Station," located off the coast of Cam Rahn Bay. Usually two carriers were assigned to the Task Force, but beginning in 1966 the number varied between three and four. There were seven deployed in June 1972, and again in January 1973.

In all, 19 aircraft carriers served in the war, most on multiple tours. Carrier air wings contained between 65 and 90 aircraft of multiple types, though the smaller Essex Class ships could not accept large aircraft such as the F-4 Phantom.

The Essex Class was the largest class of aircraft carriers ever built. The original plan was to have 32 in the class, but 26 were actually built and 16 were used in World War II. They formed the backbone of the carrier fleet into the 1960s, and some were used well into the 1980s as training ships. Smaller than the later fleet carriers, they could not accommodate larger aircraft, such as the F-4

Phantom or A-6 Intruder, so the air wings contained A-1s, A-4s, and A-7 Corsairs. There were two different size carriers in the Essex Class. The larger one had an angled deck, added during a rebuild, and the smaller was a straight-deck carrier.

The Midway Class aircraft carriers were so extensively modified during the 1950s that they were sister ships in name only. No two were alike.

The Forrestal Class of aircraft carriers was the first one built after World War II. The final approval came after a brutal inter-service struggle between the Air Force and the Navy over roles and missions that resulted in the "Revolt of the Admirals," where a number of senior Navy officers ruined their careers in order to carry the day politically.

The Kitty Hawk Class was essentially an updated Forrestal carrier, differing mainly in a number of technical details.

CVAN-65, the nuclear-powered USS *Enterprise*, displaced 89,084 tons, and was the largest warship afloat when she entered the fleet in 1961. She was also the fastest carrier ever built, exceeding 35kt during builder's trials, though the Navy listed her "official" speed as 32kt. With a ship's complement of 5,287 and 90 embarked aircraft, the *Enterprise* served six tours off the coast of Vietnam.

Above: The attack aircraft carrier USS *Hancock* and the destroyer USS *Robinson* refuel while underway.

The Essex Class

Name	*Displacement	Built	Speed	A/C	Crew	Tours	Hull No.
Yorktown	40,600	1943	30kt	80	2,905	3	CVS-10
Hornet	40,600	1943	30kt	80	2,905	3	CVS-12
Bennington	40,600	1944	30kt	80	2,905	3	CVS-20
Kearsarge	40,600	1946	30kt	80	2,905	4	CVS-33
Oriskany	40,600	1950	30kt	80	2,905	7	CVA-34
Intrepid	43,060	1943	29kt	80	2,545	3	CVS-11
Ticonderoga	43,060	1944	29kt	80	2,545	5	CVA-14
Hancock	43,060	1944	29kt	80	2,545	8	CVA-19
Bon Homme Richard	43,060	1944	29kt	80	2,545	6	CVA-31
Shangri-La	43,060	1944	29kt	80	2,545	1	CVS-38

Below: The USS *Midway* underway in the South China Sea.

* Wartime, including full complement, fuel, ammunition, and stores.

Above: The carrier USS *Oriskany* and several escorts trail the carrier USS *Constellation* on Yankee Station.

Below: The nuclear-powered USS *Enterprise* prepares to recover aircraft on her angled deck while on Yankee Station.

The Midway Class

Name	*Displacement	Built	Speed	A/C	Crew	Tours	Hull No.
Midway	62,614	1945	31kt	90	4,060	3	CVA-41
Franklin Delano Roosevelt	62,614	1945	31kt	90	4,060	1	CVA-42
Coral Sea	62,614	1947	31kt	90	4,060	6	CVA-43

The Forrestal Class

Name	*Displacement	Built	Speed	A/C	Crew	Tours	Hull No.
Forrestal	78,509	1955	33kt	90	4,676	1	CVA-59
Saratoga	78,509	1956	33kt	90	4,676	1	CVA-60
Ranger	78,509	1957	33kt	90	4,676	7	CVA-61
Independence	78,509	1959	33kt	90	4,676	1	CVA-62

The Kitty Hawk Class

Name	*Displacement	Built	Speed	A/C	Crew	Tours	Hull No.
Kitty Hawk	80,945	1961	34kt	90	4,685	6	CVA-63
Constellation	80,945	1962	34kt	90	4,685	7	CVA-64
America	80,945	1965	34kt	90	4,685	3	CVA-66

* Wartime, including full complement, fuel, ammunition, and stores.

Air-to-Air Refueling

The war in Vietnam saw the first wide-spread use of air-to-air refueling in combat. B-52 bombers flying from Guam routinely refueled during their mission, and heavily laden F105 fighter-bombers did not have sufficient range to fly all the way to their target areas in North Vietnam and then back to bases in Thailand. Additionally, because Navy aircraft were not configured to use Air Force tankers, the Navy routinely had carrier borne tankers, notably the KA-3B and KA-6 converted from a bomber and an attack aircraft respectively, on stand by. These would tank returning aircraft that were low on fuel because of extended range missions, battle damage, or heavy usage during air-to-air combat. In 1964, when the initial strikes were flown

Above: Troops of the 2nd Battalion, 14th Infantry sprint to board their UH-1D in the Filhol Plantation during Operation Ala Moana.

into Laos and North Vietnam, the only tanker available in theater was the obsolescent KB-50J, which sustained the force for seven months before it was replaced by Strategic Air Command (SAC) refueling squadrons equipped with KC-135s. Eventually, even the search and rescue helicopters used over Laos and North Vietnam were equipped for air-to-air refueling, and specially modified C-130 cargo aircraft supported them. Without air-to-air refueling the US air effort would have been seriously restricted.

Ala Moana, Operation
From December 1, 1966–May 14, 1967, the Ala Moana Operation took place. It was a multi-battalion operation of the 25th Infantry Division designed to push Viet Cong units away from the rice growing area west of Saigon. Operation Cedar Falls was a secondary part of the operation using the 2nd Brigade of the Division as a blocking force north of Cu Chi in III Corps. Contact was sporadic throughout the operation, with only one major engagement. In February, the 3rd Squadron, 4th Cavalry and 4th Battalion, 9th Infantry fought a sharp battle in the Filhol Rubber Plantation with a mixed VC force from the 165th VC Regiment. Ala Moana continued past the end of Cedar Falls and went on concurrently with the multi-divisional Operation Junction City in War Zone C. It set the stage for an all-out attempt by the 25th Division to pacify Hau Ngia province, recognized as an area where the communists were strongest.

Allies
Forty nations provided military and non-military assistance to the Republic of Vietnam. The United States, Australia, Korea, Thailand, New Zealand, The Philippines, the Republic of China, and Spain all had uniformed personnel assigned to South Vietnam and, of course, Laos and Cambodia fought against the North Vietnamese within their own borders as well, as a part of the overall war. Additionally, there were a significant number of nations from all areas of the world that contributed non-military assistance.

Alvarez, Everett Jr
A Navy Lieutenant flying an A-4 Skyhawk attack aircraft from the USS *Constellation*, Alvarez was shot down over Hon Gai North Vietnam August 5, 1964 during a retaliatory raid for the

Nations Contributing Non-Military Assistance to the Republic of Vietnam

North America	Latin/South America	Europe	Far East	Middle East	Africa
US	Argentina	Belgium	Australia	Iran	Liberia
Canada	Brazil	Denmark	Republic of China	Israel	Morocco
	Costa Rica	Germany	Laos	Turkey	South Africa
	Ecuador	France	Republic of Korea		Tunisia
	Guatemala	Greece	Japan		
	Honduras	Ireland	Malaysia		
	Uruguay	Italy	New Zealand		
	Venezuela	Luxembourg	Pakistan		
		Netherlands	Philippines		
		Norway	Thailand		
		Spain			
		Switzerland			
		United Kingdom			

Above: A Viet Cong prisoner at Thuong Duc waits evacuation to the Americal Division POW collection Point.

Left: An MP guard walks through the Americal Division POW collection point in Chu Lai.

Gulf of Tonkin incident. He was the first American pilot captured and spent eight and a half years as a prisoner.

Amerasians
Children fathered by American servicemen, Amerasians were ostracized and discriminated against by the Vietnamese after the war. Initially ignored by America, after a great deal of criticism the government first waived proving paternity to qualify for immigration, and later passed the Amerasian Homecoming Act of 1987. Eventually 22,000 settled in the United States.

Americal Division
In early 1967, MACV formed an ad-hoc division sized unit in I Corps containing brigades from the 25th Infantry and 101st Airborne Divisions, and the 196th Light Infantry Brigade, to support Marine Corps operations along the Demilitarized Zone. Originally called Task Force Oregon, it was supplemented by support units drawn from all over Vietnam. In September 1967, the two "borrowed" divisional brigades were

VIETNAM: A VISUAL ENCYCLOPEDIA

Right: A battery of How-6s goes into position while the next wave comes ashore during an amphibious operation.

Below: A convoy of amtracs, escorted by an Ontos, moves up the beach on its way to Hoi An.

replaced by the 11th and 198th Infantry Brigades and returned to their parent units. Task Force Oregon was re-designated as the 23rd Infantry Division (Americal) the name it had been given when first formed on New Caledonia during World War II. The division operated in the southern three provinces of I Corps until it was deactivated in 1971, and the 196th Infantry Brigade returned to independent status. While it was active, the Americal Division suffered over 17,500 casualties, and one of its units committed the atrocity at My Lai.

American Friends of Vietnam
This privately funded organization was established in the mid-1950s by supporters of the Diem government to promote US interests in Vietnam. Its specific goal was to prevent a communist takeover in South Vietnam, and its membership at one time included some of the most powerful political figures in the country. However, Diem's increasingly autocratic style of leadership and corrupt practices split the organization over how it should respond. After Diem was overthrown, the organization rose to prominence again, supporting the Johnson administration's escalation of the war with the help of government funding. It was widely criticized by opponents of the war, and by 1975 it had faded into the background.

Amnesty
In the context of this book, amnesty was a pardon granted to individuals or groups who illegally avoided military service in Vietnam, namely draft evaders, deserters, exiles and less-than-honorable discharges. The number of such cases had risen to nearly 1,000,000 by December 1972. President Nixon strongly opposed any move to grant amnesty, and the Ford administration's offer of amnesty in return for 24 months of alternative service with a public service was taken up by only six percent of the 350,000 offenders. Carter offered to pardon draft dodgers but not deserters, but rather than finding a satisfactory resolution, the amnesty issue instead faded in importance in the eyes of the US public.

Amphibious Operations
An assault from the open sea by a landing force across the shore is known as an amphibious operation. The Marines retained an afloat multi-battalion organization they dubbed the Special Landing Force (SLF). It could be brought ashore to reinforce on-going operations or landed to carry out independent actions. It was used from the Mekong Delta to the DMZ early in the war. Because these operations controlled their own air and gunfire support, the Air Force in particular opposed them. This dispute became so rancorous that MACV placed them under the control of the 3rd Marine Amphibious Force in Danang and limited them to I Corps. During the Tet Offensive, the battle for Khe Sahn, and the intense combat operations along the

Demilitarized Zone, the Special Landing Force battalions spent so much time ashore that they simply became additional maneuver battalions that were available. By 1969, SLF battalion operations had essentially ceased.

An Loc, Battle of (April 1972)

Attacking from their sanctuaries in Cambodia on April 2, 1972, the VC/NVA overwhelmed the District town of Loc Ninh. Then, as a key element of the Easter Offensive, General Vo Nguyen Giap unleashed several VC/NVA Divisions against An Loc, the capitol of Binh Long province 70 miles north-northwest of Saigon in order to clear a path down highway 13 to Saigon itself. The city was defended by elements of the ARVN 5th Infantry Division. President Nguyen Van Thieu ordered the ARVN 21st Infantry Division to assist in the city's defense, but as it moved north, it was blocked by the Viet Cong 7th Division and never reached the town.

On April 13, following an extremely heavy artillery bombardment, the VC/NVA launched a massive infantry attack supported by T-54 and PT-76 tanks against the defenders of the city. Though they managed to compress the defender's perimeter into an area less than a mile square, continuous aggressive attacks by tactical air power, helicopter gunships, and fixed wing gunships managed to stabilize the situation. B-52 bomber Arc Light strikes ringed the city and prevented the VC/NVA from concentrating their forces in a manner that would allow them to simply overwhelm the defenders by frontal attack. Though they were cut off and besieged by a numerically superior force, suffered heavy casualties, and had no hope of immediate relief, the ARVN held. The siege was finally broken in June and the VC/NVA retreated into their Cambodian sanctuaries to lick their wounds.

An Nam

This Chinese term meaning pacified south, was adopted by the French as the name for the middle part of Vietnam. The principle cities were Hue, Danang, Quang Tri, and Vinh. Once the center of

Right: A twin 23mm antiaircraft gun captured by the 101st Airborne Division during Operation Apache Snow.

Below: A North Vietnamese 37mm antiaircraft gun captured during Operation Dewey Canyon.

the Champa Empire, most of the population is located along the coast among the many sheltered bays.

Antiaircraft Artillery (North Vietnamese)

The North Vietnamese employed virtually every antiaircraft artillery system in the Soviet and Chinese arsenals. Allied pilots encountered systems ranging from 12.7mm heavy machineguns to 130mm radar-directed guns. Antiaircraft guns accounted for the bulk of Allied aircraft downed during the war.

Antitank Weapons (Allied)

While North Vietnamese armor was not common in the south, it was occasionally engaged with recoilless rifles and the man-carried LAW antitank rocket. Early in the war the SS-11, a first generation wire-guided missile, was routinely carried by aerial rocket artillery helicopters and some gunships, but it only was used against bunkers and, because it had to be "flown" into the target by the gunner using a small joystick, it was not very effective. Late in the war, the US deployed the TOW missile, a wire-guided semi-automatic command-to-line-of-sight system with a large HEAT (High Explosive Anti-Tank) warhead, on both helicopters and jeeps. Their performance was impressive. The infantry was also equipped with a man-pack 90mm recoilless rifle for antitank protection. It was a highly effective weapon, but its weight and the lack of NVA armor caused many units to leave it in the base camp when they went on operations, though when it was carried it was highly effective against bunkers.

The 106mm jeep and ground-mounted recoilless rifle was also issued to both the Army and the Marines, but its weight caused it to generally be retained for base camp defense, though the Marines used it effectively in the Battle of Hue to engage enemy troops in buildings. It was also a common weapon in Special Forces camps. The Marines carried the Korean War vintage 3.5in rocket launcher, a bazooka style weapon that they used against field fortifications.

Antiaircraft Artillery (North Vietnamese)

System/Type	Caliber	Fire Control	Rate of Fire	AA Range
DShK38/ManPack	12.7mm	Ring Sight	80rpm	1,000m
ZPU-2/Towed	14.5mm	Optical	300rpm	1,400m
ZPU-4/Towed	14.5mm	Optical	600rpm	1,400m
ZU-23/Towed	23mm	Optical	400rpm	2,500m
ZSU-23/4/SP	23mm	Radar/Optical	800rpm	2,500m
M1939/Towed	37mm	Optical	80rpm	3,000m
Type 63/SP	37mm	Optical	160rpm	3,000m
ZSU-57/2/SP	57mm	Optical	140rpm	4,000m
S-60/Towed	57mm	Radar/Optical	70rpm	6,000m
M1944/Towed	85mm	Radar/Optical	20rpm	10,000m
Type 59/Towed	100mm	Radar/Optical	15rpm	13,700m
KS-30/Towed	130mm	Radar/Optical	12rpm	13,720m

Antitank Weapons (North Vietnamese and Viet Cong)

The NVA issued the RPG-2 and RPG-7 to all of their companies. They were bazooka-style weapons that fired a rocket assisted 82mm HEAT warhead and were fully capable of penetrating the armor of all Allied combat vehicles. The People's Republic of China supplied most of the ammunition for the weapons. Though NVA gunners achieved a great number of hits, the low efficiency of the CHICOM HEAT warhead, on the RPG-2 in particular, limited the amount of damage caused. The NVA and VC also sometimes used captured or Chinese 57mm and 75mm recoilless rifle to fair effect against US armor, but the firing signature and the weight of the weapons resulted in them usually being employed only in camp defense.

The NVA also had a limited number of Soviet B-10 82mm and B-11 107mm recoilless rifles, though they were rarely encountered. During the Easter Offensive the NVA employed the AT-3 "Sagger," a man-pack wire-guided anti-tank missile, against ARVN armor in I Corps. The "Sagger" is "flown" to the target by the gunner using a control stick. It has a minimum arming range of 500m and a maximum engagement range of 3,000m. It has a fairly efficient HEAT warhead and a hit devastated most ARVN armor, particularly the M41A3 light tanks. Initially the NVA had some success with the system, though their employment tactics resulted in fewer hits than might have been achieved. As the ARVN gained experience in spotting the firing sites and recognizing the missile in flight they succeeded in negating it in part.

Left: A partially disassembled 12.7mm Degtyarev heavy machine gun waits inspection.

Below: The 57mm Soviet S60 was the most commonly encountered NVA antiaircraft gun.

Right: Antiwar protesters march the two miles from the Lincoln Memorial to the Pentagon in October 1967.

Below: Abbie Hoffman, David Dellinger, and Jerry Rubin of the Chicago 8, (right to third right), arrive at the court house to face charges stemming from the riot at the Democratic National Convention in Chicago.

Antiwar Movement (United States)

This movement was a loose coalition of intellectually, politically, ethically, religiously, or economically motivated factions drawn together by their common opposition to the American involvement in the Vietnam War. Attracting members from college campuses, middle-class suburbs, labor unions, and government institutions, the movement gained prominence in 1965, peaked in 1968, and remained powerful throughout the conflict. The tactics employed were diverse: legal demonstrations, grassroots organization, congressional lobbying, electoral challenges, civil disobedience, draft resistance, self-immolations, and political violence. Some peace activists traveled to North Vietnam. Quakers and others provided medical aid to Vietnamese civilian victims of the war. Veterans also protested the war.

By the beginning of 1965, the antiwar movement base was firmly established on US college campuses. Antiwar activities quickly escalated after the US began bombing North Vietnam. Marches and teach-ins were organized and over the next two years movement leaders, still mainly students, expanded their methods and gained new allies. Perhaps the most significant development of the period between 1965 and 1968 was the emergence of Civil Rights leaders as active proponents of peace in Vietnam.

As the movement's ideals spread beyond college campuses, doubts also began to appear within the administration itself. For most dissenters within the government, it was not an ethical but a pragmatic issue—the cost of winning had simply become too high. The cracks widened in 1968.

The Tet Offensive of late January initiated another major series of demonstrations, led many Americans to question the administration's veracity in reporting war progress, and contributed to Johnson's decision to retire. During the latter half of 1968, dissent degenerated into violence, culminating in August as a brutal battle between police and antiwar demonstrators in Chicago at the Democratic National Convention.

The movement became both more powerful and at the same time less cohesive between the period 1969 and 1973. Participants questioned its effectiveness, dissented over strategies and tactics, and infighting continued to alienate activists and hamper antiwar planning. The divisions were seized upon by the US government, but were largely internally generated. Although most Americans by this time opposed the escalation of the US role in Vietnam, most also disapproved of the counterculture that had arisen alongside the antiwar movement. The movement regained solidarity when news of the My Lai massacre became public and after the announcement in April 1970 that US forces had entered Cambodia. Opposition in Congress grew stronger, and when the Pentagon Papers were first published on June 13, 1971 Americans were led to believe that military and intelligence services had lost all accountability. For moderate Americans, antiwar sentiment became a legitimate reaction against excess rather than an unpatriotic one. The antiwar cause had also become institutionalized, and in

Above: Antiwar demonstrators fight with Chicago police at the Democratic National Convention in 1968.

January 1973 Nixon announced the effective end of US involvement.

The American movement against the Vietnam War was the most successful antiwar movement in US history. During the Johnson administration, it played a significant role in constraining the war and was a major factor in the administration's policy reversal in 1968. Although at times the violent nature of antiwar protest was actually seen by moderates as disruptive and unAmerican, the movement was generally successful at eroding public support for the war. Through confrontation and demonstration, the antiwar activists, the media, and the nation's college students helped to turn public support away from the war and its supporters in the government. Indirectly, the antiwar movement influenced the outcome of Vietnam by turning public opinion against the war.

During the Nixon years, it hastened US troop withdrawals, continued to restrain the war, fed the deterioration in US troop

Above: Anti-American rioters in Saigon in 1966 pull plastic bags over their head and run as the police fire tear gas.

Left: A student of the University of California at Berkeley, demonstrating in protest at the deaths of four students at Kent State, throws a tear gas canister back at police.

morale and discipline (which provided additional impetus to US troop withdrawals), and promoted congressional legislation that severed US funds for the war. It also gave rise to the Huston Plan, prompting Daniel Ellsberg to release the Pentagon Papers. This heightened the Nixon administration's paranoia about its political enemies, and played a major part in concocting the Watergate break-in, which undermined Nixon's authority in Congress and thus his ability to continue the war.

The antiwar movement's effect also meant that people who served honorably in Vietnam were not treated as well on their return as they might have been. This led in part to a problem with the position of Vietnam veterans' service in US history.

VIETNAM: A VISUAL ENCYCLOPEDIA

51

Left: An ARVN Airborne Battalion jumps from US Air Force C-123s to reinforce beleaguered units on the ground.

positions along the canal. The Task Force Commander was wounded in the first sweep of fire, and the next senior man refused to advance. In the ensuing battle the VC shot down five US helicopters that were ferrying the ARVN troops, repulsed an armored attack, and savaged the ARVN infantry. The Division Commander reinforced the troops on the ground with an airborne battalion that parachuted into the battle area at dusk. The following morning the ARVN attacked, but the Viet Cong had escaped during the night. The communist forces suffered 18 dead, while the ARVN lost 80, as well as a significant amount of heavy equipment. General Paul Harkins, the US Commander in Vietnam characterized the battle as a significant ARVN victory because the VC had abandoned their position, demonstrating the high command's absolute lack of understanding of the type of war being waged.

Ap Bia
See Hamburger Hill.

Apache Snow, Operation
From May 10–June 7, 1969, Operation Apache Snow was a follow up to Operations Dewey Canyon and Massachusetts Striker. It was designed to disrupt NVA infiltration activities in the

Ap Bac, Battle of (January 1963)
In late December 1962, the Viet Cong 261st Main Force Battalion dug into a series of tree lines and along the canal banks between the villages of Ap Bac and Ap Tan Thoi approximately 40 miles southwest of Saigon. Units of the ARVN 7th Infantry Division, planned to trap the VC by helicopter landing a regiment north of the position, while another regimental sized force of Civil Guards, (later called Regional Forces), reinforced with armor moved in from the south. The initial landings went unopposed, and then the southern wing of the operation encountered the south flank of the VC

Right: A Viet Cong prisoner is blind-folded and taken to the POW collection point.

A Shau Valley and put pressure on their logistical infrastructure. The A Shau was a major terminus of the Ho Chi Minh Trail in I Corps, and ideally positioned to support operations against Hue, Danang, or other cities along the coast. Apache Snow involved the 3rd Brigade of the 101st Airmobile Division, the 9th US Marine Regiment, and the 3rd Regiment of the ARVN 1st Infantry Division. Although almost all of the elements involved in the operation achieved contact with the enemy, the largest engagement was at Ap Bia mountain, later

dubbed "Hamburger Hill." By the time the operation ended, several US units were rendered combat ineffective and the political fallout resulted in an order to MACV from President Nixon to avoid casualties as much as possible.

Arc Light

This was the code name for B-52 bomber raids. The first strike was flown on June 18, 1965, and the last one August 18, 1973. By the end of the war B-52s had flown 124,532 strikes and dropped more than 3.5 million tons of ordnance on

Above: A B-52 Arc Light raid strikes a target along the coast in the area of II Corps.

Cambodia, Laos, North Vietnam, and South Vietnam. Only six percent of the missions were flown over North Vietnam, 12 percent in Cambodia, 27 percent against the Ho Chi Minh Trail in Laos and the rest hit targets inside South Vietnam. After the war the North Vietnamese stated that the most feared weapon in the US arsenal was the B-52.

Above: **M48A3 tanks of C Company, 1/69th Armor cross dry rice paddies in III Corps.**

Left: **A group of marines hitch a ride back to the firebase on an M48A3 tank.**

Armor (Allied)

Though many in and out of the military considered successful armor operations in the jungle to be improbable at best, Allied armor was employed in both offensive and defensive operations throughout Vietnam. At the height of the war 12 of the 239 US maneuver battalions were armor or armored cavalry.

Armored Cars

Armored cars were widely used in Vietnam for convoy escort, airbase security, and by Military Police units for patrol and reaction forces. They were also common in Vietnamese cavalry units.

Armored Reconnaissance Airborne Assault Vehicle

The US Army adamantly insisted that the M551 Sheridan was not a light tank. The 16-ton aluminum armored vehicle with a four-man crew was highly vulnerable to mines and RPG fire, suffered numerous electrical and electronic problems and because of the caseless cartridge design

Armored Cars (Allied)

Model	Wt.	Engine	Armament	Speed/Range	Crew
M3A1 Scout Car	6T	87hp G	.50 Cal. MG 7.62mm MG	60mph/250mi	2
M8 Greyhound	8.5T	110hp G	37mm .30 Cal. MG .50 Cal. MG	55mph/350mi	4
V-100 Cadillac-Gage M706 Commando	9T	200hp G	7.62mm MG (3)	60mph/350mi	3/4

of the ammunition was considered a death trap by its crews. Armament consisted of a 152mm gun/launcher firing both conventional and guided missile rounds (no missiles were employed in Vietnam), a coaxial 7.62mm machinegun, and a .50 caliber machinegun at the commander's station. With beehive ammunition, the gun was devastatingly effective against exposed troops. Powered by a 300hp diesel, the Sheridan was governed at 45mph and had a range of 380 miles. It was assigned to some armored cavalry units in lieu of the M48A3 tank.

Below: An ARVN M-8 crew watches as an American armored column passes on Highway 1 east of Tay Ninh.

Left: A V-100 armored car provides security for the International Hotel, the billet for the 716th MP Battalion.

Below: An ARVN M8 Greyhound armored car observes traffic on Highway 4, south of Saigon.

Armored Personnel Carriers (Allied)

Model	Wt.	Engine	Armament	Speed/Range	Crew
LVTP5A1 (Tracked)	18T	810hpG	7.62mm MG	30mph/200mi	2 + 34
M113 APC (Tracked)	11T	209hp G	.50 Cal. MG	40mph/200mi	2 + 11
M113A1 APC (Tracked)	12T	215hp D	.50 Cal. MG	40mph/300mi	2 + 11
M113 ACAV	12T	215hp D	.50 Cal. MG 2 x 7.62mm M60 MGs	35mph/300mi	3
M114A1 Command and Reconnaissance (Tracked)	8T	150hp G	7.62mm MG .50 Cal. MG	35mph/300mi	3
M106A1 Mortar Carrier (Tracked)	13 T	215hp D	107mm Mortar .50 Cal MG	40mph/300mi	6
M125A1 Mortar Carrier (Tracked)	13T	215hp D	81mm Mortar	40mph/300mi .50 Cal. MG	6
M132 Flamethrower (Tracked)	13T	215hp D	Flamethrower	40mph/300mi	3
M577A1 Command Post (Tracked)	13T	215hp D	None	40mph/300mi	2

Armored Personnel Carriers

The M113 series armored personnel carriers and their variants became the workhorse armored vehicles of the war and more than 12,000 were employed. Fully amphibious, fast, reliable, and simple to maintain, they fought in all four Corps areas. It was first employed in Vietnam in April 1962 and was extensively used as an Armored Cavalry Assault Vehicle (ACAV) with additional machine guns protected by armor shields. In I Corps, the Marines sometimes used their LVTP5A1 Amphibious Assault Vehicles as personnel carriers, but this was the exception and not the rule. The M114 Command and Reconnaissance Carrier, however, proved to be so poorly designed even the Vietnamese refused to take it out on operations and it was rapidly withdrawn.

Below: A commander maintains control of his LVTP-5 amtracs by radio as they approach the beach during Operation Daring Rebel.

Above: An infantry squad exits an M113 APC to take up defensive positions.

Left: South Vietnamese troops exit an M113 APC and assault a Viet Cong position.

Self-propelled Antitank Guns

The Army and the Marines each deployed a self-propelled antitank gun to Vietnam. The Marine system, the M50A1 Ontos, was a light aluminum armored chassis with a crew of three, mounting six 106mm recoilless rifles and a 7.62mm machine gun. Basic fire control consisted of .50 caliber spotting rifles that were matched to the main weapons and fired a round with a small smoke bursting charge to tell the gunner when he was on the target. The system had to be reloaded from outside the vehicle and the armor could not withstand small arms at close range. It was used with good effect, however, in Hue and as a base defense weapon.

The Army system, the M56 Scorpion, commonly referred to by the troops as the SPAT, mounted a 90mm gun on an open, unarmored tracked chassis and fired the same ammunition as the M48 tanks. Powered by a 6-cylinder gasoline engine, the SPAT could reach 30mph and had a range of 140 miles. Though fairly mobile, the system could not be fired on a side slope because the heavy recoil of the gun would tip it over. Originally designed to give airborne units an anti-tank capability, it was used only by the 173rd Airborne Brigade and was rapidly relegated to base camp defense.

Tanks

The workhorse of Allied armor was the M48A3 variant of the Patton tank. Used by both the Army and Marines, it was issued to the Vietnamese late in the war. It had a coincidence range finder, a telescope, and a ballistics computer for fire control. Many also mounted a 1.5 million candlepower xenon searchlight with which a well-trained crew could engage targets at night over 2,000m away using visible light, and out to 1,000m using infrared. Rugged and reliable, the M48A3 proved capable of operating throughout most of South Vietnam except in the Delta.

Most Vietnamese armored units were equipped with the M41A3 Walker Bulldog light tank, though some around Saigon had older M24 Chaffee light tanks as well.

Australian tankers used the Centurion Mark 5/1. Other tanks used in the theater

Below: An Ontos crew prepares to reload after firing at an enemy position north of Phu Bai.

included the M67A2 flamethrower, M728 Combat Engineer Vehicle (with a 165mm demolition gun), M51 Heavy Recovery Vehicle, M88 VTR (Vehicle Tracked Recovery) and the M60 AVLB (Armored Vehicle Launched Bridge).

Left: An M56 SPAT crew zeros their gun before going on an operation.

Below left: An exhausted Ontos crew member sacks out during a lull in the fighting in Hue.

Below: A tank helps secure a landing zone for a CH-34 coming in to evacuate casualties.

Tanks (Allied)

Model	Wt.	Engine	Armament	Speed/Range	Crew
Centurion Mk 5/1	56T	650hp G	20pdr (83.4mm) 7.62mm Coaxial MG 7.62mm External MG	25mph/70mi	4
M24 Chaffee	20T	110hp G (2)	75mm 7.62mm Coaxial MG .50 Cal. External MG	35mph/180mi	4
M41A3 Walker Bulldog	26T	500hp/G	76mm 7.62mm Coaxial MG .50 Cal. External MG	45mph/100mi	4
*M48A2C Patton	52T	825hp G	90mm 7.62mm Coaxial MG .50 Cal. Cupola MG	30mph/160mi	4
M48A3 Patton	52T	750hp D	90mm Gun 7.62mm Coaxial MG .50 Cal. Cupola MG	30mph/300mi	4

* A limited number of M48A2Cs were deployed due to a shortage of M48A3s.

Armor (North Vietnamese)

North Vietnam employed armor in both Laos and South Vietnam. Although they had used armor in Laos several times previously, their first successful utilization of armor in South Vietnam was on the night of February 6, 1968 when they overran the Lang Vei Special Forces Camp near the Laotian border in northern I Corps. A short time later a Marine Corps M48A3 engaged and destroyed a PT-76 in the Demilitarized Zone.

In March 1969, B Company, 1st Battalion, 69 Armor, destroyed two PT-76 tanks during a night action at the Ben Het Special Forces Camp in II Corps. In the 1972 Easter Offensive North Vietnamese T-54/59 tanks were mauled by a combination of South Vietnamese armor and tactical air power. North Vietnamese armored forces spearheaded their final offensive in 1975, dramatically punching through the gate of the Presidential Palace as Saigon fell.

Left: T-54 tanks were used by the North Vietnamese during the Easter Offensive and Ho Chi Minh Offensive.

Below: The T-34 tank was a World War II design that saw active service well into the 1970s.

Armored Personnel Carriers (North Vietnamese)

Model	Wt.	Engine	Armament	Speed/Range	Crew
BTR-50PK Tracked	15.5T	240hp D	7.62mm MG	28mph/250mi	2 + 20
BTR-60PA Wheeled (8)	11T	90hp G (2)	7.62mm MG	50mph/320mi	2 + 16
Type 55 Wheeled (4)	6T	80hp G	7.62mm MG	50mph/180mi	2 + 8
Type 56 Wheeled (6)	10T	110hp G	7.62mm MG	50mph/500mi	2 + 17

Tanks (North Vietnamese)

Model	Wt.	Engine	Armament	Speed/Range	Crew
PT-76 (Amphib.)	16T	240hp D	76mm 7.62mm Coaxial MG	28mph/165mi	3
Type 63 (Amphib.)	20T	520hp D	85mm 7.62mm Coaxial MG 12.7mm AA MG	32mph/150mi	4
T-34/85	35T	500hp D	85mm 7.62mm Coaxial MG 7.62mm Bow MG	35mph/200mi	5
* T-54	40T	520hp D	100mm 7.62mm Coaxial MG 12.7mm AA MG 3	0mph/250mi	4

* The North Vietnamese also had Chinese Type 59 tanks. It is a copy of the T-54.

Above: Hmong guerrillas on the Plain of Jars in Laos captured this PT-76 tank.

Though they had a number of armored personnel carriers, they were rarely seen on the battlefield in Vietnam, but occasionally in Laos.

Arnett, Peter
Arnett was an Associated Press correspondent in Vietnam from 1962 to 1965. He frequently clashed with officials over his critical reporting of the actions of the South Vietnamese government. Though highly thought of by his peers, after the war his reputation was severely damaged by a story he reported on CNN in which he accused American forces of using nerve gas and attempting to kill American defectors. The story was proven to be false.

Arnheiter, Marcus Aurelius
Arnheiter was the commander of the USS *Vance*, a destroyer escort. He filed false position reports, wrote fictional press releases, interfered with the gun line operations of other ships, and made his officers recommend him for the

Above: PFC Dave Fodor, driver for Charlie 6, 1st Battalion, 69th Armor, appears out of the hatch at Cateka in II Corps.

Right: An Air Force C-123 delivers ammunition to an 8in artillery battery at Plei Djerang in II Corps.

Silver Star. He was summarily relieved of command, after which he launched a public relations campaign claiming he was the victim of an ingenious mutiny.

Artillery (Allied)

United States military doctrine stresses the employment of firepower in lieu of manpower. Due to the advent of the cargo helicopter, allied artillery enjoyed unprecedented mobility and, other than reconnaissance actions, there were virtually no ground combat operations undertaken without artillery cover. Both towed and self-propelled systems in calibers from 105mm to 8in were available in profusion. Artillery was constantly repositioned into small semi-fortified perimeters called Fire Support Bases, which were opened and closed as required to

Self-Propelled Artillery (Allied)

System	Caliber/Type	Max Range	*Rate of Fire	Speed	Op. Range
M53	155mm Gun	22,000m	2rpm	30mph	160mi
M55	8 Inch How.	16,800m	2rpm	30mph	160mi
M107	175mm Gun	32,700m	2rpm.	35mph	450mi
M108	105mm How.	11,500m	8rpm	35mph	220mi
M109	155mm How.	14,600m	4rpm	35mph	220mi
M110	8 Inch How.	16,800m	2rpm	35mph	450mi
LVTH6	105mm	11,500m	6rpm	30mph	200mi

* Maximum Rate of Fire

Below: A battery of M108 self-propelled 105mm howitzers supports the 3rd Brigade, 25th Infantry Division during Operation Paul Revere III.

Bottom: A 175mm gun being convoyed down highway 14 south of Pleiku on its way to Ban Me Thout.

Towed Artillery (Allied)

System	Caliber/Type	Max Range	*Rate of Fire	Shell Wt. (HE)
M101A1	105mm How.	11,270m	8rpm	21.06kg
M102	105mm How.	11,500m	10rpm	21.06kg
M114A1	155mm How.	14,600m	2rpm	46.26kg
Medium Gun	5.5 Inch	16,460m	2rpm	36.28kg

* Maximum Rate of Fire

Above: An M109 155mm self-propelled howitzer of the 199th Light Infantry Brigade backs into its firing position.

Below left: An ARVN gun crew prepares their 105mm howitzer for a fire mission.

Below: A Montagnard gun crew loads their M101 105mm howitzer for a fire mission.

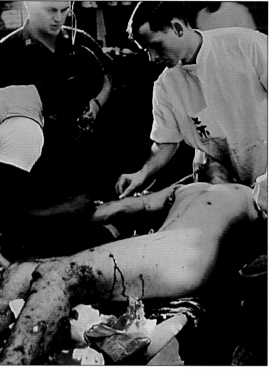

support operations. Along the coast Navy ships on the gun line supplemented the artillery and provided added fire support to engaged ground units.

Antiaircraft

The United States deployed a number of antiaircraft artillery systems to Vietnam. The M42A1 "Duster" was an open topped M41A3 tank chassis mounting two optically sighted 40mm Bofors automatic guns with a firing rate of 240rpm in a fully powered mount.

Then there were M55 Quad 50s of the Air Defense Artillery battalions (often mounted on M35 trucks) and the "Vulcan," a six-barreled 20mm rotary machine cannon mounted on an M113 armored personnel carrier chassis, with selectable firing rates of 1,000rpm and 3,000rpm.

The "Vulcan" incorporated a range-only radar. Neither gun was used in an antiaircraft role, but rather for base defense and, particularly in the case of the "Duster," as a convoy escort.

Artillery (North Vietnamese)

North Vietnamese artillery seriously out-ranged its American counterpart. However, other than light and medium guns, it was not until the very end of the war that it was found outside of I Corps, Laos, or along the DMZ.

ARVN

See Vietnam, Republic of, Army.

Above: A North Vietnamese 85mm field gun captured by the 101st Airborne in the A Shau Valley.

Below: The 122mm Soviet field gun was frequently used to support operations in I Corps and II Corps.

Above: Medics on the USS *Tripoli* treat heavy shrapnel wounds a man received during a North Vietnamese artillery raid.

Below: The 130mm Soviet field gun was the most feared artillery piece in the North Vietnamese arsenal.

Self-Propelled Artillery (North Vietnamese)

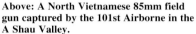

System	Caliber/Type	Max Range	*Rate of Fire	Speed	Shell Wt. (HE)
JSU122	122mm Gun	14,200	5rpm	25mph	150mi
JSU152	152mm How	9,800	7rpm	25	150mi

Towed Artillery (North Vietnamese)

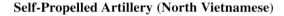

System	Caliber/Type	Max Range	*Rate of Fire	Shell Wt. (HE)
M1942/Type54	76mm/Gun	13,290m	15rpm	6.2kg
D44/Type 56	85mm/Gun	15,650m	15rpm	9.6kg
M1944/45	100mm/Gun	21,000m	8rpm	15.59kg
D74/Type 60	122mm/Gun	24,000m	5rpm	27.3kg
M46	130mm/Gun	27,150	5rpm	33.4kg
M1937	152mm/How	17,265	4rpm	43.51kg
D30	122mm/How	15,400	7rpm	21.76kg
M30/Type 54	122mm/How	11,800	5rpm	21.76kg

* **Maximum Rate of Fire**

Right: Troops cautiously approach an apparently abandoned bunker at the edge of the rubber trees.

Association of Foreign Correspondents in Vietnam (AFCV)

Press organization established to represent the interests of foreign journalists with the South Vietnamese government, the representatives of foreign governments, and other international bodies. The AFCV actively campaigned for greater press access. By 1970, the membership stood at 66. It also brought attention to the disappearance in Cambodia of foreign journalists.

Atlas Wedge, Operation

This operation targeted the 7th NVA Division, believed to be in the Michelin rubber plantation. The 1st Infantry Division, the 11th Armored Cavalry Regiment and units of the 1st Cavalry Division operated throughout the plantation from March 18–April 2, 1969. Heavy fighting erupted on March, 20 when reconnaissance elements came under fire from both sides of Highway 13. Reinforced with armor, artillery and air power they extracted a heavy toll on the North Vietnamese soldiers boxed in the killing zone. By the end of the operation, US forces had killed 421 North Vietnamese, captured tons of rice, and seized a large quantity of a small arms and ammunition. The heavy use of US armor was unusual, and served to reduce the number of casualties friendly forces sustained. The area was hammered by B-52 strikes, and a week later another major operation was initiated in the same locale. The 7th NVA division withdrew from the Michelin into sanctuaries in Cambodia to replace its losses and regroup.

Atrocities

While often considered to be synonymous with war crimes, atrocities are defined by various international treaties and conventions as inhumane acts such as murder, torture, rape, robbery and other abuses against prisoners of war and noncombatants. Most United States atrocities occurred because, faced with guerrilla tactics and often unable to confront their enemy directly, frustrated soldiers looked for a method to exact revenge for the mines, booby traps and punji-pits they continually encountered. Another contributor to the commission of atrocities by American troops was the pressure for a body count. Some commanders offered special awards to the units with highest body counts. This was occasionally interpreted as tacit approval for indiscriminate killing. My Lai, probably the best-known American atrocity, involved the murder of several hundred Vietnamese civilians by a unit of the Americal Division. The Viet Cong engaged in atrocities as well. Terrorism was a major weapon used to promote their cause. Between 1957 and 1970, they assassinated over 37,000 government officials, religious leaders, civil

Below left: City officials from Hue arrange the coffins for a mass burial of some of those executed by the NVA/VC during Tet.

Below: Two battalions of Viet Cong with flamethrowers burned out the hamlet of Dak Son, killing a large number of women and children.

Right: A CH-54 Tarhe delivers fuel to a mechanized unit during Operation Attleboro.

Below: A CH-47 Chinook lifts a howitzer and its ammunition to a new firebase during Operation Attleboro.

servants, and teachers, many of whom were disemboweled and decapitated, along with their families, in front of the village to demonstrate the primacy of the Viet Cong in a given area. The Viet Cong and North Vietnamese also routinely shelled and rocketed South Vietnamese cities to terrorize the populace, resulting in the death of thousands of unarmed civilians. During the Tet Offensive, when the North Vietnamese captured the city of Hue, they rounded up and executed several thousand South Vietnamese functionaries, burying many alive.

Attleboro, Operation
Operation Attleboro lasted from September 14–November 24, 1966. It was conducted in War Zone C and west of the Michelin rubber plantation in III Corps. The largest operation in the war up to that time, it involved the first use of large-scale multi-divisional search and destroy tactics and involved over 20,000 troops of the 1st Infantry Division, 4th Infantry Division, 25th Infantry Division, 196th Light Infantry Brigade, and the 173rd Airborne Brigade. American units uncovered an enormous communist base camp, large enough to support the entire 9th Viet Cong Division. Captured documents indicated the Viet Cong 9th Division and the 101st NVA Regiment had lost a total of 2,130 troops killed in action. The battle demonstrated that in a head-on fight between large units, the Allies would win due to their superior maneuverability and overwhelming firepower. Operations Cedar Falls and Junction City, which followed closely on behind Attleboro, confirmed that fact. Learning from these defeats the Viet Cong rarely confronted such large combat units or operations again.

Attrition Strategy
As the political decision had been made to restrict the war to South Vietnam, American military commanders were forced to devise a strategy to win that did not involve operations in the enemy homeland. They tried to break the will of communist forces by killing so many of their soldiers that they would give up. Even though the United States killed

nearly a million communist soldiers, and nearly three percent of the entire population of North Vietnam, the strategy failed. While American planners approached the war as a military

problem, the North Vietnamese look on it as both a political struggle for reunification of their nation and a total war, and were willing to accept enormous casualties to achieve their ends.

Above: The executive officer of Company D, 5th Royal Australian Regiment, radios for a helicopter extraction.

Australia

Following the defeat of the French in the Indochina War, Australian leaders steadily warned the United States that if the communists took South Vietnam all the democracies throughout the rest of Asia would be in jeopardy. Australia's military involvement began with the dispatch of a small training team in 1962, later expanded and renamed the Australian Army Training Team Vietnam (AATTV) in 1964. This small unit, which served from 1964 through 1970, also had a few New Zealanders attached from time to time. By the end of their involvement 990 men had served in the AATTV, 30 had been killed in action, and 122 wounded, of which ten were New Zealanders. At the same time, it became the most decorated unit in the history of the Australian Army. Four men earned the Victoria Cross, and there were 86 other decorations for valor awarded to team members. The US Army also

presented the team a US Meritorious Unit Citation, and the Vietnamese honored them with a collective award of the Vietnamese Cross of Gallantry with Palm, the highest decoration of that type given out by the Saigon government.

Following the Gulf of Tonkin Incident Australia added regular Army, Air Force and Navy units; the number of Australian troops reached its peak of 7,672 in 1969. The Australian Task Force officially arrived in Vietnam in May, 1965, right after the US Marines. Essentially a light infantry brigade, it had two infantry battalions, an artillery battalion, a reconnaissance company, two SAS units, and the necessary administrative and logistical forces necessary to operate independently if required. An armored squadron eventually joined them as well. New Zealand contributed about one third of the artillery assigned to the task force and, in 1967, expanded their commitment to include two infantry companies and a Special Forces platoon as well.

The Australian troops had a great deal of experience in counterinsurgency warfare, many having served against the Communist Terrorists (CT) in Malaya,

1955–1960, and also against the Indonesians during the "Confrontation," 1960–1966. For this reason they sometimes questioned the tactical proficiency of American units and commanders, repeatedly stating that the Americans were very poor at operating in the jungle because they made far too much noise. One senior Australian officer even remarked that "the Americans do not fight a jungle war, they remove the jungle and then they fight." The also chided American commanders for not being more careful with their troops lives by carrying out better planning and reconnaissance in advance of operations. They constantly characterized American troops as trigger happy and less than thorough when they operated in an area, faulting what they considered to be the indiscriminate use of air and artillery against targets that were not under observation. They also frequently turned up caches and pockets of enemy after a US unit had gone through. However, they did concede that the war against the Viet Cong in Vietnam was significantly different than what they had experienced in Malaya and against the Indonesians, simply because there was no real way to identify the combatants from the non-combatants until the shooting started, and the enemy was far more heavily armed. For their part, the US commanders believed that the Australians were very good soldiers and General Westmoreland tried, unsuccessfully, to get both Australia and New Zealand to increase their contribution to the war. Because they rotated as units rather than as individuals, with one battalion or battery replacing another after their tour was over, their units had a great deal more internal cohesion than some US units. At the same time, this served to rotate a large part of the Australian Army through the combat zone by the time their participation ended.

The Australian Navy contributed ships to the effort to both interdict North Vietnamese seaborne logistics and also to provide fire support to units in contact along the coast. Several Australian ships served in both capacities and there was almost always at least one on the gun line at any point in time. Their ships also participated in raids against North Vietnamese installations and came under fire several times from North Vietnamese shore batteries. One of the worst friendly fire incidents involved an American aircraft attack on an Australian destroyer, the HMAS *Hobart*, which killed two sailors. The HMAS *Perth* was hit by a North Vietnamese shore battery and suffered six wounded, she also received two US Navy Unit commendations, for actions during the Tet Offensive and on Operation Sea Dragon

The Royal Australian Air Force also contributed to the war, and many US soldiers will fondly recount their experiences with the courage and professionalism of the Caribou pilots of the "Wallaby Airlines," an Australian transport unit. An Australian Canberra bomber unit, 2nd Squadron, arrived in 1967 and rapidly acquired a reputation as one of the elite close support units of the war, using low level bombing tactics that they pioneered. Units in contact routinely praised their accuracy in the face of intense ground fire, and they received both the US Air Force Outstanding Unit Commendation and the Vietnamese Cross of Gallantry with Palm. The RAAF eventually deployed an F-86 squadron to Thailand as well, but it did not get involved in combat, though six pilots flew Phantoms in US squadrons.

Australia suffered 474 dead, including a nurse, and 2,940 injured during the war. Like America, Australia had a very vocal antiwar movement, although the Conscription Law that was passed in 1964 and used to maintain the manpower of the services did not attract as much opposition as the similar statute did in the United States. Even after public support for the war, once over 70 percent, had eroded more than half of the populace still supported conscription.

As the American withdrawal progressed, Australian and New Zealand withdrew their troops as well. The last Australian elements departed Vietnam in January 1973.

Australian Army Training Team— Vietnam (AATTV)

The Australian government had observed the growth of the communist insurgency in Vietnam with growing concern following the defeat of the French in 1954. In 1962, they dispatched a team of 30 jungle warfare experts, otherwise known as the Australian Army Training Team—Vietnam, to assist in the training of President Diem's fledgling Army of the Republic of Vietnam.

Below: HMAS *Hobart* served with the US 7th Fleet during the Vietnam conflict, earning a USN Commendation.

B

Baby Lift, Operation

The US plan for the evacuation by air of 2,000 orphaned Vietnamese children, some of them born to Vietnamese mothers and American fathers was codenamed Operation Baby Lift. Citing fear of the reprisals that might be meted out to children of mixed-parentage by a communist government, Operation Baby Lift relocated many children to the United States. Most analysts agree that it was staged partly to draw attention to the imminent fall of Saigon and partly as a humanitarian exercise. The operation, which took place during the first two weeks of April

Above: Emperor Bao Dai and his wife were in Paris when Premier Ngo Dinh Diem organized and held the referendum that deposed him.

Above: Vietnamese civilians at U-Tapao wait to re-board their C-141 Starlifter for transport to the Philippines at the end of Operation Baby Lift.

1975 (just before the fall of Saigon), at first met with disaster when the aircraft carrying the first group crashed. Subsequently more than 2,600 children were successfully evacuated and adopted.

Baez, Joan

The most prominent American antiwar folksinger, Joan Baez, gained notoriety by refusing to pay her income taxes because the money would go towards the war. In 1972, Baez was in Hanoi during the Christmas bombing. Upon her return to the US she falsely reported that an American prisoner of war camp had been hit by a bomb.

Ball, George W

Appointed undersecretary of State by President Kennedy, Ball opposed the buildup of US forces in Vietnam. In the Johnson administration he commonly argued against escalation. Constantly ignored, he resigned from the State Department in 1966. Following the Tet offensive President Johnson appointed Ball to the Senior Advisory Group on Vietnam, where he continued to press for disengagement from the war.

Ban Me Thout, Battle of
(March 1975)

The first major battle of the North Vietnamese final offensive against South Vietnam took place on March 10 and 11, 1975, at Ban Me Thout, the capital of Darlac province in the central highlands. Three NVA divisions smashed the ARVN defenses and over-ran the city, prompting President Nguyen Van Thieu to withdraw all South Vietnamese regular forces from the highlands. Neither the Regional Forces nor the civilian administrators were informed of the plan. Seeing the Army units moving toward the coast, the populace panicked and refugees began filling up the roads. The withdrawal rapidly became a rout. Thousands died as the NVA shelled the struggling columns.

Bao Dai

The last Emperor of Vietnam, Bao Dai became a political puppet of the French. He lost his base of support when the French were defeated by the Viet Minh and withdrew in 1954. In 1955, a national referendum stripped him of his office and turned power over to Ngo Dinh Diem, whom Bao Dai had previously appointed as Premier. He then went into exile in France.

Above: An F-100 Super Sabre climbs after unloading its bombs against a target in the jungle.

Barker, Frank A Jr

On March 16, 1968, a strike force commanded by Barker killed Vietnamese civilians in Son My village in what became known as the My Lai massacre. He submitted a false and misleading report after the action and failed to investigate indications of war crimes that were reported to him. Barker died in a helicopter crash in June 1968, before the My Lai massacre became public knowledge.

Barrel Roll, Operation

Operation Barrel Roll was the code name for covert American air operations in support of General Vang Pao in northern Laos. It was initiated on June 9, 1964 as a result of a Pathet Lao and People's Army of Vietnam offensive in the Plain of Jars in violation of the 1962 Geneva Accords, which declared Laos an independent and neutral state, and terminated on April 17, 1973. US Air Force F-100s made the first attacks on June 9. Barrel Roll was a strange operation in that the US Ambassador in Vientiane controlled all air assets and target approval. For nine years the object of this massive bombing campaign was to both interdict the Ho Chi Minh Trail and support Royal Lao Government forces in fending off a slow invasion by the North Vietnamese.

Beehive

This is a type of ammunition used in artillery shells, tank guns and aerial

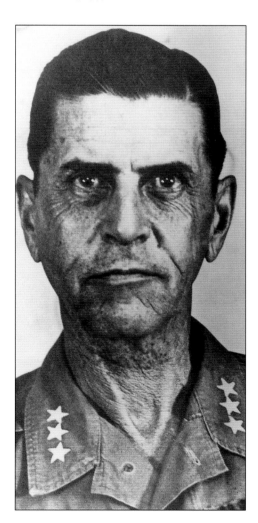

Above: Lieutenant General J Seaman proclaimed the Iron Triangle a "military desert" after Operation Cedar Falls. The Ben Suc Viet Cong Battalion reappeared within a month.

rockets. It contains thousands of small steel flechetts. When fired the flechetts deploy in an expanding cone. The round was widely used in the defense of fire-bases and against troops in the open. Sometimes helicopter gunship pilots referred to it as "nails."

Ben Hai River

On July 22, 1954, the 17th parallel was designated as a demarcation line for the regroupment of the French and Viet Minh forces at the end of the Indochina War. The Ben Hai River, which comes out of the Laotian highlands and flows into the South China Sea, roughly parallels the 17th parallel and became the defacto demarcation line.

Ben Suc

Located on the southwestern edge of the Iron Triangle, Ben Suc was a village of approximately 6,000 people. During Operation Cedar Falls, American forces destroyed the village, and miles of tunnels in and around it used by the Viet Cong. Though the villagers became forced refugees, the Viet Cong rapidly re-entered the village as soon as the Americans left, calling into question the effectiveness of both the pacification and search and destroy strategies.

Ben Tre

Ben Tre was the capital of Kien Hoa province in the Mekong Delta. During the Tet Offensive half of the city of 35,000 was destroyed by US bombs and shells. A US Army Major was quoted as saying: "It became necessary to destroy the town in order to save it." The quote

Left: Bombs impact among a group of structures along a canal outside of Ben Tre.

was later revealed to have been made up by an AP journalist to add more drama to his report.

Berrigan, Daniel

Daniel Berrigan was an antiwar activist catholic priest who joined with seven other catholics on May 17, 1968, and burned the draft records of a selective Service Office in Catonsville, Maryland. He was sentenced to three years in prison, but went underground and hid for several months before being apprehended in August 1970. He was paroled on January 26, 1972, because of ill health.

Berrigan, Philip

The founder of the Emergency Citizens' Group Concerned about Vietnam, on October 27, 1967, Berrigan and three others poured blood on the draft records of the Selective Service office in Baltimore, Maryland. He became the first catholic priest in the United States

Below: Heavy rocket and mortar fire, coupled with a significant ground probe damaged a number of buildings in Bien Hoa.

Above: A platoon leader calls for artillery on an enemy machinegun during the Battle of Bien Hoa.

ever sent to prison for a political crime. Before he could be imprisoned he joined his brother Daniel in burning the draft records at Catonsville, Maryland.

Bien Hoa, Battle of (November 1964)

Early in the war the United States constructed a large military headquarters and airfield just outside of Bien Hoa, 20 miles from Saigon. On November 1, 1964, the Viet Cong launched a pre-dawn mortar bombardment, which destroyed six and damaged the other 14 of the 20 B-57 bombers stationed there. Sappers followed up the mortar bombardment. Five Americans were killed in the attack. The attack against Bien Hoa made it clear that if the United States was going to conduct an air war over North and South Vietnam with aircraft and personnel stationed in the south, troops would be required to defend the airfields. Indirectly the attack on Bien Hoa contributed to the escalation of the conflict and the introduction of American ground forces in early 1965.

Right: Huey "slicks" wait to take on a load of troops during Operation Binh Tay.

Big Minh

See Duong Van Minh.

Binh Gia, Battle of (December 1964)

This battle was instrumental in convincing US policy makers that South Vietnamese forces required massive military assistance from the United States if they were to prevent a Viet Cong takeover of the nation.

On May 29, 1965, a force of 1,000 Viet Cong stormed the hamlet of Binh Gia near Quang Ngai, which was defended by three battalions of South Vietnamese troops. The ARVN panicked and fled the battlefield, leaving behind almost all of their weapons and even most of their uniforms. F-100 and Skyraider fighter-bombers forced the Viet Cong out of the hamlet and the ARVN reoccupied Binh Gia in June. However, on July 4, the Viet Cong attacked again, and after only an hour and a half of desultory combat, again the ARVN fled. Even though additional ARVN reinforcements were immediately available, the ARVN Corps commander requested that the US Marines intervene. The Marines attacked and drove the Viet Cong from the hamlet.

Binh Tay I-IV, Operations

During the 1970 Cambodian Incursion, Operations Binh Tay I-V were furthest north. While the main Allied attacks were in the Fishhook and Parrot's Beak areas in III and IV Corps, the US and ARVN commands decided that it was essential to attempt to disrupt NVA logistical operations farther north in Cambodia. US participation by the 4th Infantry Division was poorly executed and relatively brief. Elements of the 3rd Battalion 506th Infantry as well as the 1st Battalion 14th Infantry came under heavy fire and several helicopters were downed at the outset. As his battalions suffered significant casualties, the Commanding General of the 4th Division decided to turn the operation over to the ARVN. The ARVN 22nd and 23rd Infantry Divisions, 2nd Ranger Group, and 2nd Armor Brigade attacked into Cambodia west of Pleiku. ARVN troops discovered caches containing hundreds of weapons, tons of ammunition, and medical supplies. Their only contact was with the enemy security forces and combat was light. Toward the end of the operations on June 23, 1970 the ARVN 22nd Division, protected by

US artillery and air cavalry moved deep into Cambodia to relieve a Khmer Garrison and rescue hundreds of refugees from the NVA forces besieging it. The ARVN successfully evacuated 7,571 Cambodian troops and refugees to the Duc Co Special Forces Camp in Pleiku province.

Binh Tram

The Binh Tram were regimental-sized North Vietnamese Army units assigned both transportation and security duties along a designated portion of the Ho Chi Minh Trail. They moved matériel between logistical points and provided combat elements to oppose American Special Forces and Hmong guerrilla operations along a specific segment of the Trail.

Binh Xuyen

Prominent in the decade following World War II, Binh Xuyen was a Vietnamese criminal and political organization based in Saigon. Originally a pirate gang operating on the Sai Gon river, Binh Xuyen leader Bay Vien forged an alliance with the Viet Minh after the war, and it played a major part in fomenting the general

strike of September 24, 1945, which shut down all commerce along with electricity and water supplies. That same day in a suburb of Saigon, members of the group massacred 150 French and Eurasian civilians, including children. In 1947, Bay Vien switched allegiance to Bao Dai, predominantly to gain protection for the network of casinos, brothels, and opium dens that his Binh Xuyen controlled. In May 1955, Prime Minister Diem waged a violent crackdown against the Binh Xuyen, and its power waned.

Bird and Sons (Birdair)

Named for the owner William Bird, Bird and Sons was a small airline in Southeast Asia. It operated mainly short takeoff and landing aircraft under contract to the US Agency for International Development, and also flew clandestine missions for the CIA in Laos. Continental Airlines bought it in 1965 and absorbed the clandestine missions by operating Bird Air under a new name, Continental Air Services (CAS).

Below: A pair of OV-10 Broncos fly an armed reconnaissance mission in the Delta.

Left: C Company, 1/69th Armor, delivers dead Viet Cong in Cu Chi for the body count.

Body Count

Because success in the war in Vietnam could not be measured in terms of territory seized, American policymakers decided to use the number of enemy killed as a statistical measurement of success. Early in the war body counts were physically carried out. However, since a physical count following air and artillery strikes could rarely be carried out, estimates became common. Later, as they became a measure of professional performance for officers, the numbers were distorted. It deteriorated into a meaningless exercise and may have led to the unnecessary death of South Vietnamese civilians, who when dead were classified as Viet Cong in order to inflate the body count.

Below: A Marine 105mm Howitzer crew slams a round home and responds to a request for fire.

Black Ponies

The Black Ponies were a squadron of heavily armed Navy OV-10 Broncos that supported riverine operations in the Mekong Delta. They also provided air support to clandestine missions by Navy SEAL teams in the same area.

Blue Light, Operation

In December 1965, Operation Blue Light was the first major US Air Force airlift operation of the Vietnam War. It involved the transportation of the 3rd Brigade of the 25th Infantry Division's units from Honolulu, Hawaii, to Pleiku in the central highlands of South Vietnam using a mixed fleet of C-141 and C-133 aircraft.

It also served as an impromptu test of the C-141 Starlifter, which entered service in 1964 and was the Air Force's first all-jet transport. The operation was complicated by the fact that the Pleiku airstrip was of a marginal design and only 6,000ft long. The service limits for the C-141 stated that the minimum runway length required by the aircraft was 6,000ft. The Air Force flew 231 missions into this marginal airfield without incident, demonstrating that they could project military power into what was once considered an inaccessible area.

VIETNAM: A VISUAL ENCYCLOPEDIA

Bold Mariner, Operation

The Batangan peninsula in Quang Ngai province was one of the most strongly held Viet Cong areas throughout the war. In 1969, a joint US Marine and US Army operation was conducted to pacify the Batangan peninsula. The operation involved the forcible relocation of all civilians, and the destruction of all homes, buildings, and other property on the peninsula.

Operations began in January and by July all of the people had been removed with more than 1,000 of them detained for questioning. Army engineers destroyed over 13,000m of tunnels, as well as all of the buildings and structures they could find. The operation only served to further alienate the people from the South Vietnamese government, because no provision had been made to relocate the civilians into a place where they could live.

No lasting military gains accrued from the operation, because the Allied forces had failed to destroy the Viet Cong units operating on the peninsula. In 1970, another operation was carried out in the same area. New bunkers and tunnels had been constructed in nearly the same sites. In 1971, the Viet Cong 48th Battalion was still in action on the peninsula.

Bolo, Operation

Faced with rising losses from MiG-21 interceptors, and barred by Presidential order from bombing North Vietnamese air fields, the 7th Air Force created a trap

Above: This booby-trapped 40mm grenade, found in Quang Ngai, was carefully uncovered with a bayonet.

for the North Vietnamese fighters by exploiting a weakness in their ground controlled intercept radar system.

The North Vietnamese could determine which flights consisted of fighters and those that contained F-105 bombers by watching how they refueled. Exploiting this fact, Operation Bolo on January 2, 1967, used F-4 fighters configured for air-to-air combat to emulate the normal operations of F-105 bombers. The North Vietnamese fell for the trick. Though marginal weather caused only three of the planned 14 F-4 flights to reach the target area, in the

Left: The 2nd Battalion, 26th Marines, sweeps Hill 37 during Operation Bold Mariner on the Batangan peninsula.

ensuing intense air combat, which was the largest single aerial dogfight of the Vietnam War, 12 F-4s shot down seven MiG-21s and claimed two other probable kills against no US Air Force losses. Operation Bolo destroyed nearly half of the entire inventory of MiG-21s in the North Vietnamese Air Force, significantly reducing subsequent US losses to enemy fighters.

Bombs, Dumb (Iron)

While there were multiple kinds of bombs utilized during the Vietnam War they were divided into two general classes, dumb bombs, and smart bombs. Dumb bombs were unguided munitions dropped by aircraft. They were generally divided into standard bombs and cluster bombs. Standard bombs usually weighed 500lb, 750lb, 2,000lb, or 3,000lb. These bombs were routinely used against bunkers and troops in the jungle. They were also used against bridges and matériel targets.

A specialized type of standard bomb was the Daisy Cutter. Available in two sizes, either 10,000lb or 15,000lb, it was used to clear helicopter landing zones in dense jungle.

Cluster Bombs essentially were a carrier with a large number of submissions that were dispensed over the target. The submunitions varied in size from about 6cm in diameter to 3lb. When they detonated they blasted hundreds of small steel pellets across the impact area. Cluster bombs were used against troops in the open and area targets. For instance, a single B-52 loaded with cluster bombs could saturate an area of almost a square mile and deliver over seven million high velocity steel pellets in one pass. The antiwar movement, with encouragement from Hanoi, routinely demonstrated against cluster bombs, which they called "marble bombs."

Bombs, Smart

Smart bombs are a class of guided munitions dropped from aircraft. Two types of smart bombs were used in the Vietnam War: the laser-guided bomb and the electro-optical guided bomb. The laser-guided bomb homed on a pulsed laser beam reflected from the target. Originally developed by the US Army, it was to put into production by the US Air Force in 1965 under the code name Paveway. The laser guidance kits were attached to standard 750lb and 2,000lb. bombs beginning in the summer of 1966. The electro-optical guided bomb program led to the development by the Navy of a smart bomb known as "The 'Walleye." A miniature TV camera was fitted to the nose of the bomb and the pilot locked onto the target using a small screen in his cockpit. After release the bomb's internal computer system flew it to the aim-point. This 850lb bomb was first used over North Vietnam in 1967

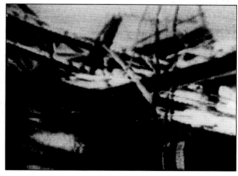

and a 2,000lb version was introduced in 1972. Though smart bombs represented less than one percent of all bombs over 500lb dropped by US forces, the numbers of targets destroyed were far out of proportion to the numbers used.

Booby Traps

Concealed devices used to inflict casualties on an unsuspecting enemy are known as booby traps. The Viet Cong utilized both explosive and non-explosive booby traps. They ranged all the way from unexploded 500lb bombs to simple pits lined with fire hardened and sharpened bamboo stakes, known as punji-pits. Antipersonnel booby traps were frequently strewn along roads and trails or within buildings that the troops could be expected to either use or enter.

Right and below: The guidance camera on a Walleye bomb tracked its path toward a highway bridge in the three small photos, the results of the attack are shown in the larger one.

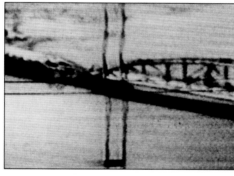

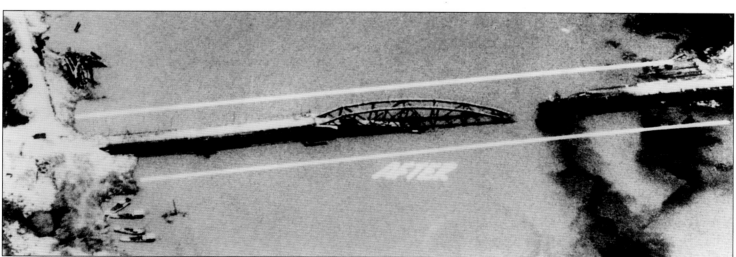

Above: A buddy comforts a soldier wounded by a booby trap, while they wait for a medic.

Right: MPs provide security for an Explosive Ordnance Disposal team while they defuse a booby trap.

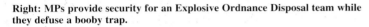

Antimatériel booby traps were usually placed on bridges, riverine chokepoints, or along a highway. Mines and booby traps reportedly accounted for more than ten percent of US fatalities and over 15 percent of the wounded.

Boun Oum, Prince

The strong man of southern Laos, Prince Boun Oum supported the military takeover of the neutralist central government in 1960. He and his co-conspirator, General Phoumi Nosavan, got US support from the CIA and US military Programs Evaluation Office. Throughout the war he was a major figure in the coalition governments of Laos.

Bowles, Chester B

In 1961, Bowles became Undersecretary of State in the Kennedy administration. He opposed the Taylor-Rostow recommendations for increased military support to the Diem regime in South Vietnam. He suggested instead that South Vietnam be neutralized like Laos. This led to his removal by President Kennedy. His removal effectively killed any opposition inside the administration to intervention in South Vietnam.

Bradley, Omar Nelson

General Bradley was one of the key American generals of World War II, where he became widely known as the "soldier's general" for his close relationship with his troops. Appointed as the first Chairman of the Joint Chiefs of Staff in 1949, he stayed in that post throughout the Korean War and was one of the few men ever promoted to five-star rank in the United States military. Although he had staunchly opposed a ground war in Asia, in 1967 he visited Vietnam and declared that the United States was fighting "the right war, in the right place, against the right enemy." In 1968, as one of the "wise men," he argued against withdrawal.

Bravo I and II, Operations

Having heard rumors of a coup against his brother's government, Ngo Dinh Nhu devised a pseudo-coup during which the plotters could be disarmed or destroyed. The plan had two phases, designated Bravo I and Bravo II. In the first phase, loyal Special Forces would be ordered out of the city to hunt guerrillas. During their absence loyal police and soldiers

Below: General Omar Bradley as a Lieutenant General in World War II.

Above: Members of the 101st Airborne Division rest as they are flown to a new operating area in II Corps.

disguised as rebels would stage a spontaneous revolt, killing selected Vietnamese and US officials. During the fighting Diem and Nhu would flee to a secure location. The leaders of the pseudo-coup would then proclaim that they were dedicated to driving the Americans out of South Vietnam and reaching conciliation with the communists. The loyal Special Forces, who would storm back into Saigon, crush the uprising, rescue the Ngo brothers, and return the rightful government to power, would spearhead the second phase. This second phase would reaffirm the legitimacy of the Diem government and strengthen it in its dealings with the Americans.

During the last week of October, 1963 it appeared that the brother's plan was unfolding smoothly. Unfortunately, the general's plot was moving ahead simultaneously, and key members of the pseudo-coup had been captured or killed. When it became clearer what was happening the brothers fled to Cholon, were there were captured and executed on November 2, 1963.

Brezhnev, Leonid Ilyich
Brezhnev replaced Nikita Khrushchev as Secretary-General of the Communist Party in 1964. He immediately increased the amount of aid the USSR was providing to the North Vietnamese, particularly high-technology items such as surface-to-air missiles and sophisticated radars. By 1970, he determined that détente with the United States was more important than victory in Vietnam and began reducing Soviet involvement in the war.

Brigade
The brigade is a standard US military organization commanded by a colonel. US divisions in Vietnam generally consisted of three brigades, containing from three to five maneuver battalions and around 3,000 men. There were also a number of independent brigades in the war. Independent brigades routinely had troops strengths approaching 5,000. Brigades were frequently moved between Corps areas in response to enemy intelligence or operations.

Bright Light
This was the unclassified code name for American efforts to rescue prisoners of war being held by either the VC or North Vietnamese in South Vietnam, Laos, and Cambodia. The Joint Personnel Recovery Center (JPRC), an element of the MACV Studies and Observations Group (SOG), was responsible for all Bright Light

was an early advocate of US involvement in Vietnam. He served as a foreign policy advisor to Presidents Kennedy and Johnson. In the 1960s and 1970s he saw communist expansion in Asia as the greatest existing threat to world peace and worked diligently to oppose it.

Buddhists

Under Ngo Dien Diem, catholicism achieved special prominence in Vietnamese affairs. Catholics were appointed to key posts in the civil service, police and military. Diem blatantly favored the catholic refugees who fled North Vietnam after the defeat of the French at Dien Bien Phu. Diem's repression contributed to a powerful resurgence of buddhist influence. On June 11, 1963, the buddhist monk Quang Duc committed self-immolation at a busy Saigon intersection in protest of Diem's policies. After Diem's assassination the buddhists filled a political vacuum in South Vietnam, and in December 1963 they organized the United Buddhist Church of Vietnam, which eventually encompassed all of the buddhist sects. In

Operations. They gathered, collated, and analyzed intelligence about VC and NVA POW camps, then organized raids in an attempt to recover prisoners. Established in 1964, SOG conducted Bright Light Operations until they were disbanded.

Brinks Hotel

On Christmas Eve 1964, two Viet Cong agents detonated a bomb in the basement of the Brinks Hotel in Saigon. Two American officers were killed and 58 were wounded. The bombing demonstrated the ability of the Viet Cong to operate anywhere in South Vietnam, even in the heavily defended capital.

Brother Number One

Khmer Rouge leader Pol Pot was designated with the codename Brother Number One. He adopted this name to confuse the Cambodian intelligence.

Brown, George Scratchley

General Brown commanded the US 7th Air Force from 1968 to 1970. During the confirmation hearings for his appointment as Chairman of the Joint Chiefs of Staff in 1973, he defended his concealment of the secret bombing of Cambodia

to Congress. He later accused Congress of selling out South Vietnam by denying them adequate aid.

Brown, Samuel Winfred Jr.

Originally a presidential campaign organizer for Senator Eugene McCarthy in 1968, Brown helped found the Vietnam Moratorium Committee in 1969. The committee sponsored the largest antiwar demonstrations held in the country on October 15, 1969, and in Washington DC on November 15. He later supported George McGovern's presidential campaign in 1972.

Bruce, David K E

As Ambassador to France, Bruce was instrumental in limiting the amount of support the United States offered to the Viet Minh after World War II. He supported the French effort to reestablish control in Indochina. He later supported a negotiated settlement to the American phase of the war, and from 1970–1971 he headed the US delegation to the Paris peace talks.

Brzezinski, Zbigniew Kazimierz

A staunch anticommunist, Brzezinski

Above: A young monk immolates himself in protest of President Diem's oppression of the buddhists.

Above: A scout dog and his handler prepare to move out near the Demilitarized Zone during Operation Buffalo.

Above right: A Marine Corps heavy recovery vehicle retrieves a damaged tank during Operation Buffalo.

Hue and Danang, led by Thich Tri Quang, the buddhists were militantly opposed to the Saigon government. Their opposition eventually led to the rise of Air Marshal Nguyen Cao Ky. In May 1966, the buddhists organized militant demonstrations throughout the country, complete with marches and widely publicized self-immolations. With tacit American support, Premier Ky flew troops to Danang and crushed the buddhists militarily. Following their crushing defeat in 1966, even though they represented 80 percent of the South Vietnamese population, their political influence was virtually nil.

Buffalo, Operation
From July 2–July 14, 1967, Operation Buffalo was conducted in an area just south of the Demilitarized Zone. It began when two companies of the 1st Battalion, 9th Marines, were ambushed and rapidly grew into a five battalion pitched battle. The North Vietnamese had moved elements of four divisions, some 35,000 troops, into areas just north of the Ben

Hai River. Supporting these units were several battalions of medium and heavy artillery, much of it arrayed north of the Marine bastion at Con Thien. By late afternoon on July 6 the Marines were unable to move due to heavy artillery fire on their positions. For example, 1,000 rounds fell on the 1/3 Marines that day. That night the enemy attacked the Marine perimeters with small arms and mortar fire, and then launched ground assaults. Re-grouping the next morning and calling air strikes, artillery raids, and naval gunfire, the Marines counterattacked north. The NVA pulled back across the Ben Hai River where the Marines could not follow them. Captured documents indicated that the 90th NVA Regiment had carried the brunt of the fighting for the North Vietnamese, who suffered over 1,250 casualties. Marine casualties were heavy with two companies reduced below 30 effectives each. The ability of the NVA to integrate long-range artillery fire into its maneuver, and the availability of such artillery, were ominous developments that later played heavily in combat along the Demilitarized Zone.

Bui Diem
As South Vietnam's ambassador to the United States from 1966 to 1972, Bui Diem served as a liaison between the US government and South Vietnam on con-

ditions for peace negotiations. He also worked behind the scenes to support President Nixon's presidential campaign, believing that Nixon would take a harder line than would Hubert Humphrey, the Democratic candidate.

Bui Tin
During the Indochina War Bui Tin fought the French in the Red River Valley and at Dien Bien Phu. In 1963 he traveled down the Ho Chi Minh Trail to assess its capability and assist the Viet Cong in their struggle. He returned to Hanoi and became the editor of *Quan Doi Nhan Dan*, the NVA newspaper. Promoted to Colonel, he returned to the south during the final offensive of 1975 and, on April 30, 1975, he accepted the surrender of the South Vietnamese government. Bui Tin later left the Socialist Republic of Vietnam and took up residence in France, though he denies that he defected.

Bundy, McGeorge
In 1961, President John F Kennedy appointed Bundy as Special Assistant to the President for National Security Affairs. He became the principal architect of the US intervention in Vietnam. In 1966, he left the administration, but continued to serve as a member of the "wise men," a group of advisers to President Johnson. In 1968, he helped

Right: NVA Colonel Bui Tin, who took the surrender of South Vietnam from General Duong Van Minh, visits the American Vietnam War Memorial.

Johnson realize that a negotiated settlement to the war was inevitable.

Bundy, William P

The brother of McGeorge Bundy, William favored covert operations, but endorsed US troop deployment. By 1964, he was responsible for much of the policy making for Vietnam. He was a strong advocate of attacks on the transportation systems, industrial areas, and military areas of North Vietnam. By 1968, he became disenchanted with President Johnson's management style and how the war was run and left the administration.

Bunker, Ellsworth

US Ambassador to Vietnam from 1967 to 1973, Ellsworth Bunker emphasized that "there is only one war, not a separate war of big battalions, a separate war of pacification, or a separate war of territorial security; these are all integral parts of the same war." Ignoring the repressive nature of the South Vietnamese government, he acted to shore it up. He enjoyed the wide respect of the Republic of Vietnam leaders. He revamped pacification and counterinsurgency efforts in the countryside, and worked closely with General Creighton Abrams to implement President Nixon's withdrawal policy. He helped Henry Kissinger persuade President Thieu to accept the Paris Peace Agreement in 1973, even though the Vietnamese believed that they were not in their best interests. He continued to believe that America's support of South Vietnam was consistent with US history, traditions, and views of individual liberty and self-determination.

Burchett, Wilfred

An Australian journalist and author, Burchett's consistent support of the communist cause in Indochina gave him access to many North Vietnamese and Viet Cong leaders and operations. His affiliation with leftist political causes alienated him from most Western governments, but his writing became popular with the antiwar movement in the United States.

Right: NVA Colonel Bui Tin, who took the surrender of South Vietnam from General Duong Van Minh, visits the American Vietnam War Memorial.

Right: Ambassador Ellsworth Bunker (right) listens to President Johnson address the troops at Cam Rahn Bay.

C-4

The military plastic explosive, the C-4, was widely used for demolitions and to make field expedient mines and booby traps. As it is insensitive to shock, even when hit by bullets, it was widely carried by the troops. Additionally, because it burned hot and clean, they often used small pieces to heat their C rations.

Cai Tang

Most Vietnamese revere their ancestors. It was important that anyone who died be buried in an ancestral graveyard. Cai Tang is the act of exhuming and rebury-ing the bodies of relatives who had not been interred properly. This was never understood by the Americans, and in some cases this led to double counting during body counts.

Calley, William Laws Jr

Lieutenant Calley commanded a platoon in Company C, 1st Battalion, 20th Infantry of the Americal Division. On March 16, 1968 at the hamlet of My Lai in I Corps, Lieutenant Calley's platoon massacred 347 South Vietnamese, most-ly women, children, and the elderly. When the event came to light in April 1969, Calley was court-martialed for the premeditated murder of 102 civilians. He was the only individual tried for what happened at My Lai. He was found guilty of premeditated murder of at least 22 South Vietnamese civilians and sen-tenced to life in prison at hard labor and dismissal from the Army. His conviction created a furor in the American public, many of whom believed that he was being made a scapegoat for higher levels

Above: Lieutenant William Calley and his lawyer confer after a session of his court-martial for murder as a result of the My Lai Massacre.

of command. During a review by the command, Calley's sentence was reviewed and reduced to 20 years. Then, in April 1974, the Secretary of the Army further reduced the sentence to 10 years. He was released from prison on parole in November 1975.

Cam Ne

The Viet Cong-controlled village, Cam Ne, was situated in I Corps. During Marine Corps operations around the vil-lage a CBS television reporter filmed Marines burning some of the huts. In his commentary he claimed that the action

Below: A Marine squad crosses an open field under fire near Cam Ne village outside Danang.

was totally unnecessary, though he had never asked why it was being done. Such uninformed reporting contributed to the beginning of the conflict between the military and the media in Vietnam.

Cam Rahn Bay

A protected natural harbor approximately half way up the coast of South Vietnam, Cam Rahn Bay became one of the largest logistical installations of the war. It had prefabricated concrete piers, a 10,000-foot jet runway, warehouses, fuel storage tanks, cargo cranes, hospitals, and barracks.

Cambodia

Ruled by Prince Norodom Sihanouk, Cambodia attempted to maintain at least a semblance of neutrality during the war. Recognizing that he could do nothing about the North Vietnamese presence along Cambodia's eastern border with Vietnam, the Prince ignored the existence of NVA base camps and staging areas there.

In 1969, President Nixon authorized the secret bombing of Cambodia by B-52s under Project Menu. Faced with both a growing North Vietnamese presence and an indigenous communist insurgency, the Khmer Rouge, Prince Sihanouk appointed Lon Nol to head a new right-wing Government of National Salvation. In March 1970, after a series of violent, government orchestrated, anti-Vietnamese demonstrations, Lon Nol publicly demanded a complete Vietnamese withdrawal, and deposed the

Prince. All-out war between the Lon Nol government and the Khmer Rouge with their North Vietnamese allies broke out. It was a war the Cambodians subsequently lost.

Cambodian Airlift

In an effort to stave off a Khmer Rouge victory in Cambodia, and over the objection of the US Air Force, the US government issued a letter contract to Bird Air to fly supplies into Phnom Penh, and a group of C-130 transports were transferred to the company. Flying from the U-Tapao Thai Air Base, by the end of 1974 Bird Air had delivered more than 450,000 tons of supplies. In February 1975, military pressure against Phnom Penh intensified when the communists succeeded in blocking the Mekong River supply route. Bird Air was issued seven additional C-130s, and directed to double their effort. While the airlift helped, the Lon Nol government was incapable of fending off the Khmer Rouge, and on April 12, 1975 Marine Corps helicopters evacuated the few remaining American personnel from Phnom Penh. On April 17, 1975 the Khmer Rouge took the city and brought the war to an end.

Cambodian Incursion

For years the US military commanders in Vietnam had pressed for authority to attack North Vietnamese sanctuaries in Cambodia. On April 25, 1970 despite opposition from Secretary of Defense Melvin Laird and Secretary of State William Rogers, President Nixon

Above left: Troops of the 6th Convalescent Hospital in Cam Rahn Bay salute President Johnson upon his arrival to visit the wards.

Above: President Johnson and General Westmoreland ride down the airstrip from Air Force 1 at Cam Rahn Bay during Johnson's 1966 visit to Vietnam.

Below: A man caught crossing the Cambodian border waits while his captors examine his documents.

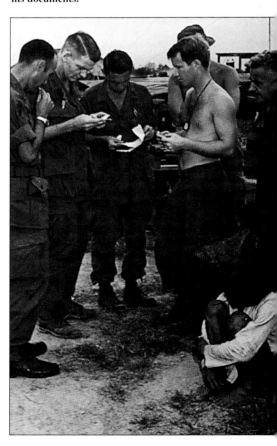

VIETNAM: A VISUAL ENCYCLOPEDIA

Above: 1st Cavalry Division troops quickly set up an M102 Howitzer at a new location west of Tay Ninh.

Left: A Montagnard village in Cambodia that was cleared by the 1st Brigade, 1st Cavalry Division.

Liberation front bases inside Cambodia. Because of intense political pressure in the United States, President Nixon directed that the operation be of limited duration and that American forces only venture up to 30km deep inside Cambodia. With this in mind, June 30, 1970 was established as the date when all US forces must withdraw. Backed by extensive support from B-52s, tactical air, and artillery, US forces overran most of their assigned operational areas rapidly. During the incursion the amount of supplies recovered was enormous. The Allies captured 23,000 individual weapons, 2,500 crew served weapons, and over 15 million rounds of small arms ammunition, as well as 100,000 antiaircraft rounds, and tons of other munitions. They also captured 435 trucks, jeeps, and motorcycles. It was estimated that the captured small arms could equip 55 enemy battalions, and there were enough

ordered ground forces into Cambodia. The Cambodian Incursion actually began in early April when Republic of Vietnam forces mounted multi-battalion raids against communist bases in the Parrot's Beak. Surprised NVA and VC forces withdrew deeper into the Cambodian jungle. The Cambodian Incursion eventually involved 50,000 ARVN and

30,000 US troops, the largest Allied operation of the war. Based on the, President's directive to commence operations in Cambodia, General Abrams ordered the II Field Force Commander, Lieutenant General Michael S Davidson, to attack within 72 hours. On May 1, the US Army commenced operations against North Vietnamese and National

Left: An aerial view of Fire Support Base Jay near the Cambodian border.

Can Lao Nhan Vi Cach Mang Dang (Revolutionary Personalist Labor Party)

This South Vietnamese political party and intelligence organization was established by Diem's brother Ngo Dinh Nhu in 1953 to promote the political career of his brother, Ngo Dinh Diem. The Can Lao ideology of personalism, which emphasized respect for the individual and humanism, was designed intentionally to contrast sharply with communism. The membership, which grew to 50,000, was secretive, manipulative and coercive, using its intelligence wing to perpetrate violence against its opponents. Along with several other parties it was disbanded by General Nguyen Kanh in 1964.

Can Tho

Located on Highway 4, south of Saigon, Can Tho was the capitol city of Phong Dinh province. On September 30, 1970 it became one of South Vietnam's autonomous cities and municipalities, and was a commercial center of the Mekong Delta. The Viet Cong considered it a critical target.

Canada

A country that remained neutral throughout the war, Canada was an original

crew served weapons to equip 82 enemy battalions, enough ammunition to provide a year's supply to 50,000 soldiers as well as enough rice to feed six enemy regiments for a year. Although the Cambodian Incursion was an overwhelming tactical victory, it was of limited strategic value because the Republic of Vietnam did not have the strength to maintain control of the region, and the NVA rapidly moved back in and rebuilt their bases.

In the final analysis the Incursion did provide the South Vietnamese a one-year breather as the Americans withdrew. President Nixon's action provoked fierce opposition in the United States. Protests erupted on hundreds of college campuses. On May 4, Ohio National Guard troops fired on a crowd of Kent State University demonstrators, killing four and wounding nine.

On May 9, more than 100,000 protesters demonstrated in Washington, joined for the first time by many ordinary citizens. On May 14, during a protest at Jackson State University, Mississippi police fired on the demonstrators killing two and wounding 12. These kinds of confrontations led to a series of congressional resolutions and legislative initiatives. By the end of 1970, Congress prohibited expenditures for US ground combat forces operating anywhere outside of South Vietnam.

Right: A pair of C-123 Providers prepare to load at the Can Tho airfield in the Mekong Delta.

VIETNAM: A VISUAL ENCYCLOPEDIA

member of the International Control Commission established in 1954 as part of the Geneva Accords. In 1973, the Paris Peace Agreements reconstituted the ICC as the International Commission for Control and Supervision, and Canada continued as a member. Canada was also a haven for around 30,000 Americans who fled there to avoid conscription.

Canister

Favored by tank crews for combat in heavy jungle or close areas, canister was a type of 90mm ammunition. The round contained 1,261 ¼in by ⅜in steel slugs. Fired at nearly 3,000ft per second, it converted the main gun into a massive shotgun and was devastating against exposed troops.

Cao Dai

The influential religious sect, Cao Dai, was founded in Vietnam in 1926, and its followers eventually included many high ranking members of the Republic of Vietnam government. The religion was established on the principle of a single God (Cao Dai, meaning "high palace," is a symbolic name for "God") who is omnipresent over Confucianism, Geniism, Christianity, Taoism and Buddhism. Followers are urged to renounce material wealth and personal prestige in favor of spiritual and moral purity, and respect friends and family. In 1941, a prominent leader of the sect, Ho Phap Pham Cong Tac, was deported for

his involvement in the independence movement. His successor, Tran Quang Vinh, accepted Japanese promises of Vietnamese independence and formed a Cao Dia army to fight the French. During the first Indochina war, Cao Dai members fought with the French against the Viet Minh. Many Cao Dai veterans of this conflict later became active in government, but the influence it had on the RVN was minimal.

Cao Van Vien

Vien, a paratrooper who was closely allied with Nguyen Cao Ky and later with President Nguyen Van Thieu, was the Chief of the Joint General Staff. He retained that position throughout numerous government upheavals. It was Vien

Left: General Cao Van Vien, the Chief of the South Vietnamese Joint General Staff, awaits refugee processing after his flight from Saigon.

Above: Marines cover their ears as a tank fires a 90mm canister round to suppress a sniper southwest of Phu Bai.

who proposed the disastrous withdrawal from the central highlands that led to the communist victory in 1975.

Capitol "Tiger" Division

In October 1965, the Republic of Korea "Tiger" Division began operating along the coast in II Corps. They remained in the country until March 1973. ROK forces were well trained, well disciplined, and had high morale. They were also ruthless with both enemy forces and the civilian population. They sometimes hung thieves on meat hooks at the gates to their firebases.

Caravelle Group

As a political lobby group, the Caravelle Group was opposed to the government of Diem. Motivated by the corruption and nepotism rife in Diem's administration, a group of 18 prominent South Vietnamese called a press conference at the Hotel Caravelle in Saigon on April 26, 1960 to denounce him and his followers, and announce a manifesto that called for total reorganization of the political and military leadership and sweeping economic reform. The group was at first ignored by

VIETNAM: A VISUAL ENCYCLOPEDIA

89

Left: The Korean "Tiger" Division receives heavy fire support from the main guns of the USS *New Jersey*.

that speeded an end to American involvement in Vietnam. The legislation was introduced by Senators Frank Church and Clifford Case, both opponents of the war, and sought to block further funding of military activities in North Vietnam, South Vietnam, Cambodia, and Laos, unless specifically approved by Congress. The bill passed through the Senate and after modification was endorsed by the House of Representatives.

Case, Clifford P
As the ranking Republican on the Senate Foreign Relations Committee, Senator Case criticized the Vietnam War from 1967 onward, arguing that it was an unwarranted extension of executive power. In 1973, he co-sponsored legislation to cut off all funding for the war. This legislation passed Congress and went into effect on August 15, 1973.

Diem but later several members were imprisoned. Despite representations by the group through US businessman Frank Gonder, the US government chose not to involve itself.

Carter, Jimmy
As the Governor of Georgia, Jimmy Carter backed President Nixon's Vietnam policy. He criticized the press for its handling of the My Lai Massacre story. As a Democratic presidential candidate in 1976, however, he denounced the Vietnam War as immoral and racist. When he became president in 1977, he issued a blanket pardon to draft resisters.

Case–Church Amendment
In June 1973 an amendment was made to the State Department authorization bill

Below: President Jimmy Carter at the SALT Talks in Vienna.

VIETNAM: A VISUAL ENCYCLOPEDIA

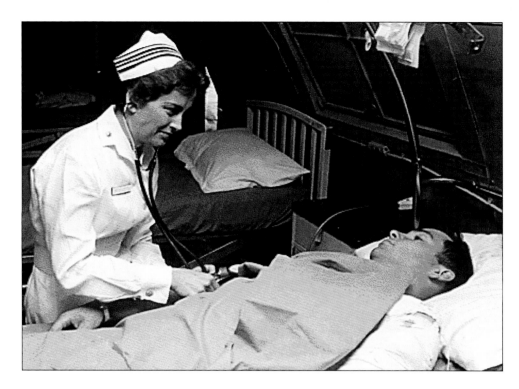

Left: A nurse checks a patient in the intensive care ward of the Navy Support Hospital, Danang.

Below: A Vietnamese woman weeps over the body of her husband, an ARVN casualty.

statistics until 1995, and then they only released gross numbers.

Catholics

First introduced to Vietnam by French missionaries in the 15th century, Roman Catholicism was at times embraced and suppressed by successive Vietnamese governments because of the influence it had over the population. Vietnamese catholics both supported and opposed the return of French colonialism after the war, but Viet Minh reprisals for collaboration were indiscriminate.

Approximately 600,000 catholics lived under the Democratic Republic of Vietnam after 1954, but its leaders were

Casualties

There are a number of enduring myths surrounding casualties in the Vietnam War. The first is that the bulk of the casualties were draftees. In fact, 77 percent of the combat deaths in the Vietnam War were volunteers, and among the 18- and 19-year-olds the percentage was even higher, 97 percent and 86 percent respectively. Second, 18-year-olds did not suffer a large number of casualties in Vietnam. In fact, there were only 101 killed during the entire war. Third, it is a myth that black troops suffered a disproportionate percentage of the casualties. In fact, 7,273 African-Americans were killed in Vietnam, or 12.5 percent of all casualties, even though African-Americans accounted for 13.5 percent of draft age males in America during that time. Another myth is that only the enlisted "grunts" fought and died. In fact, the army lost a higher ratio of its officer corps in Vietnam than it did in World War II, including 12 generals. The highest casualty rate among all Military Occupational Specialties (MOS) was for tankers (Armor Crewmen—MOS 11E). Twenty-seven percent of all armor crewmen who were assigned to Vietnam were killed in action. Additionally, the US Marine Corps suffered more casualties in Vietnam than it did in World War II.

While US and Allied casualty statistics are considered relatively firm, those for the ARVN are largely based upon estimates rather than hard data. The North Vietnamese did not release casualty

Casualty Statistics

Force	Killed In Action	Wounded In Action	Total
US Forces	47,378	304,704	352,082
ARVN	223,748	1,169,763	1,393,511
Australia	469	2,940	3,409
Korea	4,407	17,060	21,467
Thailand	351	1,358	1,709
New Zealand	83	212	295
Total	276,436	1,496,037	1,772,473
*NVA/VC	1,100,000	660,000	1,760,000

* Figures released by North Vietnam April 3, 1995.

VIETNAM: A VISUAL ENCYCLOPEDIA

Left: Marine Staff Sergeant Ermalinda Salazar
helps with the children at the St Vincent de Paul
Catholic Orphanage.

interned and places of worship confiscated. Restrictions were placed on their activities and most of the foreign priesthood fled.

RVN President Diem was a devout catholic and gave political, economic and social privileges to fellow believers during his reign, which was a factor in his downfall. The church has been tolerated since the collapse of the RVN in 1975, but the government closely monitors its activities.

Catonsville Nine

A group of antiwar activists who destroyed draft records at Catonsville, a suburb of Baltimore, in 1968 as a protest against the conflict. In May 1968, the protesters, who included catholic priest and peace activist Daniel Berrigan and eight others, invaded a Maryland Selective Service Board in Catonsville, snatched up hundreds of selective service records, carried them outside in wire mesh baskets, and set them ablaze with homemade napalm. The activists were arrested and tried in federal court, and became a nationwide cause célèbre that led to as many as 100 similar actions in protest against the Vietnam War.

Causes of the War

See Indochina War.

Cedar Falls, Operation

From January 8–26, 1967, elements of the 3rd Brigade, 1st Infantry Division, 11th Armored Cavalry Regiment, and units of the 173rd Airborne Brigade attacked the Viet Cong stronghold known as the Iron Triangle. Ben Suc, at the northwest corner of the Triangle was a village of approximately 6,000 Vietnamese residents. It served as the headquarters of the Viet Cong Long Nguyen Base Area. Attacking without the usual preparatory artillery fire, the US units achieved total tactical surprise. The local residents were all rounded up, and along with their livestock were evacuated from the area. Viet Cong tunnels beneath the village were collapsed, and Rome Plow bulldozers knocked down trees and brush.

In order to enhance their ability to return to the Iron Triangle should the Viet Cong reoccupy it, American engineer units created landing zones throughout the entire 60 square miles within its boundaries. Rome Plows cleared 2,710 acres of jungle as well. Although many tunnels were destroyed and Viet Cong operations in the Iron Triangle were disrupted, within six months they had reoccupied the area in force.

Central Highlands

An isolated plateau at the southern end of the Trung Son Mountains in west central Vietnam, the central highlands were strategically vital to the defense of South Vietnam. This sparsely occupied area was the home of the Montagnards; an indigenous minority in South Vietnam whose loyalty was absolutely critical to the successful defense of the nation. It was also the exit point for many of the spurs of the Ho Chi Minh Trail, and was the scene of fierce fighting throughout the war. The battle of the Ia Drang was

Left: A tanker investigates a small mud and log bunker after hitting it with a 90mm round.

Left: Armored vehicles of the 11th Armored Cavalry Regiment assume a defensive formation after receiving fire.

the first major battle fought between the North Vietnamese and US forces, intense fighting around Kontum blunted the 1972 Easter Offensive, and North Vietnam's final offensive began with an attack on Ban Me Thout in the southern portion of the central highlands.

Central Intelligence Agency (CIA)

Following the 1954 Geneva peace conference the CIA, led by Lieutenant Colonel Edward Lansdale, launched Operation Exodus. This propaganda campaign helped stimulate the mass migration of nearly a million people from north to south by portraying conditions under the communists in the worst possible light. Lansdale later became one of Ngo Dinh Diem's staunchest supporters. In the early 1960s, the CIA launched a clandestine campaign in Laos to attack the Ho Chi Minh Trail and brought in Special Forces teams to train and arm the Montagnards in the highlands of South

Below: View from a tank keeping watch across the flat central highlands' plateau toward Cambodia south of Pleiku.

Vietnam. Under Operation Switchback, beginning in September 1962, the Special Forces operations were turned over to the Army. At the same time however, the secret war in Laos grew ever larger as the CIA armed the Hmong tribesmen under General Vang Pao.

CIA paramilitary operations in Laos were extremely effective throughout the war, and tied down several divisions of North Vietnamese troops to secure the Ho Chi Minh trail and support the Pathet Lao, though they nearly resulted in the destruction of the Hmong. Throughout the 1960s, the CIA worked to destroy the Viet Cong infrastructure, and in 1967 initiated an intelligence program, which later became known as Phoenix. Also in 1967, based on a directive from President Richard Nixon, they initiated Operation CHAOS, a program for surveillance of antiwar critics in the United States. Early in the 1970s, the CIA came under great political pressure due to revelations of the CIA assassination of Viet Cong leaders and the discovery of the antiwar surveillance, which violated the CIA charter. In 1974, Congress passed laws limiting the CIA to only intelligence operations overseas.

Central Logistics Command (CLC)

The Central Logistics Command located in Saigon was responsible for logistical support for all the services of the Vietnamese armed forces. An ad hoc amalgam of French and American organizational and operational doctrine insured that it was only marginally responsive to the requirements of the war. Though a massive amount of supplies were delivered by the Americans to the Central Logistics Command each month, inadequate recordkeeping, graft, and corruption both slowed the delivery of needed matériel to the combat forces and insured that the Vietnamese never knew what they had or where it was.

Central Office for South Vietnam (COSVN)

COSVN was organized in 1961 by the merger of the southern and central branches of the Lao Dong Party, (Vietnam Workers Party). As an advance element of the North Vietnamese Communist Party Central Committee, its purpose was to direct the military operations of the National Liberation Front in South Vietnam. In basic terms, it was a small mobile command headquarters composed of a few people. United States military leaders, who never did make the intellectual adjustment to the difference between a guerrilla and a western style war, believed it had to be a fixed headquarters that could be located and destroyed. Throughout the entire war the Americans repeatedly launched unsuccessful operations to locate and destroy the COSVN headquarters.

Chams

Once the Chams occupied the central Vietnam coast from Vinh southward to Phan Rang. In one of the world's most devastating genocides, by the mid-18th century the Vietnamese had destroyed the Champa Kingdom and reduced the population to a struggling minority of several thousand scattered along the central coast. Unlike the Vietnamese, many Chams are muslim.

CHAOS, Operation

This secret Central Intelligence Agency program involved wiretapping and surveillance of domestic opponents of the

Below: A small mosque serves a moslem community of Chams west of Hue.

Above: General Leonard Chapman, Commandant of the Marine Corps, talks to his son in Vietnam.

war. Launched by CIA director Richard Helms (in the wake of the failed Huston Plan) to investigate the relationship between individuals in the US and foreign governments, CHAOS was in fact a direct violation of the Agency's charter and an indication of the increasing paranoia of the Nixon administration about its political opponents. Revelations in the mid-1970s about CHAOS, Phoenix and other illegal CIA programs led to the censure of the agency by Congress and restrictions were placed on the scope of its activities.

Chapman, Leonard Fielding Jr

An expert in military logistics and communications, as the commandant of the Marine Corps from 1968 to 1970, General Chapman oversaw the withdrawal of Marine combat units from Vietnam. Taking advantage of the

downsizing of the Corps as the war wound down, he administratively shed over 15,000 Marines.

Chemical Warfare

Although technically and legally the United States did not engage in chemical warfare in Vietnam because it did not use any lethal agents, the war clearly incorporated the largest use of chemicals in combat ever. America used large quantities of three different types of chemical agent, incendiaries, riot control agents, and defoliants. The North Vietnamese and Viet Cong also employed incendiaries and riot control agents.

Defoliants/Herbicides

In 1961, President Kennedy approved the first use of chemical agents in the Vietnam War when he authorized the aerial spraying of herbicides. Operational flights to deliver defoliants began in 1962 under the code name Ranch Hand, and continued until January

1971. Ranch Hand operations reached a peak in 1967 when they delivered 4.8 million gallons of herbicide across 1.2 million acres of jungle and destroyed 148,000 acres of crops.

A total of 15 herbicides were utilized during the war, however, three were of prime importance. All the herbicides were named for the color of a band painted around their shipping containers. The main three were:

Agent Orange: contains about 1.98 parts per million of dioxin, a known carcinogen. Approximately 90 percent of Agent Orange was used for defoliation and the remainder for crop destruction or to clear firebase or base camp perimeters and roads.

Agent White: a triisopropaanoline salt, was used exclusively for defoliation.

Agent Blue: cacodylic like acid, was essentially used for crop destruction, but was also used for general defoliation as well.

Many Vietnam veterans and Vietnamese

civilians alike may have died from the long-term effects of toxic chemicals, and scientific studies indicate that there may be genetic damage to the offspring of those exposed.

Incendiaries

The use of incendiary and flame weapons has been documented in nearly all the wars of human history. In Vietnam napalm and white phosphorus munitions were the common incendiaries used.

Napalm is made by mixing gasoline and detergent, which forms a jelly and burns at almost 2,000°F. It kills not only by burning, but also by asphyxiation, in that it consumes all the oxygen surrounding the area of impact, and generates enormous quantities of poisonous carbon monoxide. In Vietnam styrene plastic was mixed with napalm to ensure that it would stick to the surfaces that it hit, significantly increasing casualties. Most commonly delivered by aircraft, it

Above: Marines wait for the CS gas that they dumped on an NVA strongpoint south of Quang Tri to clear before moving up.

Right: A UH-1D sprays defoliant along a tree line in the Mekong Delta to remove the underbrush.

Above: A flamethrower team hoses down a Viet Cong structure.

Left: An F-4 Phantom dumps napalm on an NVA position in Quang Tri City in support of an ARVN counterattack during the Easter Offensive.

was also used by both sides in portable flamethrowers. The US Marines and the Army also used mechanized flamethrowers, while the Navy mounted them on Riverine Monitors.

White phosphoros rounds were used for marking, to provide smoke screens, and for psychological effect against the enemy in trenches. They were fired from helicopters, tanks, and artillery.

Occasionally, when dug-in North Vietnamese or Viet Cong troops were in a difficult location, 55-gallon drums of either napalm or raw gasoline were dropped on them from a helicopter. Following saturation of the area, the fuel was ignited by either dropping a fused napalm container or firing tracer munitions into the target. In April and May of 1970 the 101st Airborne Division dropped over 2,000 such drums.

Riot Control Agents

These were commonly used to drive Viet Cong and NVA troops out of bunkers and tunnels, particularly the powerful tear agent known as CS. Its value for close in fighting was particularly evident during the 1968 Tet Offensive. Sometimes CS would be mixed with DM, a vomiting agent. The North Vietnamese and Viet Cong used a somewhat weaker tear agent than CS and a vomiting agent akin to DM.

Chennault, Anna

Anna Chennault was the Chinese born wife of World War II General Claire Chennault of "Flying Tigers" fame. Working with representatives of Richard Nixon's presidential campaign, Anna Chennault successfully urged South Vietnamese President Nguyen Van Thieu to delay committing to, or attending the Paris peace talks in order to help Nixon's election chances.

Chicago Eight

The eight radicals accused of conspiring to incite a riot at the 1968 Democratic National Convention in Chicago were the noted antiwar protesters: Abbie Hoffman, Jerry Rubin, David Dellinger, Tom Hayden, Rennie Davis, John Froines, Lee Weiner, and Bobby Seale. The trial began on September 24, 1969 but the defendants had soon turned it into it a farce, using the publicity they attracted through their contemptuous behavior in court to bring attention to the war.

On February 20, 1970, Judge Hoffman sentenced five of the defendants to five years imprisonment as well as giving a $5,000 fine. The Seventh Circuit Court of Appeals reversed all convictions on November 21, 1972, citing Hoffman's refusal to allow inquiry into the cultural biases of potential jurors, and the fact that the FBI, with the knowledge and complicity of Judge Hoffman and prosecutors, had bugged the offices of the defense attorneys.

Chieu Hoi (Open Arms) Program

Ngo Dinh Diem initiated the Chieu Hoi Program on April 17, 1963. It was a psychological operation designed to encourage enemy defection.

From 1963 to 1973 more than 159,000 communists defected with over 10,000 individual and more than 500 crew-served weapons. Its most successful year was 1969, when more than 47,000 Viet Cong and NVA soldiers rallied to the government, their reasons were primarily because of the disasters that befell them during the Tet Offensive.

Above: A tunnel rat patiently waits with his mask on for CS riot control gas to be pumped into a tunnel south of Danang.

China, People's Republic of (PRC)

The People's Republic of China was the first communist government to recognize the National Liberation Front in South Vietnam. Immediately following the Gulf of Tonkin incident the PRC sent a squadron of MiG fighters to North Vietnam. In 1965, following the introduction of US ground forces into the war, it signed an agreement under which more than 320,000 Chinese air defense, engineering, and rail repair troops served as trainers and to expand the lines of communication and maintain the transportation routes to China. The Chinese claim that between 1965 and 1971, 1,000 of their troops were killed and they supplied over 70 percent of the military matériel used by the Viet Cong and North Vietnamese Army. The PRC initially took a hard line toward negotiations between Hanoi and Washington. However, a worsening relationship between the Soviet Union and China and the warming Sino-American friendship played a significant role in bringing the Vietnam War to an end. President Nixon's February 1972 visit to China was a severe shock to the North Vietnamese leadership. However, this did not prevent the Chinese from providing matériel to rebuild the North Vietnamese Army following the disastrous Easter Offensive. Without this the final 1975 invasion of South Vietnam could not have taken place.

China, Republic of (Taiwan)

On several occasions Taiwan offered to send troops to South Vietnam. However, because of Vietnam's long antipathy towards them they were routinely refused. The CIA did use Chinese pilots

and some commandos for deniable operations in Laos, and North Vietnam, and Taiwan operated a major repair depot for damaged armored vehicles.

Chinese in Vietnam

The Chinese were the largest minority in South Vietnam. During the Vietnam War they controlled most of the country's commerce, industry, and trade. They were only represented by token numbers of people in the upper and middle ranks of the Vietnamese government and army, and played virtually no active military role. Oppressed by the South Vietnamese government, the Chinese welcomed the North Vietnamese troops to Saigon hoping that prosperity would resume. Instead the new government expelled hundreds of thousands of Chinese, confiscating nearly everything they owned.

Cholon

The economic hub of the Republic of Vietnam, Cholon was originally a separate city located outside of Saigon and populated almost exclusively by Chinese. At the height of the Vietnam War its population exceeded 1 million. As Saigon grew and expanded, it eventually brought Cholon into the Saigon metropolitan area. During the Tet Offensive some of the heaviest fighting in Saigon actually took place in Cholon, which was badly damaged and never really recovered.

Chou En-Lai (Zhou Enlai)

From 1949 to 1976, Chou En-Lai was the premier of the People's Republic of China. At the 1954 Geneva conference he convinced Ho Chi Minh to accept a

compromise that resulted in the partition of Vietnam. When hostilities resumed, he supported the Vietnamese communists by providing military aid, although the North Vietnamese never really trusted him again.

Above: A North Vietnamese soldier decides he has had enough and "Chieu Hois" to Marines near the DMZ.

Below: Rubble lines the streets of Cholon after very heavy fighting to eject the Viet Cong during the Tet Offensive.

Chu Huy Man

A Montagnard and one of the first people to join Ho Chi Minh, Chu Huy Man was a member of the first armed propaganda team with Giap at Cao Bang. Man came south in 1965 as Deputy Commander and Political Commissar of the 5th Military Region, which included much of the South Vietnamese highlands.

Two years later he was named as the Commander of the B-3 Front. Eventually, as it grew in size and importance, General Tranh Van Tra was installed over him and he became Tra's deputy. General Dung in his memoirs says that Man commanded the final successful NVA sweep from Ban Me Thout to the sea and then south to Saigon.

Church, Frank Forrester

An outspoken liberal member of the Senate Foreign Relations Committee, Frank Church broke with the Johnson administration on Vietnam policy in 1966. In 1970, he co-sponsored the Cooper–Church amendment to prohibit US ground forces in Cambodia. This amendment failed. However, in 1972 he co-sponsored the Case–Church amendment that did pass and which cut off all funding for US military operations in Southeast Asia.

Chuyen, Thai Khac

Thai Khac Chuyen was a Vietnamese intelligence agent assigned to Project Gamma, a clandestine intelligence operation in Cambodia. In the spring of 1969, a reconnaissance unit captured a roll of film and other documents in a Viet Cong base area. On the roll of film was a picture of Chuyen with a group of North Vietnamese intelligence officers. On June 20, 1969 he was executed and his body dumped into Nha Trang Bay. General Abrams, the Commanding General of MACV, discovered that the execution had taken place, arrested, and brought court-martial charges against the commander of the 5th Special Forces Group, six Special Forces officers, and one senior NCO for murder. The CIA, who oversaw Project Gamma, refused to cooperate in the subsequent investigation, and on September 29, 1969 the Secretary of the Army ordered all charges dropped for lack of evidence.

Circle Pines, Operation

In April 1966, the first major ground operation of the Vietnam War controlled by an armored unit, Operation Circle Pines, took place. The 1st Battalion, 69 Armor, and attached infantry attacked Viet Cong units in the Filhol Plantation and Boi Loi Woods northwest of Cu Chi. Having trained in Hawaii, the units of the 25th Infantry Division were accustomed to armor/infantry jungle operations.

They severely mauled the Viet Cong main force, Cu Chi Battalion, and uncovered part of a vast tunnel network. The number of casualties suffered by friendly forces were reduced because of the presence of heavy armor firepower. For this reason, Major General Fredrick Weyand, the Commanding General of the 25th Division, directed that all future operations should incorporate armor, if possible.

Civic Action

One component of pacification, civic action, was euphemistically described as "winning hearts and minds." Projects were specifically designed to create social and economic improvements for the people, as well as increase support for the South Vietnamese government.

Right: A column of 1st Battalion, 69th Armor APCs moves through the Filhol Plantation during Operation Circle Pines.

Below right: Casualties are loaded into the back of a medic track during Operation Circle Pines.

Below: C Company, 1st Battalion, 69th Armor plows through heavy jungle during Circle Pines..

camps, such as A Shau and Kham Duc, were overrun. As the US military began to withdraw, the US Special Forces were moved out of the camps and the Vietnamese converted them to Ranger organizations. Due to the long-standing animosities between the Vietnamese and the minorities, this conversion was only marginally successful and many camps were closed. After the fall of Saigon many of the CIDG continued to fight until as late as 1993.

Civil Operations and Revolutionary Development Support (CORDS)

Pacification was the bastard child of the Vietnam War. The US military paid only lip service to carrying out that function, and the civilian elements of the country team did not have either the assets or

Left: An Air Force nurse examines a pregnant girl during a civic action project.

Right: Jarai CIDG Strikers bring a wounded NVA prisoner into the Duc Co Special Forces Camp in II Corps.

Below right: A group of CIDG Strikers prepares to mount an operation from the Bu Prang Special Forces Camp.

The MEDCAP, medical treatment of villagers by US military doctors and medics, was perhaps the best-known form of civic action project.

Civilian Irregular Defense Group (CIDG)

The CIDG program was a CIA operation begun in 1961 to prevent Viet Cong control of the Vietnamese minorities. Initially begun with the Montagnards, it was gradually extended to other minorities such as the Khmers, Nungs, and religious minorities such as the Cao Dai and Hoa Hao sects. By mid 1963 there were over 12,000 participants.

In late 1963, the program was removed from under the CIA and placed under the control of MACV. Originally conceived as a program by which infiltration across Vietnam's western borders could be monitored, after the Army assumed control it became more militarily aggressive.

By the mid 1960s the North Vietnamese assigned high priority to the elimination of the CIDG camps along the Laotian and Cambodian borders. Isolated and difficult to reinforce, many

Right: Thai children are given a medical examination by a civic action team from Nakom Phanom Air Base.

Above: A CIDG company moves down the road toward the Ben Het Camp during the fighting around Dak To.

organization to assume it. The Office of Civil Operations and Revolutionary Development Support was instigated by Ambassador Henry Cabot Lodge in 1967. It consolidated all civilian agencies involved in the pacification effort under a military chain of command reporting to the MACV. Robert Komer, a special assistant to President Johnson, was assigned to head it up. Given the rank of ambassador, and the military equivalent rank of three-star general, Komer reported directly to General William Westmoreland. Komer established unified military-civilian advisory teams in all the provinces of South Vietnam and over 250 districts. By 1969, he had more than 6,500 military and 1,100 civilian personnel involved in pacification. Although CORDS claimed credit for some significant gains in pacification, actual gains in bringing the Viet Cong over to the side of the government

Right: A CORDS advisor demonstrates an M60 machinegun to a group of popular forces soldiers near Bong Son.

VIETNAM: A VISUAL ENCYCLOPEDIA

were minimal. When Komer departed Vietnam, William Colby assumed control of CORDS. Major efforts were made under both Komer and Colby to improve the effectiveness of Regional and Popular Forces (RF/PF) units by increasing both manpower and their firepower. By the end of 1969, the RF/PF had grown to over 475,000 men and their effectiveness had increased dramatically. After the January 1973 Paris Peace Agreements, the rationale for CORDS ceased to exist, and in February 1973 it was disbanded.

Clark, Ramsey

As the Attorney General from 1967 to 1969, Clark opposed the Vietnam War. After leaving office in 1969 he joined the antiwar movement and, in 1971, represented the Vietnam Veterans Against the War in legal efforts to obtain permission

Left: A marine and a Ruff-Puff hoist the American flag over their small outpost during a clear and hold operation near Chu Lai.

Below: A Marine patrol walks along a paddy dike on a clear and hold mission west of Danang.

for demonstrations in Washington DC. He visited North Vietnam in 1972 and claimed the United States bombing campaign had returned it to the 17th century.

Claymore

The Claymore was the most widely used US antipersonnel mine of the war. It consisted of a C-4 plastic explosive embedded with several hundred steel balls, all enclosed in a curved plastic case, and was designed to produce a directional, fan-shaped pattern of fragments. As it was light, easy to carry, and specifically designed to be command detonated, it was a favorite for perimeter defense, and for ambushes.

Clear and Hold

A strategy that emphasized population security over battle attrition, clear and hold was never implemented by the US Army. However, the US Marines employed clear and hold tactics in I Corps with their Combined Action Platoons from 1966 to 1971 with significant success.

Clergy and Laymen Concerned About Vietnam (CALCAV)

An organization of religious leaders was established in 1965 to oppose the war. The group underwent numerous name changes, but maintained its support for moderate forms of protest which contrasted with the more radical measures espoused by other antiwar groups. CALCAV demonstrated at the Democratic National Convention in Chicago in 1968. Its most famous chairman was Dr Martin Luther King, who initiated the "Fast for Peace" in February 1967.

Clifford, Clark M

As an adviser to President Johnson, Clifford first participated in Vietnam policy decisions in 1965 during the debate concerning the commitment of ground combat forces. He joined Undersecretary of State George Ball in arguing against such an escalation. Throughout 1966 and 1967 he argued strongly against periodic requests by the Johnson administration to halt bombing, and supported further escalation. Replacing Robert McNamara as the Secretary of Defense in 1968, he began to have doubts about whether the war was winnable. As a member of the "wise men" he advised President Johnson to disengage and spent the last months of the Johnson presidency laying the groundwork for withdrawal.

Cluster Bombs (CBU)

These types of bombs were a major innovation in antipersonnel munitions during the Vietnam War. They are essentially an assembly of smaller bombs carried in a container dropped from the air. These sub units, usually fragmentation or incendiary bomblets, are ejected as the weapon falls, significantly broadening the area of impact.

The CBU 24 contained 600 golf ball sized bomblets, each with 300 steel pellets. The CBU 46 submunitions had offset fins, which caused a wider dispersal before detonation. The Wide Area Anti-Personnel Munition (WAPM) shot out dozens of fine wires upon impact, which when touched triggered the explosion of a small mine. A fuel-air-explosive unit was also tested. It consisted of a large canister filled with gaseous explosives that spread out at a preset altitude, creating a cloud that was then detonated as it approached the ground, thereby creating an overpressure and crushing or maiming the personnel underneath the cloud. Antiwar protesters objected most to the use of cluster bombs.

Coast Guard

South Vietnam had over 1,200 miles of coastline. Very early in the war it became clear that North Vietnam was moving a significant amount of military matériel into the south by sea.

To strengthen coastal surveillance, in May 1965 President Johnson sent Coast Guard patrol boats to Vietnam. In Operation Market Time, working in conjunction with the Vietnamese Junk Force and Coastal Surveillance Force, US Coast Guard units patrolled the entire South Vietnamese coast. They operated from bases in Danang, Quang Ngai, Nha Trang, Vung Tau, and An Thoi, confiscating hundreds of tons of supplies, and performing over 6,000 gunfire support missions. When they withdrew in 1971, the Coast Guard turned over all of their patrol boats and four cutters to the Republic of Vietnam.

Coastal Surveillance Force

In order to cut off North Vietnamese sea borne supplies, the US 7th Fleet created a Coastal Surveillance Force to blockade the coast of South Vietnam. They transferred a number of destroyer escorts and Radar picket ships from the North Atlantic, and used surveillance aircraft to patrol the coast up to 150 miles offshore. With the addition of a Coast Guard Squadron consisting of nearly 100 50-foot swift boats and 26 83-foot cutters, supplemented by the Vietnamese Navy, the Surveillance Force attempted to track literally thousands of small junks and fishing craft operating along the coastline. Because they were reasonably successful, a great deal of Hanoi's seaborne logistics was diverted to the Cambodian port of Sihanoukville, a much longer and more difficult supply line.

Cochin China

Before the French-Indochina War geographers generally divided Vietnam into three areas: Tonkin, Annam, and Cochin China. Cochin China encompassed the six southern provinces of Vietnam. Until the arrival of the French in the late 19th century, much of Cochin China was part of the Khmer empire and a significant Cambodian minority lives there.

Coffin, William Sloane Jr

A Presbyterian minister and committed antiwar activist, Coffin was an officer of the National Emergency Committee of Clergy Concerned About Vietnam, and traveled widely encouraging draft resisters. He was indicted and convicted

Below: Units of the Vietnamese Junk Force rest at anchor waiting for a Coast Guard cutter before leaving on patrol.

In 1968, he returned to Vietnam with ambassadorial rank as the Deputy Commander of MACV for Civil Operations and Revolutionary Development Support. He oversaw the Accelerated Pacification Campaign, which was initiated in November 1968, and significantly strengthened both the Phoenix Program and People's Self-Defense Force. In 1970, he began transferring planning for pacification and rural development to the South Vietnamese in accordance with American Vietnamization plans.

Charges of torture and assassinations under the Phoenix Program brought him before several congressional committees. He maintained that nearly all of the 20,000 people killed by Phoenix had died in combat action. However, he never denied that assassinations had occurred. He became the Director of the CIA in 1973 and retired three years later.

Collins, Joseph Lawton

Sent by President Eisenhower to South Vietnam in November 1954 to recommend the level of assistance needed for President Diem's Army, Collins instead recommended reducing US support. He stated that, "Diem does not have the capacity to unify the divided factions in Vietnam." He also said that Diem could not "prevent the country from falling under communist control." He was recalled in May 1955.

for conspiracy to assist draft evaders. The conviction was eventually overturned. Ironically he also worked as a Soviet expert for the CIA in the 1950s.

COINTELPRO, Operations

The US Justice Department and FBI designed covert programs to infiltrate subvert and monitor groups perceived to be a threat to domestic security. Both Johnson and Nixon believed that antiwar groups were sponsored by communists and used the power of the Justice Department and its investigatory body the FBI to infiltrate them. In 1965, FBI operatives began operations against antiwar groups and placed individuals as well as opposition politicians under surveillance. COINTELPRO activities increased under Nixon.

Colby, William Egan

William Colby was an officer in the Office of Strategic Services during World War II where he worked with the French

resistance. After the war he joined the CIA. In 1959, he became the CIA's Station Chief in Saigon, where he played a major role in developing the Civilian Irregular Defense Groups (CIDG). From 1962 to 1968, he was the Far East Division Chief at CIA Headquarters.

Right: William Colby, who headed up CORDS and oversaw the Phoenix Program, testifies before Congress in 1971.

Left: A corpsman assigned to a Combined Action Platoon gives a group of small children a bath.

Combined Action Program (CAP)

The Combined Action Program paired squads of US Marines with platoons of Popular Forces. The Marines lived and operated with their Vietnamese counterparts to provide greater security for the villages in I Corps. While the effectiveness of the program remains debatable, most available statistics and personal testimony suggests that it was.

Comfy Cougar

An electronic warfare version of the C-130 transport operated by the National Security Agency was given the radio call sign of Comfy Cougar. It routinely flew missions along the Ho Chi Minh Trail west of Tchepone monitoring North Vietnamese radio traffic in an attempt to find prisoners moving up the trail.

Commander-In-Chief Pacific (CINCPAC)

CINCPAC was a unified command in the Pacific held by a naval officer. The Commander of MACV reported to CINCPAC, as did all US Air Force, Navy, and Marine forces in Vietnam. CINCPAC reported directly to the Joint Chiefs of Staff in Washington. This division of command responsibility was later determined to have been a major strategic mistake.

Commando Hunt, Operation

From November 15, 1968 to April 10, 1972, Operation Commando Hunt targeted the Ho Chi Minh Trail in southeastern Laos. Its primary objective was to reduce the flow of North Vietnamese troops and supplies into South Vietnam and Cambodia. A secondary objective was to destroy trucks, supply caches, storage bases, and the manpower support structure for the Trail. The US Navy, Marines, and the Royal Laotian Air Force all attacked the Trail in this area but the US Air Force carried out the bulk of the bombing. B-52s and fighter-bombers hammered the area during the day, while at night AC-130 and AC-119 gunships, along with specially modified B-57Gs

Below: Members of a Combined Action Platoon pose with some of the villagers they work with.

attacked trucks and troops moving down it. Special attention was also given to the four passes leading from North Vietnam into Laos. As a measure of success, the Air Force began issuing a count of trucks destroyed or damaged, however the statistics were essentially meaningless in that they claimed to have destroyed or damaged over 20,000 vehicles, while the CIA estimated that the North Vietnamese never had more than 10,000 trucks during the entire war.

Commandos

The commandos were South Vietnamese teams trained by the CIA to infiltrate North Vietnam for the purposes of sabotage and collecting intelligence information. Several hundred were inserted into North Vietnam and were controlled by SOG. However, they were all betrayed by Viet Cong agents in the South Vietnamese military structure and captured. The CIA declared them all dead, but many had in fact survived and were eventually released by North Vietnam.

In 1996, Congress passed legislation recognizing their contribution to the American effort and granting the survivors compensation for the hardships they suffered as prisoners. This was all thanks to the efforts of Sedgwick Tourison, who was a Defense Intelligence Agency analyst.

Con Son

This notorious prison was found on Poulo Condore, one of the 14 islands of the Con Son group in the South China Sea. Built by the French colonial administration to house political opponents, the

Above: An F-105 Thunderchief prowls the skies over Laos during Operation Commando Hunt.

Below: Lieutenant Colonel John Prodan is doused with water as a "tribute" from the ground crew after his last mission over Laos in an RB-57G.

prisoners were incarcerated in cells 5ft x 9ft known as "Tiger Cages." During French rule, it was the prison of many leading Vietnamese revolutionaries. After the collapse of the French administration, the RVN used the island to hold non-Viet Cong communists and other government opponents. The brutality continued. Both RVN and US leaders denied this until 1970, when an investigative team sent to South Vietnam by Nixon uncovered widespread breaches of the Geneva Convention at the prison. The revelations influenced Congress' decision to cut funding to the RVN.

Con Thien, Battle of (September 1967)

In the spring of 1967, MACV ordered the US Marines to construct an anti-infiltration barrier across the DMZ. Strong points were to occupy prominent terrain features and artillery positions would provide fire support and house reaction forces to reinforce the strong points. Con Thien is located in I Corps 14 miles from the coast and only two miles south of the DMZ on a group of three small hills, the largest of which is 160m high.

As Con Thien provided a clear view of Dong Ha, the major logistics base supporting the 3rd Marine Division, it was considered a critical area to control. As a precursor to the offensive against South Vietnamese cities in 1968, General Giap instigated a series of border battles to draw American and ARVN forces away from the populated areas.

The siege of Con Thien was the first of the border battles. Throughout the summer of 1967, the base had routinely received sporadic artillery and rocket fire from the mountains along the DMZ. In September, the artillery fire intensified and North Vietnamese ground activity increased as several North Vietnamese regiments engaged the Marines.

On September 25, 1967, more than 1,200 rounds of heavy artillery struck the outpost and attacking North Vietnamese infantry got as far as the wire, but failed to breach the defenses. By September 27, the Marines had received more than 3,000 rounds of artillery on their positions. Concentrated B-52 strikes, tactical air support, and naval bombardment, coupled with tenacious defense, eventually caused the NVA 324B Division to abandon the siege.

General Westmoreland described the fighting around Con Thien as a "crushing defeat" for the NVA. However, while MACV estimated NVA deaths at 1,117, over 1,800 marines had been killed and wounded and the 2nd Battalion, 4th Marines was reduced in strength from 952 men to about 300, indicating that it might have been a Pyrrhic victory.

Conein, Lucien Emile

A French born CIA officer, Conein served for many years in Vietnam. First he served with the OSS in 1945, then with Edward Lansdale from 1954 to 1956, and finally as the go-between for the South Vietnamese generals and the US Embassy during the coup against Ngo Dinh Diem. Conein indicated to the generals that the US wanted Diem to go.

Conduct of the War in Vietnam (COWIN) Report

Report on General Westmoreland's personal blame for My Lai and other war crimes in Vietnam. The 14-week investigation was prompted by a book by Nuremberg war crimes tribunal veteran Telford Taylor, whose publication *Nuremberg and Vietnam* accused the US of violating international law. The Conduct of the War in Vietnam (COWIN) report was published in May 1971 and exonerated Westmoreland of all charges.

Congressional Medal of Honor (CMH)

The Medal of Honor is usually referred to as the CMH in military jargon, and often erroneously referred to as the

Below: This M109 155mm howitzer was destroyed by North Vietnamese counter-battery fire outside Con Thien.

Left: A machinegun team engages NVA troops attempting to break contact during the Battle of Con Thien.

objection. However, in 1970 the court refused to recognize the concept of selective conscientious objection for those who objected only to the Vietnam War and not to all wars.

Objection on the grounds of conscience was far more difficult. There were three classifications of CO status, IAO (available for non-combatant military service only), IO (available for civilian work in public services) and IW (performing civilian work in public services). Between 1960 and 1970 almost 170,000 were granted IO status, by far the most sought after by applicants.

Containment Policy

During the Cold War, the Containment Policy was created by the United States government to limit the expansion of communism across the globe. The idea of containing Soviet expansionist tendencies appeared during World War II, when officials advised the need for a dual policy that would enable the Allies to both defeat Germany and contain the Soviets, but this was rejected by Roosevelt. The term "containment" was

Congressional Medal of Honor. It is the highest US military decoration for bravery in combat and is awarded by the president in the name of the Congress of the United States. During the Vietnam War 239 were awarded, 64 percent posthumously. The troops sometimes referred to the CMH as the "Casket with Metal Handles" because of the high number of posthumous awards.

Conscientious Objectors

Individuals who seek to avoid combat service on the basis of moral or religious objections are given the US military classification of "conscientious objectors." US law has always recognized conscientious objection to war on specific religious doctrinal grounds. COs included traditionally pacifistic groups such as the Quakers, Mennonites, and Jehova's Witnesses, but any religious objector had to present convincing evidence to the draft board to avoid service. Many muslims, including the famous boxer Muhammad Ali, were refused exemption from service. In 1965, the Supreme Court decided that religion did not have to be church-based in order to satisfy the conditions for conscientious

Below left: President Richard M Nixon presents a posthumous Medal of Honor to the family of Sergeant William Bryant.

Below: President Richard M. Nixon at a Medal of Honor ceremony.

first introduced into the public debate in February 1946 by George F Kennan, a diplomat and US State Department adviser on Soviet affairs, who has been called the "architect" of containment. In his famous anonymous X-article Kennan suggested a "long-term, patient but firm and vigilant containment of Russian expansive tendencies." Kennan's theory of containment was readily adopted by US policy makers paranoid of Soviet expansion, though they implemented the doctrine through both military and economic means.

The Strategy of Containment found its first application in the Truman Doctrine of 1947. This guaranteed immediate economic and military aid to friendly nations, and was the logic behind the military assistance programs and escalating involvement of US military forces in communist-threatened South Vietnam.

Contemporary Historical Evaluation of Combat Operations (CHECO)

Headquarters, Pacific Air Forces, created the CHECO Project in 1964 to conduct in-depth studies of operations in Vietnam. The project was staffed by professional historians and analysts, who produced more than 200 major studies and several million frames of microfilmed documents.

Continental Air Services (CAS)

A wholly owned subsidiary of Continental Airlines, CAS began operation in September 1965 when Continental bought Bird Air and assumed the mission of supporting the Hmong guerrillas in Laos. Less well known than Air America, CAS performed exactly the same functions. It was disestablished in December 1975.

Convoy of Tears

As a reaction to North Vietnamese success early in their 1975 offensive, President Thieu ordered ARVN forces to withdraw from the central highlands. Due to a series of incredible blunders, the ARVN chose to withdraw down a route which was more of a dirt track than a highway. Frightened by the movement of troops from Pleiku and Kontum, the civilian populace panicked and attempted to accompany the Army movement. The result was a long column of mixed military units and refugees, which rapidly devolved into a struggling mess. Surprised by their own success and excited by the apparent possibility of

inflicting a serious defeat on the retreating ARVN, the North Vietnamese rapidly maneuvered to attack the column. Through a combination of artillery fire and ground assault the NVA cut the retreating column to pieces. As thousands of civilians that were caught between the two military forces died, journalists coined the term "Convoy of Tears" to describe what was happening.

Cooper, Chester A

A longtime CIA agent, Cooper served as Deputy Director of Intelligence on the National Security Council in 1963 and 1964, then joined McGeorge Bundy's staff. He consistently advocated a political solution to the conflict. In 1966, Cooper supported Operation Marigold, a diplomatic mission led by the Poles to negotiate with Hanoi. He opposed the Cambodian Incursion and advocated a hard-line with respect to the South Vietnamese on negotiations.

Cooper–Church Amendment

Amendment to the US defense appropriations bill forbidding the use of any US ground forces in Laos or Cambodia. In the spring of 1970, against a background of national protest that culminated in a 100,000 strong demonstration in Washington, Senators John Sherman Cooper and Frank Church sponsored legislation prohibiting funding of US ground forces and advisers in Cambodia after June 30, 1970. Although it passed in the Senate it failed in the House, but a revised version was passed on December 22, 1970 as part of the defense appropriations bill.

Cooper, John Sherman

In response to the Cambodian invasion in 1970, Cooper, a Republican Senator from Kentucky, co-sponsored an amendment to a foreign military sales bill with Democratic Senator Frank Church of Idaho. The bill was intended to prohibit the spending of funds without congressional approval for combat operations in Cambodia. After bitter debate the Cooper–Church amendment was adopted on June 30, 1970, but it was later dropped from the final bill in a House-Senate Conference Committee.

Coral, Battle of (May 1968)

The Australian Army prided itself on its ability to engage in jungle warfare. They viewed themselves as the hunter in the jungle and never the hunted. For 26 days

during May and June 1968, the First Australian Task Force fought a series of actions around Fire Support Base Coral north of Saigon. In the battle at Coral, the 7th NVA Division, supported by local Viet Cong units, reversed those roles and actively hunted units of the First Australian Task Force, repeatedly closing to hand-to-hand ranges.

Having received intelligence information that the North Vietnamese intended to launch a mini-Tet offensive against Saigon, General Frederick Weyand, the Field Force II Commander, moved the Australians into blocking positions north of the city. Within days, the Australians were forced to switch their tactics from patrolling and ambushing to close quarter combat, where for the first time their armor and artillery support were to prove decisive. Among the final actions that broke the back of the NVA attack was an armored sweep by C Squadron, 1st Armored Regiment, during which the Australian tankers engaged some targets with their main gun at under 10m, and crushed some bunkers and enemy troops with their tracks. General Weyand credited the victorious struggle between the Australians and the 7th NVA Division as a key element in the failure of the North Vietnamese mini-Tet.

Corps

A Corps is a standard military formation consisting of two or more divisions and supporting artillery, reconnaissance and logistical units. Because the Vietnamese used Corps to denote a geographical area, the Americans designated their Corps formations Field Force I and Field Force II. However, XXIV Corps was formed in I Corps during the war and assumed control of combat operations there with the withdrawal of the Marines.

I Corps

The northern five provinces of South Vietnam made up I Corps. The Demilitarized Zone formed its northern border and Laos was to its west. The A Shau Valley in western I Corps was a major terminus of the Ho Chi Minh Trail and a logistical staging area for the North Vietnamese. The major cities in this area were Quang Tri, Hue, Danang, Tam Ky, and Quang Ngai. Throughout most of the war I Corps was the responsibility of the III Marine Amphibious Force, the 101st Airborne, and the Americal Divisions. Unlike the rest of Vietnam, from the outset the war in I Corps was essentially

against North Vietnamese regulars, organized as regiments and divisions, and supported by artillery. More than half of all US casualties occurred in I Corps.

II Corps

Made up of 15 Provinces directly south of I Corps, II Corps stretched along the Laotian and Cambodian borders and formed the bulge along the seacoast of central South Vietnam. The major cities were Kontum, Pleiku, Ban Me Thout, Da Lat, Qui Nhon, Tuy Hoa, Nha Trang, and Cam Rahn Bay. The central highlands lie within II Corps. It is a sparsely

Above: A Marine patrol calls an air strike on a target in I Corps.

Right: Troops wait to be evacuated after they were wounded during an operation northwest of Tam Ky in I Corps.

Above: A concrete capped corner bunker in the Thuong Duc Special Forces Camp overlooks the district town.

populated area, and the home of a significant percentage of the Montagnards of Vietnam. The heaviest fighting and most frequent combat occurred in the three northern provinces of the Corps, Kontum, Pleiku, and Binh Dinh. Combat in II Corps involved significant NVA units, but also included large numbers of Viet Cong. The 1st Cavalry Division frequently operated there, while the US 4th Infantry Division and the two Korean infantry divisions spent almost all of their time there.

III Corps

Ten provinces were included in III Corps, stretching from where the central highlands blended into the flat alluvial plain of the northern Mekong Delta to the Delta itself, and from the Cambodian border in the west past

Right: Marines evacuate a family from a contested village north of Qui Nhon in II Corps.

Opposite, top: A CH-47 delivers matériel to construct a firebase to a hilltop in II Corps.

Opposite, bottom: An M48A3 tank plows through the brush around a Montagnard village situated in II Corps.

Saigon to the South China Sea. The major cities were Tay Ninh, Bien Hoa, and Vung Tau. While it surrounded the Saigon Capital Special Zone, Saigon was not a part of III Corps. The 1st and 25th Infantry Divisions, the 11th Armored Cavalry Regiment, a brigade of the 82nd Airborne Division, the Thai Black Panther Division, the Australian Task Force, and most major headquarters were located in III Corps. The heaviest combat took place along the Cambodian border, in War Zones C and D, and in the Iron Triangle. Until the Tet Offensive of 1968 most of the fighting was against Viet Cong Main Force units.

IV Corps

The entire Mekong Delta south of Saigon formed IV Corps. Crisscrossed with canals, rivers, and small watercourses, it is the breadbasket of Vietnam and rice paddies are everywhere. The major cities are My Tho, Ben Tre, Can Tho, Vinh Long, Chau Doc, and Camau. Though heavily infiltrated by the Viet Cong, who had significant base areas in the U Minh Forest at the southern tip of Vietnam and the Plain of Reeds along the Cambodian border, the NVA presence in IV Corps remained minimal throughout

Left: Troops of the 25th Infantry Division take a water break near Duc Pho.

Below left: South Vietnamese Special Forces (LLDB) troops familiarize themselves with the M79 grenade launcher.

Right: Tankers from the 11th Armored Cavalry Regiment observe a close air support attack in III Corps.

Below: Troops of the 173rd Airborne scramble to cross a bomb crater from an Arc Light in War Zone D.

Right: Troops of the 9th Infantry Division cross a muddy stream on an operation near My Tho in the Mekong Delta.

the war. Riverine forces and Navy SEAL teams operated throughout the region, but the only large US unit stationed in the Mekong Delta was the 9th Infantry Division.

Counterinsurgency

Short of conventional war, counterinsurgency is a combined political and military strategy for defeating a guerrilla war during all of its stages. Though supported by President John F Kennedy, who sought to develop special forces capable of performing a counterinsurgency mission, the hierarchy of the US military considered counter-guerrilla warfare as simply an added duty for regular forces. The American approach was naïve at best, oversimplifying counterinsurgency into the slogan "winning the hearts and minds of the people."

General Westmoreland never believed that his mission was counterinsurgency or pacification. By the time the US formally recognized the importance of the political and pacification elements of the war of it was far too late.

Below: A patrol plows through a rice paddy near Muc Hoa in IV Corps.

Right: A group of villagers board a CH-3 to flee heavy fighting around their village in IV Corps.

Credibility Gap

A phrase coined by reporter David Wise of *The New York Herald Tribune* in 1965, "credibility gap" referred to the disparity between official pronouncements on the war and what objective observers discovered was actually happening on the ground. In 1968, the Johnson administration was suffering from just such a "credibility gap," due to public disillusionment produced by falsely optimistic statements about the war. These often contrasted markedly with the reports filed by journalists in the field and the pictures the American public saw every night on TV. In fact, inaccurate statistics and overly optimistic reports on the progress of the war had been endemic from the very start of American involvement, and had already disillusioned many military and government observers of the conflict. Misrepresentation to Congress also occurred, notably over the Gulf of Tonkin incident.

Cronkite, Walter Leland

Many people called Cronkite, who was the CBS Evening News anchor, "the most trusted man in America." Until the 1968 Tet Offensive, Cronkite had offered viewers an optimistic view of the war. Following a visit to Vietnam during Tet, in a special broadcast he concluded that the war would end in stalemate. Hearing that President Johnson reportedly stated, "If I've lost Walter Cronkite, I've lost Mr Average Citizen. "

Cu Chi

A small village 25 miles north of Saigon, Cu Chi became the headquarters of the 25th Infantry Division. It was located on top of an underground Viet Cong headquarters complex. The Americans tried everything they could think of to clear the extensive tunnel complex when they discovered it. Nothing worked, so they began sending infantrymen armed only with pistols into it to hunt down the enemy. This was the beginning of what later became known as the "tunnel rats."

Cunningham, Randall "Duke"

Randall Cunningham, who was nicknamed "Duke" by his shipmates, was the

Right: Walter Cronkite interviews Professor Mai of the University of Hue during fighting in the city.

Right: Lieutenant Randall Cunningham explains how he shot down three MiGs in one engagement.

first ace fighter pilot of the Vietnam War. Flying a US Navy Phantom he completed over 300 combat missions in Vietnam. On his second tour, on January 19, 1972, he shot down a MiG-21, then on May 8, 1972 he downed a MiG-19, and finally, on May 10, 1972, he nailed an unprecedented 3 MiG-17s. While returning from this mission he was shot down by a surface-to-air missile at the mouth of the Red River. He and his Radar Intercept Officer (RIO) Lieutenant (jg) Bill Driscoll, were picked up by a search and rescue helicopter and returned to his carrier, the USS *Constellation*.

Cushman, Robert Everton Jr.

Commander of the 3rd Marine Amphibious Force from 1967 to 1969, Cushman was the Deputy Director of the CIA from 1969 to 1972, and the Commandant of the Marine Corps from 1972 to 1975. During his tour in Vietnam the Marines engaged in the defense of Khe Sahn, and the struggle to retake Hue.

Below: General Robert Cushman, Commander of III MAF, listens as General Westmoreland addresses his troops.

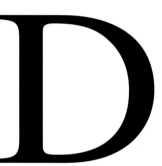

Da Lat

Founded by the French in 1897, Da Lat is a resort city in the cooler climate of the southern central highlands of Vietnam. It was the home of the Da Lat Military Academy, the South Vietnamese equivalent of West Point.

Dai Viet Quoc Dan Dang (National Party of Greater Vietnam)

Vietnamese nationalist party established in 1936 on principles that stressed economic progress and welfare programs. After the war it was allowed to serve in the National Assembly, but without real power, and acting President Vo Nguyen Giap subsequently purged its leadership. The party was revived in the early 1950s and its leader Nguyen Quu Tri was governor of northern Vietnam for most of the Indochina war.

Dak To, Battle of
(June–November 1967)

This was actually a series of battles around the Special Forces Camp of Dak To, north of Kontum in II Corps. The Battle of Dak To was initiated by the North Vietnamese on June 17, 1967 by a heavy mortar bombardment of the Camp. The 173rd Airborne Brigade and elements of the 4th Infantry Division reinforced the camp. Throughout the

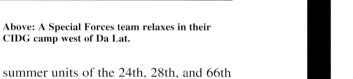

Above: A Special Forces team relaxes in their CIDG camp west of Da Lat.

summer units of the 24th, 28th, and 66th NVA Regiments laid siege to Dak To and Ben Het, another Special Forces Camp nearby. During one attack, mortar fire struck the 4th Division ammunition dump and the resulting explosion virtually leveled the camp.

Below: Troops from the 173rd Airborne Brigade destroy NVA bunkers after taking Hill 875 near Dak To.

VIETNAM: A VISUAL ENCYCLOPEDIA

As the North Vietnamese deployed more units south in preparation for the Tet Offensive, General Giap intensified the action around Dak To by reinforcing the regiments already in place in an attempt to draw additional Allied forces away from the cities and towns. He was successful, as elements of the 1st Cavalry Division, the ARVN, and another battalion of the 173rd Airborne Brigade were deployed there in October. In November, the 173rd Airborne triggered a major battle on Hill 223 when three companies of the 1st Battalion, 503rd Infantry were surrounded and came under heavy attack. Two additional battalions of the 503rd moved in to reinforce their comrades, and were themselves attacked on Hill 875 by the newly arrived 174th NVA Regiment. The NVA overran Company A, 2nd Battalion,

503rd Infantry, and then surrounded the remnants as well as Companies C and D. In late afternoon, an Air Force fighter dropped a 500lb bomb in the middle of Company C, killing 42 and wounding 45. Throughout the rest of the day the survivors fought off repeated NVA attacks. They were reinforced that night by the 4th Battalion, 503rd Infantry while at the same time, units from the 4th Division and the 42nd ARVN Infantry Regiment encountered NVA troops southwest and northeast of Dak To.

The MACV Chief of Intelligence characterized the battle as an American victory, and stated that the NVA attempt to disperse American forces to the border was a failure. However, though the NVA regiments committed around Dak To were severely mauled, General Giap had succeeded in luring additional US units

Above: A platoon of Company A, 1st Battalion, 503rd Infantry, digs in while under fire west of Dak To.

to the periphery of South Vietnam as he prepared for the Tet Offensive, and though it remained in Vietnam for several more years, the battered 173rd Airborne Brigade was never again assigned an independent mission.

Daley, Richard Joseph

Daley was the Democratic Mayor of Chicago from 1955 to 1976. In 1968, The Democratic National Convention was held in Chicago. There were large antiwar demonstrations and Mayor Daley ordered the police to use any means necessary to stop them. The result was later called a "police riot" when officers violently attacked demonstrators

Above: The crew of a CH-54 "Flying Crane" performs maintenance at Freedom Hill near Danang.

with dogs, horses, billy clubs, and mace. The mayor praised the police department for the effectiveness of their actions in suppressing the protest.

Dan Ve

The Dan Ve were village militia units comprised of local supporters of President Diem. They were armed with archaic weapons, riddled with corruption, and in some cases were largely Viet Cong. They were the precursor of the Popular Forces.

Danang

The most important port city in the central lowlands of Vietnam, Danang was the headquarters of the ARVN I Corps and a major airbase. The beginning of the US commitment of ground forces to the war occurred on March 8, 1965 when the US landed two battalions of Marines to protect the airbase.

In 1966, Danang was the scene of the buddhists "Struggle Movement" against Prime Minister Nguyen Cao Ky's government. Ky dispatched a thousand Vietnamese marines to Danang and smashed the movement. As the US commitment grew, the headquarters of the 3rd Marine Amphibious Force, a naval

Left: Members of Underwater Demolitions Team 12 rig a shelter after sweeping the beach prior to the Marine landing in Danang in 1965.

VIETNAM: A VISUAL ENCYCLOPEDIA

hospital, a major logistics installation, and a major prisoner of war camp were all established there.

Danang, Battle of (March 1975)

The 1975 final offensive created total chaos in Danang. With the fall of Hue on March 26, and the earlier loss of Thoung Duc, Quang Ngai, and Tam Ky, more than a million refugees were trying to crowd into the city. The Vietnamese Marines, who had retreated from Hue in good order, were dug in at Hai Van Pass 15 miles north of the city. To the west and south the battered 3rd Infantry Division and the remnants of the 1st Infantry Division were taking up defensive positions. By the afternoon of March 28 the military situation was bleak, and ships and planes began evacuating important civilians and troops.

Seeing this happening, the civilians panicked and attempted to crowd aboard any means of transportation that was departing the city. At 9 o'clock that night the NVA shelled the city and virtually within minutes chaos reigned and the western and southern defenses collapsed. On March 29, Danang, the most heavily

defended city in the entire country other than Saigon, its warehouses packed with food, ammunition, and weapons for months, fell to two truckloads of guerrillas, more than half of them women, who came up from the south.

Daniel Boone, Operation

Beginning in May 1967, Daniel Boone was the code name for clandestine operations into Cambodia. The purpose was to conduct reconnaissance, gather intelligence, plant mines, and carry out the sabotage of installations being used by the North Vietnamese. The Daniel Boone operations provided much of the intelligence that led to the planning of the secret bombing of Cambodia, Operation Menu, in 1969, and the planning for the 1970 Cambodian Incursion. They were authorized and conducted in a manner specifically intended to prevent congressional awareness, and their legality was debatable in that US law forbids attacking nations with which the United States is at peace and has diplomatic relations.

Right: A soldier keeps track of his DEROS with a "short timer" calendar on his helmet cover.

Above: Crewmen of the USS *Durham* take aboard refugees fleeing the fall of Danang in 1975.

Date of Estimated Return from Overseas (DEROS)

American troops served a one-year tour in Vietnam. (The Marines served 13 months.) Upon arrival in the country

each individual was given a DEROS, which established the exact day he would return to the United States. It became a goal that each individual carefully tracked.

Dau Tranh

A powerful and highly emotional term in Vietnamese, Dau Tranh loosely translates as "The Struggle Movement," and was adapted by General Giap as the basic North Vietnamese strategy for the war. There are two elements of the strategy, Political Dau Tranh, and Armed Dau Tranh. That the two must operate together, rather like a hammer and anvil, is absolutely axiomatic. The strategy recognizes that only by combining armed violence with politics can victory be achieved. Armed Dau Tranh is the military program. It incorporates the full spectrum of violence from terrorism to conventional attack. Political Dau Tranh encompasses actions which are not mere politics as the term is used elsewhere.

Below: Amtracs surge toward a landing during an amphibious operation.

Political Dau Tranh encompasses a systematic form of coercive activity that involves motivation and social organization, propaganda, and the mobilization of manpower and support. Boiled down to its simplest definition, it would be described as "the people as an instrument of war." The Dau Tranh strategist does not deal with legitimate grievances because they're too unpredictable; he manufactures grievances to fit his purpose. Spontaneity is to be avoided and the action generated is directed from the central planner, not from the heart. Since the goal is a totally new social order it demands total involvement, and total immersion at every point of the participant's existence.

Davidson, Phillip Buford Jr

General Davidson was the chief of MACV Military Intelligence from 1967 to 1969. It was during his tenure that the controversial enemy order of battle estimates, which later resulted in a libel suit by General Westmoreland against CBS, were compiled. He was a witness for General Westmoreland in that suit.

Davis, Rennard "Rennie" G

"Rennie" Davis was a leader of several radical groups, such as the Students for a Democratic Society and the May Day Tribe. He was also a leader in the demonstrations that led to the 1972 riot at the Democratic National Convention in Chicago.

Dean, John Gunther

Dean was a career diplomat with broad experience in Southeast Asia. He served in CORDS in South Vietnam, and as Deputy Chief of Mission in Laos. He was assigned as the ambassador to Cambodia in 1974, where he attempted to broker a settlement of the war between the Lon Nol forces and the Khmer Rouge. His efforts failed and he oversaw the embassy evacuation, code-named Eagle Pull, as the Khmer Rouge prepared to enter the capital in April 1975.

Defiant Stand, Operation

The first amphibious assault ever conducted by the Republic of Korea Marine Corps was Operation Defiant Stand. It was also the last of 62 Special Landing

Force operations in Vietnam. On September 7, 1969, the 1st Battalion, 26th Marines and a battalion of Korean Marines landed on Barrier Island south of Danang. As the Marines swept inland, naval patrol boats cruised offshore in order to prevent the Viet Cong from escaping. The combined Marine force swept the island, however the Viet Cong only offered token resistance and avoided them. Operation Defiant Stand was declared a success, even though little was accomplished.

Defoliation
See Chemical Warfare.

Dega Highlands Liberation Front (DHLF)
The military wing of the Dega Highlands Provisional government was known as the Dega Highlands Liberation Front. It was established in 1974–75 to oppose Vietnamese communist takeover of the Montagnard lands in the Dega Highlands. At its peak the DHLF had some 2,000 troops, who held out against the Vietnamese communist forces until 1984, when they abandoned the struggle.

Dega Highlands Provisional Government
A political administration established in 1974–75 to represent the interests of the Montagnard people, this government was essentially a reborn FULRO (see Front Unifie de Lutte des Races Opprimees, Le). During the advance south by North Vietnamese forces communist cadre promised full autonomy to the Montagnard peoples who occupied the strategically vital central highlands in return for their cooperation, but the promise went unfulfilled. The DHPG and its military wing the DHLF (see previous entry) then resisted the communist takeover of their lands.

Delaware—Lam Son 219, Operation
From April 19–May 17, 1968 Operation Delaware took place in the A Shau valley. As a joint US Army and ARVN operation, it included elements of the US 1st Cavalry Division, 196th Light Infantry Brigade, and 101st Airborne Division as well as ARVN units from the Airborne Task Force and the ARVN 1st Infantry Division. Heavy NVA antiaircraft fire downed over 30 American helicopters and one C-130 transport. During intense ground fighting heavy casualties were suffered by both sides. Though large quantities of supplies and a number of vehicles were captured, and a logistical center of the 559th NVA Transportation Group was overrun, when the US forces withdrew the NVA reoccupied the area within a matter of weeks. Early in 1969 enemy logistical installations in the A Shau valley were again fully operational.

Delinger, David
David Delinger was a long time, self-described, radical pacifist. In October 1965, he coordinated the first major anti-war demonstration in New York City. In 1967, he was a judge in Lord Bertrand Russell's International War Crimes Tribunal at Stockholm, which found the United States guilty of war crimes in Vietnam. In the same year, he headed the National Mobilization Committee to End the War in Vietnam, and led a march on the Pentagon that attracted 150,000

Below: A Delta Project instructor grades a LRRP team in training at the Recondo School near Nha Trang.

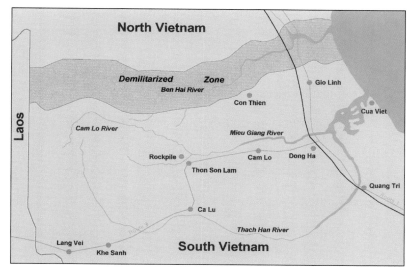

Above: This map depicts the relative location of the Demilitarized Zone to many of the major Marine Corps Bases in northern I Corps.

Left: A combat patrol moves toward the Ben Hai River during operations in the Demilitarized Zone.

people. He became a key link between the American peace movement and North Vietnam and, capitalizing on his antiwar credentials, arranged for the release of six prisoners of war.

As a leading figure in the antiwar demonstrations that took place at the Chicago Democratic National Convention in 1972, he was convicted of inciting a riot and contempt of court. He was sentenced to five years in prison, but the conviction was later overturned on appeal.

Delta, Project

Project Delta was an informally organized reconnaissance operation controlled by the 5th Special Forces Group in Vietnam. Established in 1964, it eventually was expanded to include an ARVN Ranger Battalion, a group of Vietnamese Special Forces, a CIDG company, a Nung Security Company, a mortar platoon, and other specialized troops. Normally inserted at dusk or at night by helicopter, Delta teams collected intelligence, directed air or artillery strikes, monitored Viet Cong movements, and captured prisoners. It also ran the MACV Recondo School. By the time it was deactivated on July 31, 1970 it had accumulated significant amounts of intelligence and inflicted extensive losses on the NVA and Viet Cong.

Right: Senator Jeremiah Denton speaks to the families of servicemen listed as missing in action.

Demilitarized Zone

The Geneva Conference in 1954 established a 10km-wide, temporary buffer zone between North Vietnam and South Vietnam at the 17th parallel. From the South China Sea to the village of Bo Ho Su, the demarcation line roughly followed the Ben Hai River, and then went straight west to the Laotian border. The buffer zone eventually became the defacto border between the two countries.

Denton, Jeremiah A Jr.

When he was shot down on July 18, 1965, Commander Denton became one of the most senior prisoners of war. He

Above: The radioman in front tries to keep his battery pack dry while crossing a muddy stream.

spent seven and a half years in captivity. He was at the center of a storm of controversy when he blinked the word "torture" in Morse code during a televised interview in April 1966. When he deplaned at Clark Field in the Philippines following his release in 1973, he rendered a smart salute and said: "Reporting for duty," endearing himself to the American public.

DePuy, William E

As the Chief of Operations for MACV from 1964 to 1966, General DePuy was the architect of the search and destroy tactic. He later aggressively implemented the Attrition Strategy and search and destroy tactics as the commanding general of the 1st Infantry Division. Other units, notably the 25th Infantry Division and the US Marines, emphasized pacification but were overruled by MACV.

Deserters

The US military defines desertion as being "absent from the place of duty with the intention to remain away permanently." Nearly 500,000 of the 7.6 million Americans who served in the military from 1965 to 1973 deserted, though fewer than 100,000 remained absent for more than 30 days. The bulk of these desertions took place outside of Vietnam, while there were nearly 5,000 that took place in country. The overall Absent Without Official Leave (AWOL) rate during the Vietnam War was lower than that during World War II. However, at the peak of the war, one US soldier went AWOL every two minutes, and another deserted every six. Deserters who were located were given less than honorable discharges. The highest desertion rates in the Vietnam War occurred in the ARVN, with an annual rate of approximately 120,000. The Regional Forces had a low desertion rate and there were virtually no deserters in the village based Popular Forces. Desertion from the North Vietnamese Army and the Viet Cong averaged just over 20,000 per year throughout the war.

DeSoto Missions

Beginning in the 1950s, DeSoto was a code name for naval intelligence missions against the People's Republic of China, North Korea, the Soviet Union, and North Vietnam. Intelligence agents or commando units would harass coastal radar transmitters so that American electronic intelligence destroyers could monitor the transmissions and pinpoint their locations. In the spring of 1964, South Vietnamese commando units carried out operations designed to harass North Vietnamese coastal installations. The destroyer USS *Maddox* was assigned to initiate an intelligence collection program associated with these South Vietnamese raids. It was these missions that led to the Gulf of Tonkin Incident and the escalation of the Vietnam War.

Dewey Canyon I, Operation

From January 22–March 19, 1969 three battalions of the 9th Marine Regiment conducted a search and destroy operation into Base Area 611 and the Da Krong valley west of Hue, which was a feeder for route 548 from Laos through the A Shau Valley. Because the Marines were heavily dependent on helicopters for logistical support, bad weather hampered the early phases of their operation. Though the North Vietnamese reinforced the units they had in contact, the Marines successfully overran much of the logistical support structure in the valley, and captured two 122mm field guns after heavy fighting in a bunker complex. From February 24–March 3, three companies of the 2/9th Marines crossed over into Laos and successfully ambushed NVA units moving down Route 922. In early March, the weather hampered logistical support and the movement of

Above right: Two buddies help a marine wounded during an NVA probe to an evacuation point northwest of the A Shau.

Right: Two Marine F-4B Phantoms on their way to provide close air support during Operation Dewey Canyon.

supplies again. On March 18, Operation Dewey Canyon was terminated. It was considered the most successful Marine Corps high mobility regimental sized action of the war.

Dewey Canyon II, Operation

Between January 30–February 7, 1971 some 9,000 US troops supported the Vietnamese incursion into Laos known as Operation Lam Son 719. Between January 30–February 5, an armored cavalry unit from the 1st Brigade, 5th Infantry Division secured Route 9 from Quang Tri to Khe Sahn, while the 101st Airborne launched a diversionary assault into the A Shau Valley in an attempt to draw NVA forces away from the ARVN route of march to Tchepone. Following B-52 strikes, US helicopter gunships attacked NVA weapon sites and troop emplacements north and south of Route 9. ARVN armor advanced into Laos while US helicopters inserted the equivalent of two ARVN Divisions into their landing zones. Intense antiaircraft fire severely hindered helicopter operations, and the ARVN advance was hit by

Left: The crew works on the engine compartment of a Sheridan during Operation Dewey Canyon.

Below: A helicopter flight crew takes a break while they wait for their next mission during Operation Dewey Canyon.

Right: A mixture of US and ARVN troops moves along a road during Operation Dewey Canyon.

heavy NVA counterattacks. The ARVN took Tchepone, and Lam Son 719 was proclaimed a strategic and tactical success. However, by that time the NVA had reinforced with elements of five divisions, three tank regiments, and 20 anti-aircraft units, heavily outnumbered, the South Vietnamese withdrew. Coming under intense pressure, parts of the withdrawal degenerated into a rout. Although Dewey Canyon officially ended February 7, US artillery and helicopter units continued to support the ARVN withdrawal throughout most of March.

Diem
See Ngo Dinh Diem.

Dien Bien Phu
See Indochina War.

Dink
More commonly encountered in the army than in the other services, "dink" was a derisive term generally applied to both the North Vietnamese and Viet Cong. At times it was also used to depict any Vietnamese person.

Division
A division is a nearly universal military organization, usually commanded by a Major General. In Vietnam most US Army divisions contained approximately 20,000 men. Marine divisions were somewhat larger at nearly 26,000 troops. South Vietnamese divisions had about 15,000 men, and North Vietnamese divisions were smaller at around 10,000.

Dixie Station
Dixie Station was the southern of two staging areas used by US aircraft carriers during the war. It was located off the coast of Cam Rahn Bay. Most strikes launched from Dixie Station supported operations in South Vietnam, southern Laos, and Cambodia.

Do Cao Tri
Under Diem, Tri suppressed the militant buddhists in Hue for which he was made a general. Shortly after that, he then supported the coup that removed Diem from power. He was one of several buddhist

Right: An A-4 Skyhawk is positioned on the catapult of the USS Intrepid on Dixie Station.

131

Above: The deck crew takes up tension on the port catapult bridle as the USS *Hancock* prepares to launch an A-4.

generals that Nguyen Cao Ky exiled when he came to power. After the Tet Offensive he was recalled and given command of III Corps. At one point General Westmoreland called him South Vietnam's George Patton.

Doan Khue

A key figure in the Vietnamese Communist Party, General Khue was known as an intelligence specialist. During the Vietnam War he fought in central Vietnam from 1964 to 1975. After the war he was appointed the Minister of Defense of the Socialist Republic of Vietnam.

Dobrynin, Anatoly Fedorovich

During the Vietnam War, Dobrynin was the Soviet Ambassador to the United States. He frequently acted as a conduit for messages from the US State Department to the Democratic Republic of Vietnam regarding negotiations.

Domino Theory

The view, widely held by US policymakers during the Cold War, that countries neighboring those in which communist governments had recently been established were themselves highly susceptible to communist takeover. It was first outlined by President Dwight D Eisenhower during a presidential press conference on April 7, 1954 in response to a request to comment on the strategic importance of Indochina:

"You have a row of dominoes set up, you knock over the first one, and what will happen to the last one is the certainty that it will go over very quickly. So you could have a beginning of a disintegration that would have the most profound influences."

With containment, the "Domino Theory" formed one of the cornerstones of US foreign policy during the 1950s and through the 1960s and was used by a succession of presidents and their advisors to justify ever-deepening US involvement in Vietnam. While Laos and Cambodia both fell to the communists along with South Vietnam, today the Domino Theory is viewed as having been discredited.

Dong Ap Bia

See Hamburger Hill.

Dong Ha, Battle of (April 1968)

Due to its location and transportation access, Dong Ha became a major supply center for 3rd Marine Amphibious Force

unit's operating in Quang Tri province, and the headquarters of the 3rd Marine Division. It was located at the junction of highways 1 and 9, the major north-south and east-west roads in I Corps. It was also accessible up the Cua Viet River.

On April 29, 1968, while the 3rd Marine Division was preparing a counteroffensive to attack NVA units along the DMZ, the North Vietnamese 320th Division beat them to the punch and attacked south out of the DMZ. The battle began when the 1st and 2nd Regiments of the 1st ARVN Division made contact with an NVA regiment along Route 1 north of Dong Ha. The 2nd Battalion, 4th Marines, reinforced the ARVN and engaged the NVA main force in a bitter three day battle at Dai Do hamlet northeast of Dong Ha. Reinforced with additional Marines and elements of the 196th Light Infantry Brigade, the

Above: A "grunt" steps aside as an amtrac load of troops moves up during the Battle of Dong Ha.

Left: A column of troops wades a stream on their way to join their company at Dong Ha.

VIETNAM: A VISUAL ENCYCLOPEDIA

Right: Loretta Clause, a Red Cross "Donut Dollie," plays cards with the troops during a stand down in the rear.

battle continued until May 15, 1968. On May 16, having lost over 2,000 dead, the NVA 320th Division finally broke contact and retreated back across the DMZ.

Dong Xoai, Battle of (June 1965)

Early in the morning of June 10, 1965 1,500 Viet Cong armed with AK-47s and flamethrowers attacked the Dong Xoai US Special Forces Camp, manned by 400 Montagnard CIDG troops and 24 Seabees. Under intense Republic of Viet Nam Air Force (RVNAF) air strikes, and after the Vietnamese 42nd Ranger Battalion air assaulted into the area, the Viet Cong retreated. However, on June 12 the Viet Cong struck the Ranger unit and the ARVN deserted their positions and ran into the surrounding jungle. Following in the wake of the disaster at Binh Gia, the Battle of Dong Xoai undermined American confidence in the ability of ARVN troops to oppose the Viet Cong and made the commitment of American ground forces inevitable.

Donut Dollies

Female Red Cross recreation service workers were known worldwide by the nickname of "Donut Dollies." A significant number of them served in Vietnam where they frequently visited firebases and base camps. Their visits were always appreciated and looked forward to by the troops in the field.

Double Eagle, Operation

The 3rd Marine Amphibious Force and the Army 1st Cavalry Division launched an operation in conjunction with the ARVN 2nd and 22nd Infantry Divisions to trap the 18th NVA Regiment and VC Main Force units in Quang Ngai province. This was in reaction to intelligence that Viet Cong and NVA units were gathering in the area in late 1965. The Marines began the operation by landing north of Duc Pho on January 28, 1966. As the units began to converge, weather and dense jungle slowed the Marines. The 1st Cavalry Division encountered heavy NVA resistance almost immediately, but the bulk of the communist forces evaded contact and

Right: Using the "buddy system" a patrol climbs up an elevated paddy dike during Operation Double Eagle.

escaped. The slow linear tactics employed by the US and ARVN in order to coordinate the movement of large formations allowed the faster moving NVA more than enough time to escape. The US military repeated this mistake on many occasions.

Doumer Bridge

Built between 1896 and 1902, all of the supplies coming into Hanoi by rail passed over the Doumer Bridge. The 5,532ft, 19-span, steel bridge crosses the Red River in an area of low, flat, floodplains. It was not attacked until 1967 because it lay in an area near Hanoi that had been declared off-limits. It was struck on August 11, 1967 by 36 bombers carrying 3,000lb bombs, and rendered unserviceable. Repeatedly repaired, and heavily defended by the North Vietnamese, it was struck again and again. In 1967 and 1968, 177 sorties dropped 380 tons of ordnance on the bridge. Following the bombing halt of 1968 it was again attacked in 1972. However, by this time the development of guided bombs simplified the process, and it was quickly dropped again.

Draft

The Selective Training and Service Act was passed in 1940, and the draft in

various forums was a fixture in the United States until 1973. The system was operated by nearly 4,000 local draft boards. Unpaid volunteers, predominantly World War I and World War II veterans, who had great discretionary power as to who would be deferred and for what reason, staffed the boards. Discrimination and favoritism were the norm. Women were not allowed to serve on the draft boards until 1967. All males were required to register for the draft on their 18th birthday and over 2 million

men were inducted into military service during the Vietnam War. President Nixon ended all draft calls in December 1972. President Ford terminated the draft registration requirement in 1975. President Carter reintroduced draft registration in 1979, and it is still in effect.

Dragon's Jaw Bridge

The Than Hoa Bridge spanned the Song Ma River three miles north of the town of Than Hoa, the capital of Annam Province. It was 540ft long, 56ft wide, and consisted of two steel-truss spans resting on a massive 16ft diameter steel reinforced concrete pier, and concrete abutments at either end. The Vietnamese called it the Ham Rung, which means Dragon's Jaw. Resting between two hills festooned with antiaircraft emplacements, the bridge was repeatedly attacked from 1965 until the bombing halt in 1968. In one massive attack, beginning at 5:00am, January 28, 1968, and lasting three and a half hours, the Navy and Air Force dropped three tons of bombs on the bridge every four and a half minutes, to no avail. It wasn't until May 13, 1972, during Operation Linebacker I, that the bridge was finally destroyed using laser-guided bombs.

Right: Smoke, and dust boils around the Phoung Dinh railroad bypass bridge, known as Dragon's Jaw Bridge, six miles north of Than Hoa as an A4 Skyhawk pulls away.

Drugs

During the first three years of the war the tempo of combat operations was such that very little opportunity for drug abuse, other than alcohol, presented itself. The military made alcohol available to the troops, either in service clubs established in rear areas or by issuing beer to the troops forward. After the 1968 Tet Offensive, drug use rose dramatically, and marijuana was the drug of choice. As it became clear that the United States intended to withdraw, marijuana gave way to epidemic levels of heroin use, combat effectiveness declined and the US population became increasingly concerned over the number of drug addicts returning from Vietnam.

In 1969, a Defense Department study indicated that over 25 percent of the troops in Vietnam were using drugs, either occasionally or frequently. In mid-1970, it was determined that heroin addiction was becoming a major problem. The full extent of the problem was documented in a 1974 Office for Drug Abuse Prevention survey report that indicated fully 34 percent of the troops in Vietnam had used heroin. The military attempted to explain away a portion of the problem by pointing out that men who abused drugs before they came to Vietnam accounted for the vast bulk of the user population.

When heroin use among US soldiers in South Vietnam exploded in 1969, the US expended a great deal of effort to discover the source. They determined that Allied military forces in Laos played a key role in the drug traffic. The senior commander of the Laotian military owned the region's largest heroin laboratory, and exported it to South Vietnam using troops and aircraft of the Royal Lao Air Force for that purpose. Although the CIA eventually pinpointed the locations of many of the heroin labs in northwestern Laos, they were never able to eradicate the problem. General Ouane, the Laotian Chief of Staff, who ran the operation, was politically untouchable.

Dulles, Allen Welsh

During his time as Director of the CIA from 1953 to 1961, Dulles convinced President Eisenhower to support the Diem government. He, along with his brother John who was Secretary of State, also convinced the President to support Diem in blocking the elections called for under the 1954 Geneva Accords.

Dulles, John Foster

As the Secretary of State from 1953 to 1959, Dulles regarded the Viet Minh as an instrument of communist aggression. He reluctantly participated in the Geneva Conference of 1954, but instructed the US delegation to act only as an interested nation. He later negotiated the Southeast Asia Treaty Organization treaty, and enthusiastically supported Ngo Dinh Diem.

Duong Quynh Hoa

A French trained doctor, Hoa was one of the founders of the National Liberation Front. Appointed as the health minister of the Provisional Revolutionary Government, she fled Saigon after the Tet Offensive and traveled abroad on propaganda missions for North Vietnam. Disillusioned by the actions of the North Vietnamese following the fall of South Vietnam, she became a prominent critic of the communist government.

Duong Van Duc

A native of the Mekong Delta, Duc graduated from the Vietnamese Military Academy at Da Lat in 1946, and the French Staff School in 1953. Promoted to Brigadier-General in 1956, he served as the representative to the Republic of Korea, then commanded a paratroop unit near Saigon. In 1964, he led his troops into Saigon and participated in an abortive coup, which collapsed in only 24 hours.

Duong Van Minh

In 1955, Minh, known as "Big Minh," became the ranking army officer in Ngo Dinh Diem's new Republic of Vietnam. A year later he crushed the Hoa Hao sect, and Diem removed him from military command because of his rising popularity. In 1963, he was a leader of the coup that deposed Diem. He was exiled in January 1964 by another coup. He returned to Vietnam after Nguyen Van Thieu came to power and in April 1975 assumed the South Vietnamese Presidency after Thieu resigned, surrendering the country to the victorious North Vietnamese.

Durbrow, Elbridge

In 1957, President Eisenhower appointed Durbrow as US Ambassador to South Vietnam. As ambassador he was sharply

Below: General Duong Van Minh accepts the Presidency of South Vietnam the day before Saigon fell.

critical of the corruption and nepotism in the Diem government. He also repeatedly clashed with Diem's US military advisers, and blamed governmental repression for the rise of the Viet Cong. Undermined by Edward Lansdale and his military opponents, President Kennedy replaced him soon after assuming the presidency.

Dustoff

Originally the radio call sign assigned to the 57th Medical Detachment (Air Ambulance) in 1962, within a very short time "Dustoff" became the universal short hand term for helicopter medical evacuation from the battlefield. As time

Right: A helicopter takes off from a Landing Zone on a Dustoff mission.

Below: A Dustoff helicopter prepares to set down on a battered hilltop during the Battle of Dak To.

Left: A 1st Infantry Division medic stabilizes a wounded soldier and looks for a Dustoff to evacuated them from the field.

went on Dustoff and Medevac became synonymous in military parlance. The operating ethos of the Dustoff helicopter crews demanded skill, dedication, and bravery: "No compromise. No rationalization. No hesitation. Fly the mission. Now!" There could be no refusal to fly a mission, the wounded always came first. Since the Vietnam War the term "Dustoff" has entered the American lexicon and is routinely used for helicopter medical evacuations.

Dye Marker, Operation

Secretary of Defense Robert S McNamara, acting on a 1966 recommendation of Harvard professor Roger Fisher, ordered the building of a barbed wire, mine and sensor strip along the Demilitarized Zone. This project, the final code name of which was Dye Marker, became known as McNamara's Line or McNamara's Wall.

The Defense Department was convinced that construction of such a barrier would eliminate the need to further reinforce the troops in I Corps. General Westmoreland endorsed the concept, however the Marine Corps was adamantly opposed to it. The Marines argued, unsuccessfully, that it would be expensive, probably unworkable, and that technology could not really stop infiltration, to do that required troops on the ground. Although some elements of the barrier were constructed, the subsequent siege of Khe Sahn proved that technology could not forestall infiltration and that the plan was, at best, naïve.

Dylan, Bob

An American musician and social protester, Dylan's songs frequently criticized the Vietnam War. Two of his songs, "Blowin' in the Wind" and "The Times They are a Changin'" became the anthems of the civil rights and antiwar movements respectively.

Left: A rifleman jumps across a breach in a paddy dike during reconnaissance of an area to be cleared for Operation Dye Marker.

Eagle Flight

Coined by the Marines in 1963, Eagle Flight was a term that described the use of airmobile strike forces to raid and harass the Viet Cong, or quickly reinforce reconnaissance elements in contact. As the war expanded it came to mean an infantry element supported by gunships that could be quickly inserted.

Eagle Pull, Operation

The evacuation of the US Embassy in Phnom Penh, Cambodia, on April 12, 1975 was known by the code name Eagle Pull. On April 10, as the Khmer Rouge closed in on the capital, the US Ambassador requested air evacuation no later than the April 12. At 8:50am on the April 12, an HH-53 landed a four-man Air Force combat control team to coordinate the operation. By 10:00am, Marine Corps CH-53s had evacuated 82 Americans, 159 Cambodians, and 35 other foreign nationals to US Navy assault ships in the Gulf of Thailand. There were no casualties.

Easter Offensive
(Nguyen Hue Campaign)

On March 30, 1972 North Vietnam launched a massive three-pronged attack designed to achieve a conventional military victory over the south. The North

Above: The troops debark their helicopters as an Eagle Flight recovers back to the airstrip.

Vietnamese decided to employ conventional tactics, because they did not believe that the 65,000, mostly logistical support troops, the US had remaining in Vietnam were capable of intervening. General Giap struck with 14 infantry divisions and 26 separate infantry regiments—almost 120,000 troops—backed up by 1,200 tanks and other armored vehicles, as well as a significant quantity of artillery. On April 2, Camp Caroll, the strongest position in northern I Corps surrendered, providing the NVA an almost unrestricted route east to Quang Tri City. A short time later, as NVA tanks rolled south, ARVN armor, supported by elements of the Vietnamese Marine Brigade, stopped them cold at the Dong Ha Bridge, only to be outflanked at the Cam Lo Bridge seven miles to the west. By April 28, the ARVN 3rd Infantry Division, a relatively new and inexperienced organization defending Quang Tri, disintegrated. Lieutenant General Ngo Quang Troung, arguably the best South Vietnamese General, assumed command of I Corps and stabilized the situation. He succeeded in rallying his forces and then counterattacked. Though he regained Quang Tri City in September,

Left: A group of Marines prepare to go secure the Landing Zone to evacuate the embassy from Phnom Penh.

Below left: A South Vietnamese armored personnel carrier passes a truckload of refugees fleeing south from Quang Tri during the NVA Easter Offensive.

the NVA remained in control of the bulk of the province. In the central highlands the NVA opened the fighting along the coast in Binh Dinh province in an attempt to draw ARVN forces away from Pleiku and Kontum. The ruse failed. The NVA then launched a massive attack at the small town of Tan Canh and the firebase at Dak To north of Kontum. The two defending regiments of the ARVN 22nd Infantry Division disintegrated, opening the route to Kontum. Inexplicably the NVA delayed following up on their attack for almost three weeks. The ARVN, by reinforcing Kontum and employing massive B-52 strikes, turned back the assault. The third (southern) prong of the offensive, three divisions attacking out of Cambodia, overran Loc Ninh and then surrounded An Loc 65 miles from Saigon. NVA armor played a larger role at An Loc than anywhere else during the Easter Offensive. T-54 tanks punched their way into the city on April 13, but the South Vietnamese defenders managed to separate them from their

supporting infantry and, using hand-held antitank weapons such as the LAW, and shoulder-fired recoilless rifles, destroyed large numbers of them. The NVA then attempted to reduce An Loc using classic siege tactics. The ARVN countered with massive air strikes and bitterly contested every square yard of ground. An Loc held, with terrible losses on both sides. Reacting to the North Vietnamese attack, President Nixon ordered the American Navy and Air Force to intervene with the maximum power available. Operation Linebacker I inflicted severe losses on the NVA, and included the mining of Haiphong Harbor and other North Vietnamese ports. General Giap lost an estimated 100,000 troops, and at least half of his large caliber artillery and armored vehicles. It was not until 1975 that the NVA had rebuilt their forces to the point where they could again launch a conventional assault.

Eden, Anthony

British Foreign Secretary, Anthony Eden, together with Soviet Foreign Minister Molotov, co-chaired the 1954 Geneva Accords. He opposed US Secretary of State John Foster Dulles' push for military intervention, and acting as an intermediary between the Soviets, Chinese, and Americans, brokered the political division of Vietnam, conceding the North to the communists.

Above: Dwight D Eisenhower supported US involvement in Vietnam during and after his presidency.

Eisenhower, Dwight David

As President, Eisenhower actively considered the use of nuclear weapons to support the French at Dien Bien Phu, and later established the first Military Advisory Group for Vietnam. After leaving office he continued to support US involvement in Vietnam but privately criticized both President Kennedy and President Johnson's policies.

El Paso, Operation

Operation El Paso was conducted by the 1st Infantry Division along Route 13 through War Zone C in June and July, 1966 to prevent a 9th Viet Cong Division thrust at An Loc. The battle opened when the VC 272nd Regiment ambushed an armored cavalry troop on June 8, 1966, disabling a number of tanks and armored personnel carriers. Three days later the 2nd Battalion, 28th Infantry, slugged it

Left: A soldier standing near a cloud of colored smoke guides a helicopter in for a landing on a cold landing zone.

out with the VC 273rd Regiment in a bunker and trench line northwest of Loc Ninh. On June 30, the VC 271st Regiment ambushed another armored cavalry troop, destroying several tanks and inflicting heavy casualties. Only heavy US air strikes prevented a major communist victory.

Elections, Vietnamese National

National elections were held in the Republic of Vietnam in 1955, 1967, and 1971. Each of them was heavily influenced by the US government, which used its influence with successive RVN administrations to promote reform and greater self-determination for the Vietnamese, while ensuring that US interests were secure. The 1956 reunification elections called for in the Geneva Accords never took place, mainly because Diem knew he had no chance of defeating the communists. Instead he called a referendum in South Vietnam between himself and Bao Dai, held on October 23, 1955. It was heavily rigged and Diem took 98.9 percent of the vote. Diem's close advisers drew up the resulting constitution, but this underwent important modifications prior to the 1967 elections, which allowed for the existence of political opposition and an effective judiciary. Nevertheless, the most powerful slate, that of Thieu and Ky, intimidated its most threatening opponents and carried the election with just 34.8 percent of the vote, the other votes spilt between 10 other such slates. In the four years preceding the 1971 election Thieu was able to implement legislation that effectively disbarred minority candidates. In the election his main opponents were Duong Van Minh and Vice-President Ky, the latter failing to generate the votes in the national assembly needed to certify his candidacy. Both men withdrew from the election as a result, Ky calling for a new election organized by the Senate. Thieu offered instead to resign if he did not receive at least 50 percent of the vote. In the election, which he would have won even had it not been rigged, he took 90 percent of the vote.

Electronic Intelligence (ELINT)

ELINT involves the collection and analysis of the electronic "signatures" of

weapons and surveillance systems in order to determine vulnerabilities and devise countermeasures. Electronic Intelligence was the primary method for obtaining information on the capabilities of the rapidly expanding North Vietnamese air defense systems. Specially configured ships and aircraft recorded their radar and communications signals, which helped the US to build the jammers and devise countermeasures to allow them to operate over North Vietnam.

Electronic Warfare (EW)

The implementation of a Soviet designed integrated air defense network of radars, guns, missiles, and ground-controlled interceptors by the North Vietnamese quickly made it necessary for the US to deploy some form of electronic countermeasures. The first of these involved assigning EB-66C Destroyers equipped with four types of radar warning receivers and nine different jammers to escort raids. Initially this proved fairly effective, but the addition of the MiG-21 to the NVA weapons mix and more aggressive tactics eventually relegated the EB-66C to lower North Vietnam. Equally important were the Big Eye, later renamed College Eye, and Rivet Top Lockheed EC-121 airborne early warning aircraft that could warn

American pilots of the presence of MiGs and assist in vectoring them to and from the targets, or plot their positions in the event of damage or shoot down. Initially, while the North Vietnamese Ilyushin Il-28 bombers were still considered a threat, the Big Eye also provided airborne early warning coverage over South Vietnam as well. This mission continued until 1967. Rivet Top specialized in pinpointing SAM sites and, with the advent of the Wild Weasel, vectoring Iron Hand missions against them. The signals intelligence, SIGINT, workhorse was the venerable RC-135 Combat Apple, which flew out of Kadena on Okinawa. Specialized electronic warfare missions were carried out by Ryan 147D drones launched from DC-130E Hercules control aircraft. They routinely challenged North Vietnamese air defenses and recorded then transmitted the fire control and guidance signal information to RB-47Hs orbiting off the coast.

Their greatest coup occurred on February 13, 1966 when a model 147E drone captured and transmitted to an RB-47H the details of the SA-2 radar guidance link, proximity fuze frequency and operation, and warhead functioning before it was destroyed, allowing the US to devise specific countermeasures for the system.

Ellsberg, Daniel

One of Secretary McNamara's "whiz kids," RAND researcher, and intelligence analyst, Ellsberg was assigned to help compile the comprehensive classified study of American policy in Vietnam. He became disillusioned with the war and copied the study, which he then provided to the Senate Foreign Relations Committee. When they didn't respond, in 1971 he gave it to *The New York Times*, where parts were published as the "Pentagon Papers."

Enclave Strategy

When the first US combat units arrived in Vietnam, Ambassador Maxwell Taylor and General Harold Johnson, the Army Chief of Staff, proposed limiting their operations to a 50-mile zone around coastal base areas. The strategy was opposed by General Earl Wheeler, Chairman of the Joint Chiefs of Staff, and General William Westmoreland, Commander of MACV, whose contention was that hunkering down in an enclave simply made a lucrative target. Officially the Enclave Strategy lasted a year; unofficially it simply was never

tried. As US casualties increased, retired General James Gavin recommended a return to the Enclave Strategy rather than increase the presence of troops, as a way to return the primary combat role to the ARVN. President Johnson dismissed this recommendation out of hand.

End Sweep, Operation

In reaction to the Easter Offensive, President Nixon ordered the mining of North Vietnam's harbors and rivers. Beginning on May 8, 1972 and continuing to the end of the year thousands of mines were laid. The mining prevented 85 percent of all North Vietnamese imports, and combined with the Linebacker bombing campaign, eventually induced the North Vietnamese to negotiate an end to the war. In response to the Paris Peace Agreement, the United States Navy launched Operation End Sweep to clear the mines from Vietnamese waters. The operation was initiated on February 5, 1973 and by June 18 the North Vietnamese ports of Haiphong, Hon Gai, and Cam Pha were declared clear. The operation terminated on July 18, 1973.

Above: A Marine M67A1 flame-tank fires at a small trench line during operations geared to clear the area around the Air Base at Danang.

Enhance Plus, Operation

Operation Enhance Plus was an outgrowth of Operation Enhance, which was designed to replace equipment South Vietnam lost during the Easter Offensive. On October 12, 1972 the Nixon administration began transferring billions of dollars worth of military equipment to the Republic of Vietnam. The hope was that the ARVN would use the equipment to improve its position on the battlefield and strengthen its hand during negotiations following the Paris Peace Agreement. This massive influx of matériel was named Operation Enhance Plus. By January 1973, the United States had provided over $2 billion worth of military equipment to the Republic of Vietnam and its Air Force was the fourth largest in the world. This buildup of logistical supplies was instrumental in overcoming President Thieu's opposition to the peace negotiations.

Above: A mine detonates in Haiphong Harbor during the US Navy mine clearance effort in 1973, known as Operation End Sweep.

Enuol, Y Bahm

Y Bahm Enuol was a Rhade Montagnard nationalist. He was a founder and President of Le Front Unifie de Lutte des Races Opprimees (FULRO), which translates as The United Front for the Liberation of Oppressed Races. It was created in opposition to President Diem's program for resettlement of Vietnamese refugees on Montagnard lands in the central highlands. As the FULRO President, he represented the Montagnards in negotiations with the Cambodian and South Vietnamese governments, the North Vietnamese, and the

Viet Cong. In 1964, during an armed uprising at Special Forces Camps around Ban Me Thout, he delivered a FULRO manifesto calling for action to reclaim Montagnard lands. Threatened with imprisonment he fled to Cambodia. Montagnard security deteriorated and in 1968 he attempted to return, but was overthrown by more militant tribesmen. He again fled to Cambodia where he was captured by the Khmer Rouge and executed in 1975.

Enterprise, Operation

On February 13, 1967, the US Army 9th Infantry Division and South Vietnamese Regional and Popular Forces, in conjunction with riverine elements, launched Operation Enterprise to clear the Viet Cong out of Long An province, south of Saigon. Allied forces incurred

considerable losses as they swept the area through April 11, 1967, while the Viet Cong successfully dispersed and evaded their patrols. Though the operation lasted until March 11, 1968, it still failed to clear the province and the Viet Cong remained both a popular and powerful presence.

Enthoven, Alain

One of the "whiz kids" brought to the Defense Department by Secretary McNamara; Enthoven was one of the few senior advisers who continually disagreed with the rosy picture portrayed by the military. He maintained that the Attrition Strategy supported by Westmoreland would not work because the North Vietnamese controlled their casualty rate and would outlast the Americans indefinitely.

Fairfax, Operation

By 1966, security around Saigon had deteriorated so badly that General Westmoreland decided to use US battalions to strengthen it. In Operation Fairfax, one US battalion was assigned to each district in Gia Dinh. Three ARVN battalions were assigned to operate in the same area, each linked to a US unit, until security improved.

By the end of 1967, the operation was declared a success though, due to a reluctance to share intelligence, the Viet Cong infrastructure was virtually intact. Robert Komer studied Operation Fairfax when he was assigned as head of the US pacification effort. His study culminated in the establishment of the Phoenix (Phung Huong) Program.

Above: A Patrol Air Cushion Vehicle is used to salvage parts from a shot-down Huey during Operation Fairfax.

Below: A group of Viet Cong suspects await interrogation during a cordon and search operation.

Fall, Bernard B.

Dr Fall was Professor of International Relations at Howard University. He first came to Vietnam in 1953 to do research for his doctorate, and returned repeatedly as the war unfolded. A critic of both French colonialism and American intervention, he had great respect and admiration for both the Viet Minh and the Viet Cong. His insights were also widely admired by the US military. On February 21, 1967 he was killed by a Viet Cong booby trap while accompanying a Marine patrol on the Street Without Joy in I Corps.

Farm Gate, Operation

Operation Farm Gate represented the first direct combat involvement of US units in the Vietnam War when President Kennedy dispatched detachment 2A, 4400th Combat Crew Training Squadron to Binh Hoa. Ostensibly there to train Vietnamese pilots and air crews, on December 6 the Joint Chiefs of Staff authorized Farm Gate to undertake combat missions, provided that at least one Vietnamese National was aboard the aircraft. Flying obsolescent B-26 bombers and T-28 trainers converted to strike aircraft, the detachment became the nucleus of an expanding US Air Force presence.

In 1962, President Kennedy approved an expansion of Farm Gate, and in July the contingent at Binh Hoa became the 1st Air Commando Squadron, part of the Pacific Air Forces. In 1964, the B-26s and T-28s were replaced by A-1Es, and the older aircraft were transferred to Laos to support Hmong guerrillas fighting the Pathet Lao. In March 1965, the requirement for South Vietnamese Nationals to be carried on the aircraft was dropped, and as the US Air Force presence in Vietnam increased by the end of 1967, Farm Gate disappeared.

Faure, Edgar

In 1955, the Prime Minister of France, Edgar Faure, clashed with US Secretary of State John Foster Dulles over supporting the Diem regime in Vietnam. Faure considered Diem incapable, and the Eisenhower Administration's support of Diem caused the French to shift their attention from Vietnam to North Africa. The removal of France's influence allowed the United States to embark on its own independent political path in South Vietnam.

Federal Bureau of Investigation (FBI)

The investigative branch of the US Justice Department is known as the FBI.

During the Vietnam War FBI Director, J Edgar Hoover, worked closely with Johnson and Nixon to investigate alleged breaches of federal law committed by opponents of the war. Fearful of the consequences, Hoover refused to cooperate with Nixon when the latter sought to create the unified intelligence force suggested by the Huston Plan, but his caution could not prevent the FBI suffering a major crisis in the aftermath of Watergate and the Vietnam War.

Fellowship of Reconciliation (FOR)

The US antiwar movement, the Fellowship of Reconciliation, has been active from the mid 1960s until the present day. Although not the most public of the many protest groups, the FOR was the first to publicly advocate draft resistance in 1965. It acted as a focal point for the antiwar movement and had a moderating influence.

Felt, Harry D

Admiral Felt was the Commander-in-Chief Pacific from 1958 to 1964.

Below: Admiral Harry D Felt, Commander-in-Chief Pacific, welcomes General Lyman Lemnitzer, Chairman of the Joint Chiefs of Staff, and Secretary of Defense Robert McNamara to the Honolulu Conference.

Originally he recommended not sending US troops to South Vietnam in 1961. Later, however, he became a strong supporter of intervention. He presided over the rapid buildup of Special Forces and air units, and also supported the use of fast attack craft against North Vietnam under OPLAN 34A, which contributed to the Gulf of Tonkin Incident.

Fernandez, Richard
Clergy and Laymen Concerned About Vietnam (CALCAV) was America's largest religiously oriented antiwar organization. Its executive director, Richard Fernandez, though a highly effective organizer, did not establish formal ties to other antiwar coalitions. He was concerned that their radical leadership and inflammatory rhetoric might alienate his core constituency.

Field Force I
Field Force I was a Corps level headquarters in Nha Trang commanded by an Army three-star general. It controlled all US and Allied units in II Corps. Originally called Task Force Alpha in 1965, in 1966 it was renamed Field Force I because the Vietnamese had used the term Corps to designate geographical, as well as military command areas.

Above: A Field Force II AH-1G Cobra gunship returns to base to rearm after expending most of its rockets.

Field Force II
Commanded by an Army three-star general, Field Force II was a Corps level headquarters located in Long Binh, just outside Bien Hoa. It controlled all US and Allied units in III Corps, the Saigon Special Zone, and northern IV Corps. It was named Field Force II because the Vietnamese had used the term Corps to designate geographical, as well as military command areas.

Fire Support Base (FSB)

Usually helicopter supplied, Fire Support Bases were self-contained US and South Vietnamese bases. They provided artillery fire for patrolling units and served as a forward operational base for combat units. Some developed into semi-permanent installations, though most were opened or closed as the combat tempo dictated.

A typical firebase usually had a battery of artillery, six guns with crews, and a fire direction center, and a platoon or company of infantry for security. Some were smaller, with a couple of guns and an infantry squad, and some larger, with a battalion or more of artillery and several companies of infantry.

Fishel, Wesley Robert

A political science professor at Michigan State University (MSU), Robert Fishel, met Ngo Dinh Diem in Japan in 1950. When Diem came to power in South Vietnam in 1954 he contracted with Michigan State University to assist the South Vietnamese in setting up a government. Fishel headed the effort. The anti-war movement accused the MSU program, especially its police-training component, of being a front for the CIA. As the head of the American Friends of Vietnam, Fishel pushed hard for US military involvement. Though he later

became a critic of Diem, he remained pro-war throughout.

Fishhook

A vaguely hook-shaped geographical area of Cambodia, approximately 50 miles northwest of Saigon, was known as the Fishhook. American military and political officials suspected that the Viet Cong Central Office for South Vietnam (COSVN) was located there. In 1970, President Nixon, whose aim was to destroy COSVN, decided to target the region as the central thrust of the Cambodian Incursion.

Five o'clock Follies

The name given by press representatives to the daily bulletins by the Military Assistance Command was the "five o'clock follies." The name stemmed from the widely held feeling among the media that the military was misrepresenting the war to them through overly optimistic statistics and reports, which contrasted to their own experiences in the field.

Flaming Dart, Operation

The code name for the US retaliatory air raids against North Vietnam that took place on February 7–8, 1965 was Operation Flaming Dart. It was launched in response to the February 6, Viet Cong

Above: Fire Support Base Thunder, between Long Binh and Loc Ninh, was steadily enlarged.

mortar attack on the US airbase at Pleiku. The strikes were launched from the attack carriers *Coral Sea*, *Hancock*, and *Ranger* against barracks and port facilities in southern North Vietnam. Forty-eight hours later, the Viet Cong killed 23 Americans at Qui Nhon and President Johnson ordered Operation Flaming Dart II, a second series of sorties that marked the onset of Operation Rolling Thunder.

Flexible Response

A US military defensive strategy was developed in the late 1960s by Maxwell Taylor, a former Army General and military adviser to Kennedy, known as "Flexible Response." It was based on the idea that military forces should be able to adapt and react effectively to any enemy threat or attack with appropriate action for the specific circumstances. Under Eisenhower US defensive strategy rested on the idea of "massive retaliation" with nuclear forces. Taylor surmised that

Above right: Troops keep watch from the bunker line of a Fire Support Base south of Phu Bai.

Right: Home is where you dig it. These troops add a little humor to their war.

148

"massive retaliation" was too inflexible, and stressed the value of having "multiple options" available should a crisis arise. He argued that having multiple options enhanced the credibility of the US deterrent (reassuring allies while deterring the opponent) and at the same time, made it improbable that the US would want or need nuclear attack. Conventional forces were to serve two functions, a deterrent function and the function to fight limited wars. Kennedy's adoption of "Flexible Response" enhanced the ability of US forces to respond to local, nonnuclear or "brush-fire" wars, and prepared it for the Vietnam conflict.

Fonda, Jane Seymour

Though named by the Pentagon in 1962, as "Miss Army Recruiting," throughout the 1960s Fonda became an increasingly vocal and strident antiwar protester. In

Below: President Gerald Ford awards the Medal of Honor to three former prisoners of war.

1971, she provided financial support to the "Winter Soldier Investigation" in Detroit, where a group alleging to be Vietnam veterans testified about atrocities and war crimes they had committed or witnessed in Vietnam. In the summer of 1972, she went to Hanoi and spoke with selected American prisoners, then made a propaganda broadcast on Hanoi Radio. She donned a helmet and posed on an NVA antiaircraft gun, causing journalists to christen her Hanoi Jane. Following her return to the United States, she accused American prisoners of war of lying when they claimed they had been tortured. Many conservative Americans and Vietnam veterans consider her to be an unpunished traitor.

Forces Armees National Khmer (FANK)

Following the collapse of Prince Norodom Sihanouk's neutral Cambodian government in 1970, President Nixon authorized military aid for the new Lon Nol regime. US Army Special Forces, Australian, and New Zealand jungle

instructors created an entirely new National Army for Cambodia consisting of 86 infantry and marine battalions. This was known as the Khmer National Armed Forces, or FANK.

Ford, Gerald R

A moderate Republican congressman from Michigan, Ford was nominated by President Nixon to replace Spiro Agnew, who resigned as Vice President in 1973. After succeeding Nixon as a result of the Watergate scandal, Ford struggled with an increasingly hostile Congress for funding to shore up the sagging Cambodian and South Vietnamese governments. As South Vietnam collapsed, President Ford declared that the war was "finished as far as America is concerned." However, shortly after the fall of Saigon and Phnom Penh, the Khmer Rouge government captured the Mayaguez, a US merchant vessel. Ford ordered the military to rescue the crew, even though Cambodia had already agreed to release them. Ford, unable to fully distance himself from the Nixon

Above: A pair of Forward Air Controllers fly at a very low altitude along a tree line to search for the enemy in their O-1 Bird Dogs.

administration, narrowly lost the 1976 presidential election to Jimmy Carter.

Forrestal, Michael V.

As head of the National Security Council Vietnam Coordinating Committee in 1960, Forrestal was the co-author of a report with Roger Hilsman, Director of Intelligence for the State Department, that expressed doubt about the survival of the Republic of Vietnam.

The report also cast serious doubt on the accuracy of official estimates of progress in Vietnam. Believing that Ngo Dinh Diem had become a part of the problem rather than the solution, Forrestal was one of the central figures in obtaining President Kennedy's approval of a recommendation for the overthrow of his government.

Fort Hood Three

A trio of US Army privates, James Johnson, Dennis Mora, and David Samas, became known as the "Fort Hood Three." In 1966, they gained national acclaim for their refusal to serve in Vietnam. The three signalers with the 2nd Armored Division at Fort Hood, refused service on the grounds that they believed the war to be illegal, immoral, and unjust. They were charged with insubordination and sentenced by a military court to imprisonment.

Fortas, Abe

Associate Justice of the US Supreme Court, Fortas was a trusted friend and informal adviser to President Johnson. Almost from the outset he vigorously advocated escalation of the war and opposed any halt to bombing. As Johnson became more concerned about the war, Fortas consistently urged that he stay the course. When recommended by Johnson to become the Chief Justice of the Supreme Court, he was charged with improperly involving himself in the executive branch decision-making, and his nomination was defeated.

Forward Air Controller (FAC)

Air Force pilots who flew slow, single-engine, propeller driven aircraft, such as the O-1 Bird Dog and twin turboprop OV-10 Bronco, were known as Forward Air Controllers. Their primary mission was to call in air strikes on enemy positions, by flying at a very low altitude and using visual reconnaissance to find their targets. They identified Viet Cong and North Vietnamese locations and relayed the information to fighter-bombers, bombers, or helicopter gunships.

Above: President Charles de Gaulle of France rejects a reporter's suggestion that France attempt to mediate the Vietnam War at a 1966 press conference.

Four-party Joint Military Commission

The commission created at the Paris Conference on January 27, 1973 to implement such provisions as the withdrawal of foreign troops and the release of prisoners was named the Four-party Joint Military Commission. It formed part of the cease-fire signed by the United States, South Vietnam, North Vietnam, and the Provisional Revolutionary Government of the National Liberation Front (NLF), the civilian arm of the South Vietnam communists. An International Commission of Control and Supervision (ICCS) was established to oversee the ceasefire.

Based in Saigon, the Four-party Joint Military Commission first met in February 1973, and was disbanded at the end of March. Although the Commission successfully oversaw the repatriation of US POWs and the withdrawal of remaining US or Free World military forces, it was not able to enforce the ceasefire and resolve the issue of troops reported Missing In Action.

Fragging

An attack on an officer or an NCO by his own troops, usually with a fragmentation grenade, was known by the slang term "fragging." While virtually unheard of before 1969, between 1969 and 1972 there were 788 fragging incidents that killed 86 people. They were indicative of a serious breakdown in the morale and discipline of American troops, who failed to see the purpose of dying in a war that their government had decided to abandon. Some fragging incidents in combat were attempts to remove leaders the troops believed to be incompetent and a threat to their survival. Most incidents however, occurred in rear echelon units where drug use and racial tension were rampant.

France

Following their defeat at Dien Bien Phu in 1954, and the subsequent Geneva

Above: Protesters fill the streets of Paris as the antiwar movement spreads to Europe.

Accords, France attempted to distance itself from the Indochina conflict. Though the terms of the ceasefire assigned France a role in South Vietnam, constant bickering with the United States gave them the opportunity to fully withdraw. Throughout the American phase of the war the French consistently pushed for the neutrality of Vietnam and opposed most American initiatives. (See also Indochina War.)

Francis Marion, Operation

Operation Francis Marion was one of the last of a series of screening operations along the II Corps–Cambodian border in 1967. It resulted in a series of eight battles between the US 4th Infantry Division and North Vietnamese units in the Ia Drang Valley and around the Duc Co Special Forces Camp west of Pleiku. Beginning in April and lasting into October, 4th Division units engaged regiments assigned to both the 1st and 10th NVA Divisions. Every battle resulted in heavy losses to the North Vietnamese, and by early fall it became apparent that the NVA had shifted the focus of its attention away from Pleiku and north to Kontum. On October 12, 1967 Francis Marion was combined with Operation Greeley and renamed Operation MacArthur, which precipitated the pivotal battle of the central highlands Campaign, the Battle of Dak To.

Free Fire Zones

Areas established by US units in coordination with the South Vietnamese district or province chiefs were known as Free Fire Zones. In a Free Fire Zone, all structures and personnel were considered to be enemy and could be attacked without warning or further consultation.

Free World Assistance Program (FWA)

During the 1950s, a program of economic and military aid was developed by the Free World Military Assistance Office of the United States government. Thirty-three nations were members of the Free World Assistance Program (FWA), furnishing what were described before the Senate Committee on Foreign Relations as "all kinds of materials and services needed in Vietnam, such as medical supplies, hospital equipment, refugee relief supplies, schools and hospital construction and so forth." Although coordinated by the US State Department, the Free World Assistance Program was sponsored by the Pentagon.

Free World Military Assistance Council

A council was established to provide operational guidance to, if not direct control of, the Free World Military Forces of Australia, New Zealand, Thailand, and the Republic of Korea committed to the aid of the Republic of Vietnam through the Free World Assistance Program. The council was composed of the chief of the Vietnamese Joint General Staff, the most senior Korean officer in Vietnam and the commander of US Military Assistance Command, Vietnam.

VIETNAM: A VISUAL ENCYCLOPEDIA

CLEAR-ALL-WEAPONS

Above: Happy troops at Bien Hoa line up to board a National Airlines Freedom Bird and depart Vietnam.

Free World Military Forces

In order to emphasize that nations other than the United States were also supporting South Vietnam, and to clearly distinguish themselves from the communists, the official title promulgated for the Allies fighting in South Vietnam was the Free World Military Forces. All newly arriving troops were issued a small plastic pocket badge that identified them as "Free World Military Forces," though few ever wore it

Freedom Bird

The aircraft that troops departed Vietnam on at the end of their tour was called the Freedom Bird. It signified both their freedom from the exigencies of combat and, for many, their pending release from the United States military.

Freedom Train, Operation

As a response to the North Vietnamese Easter Offensive the US launched Operation Freedom Train, one of the heaviest bombing campaigns of the war. Initially it employed those Air Force, Navy, and Marine Corps aircraft that were immediately available. However, President Nixon immediately ordered additional aircraft carriers to Yankee Station and made additional B-52 bombers available to carry on strikes both against the advancing North Vietnamese forces and military targets in North Vietnam. As the attacks built to their full fury, the operation was renamed Linebacker I.

Frequent Wind, Operation

Before dawn on April 29, 1975, a heavy North Vietnamese artillery and rocket assault on Tan Son Nhut Air Base outside Saigon signaled that the final assault was under way. With the runways unusable, Ambassador Graham Martin, who had inexplicably delayed the evacuation of both Americans and key Vietnamese, was faced with the necessity of organizing a helicopter withdrawal. The Marine commander of the airlift had not planned on a large-scale evacuation from the embassy and had not been informed that several thousand people were to be lifted out. Only one CH-53 at a time could land in the embassy courtyard, and a smaller CH-46 could use the rooftop pad. At 4:30am of April 30, by Presidential order, only the remaining Americans were to be evacuated. At 5:00am Ambassador Martin left, and nearly 500 Vietnamese employees, as well as the Korean Ambassador who had been told he would be evacuated from the American Embassy, were abandoned to their fate.

Friendly Fire

Sometimes called "Blue on Blue," friendly fire is the inadvertent engagement of one friendly unit by another one. It most commonly occurs through misdirected artillery fire or inaccurate bombing. While the US military does not keep statistics on friendly fire casualties, in Vietnam some observers believe they accounted for between two and ten percent of all casualties.

Front Unifie de Lutte des Races Opprimees, Le (FULRO)

FULRO (The United Front for the Oppressed Races) was created from var-

Left: An F-105 refuels on its way to North Vietnam during Operation Freedom Train.

ious ethnic political groups to oppose Diem's Land Development program, which sought to displace the Montagnard from their lands in the central highlands. The group staged a military uprising at Ban Me Thuot in 1964, but the threat of reprisals from the RVN forced it into exile in Cambodia.

In 1968, FULRO leader Y Bham Enoul agreed to integrate FULRO army units into Regional Force units to allow them to return to Vietnam to protect Montagnard villages, but he was overthrown by militants within the group and forced into exile. The movement faded from view in 1969, only to emerge again

Below: A pair of Marine CH-53s wait for the people they are supposed to evacuate during Operation Frequent Wind.

Left: During the fall of Saigon, a Navy boat goes to retrieve South Vietnamese refugees from a ditched Huey.

Below: A Marine Corps CH-53 sets down on a parking lot ready to pick up evacuees from Saigon.

Right A Marine security guard escorts a South Vietnamese helicopter pilot and his family along the deck of the USS *Hancock*.

in 1974 as the Dega Highlands Provisional Government.

Fulbright, William J

Although Fulbright, the Chairman of the Senate Foreign Relations Committee, helped President Johnson get the Gulf of Tonkin Resolution through Congress in 1964, he soon became a critic of the war. Throughout 1967 and 1968 he gave critics of American foreign policy a high-level forum for expressing their views by holding open public hearings of the Foreign Relations Committee.

G

Game Warden, Operation

In 1965, it became apparent that although Operation Market Time had significantly reduced Viet Cong and North Vietnamese seaborne logistics traffic, it could not prevent enemy movement on inland waterways. Task Force 116 was formed to interdict Viet Cong activities along major rivers of the Mekong Delta. US Navy fiberglass hulled river patrol boats (PBRs) based either around tank landing ships (LSTs) anchored at the mouth of rivers or at shore installations, were formed into River Divisions. In 1967, a squadron of 24 Huey helicopters, the "Seawolves", were added to provide air support. A squadron of heavily armed OV-10 Broncos, the "Black Ponies," were added in 1969. Game Warden forces, generally divided into two boat patrols, conducted around-the-clock operations to inspect Vietnamese river craft, enforce curfews, conduct ambushes, and provide both logistical and fire support to Allied troops ashore. They landed US Navy SEAL teams to collect intelligence data and assault Viet Cong units in the Delta. They also swept the vital Long Tau shipping channel for mines. Beginning in 1968, the Navy's Vietnamization program shifted Game Warden matériel to the Republic of Vietnam Navy, and Task Force 116 was disestablished in December 1970.

Right: A Navy River Patrol Boat, PBR, moves up a crowded waterway near Chau Doc.

Below right: A Navy Huey flies toward the smoke from an engagement in the Delta.

Below: A light fire team from the Seawolves patrols a section of the Mekong River.

Above: The Geneva Conference eventually produced the Geneva Accords of 1954, ending the French-Indochina War.

Gamma Project

One of the most highly classified operations of the Vietnam War, Project Gamma was a clandestine Special Forces intelligence operation targeted against North Vietnamese and Viet Cong base camps in Cambodia, and the Cambodian government's cooperation with the North Vietnamese. On February 28, 1968 Detachment B-57 was relocated from Saigon to Nha Trang and designated as Project Gamma headquarters. Operating from Special Forces camps along the Cambodian border from the Mekong Delta to the highlands, by early 1969 it was providing the bulk of the intelligence upon which the Cambodian Incursion was based.

Garwood, Robert "Bobby" R

A US Marine Corps jeep driver who was taken prisoner in September 1965 in Quang Nam province, Bobby Garwood was not released with the other prisoners in 1973. In 1979 he passed a note to identify himself as an American to a Finnish diplomat, and the publicity surrounding his case led to his release. Accused by numerous prisoners of war of having been a collaborator with the North Vietnamese, Garwood was tried by a Marine Corps court-martial. He was found guilty of serving as a guard for the NVA, informing on his comrades, taking part in interrogations of other prisoners, and assaulting another American prisoner. Political intervention during the review process of his sentence resulted in his release rather than imprisonment.

Gavin, James M

A retired Army Lieutenant General and former Ambassador to France, James Gavin was one of the few military figures who publicly opposed US policy in Vietnam from the outset. He pronounced the war both wasteful and without purpose, urged the Johnson administration to adopt the Enclave Strategy, and pointed out that the US leadership had failed to articulate any clear military objective in Vietnam.

Gayler, Noel Arthur Meredyth

Admiral Gayler was the former head of the National Security Agency before he was appointed as Commander-in-Chief Pacific in September 1972. As the last CINCPAC during the war in Vietnam, he was responsible for Operation Frequent Wind. He tried repeatedly to persuade Ambassador Martin to implement an evacuation plan, but Martin refused until it was almost too late.

Gelb, Leslie H

As Deputy Director of the Defense Department Policy Planning Staff in 1967 and 1968, Gelb was responsible for producing the 7000-page history of US policy and involvement in Vietnam, which later became known as the Pentagon Papers. He believed that a seriously flawed decision-making process led the US deeper into Vietnam, even after the leaders were aware that success was highly unlikely.

Geneva Accords (1954)

The international agreement, known as the Geneva Accords, brought the war in Indochina to an end. On May 8, 1954 the Geneva Conference on Indochina opened. In attendance were representatives of Cambodia, the Democratic Republic of Vietnam, France, Laos, the

People's Republic of China, the State of Vietnam, the Union of Soviet Socialist Republics, the United Kingdom and the United States of America, all meeting to negotiate a solution for Southeast Asia. On July 21, 1954 after more than a month of debate, the Geneva Accords were signed, which agreed to divide Vietnam in half at the 17th parallel. Ho Chi Minh's communists were ceded the north, and Bao Dai's regime granted the south. The accords also provided for elections to be held in the whole of Vietnam within two years to reunify the country. However, the US opposed the unifying elections, fearing a likely victory by Ho Chi Minh.

Geneva Agreement (1962)

A declaration on the neutrality of Laos was signed on July 23, 1962 by the US and 13 other nations, which prohibited the US from attacking sections of the Ho Chi Minh Trail that lay inside eastern Laos. Although this had already been guaranteed under the Geneva Accords, the threat to the country by the communist Pathet Lao which emerged in the late 1950s forced the issue to the fore. Not wishing to commit military forces, Kennedy sought instead to negotiate the neutralization of the country at Geneva. During the talks the Pathet forces, aided

by North Vietnamese regulars (PAVN), made major territorial gains along the route of the Trail. The agreement, which required the withdrawal of foreign troops from Laos, was never adhered too and for the remainder of the war a façade of neutrality pervaded, while the southeastern area of the country proved to be a major supply and infiltration route for PAVN and Viet Cong irregulars.

Genovese, Eugene Dominick

A Marxist history professor at Rutgers University, Genovese declared at an anti-war teach-in, "I do not fear or regret the impending Viet Cong victory. I welcome it." Nixon called for his ousting from the faculty and Barry Goldwater denounced him as a traitor. He left Rutgers in 1967 and taught in Canada for two years. He returned to the United States in 1969 and subsequently became one of the best-known American historians on the subject of slavery in America.

Geography of Vietnam

Vietnam occupies the eastern side of the Indochinese peninsula. It's located in the Northern Hemisphere between the 8th and 23rd parallels, bordered on the north by China, and on the west by Laos and Cambodia. The Gulf of Tonkin and the South China Sea form the eastern border,

while to the south and southwest is the Gulf of Thailand. Vietnam's two broad deltas, the Red River in the north and the Mekong River in the south, are linked by a long, thin coastal strip approximately 50 miles wide, that quickly gives rise in the west to a highland plateau that is the home of the Montagnards. The Annamite Cordillera, rising to some 3,000m, stretches along the Laotian and northern Cambodian borders.

Germany, Federal Republic of

Germany officially supported US policy in Vietnam, and contributed both economic and humanitarian aid. In 1966, the Federal Republic of Germany sent the hospital ship SS *Helgoland* to Vietnam, and also provided approximately $7.5 million annually in foreign aid. As the war dragged on, the German public became more critical of US Vietnam policy and antiwar demonstrations erupted in 1968. In January 1973, Chancellor Willy Brandt criticized the Christmas bombing of North Vietnam.

Giap

See Vo Nguyen Giap.

Below: The German Hospital Ship SS *Helgoland*, usually anchored in Danang, provided civilian medical support in I Corps.

Godley, George McMurtrie

Godley was the Ambassador to Laos from 1969 to 1973. By presidential order he was responsible for the "overall direction, coordination, and supervision" of all military operations in Laos. Building on his previous experience in suppressing a Chinese-backed rebellion in the Congo in 1964, he carefully orchestrated both the ground and air operations. In January 1972, the North Vietnamese expanded the war in Laos by sending two divisions to deal with the CIA-led Hmong forces there. Godley obtained several battalions of Thai "volunteers," and numerous sorties of B-52 bombers to use against NVA troop concentrations. With this support the Hmong turned back the NVA offensive, though with serious losses. When Godley departed Laos in 1973 a peace agreement had been signed and a coalition government established. Within two years Laos was communist.

Goldberg, Arthur Joseph

In 1965, President Johnson persuaded Arthur Goldberg to leave the US Supreme Court and become the US Ambassador to the United Nations, where he routinely supported the US position on Vietnam. By 1968 he had come to regret leaving the Supreme Court, and believing he was being ignored by the Johnson administration, resigned as the Ambassador to the United Nations. In 1970, he endorsed the massive antiwar protests and claimed he had always favored a negotiated settlement to war.

Goldwater, Barry Morris

An archconservative Republican politician, Goldwater lost the presidential bid in 1964 to Lyndon Johnson, largely due to significant differences concerning the war in Vietnam.

As a Senator he urged the president to carry the war to North Vietnam, castigated liberals for strengthening the hand of the North Vietnamese during peace negotiations, opposed amnesty for draft dodgers, and vehemently stated that the war was lost at home, not on the battlefield. He was also one of the key Republicans to convince President Nixon to resign after Watergate.

Gravel, Maurice Robert

A Democratic senator from Alaska from 1969 to 1981, Gravel was a vocal critic of the Vietnam War. In 1971, following the indictment of Daniel Ellsberg for the theft of the documents known as the Pentagon Papers, Gravel read from them for three hours in an open meeting of his Congressional Subcommittee. The next day the US Supreme Court ruled that senatorial immunity did not protect him or his aides from prosecution. Nothing came of it, and in 1972 he published a five-volume edition of the study.

Great Britain

Britain co-chaired the 1954 Geneva Accords and supported the partition of Vietnam at the 17th parallel. Until 1962, the British government openly opposed military intervention in Vietnam. From 1962 to 1968, Prime Minister Harold Wilson prevented any formal British participation in the war. However, Britain attempted three separate peace missions in 1965 on behalf of the United States and frequently acted as an intermediary between the United States and the Soviet Union in attempts to establish negotiations with the North Vietnamese.

Great Society Program

The term coined for the program of liberal reforms under the President Johnson's administration was the Great Society Program. Johnson was a great admirer of Roosevelt and took his New Deal as a model for his own plans for greater social justice, economic equity, and racial equality. Along with the civil rights movement, the Great Society Program brought a greater awareness of poverty and inequality, and legislation enacted under it granted federal aid to impoverished children, healthcare for the elderly and gave voting rights to African-Americans. However, the Vietnam War diverted both attention and funds from the program, and it had no lasting impact on American society.

Greeley, Operation

In 1967, Operation Greeley, north of Kontum and west of the Dak To Special Forces Camp, was a complementary border screening operation to Francis Marion west of Pleiku. Reacting to intelligence that a NVA Division was present, General Westmoreland deployed the 173rd Airborne Brigade, along with 1st Cavalry and 4th Infantry Division elements, to the area. Two ARVN airborne battalions, and a battalion of the 42nd ARVN Regiment further reinforced them. Throughout July both the 4th Infantry Division and the 173rd Airborne Brigade suffered heavy casualties during engagements with NVA units dug-in along the ridges west of Dak To. The fighting began to taper off, and on July 25 the 1st Cavalry Division units were sent back to the coast. In early September, MACV believed that the heavy fighting was over and the 173rd was also withdrawn. MACV was wrong. On October 12, Operation Greeley became part of Operation MacArthur and the decisive Battle of Dak To began.

Green Berets

The popularized name for the US Army Special Forces is Green Berets. It originated following the approval of a distinctive green beret as the official Special Forces headgear by President John F Kennedy. (See Special Forces.)

Greene, Wallace M.

As the Commandant of the Marine Corps from 1964 to 1968, General Greene was a strong public supporter of US policy in Vietnam. Following the entry of the first Marine combat units in 1965, he pressed for a larger combat role by stating "you don't defend a place by sitting on your ditty-box." He promoted the Marine Combined Action Platoons, but stated that pacification would take more than a decade. He retired in January 1968, just prior to the Tet Offensive.

Grenades (Allied)

The Allies in Vietnam used five types of grenades. High explosive antipersonnel hand grenades, both the classic pineapple-shaped World War II type with a serrated cast-iron body that sprayed heavy fragments over a radius of approximately 10m, and newer, wire-wrapped fragmentation grenades that showered the target with small pieces of wire when detonated. They also used white phosphoros grenades to create casualties and to mark either a target or to provide screening smoke. The most common type of grenade found in Allied units was a smoke grenade. These were routinely used to mark targets and landing zones, and for signaling. Gas grenades, sometimes called bug-out bombs, either contained CS or CN tear-gas. The Allies also made wide use of 40mm grenades of various types fired from either a shoulder launcher or an automatic system on board a helicopter or a patrol boat.

Grenades (North Vietnamese and Viet Cong)

The NVA and VC used a variety of

Right: A grenadier fires at a sniper in a building as the Marines advance toward the Citadel in Hue.

Russian and Chinese-designed grenades. The most common was a stick type fragmentation grenade that was frequently made of cast aluminum rather than cast-iron. While nominally it had a burst radius of 10m, many of them either failed to function or resulted in very small fragment patterns. They also used a type of egg-shaped grenade with a smooth steel body wrapped around a fragmentation liner. This grenade generally had an effective fragment radius of about 15m. Their most dangerous grenade was a rocket-propelled grenade (RPG). Propelled by a 40mm rocket, this grenade had either an 80 or 82mm High Explosive Anti-Tank (HEAT) warhead and was a development of the World War II German Panzerfaust. It could be used against armor, bunkers, or troops. While the burst radius was small, because it was fired from a launcher it could be very accurately placed. The Viet Cong also made use of a number of field expedient grenades created from abandoned C-ration and soda cans.

Group
A United States Army Group is formed to command or control several units,

Below: The Marines introduced the 40mm automatic grenade launcher to ground combat.

163

Left: The American and South Vietnamese Presidents, Johnson and Thieu, met at Guam in 1967 to discuss the progress of the war.

Guns and Butter

Classic economic debate over defense spending or social development, commonly known as the "guns versus butter" debate. Butter is a symbol of economic prosperity and well-fed citizens. Johnson's desire for both guns and butter (his belief that he must stem the advance of communism in Southeast Asia while pursuing a Great Society at home) has been acknowledged by many analysts and former policymakers in the Johnson administration as a crucial factor in the way the United States escalated their involvement in Vietnam. Johnson was painfully aware of what happened to Woodrow Wilson's and Franklin D Roosevelt's comparable reform programs when they fell victim to "guns-over-butter" decisions. Escalating involvement by stealth in Vietnam, Johnson was able to have "guns and butter" without increasing taxes to pay for both projects. This decision had a profound impact on the American economy.

normally battalions. Other than in the US Special Forces, where the largest organized element is a numbered Group, they are most frequently found in corps level artillery and in support commands.

Gruening, Ernest Henry

A liberal Democratic Senator from Alaska, Gruening was one of the first to oppose American involvement in Vietnam. In a speech on March 10, 1964 he said, "All Vietnam is not worth the life of a single American boy." He joined Senator Wayne L Morse in opposing the Gulf of Tonkin Resolution, which he said violated the constitution by giving the president "war making powers in the absence of a declaration of war."

Guam Conference

The third in a series of summits held between the governments of the US and Republic of Vietnam was the Guam Conference, staged from March 20–21 on the Pacific island of Guam. The summit was attended by 22 high-ranking delegates from each camp, headed by President Johnson and Premier Ky. The agenda amounted to a review of the war and recent UN peace initiatives. It also introduced the replacements Johnson had chosen for Ambassador Lodge

(Ellsworth Bunker) and General Westmoreland (Creighton Adams), and served as an opportunity for Johnson to pressure Ky to hold national elections.

A call for an additional 200,000 US troops for Vietnam from Westmoreland was scaled down to 55,000, and a request for a stepping up of the bombing campaign against North Vietnam from Ky went unheeded.

Gunships, Fixed Wing

The fixed wing gunship was one of the major weapons innovations of the Vietnam War. Mounting a variety of high firing rate machineguns and light cannon, or in the case of the later versions of

Right: A cone of fire forms as an AC-119 gunship works over a suspected Viet Cong mortar position.

Above: An AC-130 Spectre gunship is hooked up to a generator cart.

Left: The crew feeds a belt of 7.62mm ammunition into the rear mini-gun magazine on an AC-47 gunship.

Gunships, Fixed Wing

the AC-130 Spectre, a 105mm howitzer, they delivered a highly accurate high volume of fire against area targets on the ground. On numerous occasions the arrival of a gunship spelled the difference between survival and death for heavily outnumbered allied forces.

Type:	Gunship I	Gunship II	Gunship III	Gunship IV	Prototype
Aircraft:	AC-47	*AC-130A	AC-119G	AC-119K	AU-23
Nickname:	Spooky/Puff	Spectre	Shadow	Stinger	Peacemaker
Armament:					
7.62mm	3/4	4	4	2	
Mini-guns					
20mm		4—Vulcan		2—Vulcan	1 XM-197
40mm		2—Bofors L60			
105mm		1—M102 Mod.			
Fire Control:	Visual	Computer	Electronic	Electronic	Electronic
Illumination Flares:	24–56	24	24	24	
S/L:		1.5mcp	1.5mcp	1.5mcp	
Firing Alt.:	3,000ft	3,500ft	3,500ft	3,500ft	3,000ft
Endurance:	7hrs	6.5hrs	6.5hrs	5hrs	3.5hrs
Crew:	7	14	8	10	2
Available:	1964	1967	1968	1969	1974

* Originally armed with four 7.62mm mini-guns and four 20mm Vulcan Gatling guns, later two of the 20mm Vulcans were replaced by two Bofors 40mm L60s, and later yet, one Bofors was replaced by a modified M102 105mm howitzer.

Above: The crew rearms their UH-1 B Huey gunship after a mission.

Right: A pair of Huey gunships keep an eye on river traffic.

Gunships, Helicopter

The first helicopter gunships were created by adding pods containing 2.75in folding fin rockets and a pair of 7.62mm machineguns to the UH-1B utility helicopter. As the war went on, a variety of weapons packages were created to enhance the capabilities of the later models, but the gunship was still an adapted utility helicopter. In 1966, the Bell AH-1G Cobra began arriving in Vietnam. It was a purpose built helicopter gunship. They were generally armed with a 7.62mm mini-gun and a 40mm grenade launcher in chin turrets, and up to 52 folding fin rockets in four rocket pods mounted on stubby wings. The Cobra was light, narrow, and fast, with a crew consisting of the gunner and a pilot. Operating in all sorts of weather and from forward locations helicopter gunships provided the committed infantry on the ground almost instantaneous air support. Following the Vietnam War helicopter gunships were developed into heavily armed antitank weapons systems.

Right: A Cobra gunship prowls across a flat stretch of terrain near Xuan Loc.

Habib, Philip Charles

A career foreign service officer who served in the US embassy in Saigon from 1965 to 1967, Habib did not believe that South Vietnam could survive without US military support, and strongly advocated negotiations. In 1968, he was the highest ranking career diplomat on the US negotiating team at the Paris peace talks. When Henry Cabot Lodge and Lawrence Walsh resigned in November 1969, he became the acting head of the delegation before he was replaced by David Bruce in July 1970.

Hai Van Pass

At the boundary between Quang Nam and Thua Tien provinces north of Danang, a spur of the Annamite Cordillera pushes east to the sea. Highway 1, the only usable north-south road connecting the port of Danang with Hue and Quang Tri further north, crosses the mountains at Hai Van Pass. This supply line was crucial to the American war effort in I Corps, and the Marines expended considerable effort keeping the pass open.

Haig, Alexander Meigs Jr

In 1968, Alexander Haig was the military advisor to Kissinger's National Security Council. By 1972, he had so impressed President Nixon that he was promoted over the heads of 240 senior officers to four-star general rank and assigned as Army Vice Chief of Staff. He advocated the 1972 Christmas bombings, and personally delivered the ultimatum to President Thieu to accept the peace agreement. Because of his relationship with President Nixon, his power was so extensive that Watergate special prosecutor Leon Jaworski called him the country's $37\frac{1}{2}$th President. He continued as President Ford's National Security Advisor and later was the Secretary of State in the first Reagan administration.

Below: General Alexander Haig (left) after becoming Secretary of State.

Haiphong

The primary port and a major industrial center of North Vietnam, Haiphong is located on the Cua Cam River, 30 miles inland from the Gulf of Tonkin. Railroads, rivers, and roads connect Haiphong and Hanoi, 70 miles northwest. The Hanoi-Haiphong corridor was the economic center of North Vietnam during the war.

In September 1967, President Johnson authorized air raids to disrupt transportation routes into and around the city, however, the port and the dock facilities remained off-limits. Following North Vietnam's Easter Offensive, in April 1972 President Nixon authorized extensive bombing of military installations and storage areas in Haiphong. Later that year he approved the mining of Haiphong Harbor, and ordered a massive bombing of the Hanoi-Haiphong corridor. During the Christmas bombings of December 18–29, 1972, US planes dropped 17,000 tons of ordnance on targets around Hanoi and Haiphong, and throughout the corridor. Following the signing of the Paris Peace Agreements in 1973, the US Navy cleared the harbor of mines to reopen the port.

Halberstam, David

As a correspondent for *The New York Times* in Vietnam from 1962 to 1964,

Above: A fuel storage area outside Haiphong burns after an attack by planes from the USS *Oriskany*.

Right: The sun shimmers off the sea near a petroleum depot in Haiphong as Navy aircraft bore in on it.

Halberstam won a Pulitzer Prize for his coverage. Because he reported on the deteriorating, military situation and the lackluster performance of both the South Vietnamese military and government, President Kennedy personally recommended to *The New York Times*' publisher that Halberstam be removed from Vietnam. Halberstam was the author of *The Best and the Brightest*, a critique of American policy in Vietnam, and of American policymakers.

Halperin, Morton H

In December 1965, Halperin was one of 190 American academics that signed a petition supporting President Johnson's conduct of the war. In January 1969, he became a senior staff member on Kissinger's National Security Council. By September 1969, he had become highly critical of US involvement in Vietnam, and was accused by some members of the Nixon administration of leaking sensitive material to the press. Even after he resigned, President Nixon and Henry Kissinger ordered a 24-hour wiretap on Halperin's phone, from 1969 to 1971.

Hamburger Hill (Dong Ap Bia), Battle of (May 1969)

The major engagement of Operation Apache Snow, the Battle for Hamburger Hill (Dong Ap Bia) began when the 3rd Battalion, 187th Infantry, ran into the 7th and 8th Battalions of the NVA 29th Regiment in heavily fortified positions on Ap Bia Mountain, precipitating a ten-day battle. In the opening round, three Americans were killed and 33 wounded. The next morning friendly fire from two Cobra gunships killed two and wounded 35 more of the 187th. The units maneuvered for a coordinated assault on the mountain. On May 14, companies B, C, and D of the 187th assaulted Hamburger Hill, but were thrown back after 12 were killed and more than 80 wounded. On May 15, companies A and B tried another assault but were stopped by 36 additional casualties. Heavy air strikes battered the NVA positions. Two more battalions of the 101st Airborne, and one battalion of the ARVN 1st Infantry Division, came in as reinforcements. On May 18, two full battalions, 3/187th and 1/506th Infantry assaulted, only to be stopped short of the summit by a torrential monsoon downpour that turned the chewed up landscape into a sea of mud.

Finally on May 20, a simultaneous four-battalion assault from multiple directions managed to take the crest of Hamburger Hill and the NVA withdrew into Laos. The North Vietnamese, uncharacteristically, had decided to stay put and "take on" the Allies in a stand up battle. During the action the Air Force pounded the NVA fighting positions with over 500 tons of bombs and 70 tons of napalm, while American artillery and helicopter gunships kept up a veritable drumfire against them. In the end, however, the

position had to be taken by a determined infantry assault and hand-to-hand combat during a brutal bunker-by-bunker action that captured an enormous amount of media attention. The Americans, once the NVA retreated to their sanctuaries in Laos, spent a few days policing the battlefield and then, within a week, left the mountain. This pattern of heavy combat, and then abandoning terrain that was so dearly bought without any seeming relationship to obtaining a victory, resulted in a great deal of controversy and a decline in public support for the war. President Nixon subsequently passed the word to his commanders in Vietnam that he wanted casualties limited during Vietnamization, indirectly handing the North Vietnamese a substantive victory for their efforts at Dong Ap Bia.

Hamlet Evaluation System (HES)
The Hamlet Evaluation System (HES) was devised by Robert Komer in 1967 as a means to evaluate the progress of pacification. Using 18 political, economic, and military variables, 250 MACV district advisors filled out a computer worksheet for 9,000 of South Vietnam's 13,000 hamlets. The hamlets were then classified into one of five categories, depending on their supposed depth of loyalty to the Saigon government. Hamlets rated A, B, and C were considered "relatively secure." Those rated D and E were classified as "contested." The 4000 hamlets that were acknowledged to be Viet Cong controlled were simply ignored. According to the HES, by late 1971, 97 percent of the evaluated hamlets were rated C or above. In retrospect it is clear that command pressure, (a District Senior Adviser's fitness report depended on improvements in pacification), caused a serious and unrealistic inflation of the ratings.

Hanoi
Located in the center of the Red River Delta, 70 miles inland from the South China Sea, Hanoi is one of Vietnam's oldest cities. With a population of about 2.6 million it is the main industrial center and transportation hub of North Vietnam. Though periodic bombing was conducted around Hanoi from 1966 to 1968, the city itself was never targeted, and from 1968 to 1972 American bombers were forbidden to operate that far north.

Left: Members of the 1st ARVN Division move up to prepare for an assault at Hamburger Hill.

VIETNAM: A VISUAL ENCYCLOPEDIA

However, in reaction to the North Vietnamese Easter Offensive, most restrictions were removed and a number of targets that had been off-limits were struck by both fighter-bombers and B-52s during Operations Linebacker I and II. During the Christmas bombings of December 1972, over 17,000 tons of bombs were dumped on Hanoi in 12 days. However, Hanoi was never subjected to the kind of saturation bombing inflicted on the Germans and Japanese in World War II. Only about 1,300 civilians were killed, and very few nonmilitary targets were damaged.

Hanoi Hannah

Tri Thi Ngo, a Vietnamese woman who broadcast propaganda over Radio Hanoi in English from 1965, was given the nickname Hanoi Hannah by the troops. Most of the propaganda efforts were clumsy at best, but many listened to her broadcast because she played the latest American music.

Hanoi Hilton

The Hanoi Hilton was a name applied by American prisoners of war to the Hoa Lo Prison, built by the French near the center of Hanoi. Occupying an entire city block, it had walls 4ft thick and 20ft high. Shards of glass were imbedded in the top and crowned by another 5ft of electrified barbwire. It was divided into sections that the prisoners named "New Guy Village," "Heartbreak Hotel," "Little Vegas," and "Camp Unity."

Above: Victorious Viet Minh troops cross the Paul Doumer Bridge into Hanoi after the 1954 Geneva Accords.

Below: A low-flying reconnaissance aircraft snapped this picture of the notorious "Hanoi Hilton" POW camp.

Harassment and Interdiction Fires (H&I Fires)

US Army field manuals define harassment fire as "fire delivered for the purpose of disturbing rest, curtailing the movement, and lowering the morale of enemy troops by the threat of casualties or losses and destruction of matériel." The same publication states that Interdiction Fire is " fire delivered for the purpose of denying the enemy the unrestricted use of an area or point." H&I fire is generally unobserved and of short duration. Numerous evaluations determined that H&I fire was ineffective in Vietnam. However, the NVA began their Easter Offensive with H&I fire on ARVN positions from across the DMZ.

Harkins, Paul D

In 1962, as part of the Kennedy administration's Project Beef-up, which converted MAAG–Vietnam to MACV, General Harkins was assigned as the first

Left: A 175mm gun at Camp Carroll fires a harassment and interdiction mission into the Demilitarized Zone.

Below: A pair of M107 self-propelled 175mm guns at Fire Support Base Elliott fire an harassment and interdiction (H&I) mission.

VIETNAM: A VISUAL ENCYCLOPEDIA

Left: General Paul D Harkins pins the rare third award of the Combat Infantry Badge on Master Sergeant Wiley Johnson.

Harris, David

In 1967, David Harris was one of the founders of the Resistance, an antiwar group that encouraged opposition to the Selective Service System. He made hundreds of speeches promoting draft resistance, and organized the turn in or burning of thousands of draft cards. In May 1968, a jury convicted Harris for refusing induction. The verdict was upheld on appeal and he spent nearly two years in a federal prison.

Harvest Moon, Operation

Operation Harvest Moon was an early test of Westmoreland's search and destroy strategy. Carried out from December 8–20, 1965 in the Phuoc Hoa and Que Son Valleys in Quang Nam and Quang Tin provinces of I Corps, the operation was intended to prevent the NVA from overrunning the Que Son Valley and taking the ARVN garrisons at Viet An and Que Son. Originally designed to be a joint operation with the ARVN 5th Regiment, the operation got

Commanding General of MACV. He was a strong supporter of President Diem, and his opposition to the coup that eventually toppled the Diem regime put him at odds with Ambassador Henry Cabot Lodge. Also at odds with the junta that replaced Diem, Harkins promoted a second coup by General Nguyen Khan. Many South Vietnamese labeled it "Harkins' Revenge." General William Westmoreland replaced him at MACV.

Harriman, W Averell

A longtime fixture on the US diplomatic scene, in 1962 Harriman negotiated a settlement in Laos that resulted in the withdrawal of US forces, but left the North Vietnamese in place. Throughout the war this agreement barred US ground action in Laos. A staunch believer in a negotiated settlement with North Vietnam, he took an active part in the group of "wise men" that advised President Johnson. In May 1968, Harriman became the chief American negotiator at the Paris peace talks. He remained there until Henry Cabot Lodge replaced him in January 1969.

Right: Troops move on after searching a Vietnamese village.

Above: A machinegun team watches an artillery preparation chew up a landing zone during Operation Harvest Moon.

Left: Marines assault an NVA position following an air-strike during Operation Hastings.

off to a rocky start when the ARVN were ambushed enroute and sustained heavy casualties.

The Special Landing Force, a new organization created aboard ship offshore to reinforce Marine Corps operations, was brought in by helicopter. It came under heavy fire on the selected landing zones from Viet Cong who were already there, but succeeded in getting on the ground. For the next ten days the Marines, supported by heavy B-52 strikes, fought their way up the valley. On December 20, the Marines returned to their enclaves and the Viet Cong again occupied the two valleys.

Hastings, Operation

The Marine Corps approach to the Vietnam War was to emphasize counterinsurgency and pacification. General Westmoreland wanted them to conduct large unit operations against Viet Cong main force units and the NVA Army. To placate Westmoreland, in the spring of 1966 the Marines began reconnaissance operations along the southern edge of the Demilitarized Zone in Quang Tri province. The reconnaissance operation was code-named Hastings and lasted throughout July 1966.

Marine reconnaissance teams operating between Highway 9 and the DMZ were frequently ambushed by units of the NVA 324B Division, and engaged them in a number of heavily fortified positions throughout the area. B-52 bombers from Guam supported the Marines and struck the DMZ for the first time. As a result of Hastings, the Marines

Above: Members of the 2nd Battalion, 503rd Infantry fight from old Viet Cong trenches during an NVA attack near Kontum.

shifted their main emphasis from pacification to searching out and engaging major North Vietnamese units in their Tactical Area of Responsibility.

Hatfield, Mark Odum

A liberal Republican senator from Oregon, Hatfield was a vigorous opponent of the Vietnam War and a leading critic of the Nixon administration. He proposed that it should be replaced because Nixon had failed to carry out his 1968 campaign promise to end the war. In response to the invasion of Cambodia, Hatfield, along with Senator George McGovern, offered an amendment to cut off funds for the Vietnam War after December 31, 1971, which became a rallying point for antiwar activists.

Hatfield–McGovern Amendment

An amendment to military procurement legislation that sought to end the war in Vietnam was sponsored by Senators George McGovern and Mark Hatfield. The original draft of the amendment required a complete halt in American military activities in Vietnam by the end of 1970. This was later revised to December 31, 1971, but it was nevertheless defeated in the Senate.

Hawthorne, Operation

Operation Hawthorne is sometimes referred to as the First Battle of Dak To. It began when a battalion of the 101st Airborne Division was ordered to rescue a CIDG unit that was surrounded at the Tou Morong Special Forces Camp on June 2, 1966. Following relief of the Special Forces Camp, the 1/327th Infantry pursued the NVA into the surrounding valleys. On June 6 and 7, 1966, the NVA 24th Regiment partially overran an artillery position and mauled a company of the 1/327th. The 101st Airborne Division reinforced their beleaguered unit with the 2/502nd Infantry.

That night the NVA, attacking in human waves, overran one of the companies of the 2/502nd and the company commander responded by calling napalm on his own position. While General Westmoreland promised he would recommend the commander for a Medal of Honor, a number of his surviving men threatened to kill him. As the operation wound down a company of the 1/327th engaged a small NVA Force in heavy jungle terrain and called in helicopter gunships for support. 1st Cavalry Division gunships responded and mistakenly hit the company itself, causing heavy casualties. The operation terminated on June 20, 1966.

Hayden, Thomas E.

While a student at the University of Michigan, in December 1961 Hayden was one of the founders of the Students for a Democratic Society. Throughout the early 1960s he became more and more radical. In 1968, Hayden was one of the planners of the antiwar demonstrations at the Democratic National Convention in Chicago. He was arrested, tried, and convicted of conspiracy. The conviction was overturned on appeal. In 1973, he married Jane Fonda, toned down his stridency, and entered California politics.

Headquarters 333

On April 10, 1963, President Kennedy authorized covert delivery of military supplies to both the Neutralist Lao Forces and the Hmong guerrillas fighting on the Plain of Jars. Headquarters 333, occupying a single story wooden complex at Udorn Royal Thai Air Force Base, was established by the CIA, and became the rear support headquarters for all paramilitary operations in Laos.

Above right: A squad counterattacks a group of NVA attempting to overrun an artillery position at Dak To.

Right: An airfield guard savors the early morning silence, before the choppers wind up for Operation Hastings.

Healy, Michael J

Healy was the last commander of the 5th Special Forces Group in Vietnam. He supervised the conversion of the remaining 38 CIDG camps to ARVN Ranger Battalions between 1969 and 1970, and the close out of the Special Forces in Vietnam effective March 3, 1971. Recalled again to Vietnam in 1972, he replaced John Paul Vann, who had been killed in a helicopter crash, and remained there until all US forces were withdrawn in 1973.

Hearts and Minds

Used to describe the US pacification effort, "Hearts and Minds" was a buzz phrase extracted from a 1965 speech by President Johnson. It was an umbrella term applied to all the various programs designed to win the allegiance of the South Vietnamese people to their government. Most combat troops considered it a joke.

Helicopters in Vietnam

Model	Type	Speed	Range	Payload
Bell AH-1 Cobra	Gunship	219mph	257mi	Crew of 2
Bell UH-1 Iroquois	Utility	127mph	345mi	12/15 troops depending on model
Bell OH-13 Sioux	Observation	105mph	325mi	3 seats
Bell OH-58A Kiowa	Observation	138mph	355mi	5 seats
Boeing CH-46 Sea Knight	Transport	160mph	245mi	17 troops or 7,000lb
Boeing CH-47 Chinook	Transport	190mph	230mi	44 troops or 20,800lb
Hiller OH-23 Raven	Observation	96mph	250mi	3 seats
Hughes OH-6 Cayuse (Loach)	Observation	150mph	380mi	6 seats
Kaman HH-43 Huskie	Search & Rescue	120mph	500mi	Accommodations for 4
Kaman UH-2 Sea Sprite	Antisubmarine	162mph	670mi	3 crew plus 4,000lb
MIL Mi6 "Hook"	Heavy General Purpose	186mph	385mi	90 troops or 17,600lb
MIL Mi8 "Hip"	Heavy General Purpose	155mph	311mi	28 troops or 7,000lb
Piasecki CH-21 Shawnee (Workhorse)	Transport	131mph	120mi	14 Troops or 4,000 lb
Sikorsky CH-3, HH-3, SH-3 Jolly Green Giant, Sea King	Transport/Search & Rescue	162mph	625mi	3 plus 5,000lb
Sikorsky UH-19 Chickasaw	Utility	112mph	360mi	10 troops
Sikorsky UH-34 Choctaw	Utility	123mph	185mi	18 troops
Sikorsky CH-37 Mojave	Transport	121mph	335mi	20 troops or 6,675lb
Sikorsky CH-53A/HH-53A Sea Stallion/Super Jolly Green	Transport/Search & Rescue	172mph	885mi	38 troops or 14,000lb
Sikorsky CH-54B Tarhe	Transport	127mph	255mi	22,000lb

Helicopters

The US Army officially reported 4,643 helicopters shot down, and 6,000 more so badly damaged they required rebuilding. There were more than 36 million helicopter sorties flown during the war. In 1969, the daily average was slightly over 2,500. The North Vietnamese had two models of Soviet helicopters, and they were occasionally reported operating either in Laos or in the vicinity of the Demilitarized Zone, but they were only infrequently used. None were shot down.

Right: A CH-46 "log bird" delivers rations to a forward base in I Corps.

Below: Helicopters of all descriptions were a common sight at 1st Cavalry Division Operating Bases.

Opposite, top: This battered Vietnamese CH-47 Chinook managed to escape the final fall of Saigon and waits disposition.

Opposite, bottom: UH-1D slicks come in to pick up troops from the 101st Airborne Division for an operation.

Left: A flight of UH-1H slicks and their escorting Cobra gunship return from a resupply mission into Cambodia during the Cambodian Incursion.

Above: A CH-47 Chinook delivers a 105mm howitzer and its ammunition to a firebase in II Corps.

Above right: A CH-53 delivers damaged equipment to a repair point.

Right: An H-37 helicopter recovers a downed H-21 in the Delta as two soldiers provide security.

VIETNAM: A VISUAL ENCYCLOPEDIA

Left: CH-46s from Marble Mountain transport troops to the Arizona Territory for an operation.

Helicopter Employment
During the Vietnam War the helicopter came into its own as a combat system. It was used for a wide variety of tasks: infantry assault, fire support, reconnaissance, medical evacuation, and logistical support. The US Army employed entire Airmobile Divisions built around the capabilities of the helicopter. The 1st Cavalry Division (Airmobile) was one of the first large US units deployed to Vietnam, and was widely considered to be the most effective. The US experience in Vietnam has had a profound impact on the way the American Army fights. Helicopter gunships now supplement heavy armored formations as tank killers, and utility helicopters transport soldiers and supplies into the battle area and evacuate wounded. Many of the other armies of the world have developed similar weapons and tactics.

Helicopter Valley

Helicopter Valley was a nickname the Marines gave the Song Ngan Valley in Quang Tri province during Operation Hastings. A large number of Marine Corps CH-46 helicopters were either shot down or crashed during a combat assault into the valley by the 3rd Battalion, 4th Marines, on July 15, 1966.

Helms, Richard McGarrah

President Johnson appointed Helms the Director of the CIA in 1966. He often clashed with military services over the accuracy of intelligence that was provided to the president. The most important battle occurred in 1967 when the military claimed that the Viet Cong and North Vietnamese had fewer than 50 percent of the troops contained in a CIA estimate. Eventually this disparity was made public and resulted in a lawsuit between General Westmoreland and CBS News. Though he was unpopular with two presidents, Helms served as the Director of the CIA longer than any individual except Allen Dulles.

Heng Samrin

Heng Samrin joined the Khmer Rouge in 1967. During its war against the Lon Nol government from 1970 to 1975 he was a top figure in the Eastern Zone, where Khmer Rouge policies were less draconian than in the rest of the country. After the Khmer Rouge victory he led an unsuccessful coup against Pol Pot and fled to Vietnam. When the Vietnamese invaded Cambodia and drove Pol Pot from power they named him President of the People's Republic of Kampuchea.

Herbert, Anthony

Herbert was a heavily decorated paratrooper and battalion commander in the 173rd Airborne Brigade. In 1971, he publicly accused his immediate superiors of covering up or suppressing evidence of American war crimes and violations of the Geneva Conventions. Claiming Army harassment, he retired in 1972 amid a storm of controversy. Two of his charges were later substantiated.

Herbicides
See Chemical Warfare.

Hersh, Seymour Myron

An investigative journalist, during 1969 and 1970 Hersh uncovered the story of the My Lai massacre. Later, as a journalist for *The New York Times*, he also exposed the Nixon administration's secret war in Cambodia and Air Force General John Lavelle's unauthorized bombing of North Vietnam. In 1974, he was instrumental in exposing the CIA's illegal spying on antiwar activists resident in America.

High National Council (HNC)

In August 1964, the High National Council (HNC) created to govern the Republic of Vietnam after the overthrow of Duong Van Minh's regime by Nguyen Kanh on January 30. Although Minh remained as head of state, real power lay with Kanh. In August he attempted to abolish the office of head of state and install himself as president but was met with widespread resistance on the streets, leading the Military Revolutionary Council to revoke the new constitution. In the power vacuum that followed a 17-member HNC was created, and attempts were made to introduce civilian rule, but it was inherently weak and could not prevent the subsequent military takeover.

Hilsman–Forrestal Report

A report for the Kennedy administration was made from a fact-finding mission to South Vietnam. Authored by state department official Roger Hilsman and presidential aid Michael Forrestal, the report was inspired by Kennedy's desire to know if the RVN government could be saved from collapse. The report was highly critical of the weakness and corruption in the Diem's regime, and highlighted his unpopularity. However, although warning that US involvement in Vietnam would be longer than originally anticipated, its basically optimistic tone contributed to further escalation.

Hilsman, Roger

As the Director of the Bureau of Intelligence and Research of the

Right: A guard maintains his vigil while the Chaplain holds services.

Below: After a bitter struggle in the hills, a group of Marines bathe in a stream.

Department of State, Hilsman prepared a plan titled "A Strategic Concept for South Vietnam." It defined the war as a political struggle, and correctly identified the Vietnamese peasant as the key to victory. His plan led directly to the Strategic Hamlet Program. He was also one of the instigators of the message to the US Ambassador in Saigon that provided at least tacit approval for the coup against Diem in November 1963.

Hills 881 North and South, Battle of (April–May 1967)

On April 24, 1967, Company B, 1st Battalion, 9th Marines, surprised a unit of the 325C NVA Division on Hill 861 northwest of Khe Sahn as it moved into position to attack the base camp. Reinforced on April 28 by the 2nd Battalion, 3rd Marines, the Marines launched a two battalion assault on the hill only to find that the enemy had withdrawn to two hills, both 881m high, further northwest. The Marines followed up and attacked the hills, where the NVA put up stiff resistance. Pounding the peaks with over 25,000 rounds of heavy artillery, 1,100 tactical air strikes, and 23 raids by B-52 bombers, the Marines

finally took them on May 5, and the NVA 325C division withdrew back across the Demilitarized Zone and into Laos. During the fighting the Marines, who had just been re-equipped with the M-16 rifle, lost a number of troops when it jammed in combat. As a result of their experience, following significant pressure from Congressmen who had received letters of concern both from troops and their families, the Army undertook a major investigation of the adequacy of the M-16. It was determined that the design of the rifle was adequate, however, the Army had changed the formula for the powder in the ammunition without telling anyone and the new powder fouled the action of the rifle.

Hmong

The Hmong, sometimes called Meo, were one of the principle ethnic minorities of Laos and western North Vietnam. They occupied the highest ridges in Laos and practiced a swidden agricultural system. Their involvement in the Indochina wars began during World War II when the French recruited them as guerrillas to fight the Japanese around the Plain of Jars in northern Laos. When the Viet Minh attacked Laos in 1952, a majority of the Hmong clans, led by Touby Lyfong, supported the French and later fought with them at Dien Bien Phu. The CIA recruited the Hmong to fight the

Pathet Lao after the French withdrew. While Touby Lyfong cooperated with the CIA, military command of the tribes devolved to Vang Pao, who had also fought with the French. Eventually Vang Pao commanded a secret army of nearly 30,000 guerrillas. From 1965 to 1968 Hmong guerrillas recovered downed pilots, defended the Sky-spot radars that guided B-52 raids over North Vietnam, and tied down thousands of North Vietnamese troops in defending the Ho Chi Minh trail and attempting to support the Pathet Lao. After 1968, the CIA insisted that the Hmong convert from guerrillas to ground troops. This had a disastrous effect and the Hmong began to suffer casualties that strained their total population of only about 250,000. By 1971, many families were down to the last surviving male, in many cases they were only 13 or 14 years old. In 1974, the last CIA operative left Laos, and by 1975 General Vang Pao and thousands of Hmong fled Laos, many relocating to the United States.

Ho Chi Minh

Ho Chi Minh was a founder of the Indochinese Communist Party and the President of the Democratic Republic of Vietnam from 1945 until his death in 1969. During World War II, Ho cooperated with the US Office of Strategic Services (OSS) and received both

logistical and training support in return. In August 1945, concurrent with the Japanese surrender, Ho and the Viet Minh occupied Hanoi and declared the provisional formation of the Democratic Republic of Vietnam. On September 2, 1945 he declared Vietnam independent from France, couching the declaration in language drawn from the US Declaration of Independence. By late 1946, the Viet Minh and the French were at war. In 1950, his new nation was quickly recognized diplomatically by most Soviet bloc countries, and finally won their true independence in May 1954 with the French defeat at Dien Bien Phu. Between 1954 and 1960, Ho consolidated his power in the north and anticipated the collapse of the Diem regime in the south. Recognizing that American military and economic assistance would assure Diem's survival, he authorized armed resistance in the south, and in 1960 began construction of the Ho Chi Minh trail through Laos and Cambodia into South Vietnam. He also began providing supplies and support to the Pathet Lao in Laos and the Khmer Rouge in Cambodia. Ho was an indefatigable nationalist whose legendary drive for the

Below: Ho Chi Minh meets with French General Le Clerc just before the outbreak of the French-Indochina War.

Right: Originating in North Vietnam, the Ho Chi Minh Trail transited Laos and opened out into South Vietnam at numerous points.

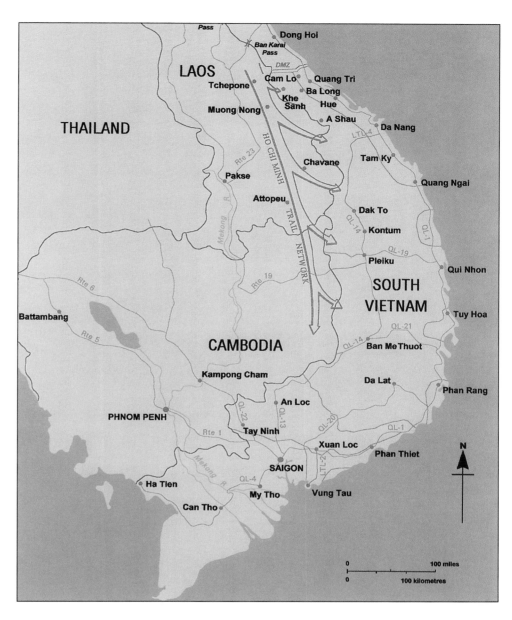

reunification of Vietnam clearly made him the "father of this country." The March 1965 military intervention by the United States significantly complicated his efforts. However, he was a masterful leader who recognized that militarily he could not achieve his ends. He therefore transitioned his war aims from one of battlefield victory to a protracted war strategy designed to wear the United States down. From his previous experience with the French, he did not believe that Westerners had the stomach for a long and indecisive conflict.

He was also a masterful politician and managed to straddle the options in the Sino-Soviet dispute in such a way that he obtained significant support from both sides. As the war dragged on and North Vietnamese casualties mounted, Ho used his leadership and prestige to mobilize his people to continue to engage in what was a total war. He died on September 2, 1969 and did not live to see his country reunified. The Viet Cong and North Vietnamese memorialized him by christening their final assault in 1975 the Ho Chi Minh Campaign, and renaming Saigon as Ho Chi Minh City.

Ho Chi Minh Campaign

Encouraged by the incredible success of the earlier attacks in I Corps and the central highlands, General Van Tien Dung convinced Hanoi that conditions were right for an all-out drive to end the war. By mid-April 1975, he had concentrated 18 NVA divisions within a 40-mile radius of Saigon. The 3rd, 304th, 324B, and 325th Divisions were poised to attack the 1st and 4th Airborne Brigades and 951st ARVN Ranger Group east of the city. In the northeast the 6th, 7th, and 314th Divisions prepared to assault Bien Hoa. Due north, the 312th, 320B, and 338th Divisions prepared to attack the ARVN 5th Division and 9th Ranger Brigade at Ben Cat and Lai Thieu. Northwest of Saigon the 70th, 316th, 320th, and 968th Divisions were to crush the ARVN 25th Division at Trang Bang and Cu Chi, then drive on to Saigon. In the west, the 3rd, 5th, 9th, and 16th NVA Divisions were to assault the ARVN 22nd Division at Tan An, and then attack the 7th and 8th Ranger Brigades outside of Saigon. The NVA 8th Division was to launch an attack against the ARVN 7th

Division at My Tho in the south to prevent it from reinforcing the city. The campaign began on April 9, 1975 with a heavy artillery barrage against Xuan Loc in the east. After unexpectedly ferocious resistance by the ARVN 18th Division, the NVA 6th, 7th, and 341st Divisions, heavily reinforced with armor, captured the city on April 20, opening the road to Saigon. The next day President Thieu resigned, blaming the United States for abandoning South Vietnam.

On April 26, Dung hurled 120,000 men at the remaining 30,000 ARVN defenders from five directions at once. Though the fighting in some areas was intense, by April 29 the city was receiving intense artillery fire and NVA units had entered the outskirts. By April 30, the last Americans had departed, and North Vietnamese tanks were rolling through the streets. NVA Colonel Bui Tin accepted South Vietnam's surrender on the

steps of the Presidential Palace. The war was over.

Ho Chi Minh Trail

In May 1959, the Communist leadership in Hanoi began enlarging and upgrading a series of trails from the panhandle of North Vietnam into Laos, southward into Cambodia, and emptying into South Vietnam. When the United States began its build up, the North Vietnamese undertook a massive effort to upgrade the trail to handle increased traffic. Aided by Russian, Chinese, and North Korean advisors, NVA Engineering Units widened footpaths and roads, strengthened bridges, and eventually laid fuel pipelines. By the end of the war most of the roads were either paved or improved gravel surfaces capable of withstanding heavy military traffic. Though repeatedly attacked by air, the trail was never seriously interdicted. The North Vietnamese

Left: The NVA constructed a small bridge to get across a fast moving stream in the Plei Trap Valley.

Below left: ARVN soldiers clean out a North Vietnamese supply cache during Operation Lam Son 719.

have stated that without the Ho Chi Minh Trail they could not have won the war.

Hoa Hao

The Hoa Hao is a buddhist sect formed in the Mekong Delta early in the 20th century. During World War II, the sect developed an independent military capability. Though they opposed the French, the Viet Minh turned them against the communists by assassinating their leader. They also opposed the government of President Ngo Dinh Diem, who crushed them militarily in 1955, then guillotined their new leader in 1956. They withdrew to An Giang province near the Cambodian border, where they maintained an armed neutrality throughout the war.

Hoang Duc Nha

Nha was President Thieu's cousin, and Information Minister. He advised Thieu to reject the peace agreement negotiated by Henry Kissinger and Le Duc Tho because it left North Vietnamese Army units in South Vietnam. He repeatedly voiced his distrust of Henry Kissinger, and emphasized that Kissinger was not honestly representing the South Vietnamese position particularly with respect to the status of the DMZ as a dividing line between the north and south. He was later removed from office at the insistence of US Ambassador Graham Martin, who made his dismissal a condition for continued US aid.

Hoang Van Thai (Hoang Van Xiem)

Hoang Van Thai was one of Giap's original military cadres. In 1945, he became the Deputy Chief of Staff of the Viet Minh Army. During the Vietnam War he commanded Military Region V, which encompassed the northern third of South Vietnam, from 1965 to 1968. In 1968, he became chairman of the COSVN Military Committee, effectively the Commander of the People's Liberation Armed Forces. In 1973, he returned to Hanoi and was appointed as the Vice Minister of National Defense.

Hoffman, Abbie

An anarchist antiwar protest organizer, Hoffman attempted to provide entertainment value in protests to attract media attention. He was a co-founder of the Youth International Party, "Yippies," and helped orchestrate the disruption of the 1968 Democratic National Convention in Chicago. Arrested for selling cocaine to an undercover officer in 1973, he eventually served one year in prison. He committed suicide in 1989.

Homecoming, Operation

Operation Homecoming, February 12–March 29, 1973, involved the release of American prisoners of war held in Southeast Asia. Those prisoners held by the Viet Cong were staged through Saigon, those held by the North Vietnamese and Pathet Lao were processed through Hanoi, and three airmen shot down over Red China came home through Hong Kong. Of the 591 US prisoners of war returned, 497 were officers, 69 were enlisted men, and 25 were civilians. All of the prisoners were flown to Clark Air Force Base in the Philippines. From there, following processing, debriefing, and medical examinations, they could go to any of 31 military medical facilities in the United States for treatment or recovery. Operation Homecoming was carefully orchestrated as a public relations event by the White House, which clearly understood that the prisoners were among the few popularly recognized heroes of the war, and that many Americans viewed their release as the

Below: Former POW, Sergeant Jon R Caviani, walks up the boarding ramp of the aircraft that will take him out of Hanoi.

VIETNAM: A VISUAL ENCYCLOPEDIA

Above: President Johnson and his key aides get ready for a meeting with Vietnamese leaders in Honolulu while in transit on board their plane.

Above left: Former American Prisoners of War cheer as their aircraft breaks ground on their way home from Hanoi.

Left: A group of Marine wives at the Naval Air Station, Miramar, await the arrival home of prisoners of war.

final episode in a national trauma. Though the POWs were accorded a hero's welcome at every stop along the way, many questions immediately arose concerning those who were still missing but had been seen while in captivity. This missing in action issue continued to cloud Vietnamese American relations for nearly 30 years.

Honolulu Conference

The Honolulu Conference was a top level meeting of Kennedy advisors charged with reconsidering Vietnam policy in the wake of the coup that toppled President Diem. Kennedy and members of his administration were apparently disturbed by the repression of the Diem regime, and had come to doubt that it could successfully prevent a communist takeover. The new military regime held the possibility of a government that

would be less repressive, and rally influential buddhist leaders and peasants behind it. At the Honolulu Conference, US officials who had assessed the post-coup situation in South Vietnam met with American diplomatic and military leaders from South Vietnam. After hearing that the peasants who made up the bulk of South Vietnam's 14-million population were still apathetic, Kennedy's representatives were cautiously optimistic that the new military regime would be able to win their support. This was seen as a critical to the defeat of the communists. In brief, the conference did not lead to any radical changes in policy over Vietnam.

Hoopes, Townsend

Townsend Hoopes was the Deputy Assistant Secretary of Defense for International Security Affairs from 1965 to 1967, and Undersecretary of the US Air Force from 1967 to 1969.

He was an advocate of the Enclave Strategy and opposed escalation of the war. Following Defense Secretary McNamara's resignation in 1968, Hoopes helped convince Clark Clifford, who was McNamara's replacement, that the war was unwinnable and the US should disengage.

Hop Tac

General William Westmoreland devised a plan to pacify the six provinces surrounding Saigon and gave it the code name Hop Tac. The basic thrust was to use ARVN troops to push the guerrillas out of the provinces and distribute American provided supplies in an attempt to win the loyalty of the peasants, while the Vietnamese police established and maintained order in the villages and hamlets.

It was based on operations the French had tried earlier, and also attempted to incorporate lessons learned from the failed Strategic Hamlet Program. In an effort to increase the number of ARVN troops available, Westmoreland convinced the ARVN to transfer their 25th Division from Quang Ngai to Saigon. Because the troops had to leave their families in Quang Ngai, desertion rates skyrocketed to the point that the 25th Division was nearly rendered incapable of combat. The police failed to do their job, and the government did not deliver the supplies that were promised to the people. In 1965, even Westmoreland admitted that the project was a failure.

Hope, Leslie Townes "Bob"

Bob Hope was a comedian who had

begun entertaining US troops for the United Service Organizations (USO) during World War II. He continued this tradition in Korea and the Vietnam War. Many antiwar protesters vilified him as a tool of the government. However, he felt that he was simply lightening the burden of the war for the troops involved. The US Congress recognized his selfless generosity and voted him a special medal.

Hot Pursuit

In 1965, MACV requested authority to pursue Viet Cong and NVA forces retreating across South Vietnam's borders into sanctuaries in Laos and Cambodia as a result of combat. This policy was called Hot Pursuit. They particularly wished to use this policy to interdict North Vietnamese supplies coming to the Cambodian port of Sihanoukville. The request was routinely refused, but became moot, in part, when President Nixon ordered the Cambodian Incursion in 1970.

Hotfoot, Project

On January 22, 1959, the Commander-In-Chief, Pacific forwarded a request to the Joint Chiefs of Staff for 12 Mobile

Training Teams to be assigned to Laos to assist in the training of the Royal Lao Army. The request was bucked down to the 77th Special Forces Group (Airborne) at Fort Bragg, North Carolina, for action. While the primary mission of the Special Forces was to

Above: The Emperor's throne in Hue, the old Imperial Capital of Vietnam.

Below: Bob Hope is welcomed to Vietnam on one of his many trips to entertain the troops.

train indigenous units, that mission was built around the Special Forces 12-man A Detachment, and the US Embassy in Laos had capped the number of personnel that could be deployed at 96. The detachments were reorganized into 8-man units and deployed to Laos on July 7, 1959 under the command of Lieutenant Colonel Arthur "Bull" Simons. The operation was code named Project Hotfoot.

Hue

Built by Emperor Gia Long early in the 19th century, Hue was the Imperial Capital of Vietnam between 1802 and 1945. Located near the coast of Thua Tien province, 45 miles south of the Demilitarized Zone, Hue was South Vietnam's third largest city. It was the center of buddhist opposition to the Saigon government. The buddhists protested against Ngo Dinh Diem in May 1963, and against President Ky in March 1966. Both protests were ruthlessly crushed by the South Vietnamese armed forces. The NVA occupied the city

during the 1968 Tet Offensive. Viet Cong agents went from house to house and arrested then executed several thousand civil servants, religious leaders, soldiers, educators, and anyone who had worked for the Americans. In March 1972, during the Easter Offensive, the NVA shelled refugee columns running for Hue and killed an estimated 20,000 people. The city fell to the North Vietnamese final offensive in March 1975.

Hue, Battle of (January–February 1968)

The bitterest and bloodiest battle of the Tet Offensive took place in Hue, the former Imperial Capital of Vietnam. At 3:30am on January 31, 1968, the 6th NVA Regiment and the 12th VC Sapper Battalion stormed the old Imperial Citadel on the northern bank of the Perfume River while the 4th NVA Regiment attacked the MACV compound on the south bank. By dawn most of the city was in communist hands, and the Citadel would remain so until February 24. The Hac Bao (Black

Above: After intense close-quarters combat the South Vietnamese flag flies again over the Citadel Fortress in Hue.

Panther) Reconnaissance Company of the ARVN 1st Infantry Division managed to retain the division headquarters inside the northeast corner of the Citadel. General Ngo Quang Troung, commander of the ARVN 1st Infantry Division, ordered an immediate counterattack by the ARVN 3rd Infantry Regiment, which was operating north of the city. Reinforced the next day by the ARVN 2nd, 7th, and 9th Airborne Battalions he undertook to clear the Citadel and the part of the city on the north bank of the river. The US committed to clear the south bank, and on February 4 the 1st Battalion, 1st Marine Regiment and 2nd Battalion, 5th Marine Regiment, supported by naval gunfire from three cruisers and five destroyers, began pushing north. The fighting quickly turned into hand-to-hand combat. On February 2, anticipating that the Viet Cong and North Vietnamese would attempt to withdraw

Above: A corpsman treats wounded Marines behind a wall during the fighting in Hue.

Left: A rifleman hides behind the door in a church and carefully surveys the street during the fighting in Hue.

Right: A well positioned sniper scans for targets during the fighting in Hue.

to the west, and in order to prevent reinforcements from reaching those NVA units already in the city, the 3rd Brigade of the First Cavalry Division and the 1st Battalion 501st Infantry from the 101st Airborne Division established blocking positions to the west. By February 9, the Marines had cleared the south bank of the river, but the ARVN 1st Division became bogged down. On February 12, two Vietnamese Marine Corps battalions and the 1st Battalion, 5th Marines reinforced the ARVN. The fighting was again from house to house and hand-to-hand, and the US Marines suffered one casualty for every yard they moved the lines forward. On February 21, the 1st ARVN Infantry Division linked up with elements of the US 1st Cavalry Division, which had launched an attack from the west. On March 2, 1968, the battle for Hue officially ended. During the battle

over 50 percent of the city was destroyed and in the aftermath the graves of 2,800 civilians who had been shot, stabbed, or simply buried alive were discovered. Another 3,000 civilians were never accounted for.

Hue, Battle of (March 1975)
In March 1975, five NVA Divisions pushed south into I Corps. Initially their advance was contained. Then on March 12, President Thieu ordered the ARVN Airborne Division at Danang back to Saigon, and the Vietnamese Marine Division, minus one brigade to withdraw from northern I Corps back to Danang. The withdrawal of the Marines significantly weakened the front and precipitated the wholesale movement of civilian refugees south toward Hue and Danang. On March 13, the I Corps Commander was told to withdraw his forces to an

enclave around Danang. Shortly after the order was put into effect it was countermanded, however, the citizens of Hue, remembering the atrocities committed by the North Vietnamese and Viet Cong in 1968, began to flee south. By March 17, soldiers of the ARVN 1st Infantry Division began to desert in order to look after their families who lived in and around Hue. This "family syndrome" literally caused the division to disintegrate. Those units that could be retrieved were evacuated south by sea, and Hue fell without a struggle on March 25, 1975.

Humphrey, Hubert H
As the Vice President, Humphrey became the heir apparent when President Johnson declined to run for a second term. He anticipated campaigning in support of the domestic programs started under the Great Society, however the

Above: A 106mm recoilless rifle crew moves their gun to add some "serious firepower" to an attack during the Tet Offensive.

unpopularity of the Vietnam War posed a dilemma. He could not break with the President, but the antiwar candidates, Robert Kennedy and Eugene McCarthy, made his position precarious. Although he won his party's nomination, internal Democratic splits concerning Vietnam caused him to lose the election to Richard Nixon by less than one percent in a three-way race.

Hun Sen

Hun Sen was a Khmer Rouge military commander during the war against the Lon Nol regime from 1970 to 1975, and remained with the Khmer Rouge until 1977. Ordered to attack Vietnamese villagers by Pol Pot, Hun Sen and 200 of his men instead defected to Vietnam. Following the Vietnamese invasion of Cambodia that expelled the Khmer Rouge from Phnom Penh, he became the foreign minister of the new government in 1979. In July 1997, he seized power in Cambodia in a coup d'état.

Huston Plan

A highly controversial Nixon administration plan, known as the Huston Plan, was drawn up to create a covert inter-agency US intelligence committee. Its specific aim was to coordinate counter intelligence activities against opponents of the war. The plan was developed in June 1970 and called for unrestricted domestic surveillance on groups believed to be working against the national interest. Although highly illegal, Nixon approved it and only the opposition of the FBI Director J Edgar Hoover and Attorney General John Mitchell prevented its actual implementation.

Huynh Tan Phat

During the French Indochina war Huynh Tan Phat led the Information Section of the Resistance Committee of the Saigon-Gia Dinh area. In 1960, he was a founding member of the National Front for the Liberation of South Vietnam (NFLSV). From 1964 to 1969 he served as the Secretary General. In 1969, he became the President of the Provisional Revolutionary Government of South Vietnam. After Saigon fell he was one of the few NFLSV leaders who were given a role in the new government.

Huynh Van Cao

Huynh Van Cao was the commanding general of IV Corps in the Mekong Delta during the disastrous Battle of Ap Bac. Promoted to high rank because of his relationship with President Diem, he was considered incompetent by both the American and most of the South Vietnamese military. However, because of his loyalty to Diem, the plotters of the November coup went to great lengths to ensure that his troops could not reach Saigon. Following the coup he was replaced and faded into obscurity.

Ia Drang, Battle of the (October 1965)

The Battle of the Ia Drang began with a North Vietnamese attack on the Special Forces Camp at Plei Me in the central highlands on October 19, 1965. The US 1st Cavalry Division (Airmobile), newly arrived from the United States, initially assisted ARVN units from Pleiku in relieving the pressure on the Special Forces Camp. On October 27, General Westmoreland ordered the 1st Cavalry to seek out and destroy the 32nd, 33rd, and 66th NVA Regiments, known to be in the area. The 1st Squadron 9th Cavalry, the Division Reconnaissance Squadron, located the North Vietnamese along the Ia Drang River and on a nearby mountain known as the Chu Pong Massif. On November 14, the 1st Battalion, 7th Cavalry unwittingly landed between two of the NVA regiments. The NVA attacked and pressed the US unit into a perimeter only 300m across. The fighting was so intense that in attempting to break through to the beleaguered Americans,

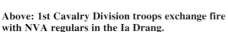

Above: 1st Cavalry Division troops exchange fire with NVA regulars in the Ia Drang.

reinforcements were forced to land some distance away and fight their way into the battle area. Though nearly overrun several times in the next 72 hours, the troops held out and the NVA withdrew. This was helped by carefully orchestrating the supporting artillery that the 1st Cavalry Division had lifted to within range, tactical air strikes, and B-52s used for the first time in direct support of a ground unit. On November 17, however, the NVA ambushed and overran the 2nd Battalion, 7th Cavalry, near the site of the original battle, killing 155 US troops. Because the battle was conducted as a group of individual combats, essentially hand-to-hand, no artillery fire or support was possible. By late afternoon company B of the 1st Battalion, 5th Cavalry, fought its way into the landing zone and the NVA withdrew. Despite the significant losses

Above: On the third day of the Battle of the Ia Drang, troops of the 2nd Battalion, 7th Cavalry, launch a probe to eliminate some snipers.

American commanders considered the Battle of the Ia Drang a victory and a successful test of airmobile tactics. More importantly, the battle committed the United States to a war of attrition and laid to rest the Enclave Strategy. General Chu Huy Man, the NVA commander, drew his own lessons from the fight. In his report to Hanoi he stated that, while US firepower posed significant problems, he believed the NVA could hold their own against US units by closing quickly and staying close to nullify part of the firepower advantage. Based on this report, though General Giap considered reorienting more toward guerrilla warfare, he didn't do it until after the Tet Offensive of 1968.

Igloo White Project

To destroy trucks on the Ho Chi Minh Trail in Laos electronic sensors were developed which could be dropped from aircraft to detect motion, sound, metallic

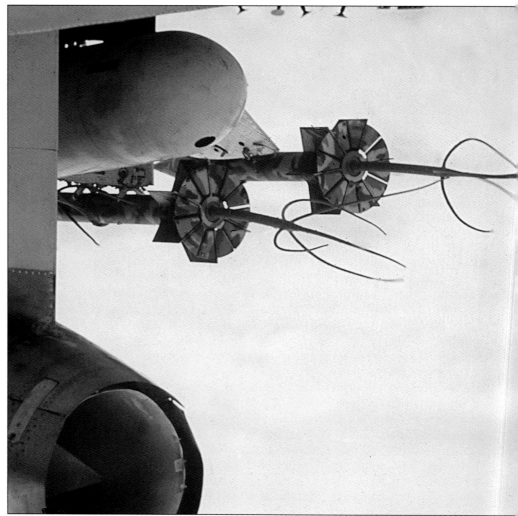

Right: A pair of sensors hang on a weapons pylon of a Navy P-2 Neptune before they are dropped in an enemy area.

objects, or the chemicals emanating from the bodies of mammals. A computer processed and sorted the data produced by the sensors, then relayed the target information to strike aircraft. Because the computer contained extensive maps of the Ho Chi Minh Trail, by comparing sensor readouts the expected path, and speed of a convoy could be predicted. Fixed-wing gunships, fighter-bombers, and even B-52s were guided to a particular point and munitions were automatically released at the predicted time of arrival of the targets. The system, code-named Igloo White, was popular in the Pentagon because it operated in all weather and required no troops on the ground. Based on the sensor readouts the Air Force claimed the destruction of large numbers of trucks. In fact their claimed number of kills exceeded the total number the CIA estimated that the North Vietnamese possessed.

Left: An Igloo White air-delivered seismic intrusion detector (ADSID) sits in the grass and bushes along a trail.

Below: French Defense Minister Pleven (left) and General Cogny, CINC French Forces in Indochina, (rear), are accompanied by Brigadier De Castreis, the Garrison Commander, on an inspection of Dien Bien Phu.

VIETNAM: A VISUAL ENCYCLOPEDIA

Above: The underground command post at Dien Bien Phu on April 3, 1954, at the start of the Viet Minh siege.

Right: Refugees crowd aboard an American ship in Haiphong for transport to the south following the 1954 Geneva Agreement.

India

After the 1954 Geneva Conference, India joined the International Commission for Supervision and Control (ICSC) along with Poland and Canada. Because it was the non-aligned member, India chaired the commission and provided the bulk of its personnel. Though officially a non-aligned nation, India was generally sympathetic to the Democratic Republic of Vietnam, and usually sided with Poland against Canada. In 1965, India called for a "Geneva type conference to address Vietnam, an end to the bombing, a withdrawal of all troops from South Vietnam, and reunification of the two Vietnams." In 1973, India withdrew from the ICSC.

Indochina War

Westerners applied the name Indochina to an area slightly larger than Texas in Southeast Asia that included Cambodia, Vietnam, and Laos. The Indochina War

Above: General Eisenhower is shown with French General Le Clerc before Le Clerc is to depart to Indochina.

refers to the Vietnamese war of independence against French colonial rule from the end of World War II to 1954. Following the Japanese defeat in World War II, Ho Chi Minh proclaimed the independence of Vietnam in Hanoi on September 2, 1945. However, the British assisted the French in returning to Saigon and the south was quickly brought back under French control. Although Ho Chi Minh had cooperated with the American Office of Strategic Services (OSS) against the Japanese, and many former members of the OSS believed that the United States should support his efforts to free Vietnam from French domination, President Truman believed that cooperation with France would be critical in opposing the rise of the Soviet Union. In a move opposed by many in his administration, the president extended the policy of containment to Asia, and looked to France to keep communism out of Indochina. In February 1950, Truman formally recognized the Emperor Bao Dai as a head of government and began funneling aid to France. The North Korean invasion of South Korea in June 1950 reinforced President Truman's belief that it was critical to continue to oppose the avowedly communist Ho Chi Minh, and by 1953 America was funding nearly 80 percent of the cost of the French war in Indochina. As the war went on, French public opinion began to oppose the nation's involvement. Then in spring of 1953, General Giap assembled a powerful force for the invasion of Laos. The new French commander, General Henri Navarre, was determined to oppose the Viet Minh thrust, which had overrun much of central and southern Laos. He established an airhead astride the Vietnam invasion route at the village of Dien Bien Phu. Reacting quickly, General Giap threw four divisions at the airhead, and quickly reduced it to a state of siege. At the request of Britain and the Soviet Union, a conference was called for in Geneva to discuss Korea and Indochina. The Viet Minh forced the French to surrender Dien Bien Phu on May 7, 1954, as the conference opened. At the Geneva Conference Chou En-Lai, the delegate from the People's Republic of China, cooperated with French Premier Pierre Mendes-France in persuading Ho Chi Minh to accept a division of Vietnam at the 17th parallel. This division allowed the southern half of Vietnam, and Saigon, to remain under Bao Dai's rule, while the Viet Minh consolidated their power in the northern portion. Political maneuvering by the United States delegates insured that the rump State of Vietnam that would exist in the south would be in position to resist later unification with the north. Nationwide elections were to be dealt within two years. Ultimately, following the consolidation of the new government under the control of Ngo Dinh Diem, the south refused to participate in the elections. Their decision was supported by the United States, setting the stage for the Vietnam War.

Indonesia

Indonesia, like India, was officially a non-aligned state. Under President Sukarno, Indonesia was a vocal critic of US policies in Vietnam. However, following a bloody 1966 coup, President Suharto more closely aligned Indonesia with the US. In 1973, Indonesia replaced India as the chairman of the International Committee for Supervision and Control.

Insurgency

The US military defined insurgency as "a condition resulting from a revolt against a constituted government, which falls short of civil war." However, the Vietnamese concept of insurgency was adapted from the teachings of Mao Tse Tung and entailed three phases.

The first was limited guerrilla attacks against the government's administrative presence in the countryside. The second involved the development of mobile warfare by larger, organized units, aimed at wearing down government forces. The third and final phase was an all-out conventional war aimed at the destruction of the government.

International Committee for Supervision and Control (ICSC)

Supervisory body established at the 1954 Geneva Conference to oversee the implementation of the armistice agreements in Vietnam, Laos and Cambodia. Initially, India, Canada, and Poland staffed the committee, which had little power other than to report on violations of the armistice. The ICSC was reactivated in 1961 to try and negotiate a peace settlement in Laos, but after 1964 its influence on the escalating war in that country declined.

International Commission for Control and Supervision (ICCS)

Supervisory body mandated at the 1973 Paris Conference. Essentially a reworked version of the ICSC, where Indonesia replaced India on the committee.

Below: A soldier helps his buddy up a slippery stream bank in the Iron Triangle.

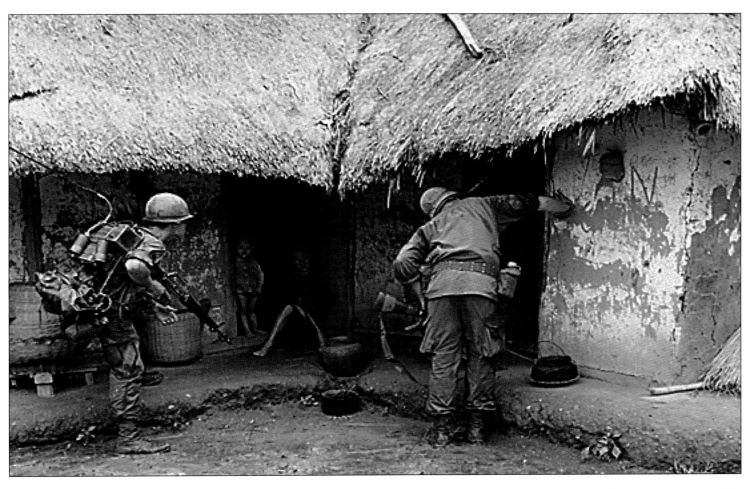

Above: 1st Cavalry Division troops check a house during Operation Irving north of Qui Nhon.

International Rescue Committee (IRC)

International humanitarian organization, which, during the course of the Vietnam War, took the leading role in the resettlement of displaced Vietnamese. The committee began its involvement in Vietnam after the 1954 division. Initially it provided emergency food, shelter, clothing and medicine to the thousands of Vietnamese who fled to the south. Later the IRC changed its focus to education, sanitation, and self-help programs, and was responsible for establishing numerous medical facilities and orphanages.

International War Crimes Tribunal

A mock tribunal was held in Stockholm, Sweden and Roskilde, Denmark from May 2, 1967, at which the US was charged with war crimes in Southeast Asia. Organized by British philosopher Bertrand Russell, the International War Crimes Tribunal heard evidence on the conduct of the war in Vietnam from leading historians, scientists, journalists, American soldiers, and Vietnamese civilians. Invitations to the American government were ignored. The charges made were of political connivance, of wholesale attacks on civilians, hospitals and schools, the torture of political prisoners, and of calculated disruption of the landscape and social structure of Vietnam. Those who questioned the tribunal's legitimacy charged that it was investigating a conflict in which its own sympathies were very clear. The "prosecution" cited the Nuremberg War Trials, which had also assumed the right of judgement, in its defense.

Iron Triangle

The Iron Triangle was a Viet Cong stronghold formed by the junction of the Saigon and Thi Tinh rivers between the villages of Ben Suc and Ben Cat. It contained a vast underground storage complex, headquarters, a hospital, munitions factories, and living quarters built during the French Indochina War. In January and February 1967, the US and ARVN threw more than 32,000 troops against the Triangle. Though they did significant damage to the installations, there was little fighting as the Viet Cong fled to sanctuaries in Cambodia. After the troops withdrew the VC returned and the Triangle was used as a staging area for the Tet Offensive. Delay-fused 500lb and 1,000lb bombs dropped from B-52s, and Rome Plows finally neutralized the Triangle in 1970.

Irving, Operation

Operation Irving began on October 1, 1967 when the 1st Cavalry Division forced the 18th NVA Regiment east, out of the Kim Son Valley and on to the flat coastal plain. The Republic of Korea Capital Division and the 22nd ARVN Infantry Division established blocking positions to the south and the 1st Cavalry Division air-landed five battalions to the west and north.

Supported by artillery, helicopter gunships, and naval gunfire, the 1st Cavalry moved swiftly to complete the encirclement. By October 24, when the operation ended, over 680 NVA had been killed and 1,000 captured. Operation Irving has been touted as the finest display of airmobile tactics during a war.

J

Jacobson, George D

George Jacobson was an Army officer who was first assigned to Vietnam in 1954. By 1962, he had become the Director of the MAAG—V Training Division. Upon retiring from the Army, he returned to Vietnam in 1965 working for the US Agency for International Development. After the Tet Offensive he became the Assistant Chief of Staff of CORDS under William Colby. He succeeded Colby as the Chief of CORDS in 1971 and was one of the last Americans to evacuate Saigon in April 1975.

Jackson State College

A higher education establishment in the state of Mississippi was the site of a major antiwar protest in May 1970 that resulted in two fatalities. America was still reeling from the shock of the tragedy at Kent State University (see separate entry), when on May 14, 1970, a similar incident occurred at Jackson State College. The predominantly African-American student population began demonstrations on May 13. They continued into the next day, and amid rising tensions police and state highway patrolmen fired into a student accommodation block that officers believed was being used by a sniper.

Two students were killed and 14 others wounded. An investigation into the incident concluded that there was no evidence of a sniper, but the tragedy received far less media attention than that at Kent State University.

James, Daniel "Chappie" Jr

The first African-American promoted to four-star general by the US Air Force was Daniel James. As the Vice Commander of the 8th Tactical Fighter Wing in Thailand, in 1967 he flew 78 combat missions over North Vietnam.

Right: General "Chappie" James addresses a group of fighter pilots at a conference in Thailand.

Right: President Johnson, John F Kennedy's successor, listens to a tape sent by his son-in-law, Captain Charles Robb, from Vietnam.

Japan

Though Japan was not an official participant in the war, under the terms of a 1960 Japanese–American security treaty the United States channeled supplies and military personnel through bases in Japan and Okinawa. However, Japan was a reluctant ally at best and it was the presence of Japanese ships in Haiphong harbor, which initially dissuaded the Americans from bombing the docks and mining the harbor. Japan actively traded with both sides and the Japanese economy profited greatly from the war.

Jason Study

A study was made by the Jason Division of the Institute of Defense Analysis on the Ho Chi Minh Trail. Infiltration of troops and supplies from the north via the Trail had become one of the most serious and pressing problems facing the US military by late 1966. The study recommended creating an electronic barrier of sensors across the infiltration routes, linked to computer arrays. Known as the McNamara Line, it went into operation in December 1967.

Javits, Jacob Koppel

A leading critic of the war, Javits was a liberal Republican senator from New York. In 1970, he sponsored legislation to restrict the ability of the president to conduct a war without Congressional authorization. His bill was passed over President Nixon's veto in 1973 and is known as the War Powers Resolution.

Jefferson Glenn, Operation

Operation Jefferson Glenn was the last major US ground combat operation of the war. During September 1970, the 101st Airborne Division began establishing firebases in the coastal lowlands of Thua Tien province. The purpose was to shield critical installations in Hue and Danang by patrolling communist rocket belts along the edge of the mountains. At the same time the division gradually transferred responsibility for the areas of operation, along with the installations and equipment, to the 1st ARVN Infantry Division. By the time the operation terminated on October 8, 1971 the US claimed that more than 2,000 casualties had been inflicted on the NVA.

Johns Hopkins Speech

Landmark speech delivered by President Johnson at Johns Hopkins University, on April 7, 1965, which underscored his commitment to the Vietnam conflict. Some analysts see the speech as the first major example of the political impact of antiwar demonstrations. The simply worded but deliberately dramatic rhetoric made reference to the threat of communist China and America's duty to "fight if we are to live in a world where every country can shape its own destiny…" He later added, "only in such a world will our own freedom be finally secure." He also referred to the past promises of America to defend the independent nation of South Vietnam: "…over many years, we have made a national pledge to help South Vietnam defend its independence. And I intend to keep that promise... We must say in Southeast Asia as we did in Europe in the words of the Bible: 'Hitherto shalt thou come, but no further.'"

Johnson, Harold K

A survivor of the Bataan Death March during World War II, General Johnson was chosen over 43 more senior generals to become the Army Chief of Staff in 1964. Following a trip to South Vietnam in March 1965, he reported to the President that he did not believe that bombing would win the war and recommended committing US combat troops. He came to regret that recommendation, but did not take any steps to get the decision reversed. He was replaced by General William Westmoreland as Army Chief of Staff in 1968.

Johnson, Lyndon Baines

While he was the US Senate Minority Leader in 1954, Johnson was instrumental in persuading President Eisenhower not to intervene on behalf of France in the Indochina War. Later, as Kennedy's Vice President, Johnson assured President Diem of South Vietnam that the United States would provide technical and financial aid, military supplies, and possibly US combat troops to prevent a communist takeover of South Vietnam. Later, he advised the President not to endorse a coup against the Diem government. Three weeks after the coup took place, President Kennedy was assassinated and the responsibility for Vietnam became Johnson's. Soon after taking office Johnson began the gradual escalation of war. In February 1964, he

Above: President Johnson waves small American and Vietnamese flags at a rally in Saigon.

Right: After President John F Kennedy was assassinated, the responsibility for Vietnam became President Johnson's who began the gradual escalation of the war.

authorized US support for South Vietnamese maritime raids against North Vietnam under OPLAN 34A. General William Westmoreland was appointed as the US commander in Vietnam, and General Maxwell Taylor as the Ambassador to Vietnam. They both favored increased military participation. Throughout 1964 he carefully prepared a number of options for intervention. A brush between US destroyers and North Vietnamese patrol boats in the Gulf of Tonkin in August provided him with a popular excuse. He obtained the Gulf of Tonkin Resolution from Congress, which authorized him "to take all necessary measures to repel any armed attack against the forces of the United States and to prevent further aggression," which was essentially an open-ended permission to engage in a war. Johnson paid lip service to the idea of a negotiated settlement, but privately insisted that

Right: The 1972 Joint Chiefs of Staff had many Vietnam Veterans. From left to right: General Creighton Abrams, Army, General John Ryan, Air Force, Admiral Elmo Zumwalt, Navy, and General Robert Cushman, Marines, all served there. The Chairman, Admiral Thomas Moorer, right foreground, was the only exception.

he was not going to be responsible for "losing" South Vietnam as China had been "lost." While increasingly absorbed in the war, Johnson actually saw his "Great Society" domestic programs as the most important facet of his presidency, and routinely attempted to divert the nation's attention from what was happening in Vietnam to his domestic agenda. In this regard, he refused to activate the military reserves and began couching all reports from Vietnam in glowing terms; a practice that led to what the press referred to as the "credibility gap." A growing antiwar movement created additional problems for the president, both on domestic and international fronts. By 1968, there were more than 540,000 troops in Vietnam, as well as powerful naval forces off the coast and bombers flying from Guam, Okinawa, and Thailand. However, in February 1968, the Viet Cong and NVA launched the Tet Offensive with an attack on Saigon and 30 provincial capitals. Even though it was a military disaster that essentially marked the end of the Viet Cong as a force on the battlefield and transformed the war into an Americans versus North Vietnamese struggle, the Tet Offensive was a strategic psychological victory. Immediately after Tet, Johnson was shocked by his near defeat at the hands of Senator Eugene McCarthy in the New Hampshire presidential primary, and depressed over the possibility that Senator Robert Kennedy would also run against him. On March 31, 1968, Johnson announced a reduction in the bombing of North Vietnam and that he would not run again for president. In reality, the Tet Offensive blocked further domestic reform, his principal goal, and essentially destroyed his presidency.

Johnson, U Alexis

A career diplomat, Johnson was the coordinator for the US delegation to the Geneva Conference of 1954. He was Assistant Ambassador to South Vietnam in 1964 and 1965 under General Maxwell Taylor. He initially opposed the introduction of American forces into Vietnam, but once they were there he believed the US should prosecute the war to the fullest. He opposed any bombing halts or attempts to open negotiations with North Vietnam. He was the Undersecretary of State for Political Affairs from 1969 to 1973. However, like most of the State Department, Nixon and Kissinger excluded him from major decisions on the war.

Joint Chiefs of Staff (JCS)

The Joint Chiefs of Staff (JCS) were created by the National Security Act of 1947. Made up of the Army Chief of Staff, the Air Force Chief of Staff, the Chief of Naval Operations, and the Commandant of the Marine Corps, along with a non-voting chairman, they were intended to be the primary military advisers for the president. John F Kennedy initiated the practice of consulting on military matters with the National Security Council rather than the Joint Chiefs of Staff, relegating them to a secondary role. By the time of Kennedy's death, the advisory circle essentially excluded the JCS. Denied direct access to the president by Secretary of Defense Robert McNamara, the JCS began to focus on ways the war

could be prosecuted, becoming direct accomplices in the failure to establish a clear objective in Vietnam. Rather than resign in protest over what they believed to be an unworkable strategy, they convinced themselves that they were needed to protect the interests of their individual services and never took any action to bring their disagreement to a head.

Joint General Staff (JGS)

The Joint General Staff (JGS), headquartered in Saigon, was the South Vietnamese equivalent of the US Joint Chiefs of Staff. The major difference was that the JGS had direct operational control over all South Vietnamese forces, and because of this South Vietnamese troops were sometimes used for political purposes in intramural struggles among the generals. General Westmoreland repeatedly tried to convince the Vietnamese that a combined staff, under his control, would significantly increase military effectiveness. The Vietnamese, for a variety of reasons, steadfastly refused to even consider it.

Joint Task Force 116

In the late 1950s, the Pathet Lao began receiving support from both the North

Right: Troops from the 1st Infantry Division call in an air strike near Suoi Da during Operation Junction City.

Vietnamese and the Russians, who air lifted weapons and matériel onto the Plain of Jars in Laos. Concerned by their expansion of communist control, President Eisenhower directed that contingency plans be created for intervention. In 1959, the Commander in Chief, Pacific, formed Joint Task Force 116 for that purpose. It included Navy, Marine, Air Force, and Army units.

Joint United States Public Affairs Office (JUSPAO)

A US Government "information" office, JUSPAO, was created in 1965 and made responsible for the daily press briefings at MACV headquarters in Saigon (otherwise known as the "five o'clock follies"). Directed by Barry Zorthian, the office coordinated the US government propaganda on Vietnam, and was the main source of information about US military activities in the country.

Jones, David C

Lieutenant General Jones was the Vice Commander of the 7th Air Force in Vietnam in 1969. He helped plan the secret bombing of Cambodia under Project Menu, and kept it concealed from Congress. He was promoted to full general in 1971 and given command of US Air Forces in Europe. He was later appointed US Air Force Chief of Staff in 1974, and Chairman of the Joint Chiefs of Staff in 1978.

Junction City, Operation

Operation Junction City was the second corps-sized operation of the war and involved 26 Allied battalions. From February 22–May 14, 1967, the allies pressed through War Zone C in an attempt to eliminate the Viet Cong 9th Division. War Zone C was a 1,500 square mile, marshy, communist controlled sanctuary along the Cambodian border. On February 22, the 173rd Airborne Brigade's 2nd Battalion, 503rd Infantry parachuted unopposed into a landing zone seven miles from the Cambodian border, which was the only major US "combat" jump of the war.

Right: A squad from the 2nd Battalion, 16th Infantry, 1st Infantry Division move through heavy jungle near the Cambodian border.

Left: A soldier watches the resupply helicopters take off from Suoi Da during Operation Junction City.

Simultaneously, 249 helicopters, in the largest mass helicopter lift of the war, inserted eight infantry battalions into the operational area. While there were some sharp engagements earlier, the three heaviest battles took place from March 19–26. During the night of March 19, the 273rd VC Regiment attacked and nearly overran the 9th Infantry Division's Troop A, 3rd Squadron, 5th Cavalry at Ap Bao Bang. Troops B and C fought their way into the beleaguered perimeter and the VC withdrew. In the early morning of March 21, the 273rd VC Regiment attacked the 4th Infantry Division's 3rd Battalion, 22nd Infantry and the 2nd Battalion, 77 Artillery at Fire Support Base Gold near Suoi Tri. Though a relief force from the 2nd Battalion, 22nd Infantry fought its way into the firebase, the fighting continued on into the day. The Viet Cong finally withdrew when they were counterattacked by tanks of the 2nd Battalion, 34th Armor. The last major fight of Junction City took place on April 1, when Landing Zone George was attacked by the 701st VC Regiment and the 1st Battalion, 70th VC Guards Regiment. A combination of artillery fire, helicopter gunships, and tactical air support caused them to withdraw. Tactically, Junction City was an Allied victory, even though War Zone C was clearly not neutralized. However, it made General Giap painfully aware that the Viet Cong base areas inside South Vietnam could not be adequately secured. As a result the Viet Cong moved their headquarters and logistics elements into Cambodia, where the NVA were already established.

Left: A radioman gives his wounded squad leader mouth-to-mouth resuscitation during Operation Junction City.

K

Kampuchea
See Cambodia.

Kattenburg, Paul
Paul Kattenburg was a State Department Indochina research analyst from 1952 to 1956. Later, between 1963 and 1964, he served as the Vietnam Desk Officer. During the 1950s and early 1960s he traveled widely in Vietnam, and came to believe that the Ngo Dinh Diem regime would lose to the Viet Cong. At a meeting of the National Security Council on August 31, 1963, he became the first American official to recommend withdrawal from Vietnam. Dean Rusk and Robert McNamara, who subsequently had him removed from the Vietnam decision-making process, both vehemently opposed his recommendation.

Katzenbach, Nicolas
As the US Attorney General in 1965 and 1966, Katzenbach ordered investigations of those who protested against the draft. While he served as Undersecretary of State from 1966 to 1969, it was Katzenbach who told the Senate Foreign Relations Committee, on August 7, 1967 that the President had the power to initiate military action and that the role of Congress was primarily to ratify the President's decisions.

Kelly, Charles L.
Charles Kelly was the Commander of the 57th Medical Detachment (Helicopter Ambulance) from January 11, 1964 until he was killed in action on July 1, 1964. It was Kelly, whose radio call sign was "Dustoff," that developed the tactics and procedures for aero-medical evacuation by helicopter. To implement his tactics he was forced to fight a running bureaucratic battle with the Surgeon General of the Army in Washington, and the US Army Support Command Chief, Brigadier General Joseph Stillwell, who both considered helicopters too valuable to risk for medical evacuation of the wounded. Though he didn't live to see it, other medevac units adopted his tactics, and "Dustoff" became the most famous call sign of the war.

Right: President John Fitzgerald Kennedy.

Kennan, George Frost

While Kennan was the Director of the State Department Policy Planning Staff in 1947, he was the architect of the "Containment Policy," a keystone of American relations with Russia and China for nearly 40 years. He believed that American intervention in Vietnam might imperil relations with the two communist giants.

In 1965, in a testimony before the Senate Foreign Relations Committee, he stated that the United States had no strategic or economic interest in Indochina, and that a communist Vietnam posed no conceivable threat to US security. He also testified that a communist Vietnam would probably pursue a foreign policy independent of both Russian and Chinese influences.

Kennedy, Edward Moore

After the assassination of his brother Robert in 1968, Edward Kennedy took up the anti-Vietnam commitment and outspokenly condemned the Attrition Strategy, calling for an implementation of the Enclave Strategy in its place. He was openly critical of what he called the "gross corruption" of the government of the Republic of Vietnam, and began calling for the immediate withdrawal of American forces after the Cambodian Incursion. He was an important figure in dealing with refugees of the war.

Kennedy, John Fitzgerald

John F Kennedy's involvement with Vietnam began in the early 1950s. A firm believer in Containment Policy and the Domino Theory, as the French began to falter Kennedy urged the Eisenhower administration to back the government of Ngo Dinh Diem in South Vietnam.

In 1956, while still a US Senator, Kennedy called South Vietnam "the cornerstone of the free world in Southeast Asia." Elected to the US Presidency in 1960, he began to increase the US commitment to Vietnam. By the end of 1963 he had increased the number of US advisers from fewer than 600 when he assumed office to more than 16,000. In addition, he authorized military advisers to participate in combat operations; supported covert operations against North Vietnam; and publicly stated that America was unequivocally committed to the preservation of a non-Communist South Vietnam.

As the political and military situation deteriorated, some officials in both Washington and Saigon urged support for a coup against the Diem regime; some recommended stronger backing for Diem; and a few urged withdrawal. Kennedy opted for the coup, but was truly surprised when the assassination of Diem was carried out.

Kennedy, Robert Francis

During the domestic debate over Vietnam policy in 1965 Robert Kennedy, the younger brother of President John F Kennedy, supported the position of the Johnson administration. In early 1966, he broke with the Johnson administration, calling for a coalition government in South Vietnam and the pursuit of "honorable negotiations." After Senator Eugene McCarthy's near victory in the 1968 New Hampshire primary, Kennedy entered the Democratic race for the Presidency, and on June 4, 1968 he won the California primary, becoming the party frontrunner. In his campaign he made the war the central issue, repeatedly calling for a negotiated solution. He was assassinated on June 5, 1968.

Kent State University

On May 4, 1970, National Guardsmen shot and killed four student protesters and wounded nine others at Kent State University, Ohio. A few days before, on May 1, 1970 amid rising opposition to the war on the nation's college campuses, President Nixon publicly denounced antiwar students as "bums blowing up campuses." The next day, Nixon announced to the nation that an "incursion" into Cambodia had been launched by the United States combat forces. In reaction to this, American college campuses erupted in protest.

At Kent State University, unrest began on Friday, May 1, 1970. On May 2, a large rally was staged on the campus, and in the downtown area damage estimated at $15,000 was caused. Subsequently, Mayor Satrom established a citywide curfew and called in the National Guard, who clashed with students on the following two nights. On Monday May 4, local and state officials decided that a planned rally should not be allowed, but by noon a large crowd had gathered in front of the college. The National Guard cleared the area with tear gas and then fought running battles with scattered groups of students. At just before 12:30pm the Guard began to march back to the Commons area, and most of the students began walking away from the area, although some continued to shout obscenities and throw rocks. As the Guard reached the crest of a hill, 28 of them suddenly fired their weapons into a group in a parking lot.

Right: A C-130 airdrops ammunition and rations while the airstrip is out at Khe Sanh.

In response to the killings, over 400 colleges and universities across America shut down. In Washington, nearly 100,000 protesters surrounded government buildings.

Kerry, John Forbes

Forbes was the commander of a "swift boat" in the Mekong Delta who became disillusioned with the war. He took part in the 1969 Moratorium to End the War in Vietnam demonstrations, and became the national coordinator for the Vietnam Veterans Against the War (VVAW). In 1971 he participated in the "Winter Soldier Investigation" during which more than 100 alleged veterans testified about war crimes and atrocities they had either participated in or witnessed. In testimony before the US Senate Foreign Relations Committee he asked how the US could demand someone to be "the last man to die for a mistake?" He was later elected to the US Senate from Massachusetts and chaired the Senate select Committee on matters concerning POW and MIA issues.

Key West Agreement

Agreement between the Joint Chiefs of Staff and US Department of Defense resulting from negotiations at the Key West Naval Base, Florida, between March 11–14, 1948. The agreement defined the hereto conflicting roles of military aviation, giving the naval air arm responsibility for close support and interdiction, and placing all land-based aircraft under the command of the US Air Force.

Keystone, Operation

The code name for the withdrawal of US forces from Vietnam was Operation Keystone. As each major ground unit was selected for withdrawal, a schedule was drawn up and the operation was code-named Keystone, followed by a bird's name. For instance, the withdrawal of the 3rd Marine Division, the first major unit to withdraw, was code-named Operation Keystone Robin.

Kham Duc

After the fall of Lang Vei during the Tet

Above: A marine closely observes the effect of a close air support mission just outside the Khe Sanh wire.

Offensive, Kham Duc became the only remaining Special Forces Camp along the Laotian border in I Corps. Located in northwestern Quang Tin province 90 miles southwest of Danang, the base was a key launch site for the Studies and Observations Group (SOG). Throughout April 1968, reconnaissance indicated that the communists were massing around the camp, and it was heavily reinforced by troops from the Americal Division. Early on the morning of May 10, two NVA reg-

iments attacked the outlying outpost of Ngoc Tavak, which fell after fierce resistance, and the defenders were scattered. Shrugging off repeated B-52 strikes, the NVA pounded Kham Duc during May 10 and May 11. On May 11, General Westmoreland ordered the camp to be evacuated, however that night all seven hilltop outposts overlooking the camp were overrun, and during the morning of May 12 a massive ground assault struck the camp perimeter. The 7th Air Force ordered all in-country and out-country units to support the evacuation. Intermittently through the day, Army and Marine helicopters lifted out survivors as Allied air strikes held off the enemy. Then, in a spectacular show of airman-

ship and courage, C-123 and C-130 transports began landing and taking out evacuees. Over 1,500 were successfully transported. Meanwhile, Army and Marine helicopters brought in ammunition and took out wounded. Two days later, helicopters rescued three Army soldiers who had escaped from one of the outposts when it was overrun on May 11 and the evacuation was complete.

Khe Sanh, Battle of (October 1967–March 1968)

General Westmoreland ordered the construction of an interconnected series of bases along the DMZ to act as an infiltration barrier. Khe Sanh was one of the outposts. Located on a plateau six miles

Left: A C-130 Hercules accelerates down the runway at Khe Sanh.

Below left: A C-130 delivers cargo to Khe Sahn by parachute low level extraction (LOLEX).

from Laos and 14 miles from the Demilitarized Zone, Khe Sanh was surrounded by heights up to 3,000ft. Between October and December 1967, the NVA moved major forces into place around the outpost. The NVA 325C Division was northwest of Khe Sanh, and two regiments of the 320th Division were northeast. An armored regiment and two artillery regiments supported these, while the 304th Division provided a ready reserve in eastern Laos. Though the Marines were reluctant to remain in a fixed base, Westmoreland, who was looking for a massive set piece battle poured in reinforcements and supplies. General Giap considered it a test on whether to proceed with the Tet Offensive. If corps-sized attacks across the DMZ were not enough to provoke a US invasion of North Vietnam, then the Tet Offensive could be safely undertaken. As the 77-day siege of the outpost began on January 21, 1968 President Johnson required a written guarantee from the Joint Chiefs of Staff that the outpost could be held. This was a move unprecedented in the relationship between the civilian and military elements of the US government. That same day the North Vietnamese hurled a corps of over 40,000 men at the outpost.

Hundreds of 122mm rockets, mortars, and artillery rounds slammed into the Marines. A direct hit detonated the Marine ammunition dump and destroyed much of their fuel supply. On February 6, the 304 Division's 66th Regiment, reinforced with PT 76 tanks, overran the Lang Vei Special Forces Camp west of Khe Sanh, and NVA infantry began a classic siege, constructing trenches, zigzag approaches, and parallels.

On February 29, the only serious ground assault occurred. The 304th NVA Division charged the ARVN 34th Ranger Battalion positions, only to be driven back. On April 1, the 1st Cavalry Division launched Operation Pegasus to reopen Road 9 and relieve the siege of Khe Sanh. Meeting only light resistance, the Cavalry linked up with the Marines on April 8, bringing the siege to an end. The battle had mixed results. Though the United States did not respond by invading North Vietnam, which assured General Giap that the Tet Offensive would probably be safe to undertake, the successful defense and heavy NVA casualties clearly indicated that the planned follow on invasion across the DMZ would not work.

Khieu Samphan

The top Khmer Rouge leader, Khieu Samphan, aligned himself with Prince Sihanouk and was elected to the Cambodian National Assembly in 1962, however, in 1966 he fled to the jungle when the Prince denounced the Khmer Rouge. After Lon Nol seized control, he reappeared as Deputy Prime Minister and Defense Minister in Sihanouk's resistance government. When the Vietnamese invaded Cambodia he returned to the jungle. He later became the senior Khmer Rouge member of the Supreme National Council.

Khmer Krom

An ethnic Cambodian group was known as the Khmer Krom. The name refers to the Khmer who live in the south of Cambodia (Kambuja). Approximately 80 percent of them live in the Mekong Delta, and a small number in other provinces throughout the southern part of Vietnam. During the Vietnam War the Khmer Kampuchea Khrom allied themselves to South Vietnam, from which it had gained promises of autonomy in return for military service.

Khmer Rouge

The Cambodian communist faction was known as the Khmer Rouge, which means "Red Khmer." In 1970, it was led by an unknown figure named Pol Pot, and lent its support to Prince Sihanouk of Cambodia after he was deposed by General Lon Nol in the March 18 coup d'état. Sihanouk, who had been out of the country at the time of the coup, aligned with the Khmer Rouge in an effort to oust Lon Nol's regime. The Khmer Rouge leadership capitalized on the enormous prestige and popularity of Prince Sihanouk to increase support for their movement among Cambodians. Pol Pot later violently ousted Lon Nol then began a radical experiment to create an agrarian utopia, resulting in the deaths of 25 percent of the country's population (2,000,000 persons) from starvation, overwork, and systematic executions. The Khmer Rouge was overthrown during the Vietnamese invasion, but even after Pol Pot's capture in 1997 it still continues to violently resist the Cambodian government.

Khmer Serai

The Cambodian resistance movement, Khmer Serai (Free Khmer), were loosely aligned with the Khmer Krom that fought against both the communists and the Cambodian government. The movement received irregular assistance from

Left: Two soldiers of the 173rd Airborne Brigade wait for a logistics helicopter to take their friend's body.

Above: A patrol recovers the bodies of a squad that was ambushed by the Viet Cong.

Left: A rifle salute to the dead is rendered in honor of those killed in action during a Marine operation near Danang.

Right: Airbursts ring a firebase as the artillery fires a well-executed Killer Junior mission near the Cambodian border.

the RVN, and regularly participated in US Special Forces operations. It was also involved in the March 1970 coup d'état against Prince Sihanouk, that brought Lon Nol to power.

Khrushchev, Nikita Sergeyevich

Although he never visited Vietnam, Khrushchev was the first Soviet Premier to show a sustained interest in Southeast Asia. In the late 1950s, he supported the communists struggle in Laos, and authorized a Soviet airlift of military equipment and supplies to the Pathet Lao on the Plain of Jars. On January 6, 1961 he formally announced that the Soviet Union would support "wars of national liberation" anywhere in the world. However, Khrushchev provided only lukewarm support to the North Vietnamese and was not trusted by Ho Chi Minh.

KIA

See Killed In Action.

Killed in Action (KIA)

This category of death in a combat zone applies to any individual who died of wounds inflicted by an enemy by either conventional means such as bullets, grenades, artillery, or unconventional methods including mines and booby traps, etc.

It does not include death due to circumstances unrelated to combat, such as drowning, or vehicle accidents. As a result, although the Vietnam Memorial Wall has the names of over 58,000 who died in Southeast Asia, only 47,378 were Killed In Action.

Killer Junior

The artillery direct fire tactic, Killer Junior, used time-fused 105mm and 155mm shells set to explode 30ft off the ground at ranges between 200m and 1,000m from the muzzle of the guns. Killer Senior was the same tactic, employed by the heavy 8in howitzer. Used to defend fire support bases, these low-level airbursts created a killing zone where nothing could survive.

King, Martin Luther

By 1965, when the Vietnam War escalation began in earnest, Martin Luther King was the premier civil rights leader in the United States. By late 1966, he became the co-chairman of the Clergy and Laity Concerned About Vietnam (CALCAV).

Disturbed by the effect of the draft on the black community, and concerned that black soldiers were suffering a disproportionate number of casualties, in 1967 King openly protested the Vietnam War. Though opposed by many civil rights leaders, he explicitly aligned the civil rights and antiwar movements, renewed his call for civil disobedience, and urged young men to seek conscientious objector status. He was assassinated on April 4, 1968.

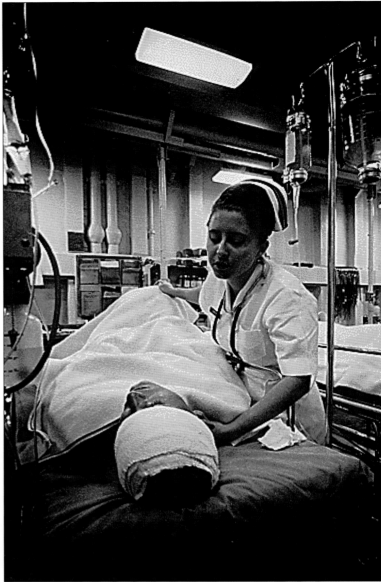

Above left: Casualties are staged aboard the USS *Tripoli* for further evacuation to hospitals in Japan or the United States.

Above: A nurse tends a patient just out of surgery on the USS *Repose*, a hospital ship positioned near Danang.

Kingfisher, Operation

From July 16–October 31, 1967, the 3rd Marine Division conducted Operation Kingfisher along the DMZ to prevent NVA entry into Quang Tri Province. Though there was little contact initially, when the Marines began withdrawing from the DMZ toward Con Thien, they encountered heavy NVA resistance. On September 10, the 3rd Battalion, 26th Marines engaged the 812th NVA Regiment and suffered more than 200 casualties. On September 21, the 2nd Battalion, 4th Marines, were hammered by the 90th NVA Regiment and forced to pull back inside the main perimeter. Between September 19–27, NVA artillery pounded the Marines with more than 3,000 rounds. By the end of September, the NVA had launched three major attacks from three different directions on the Marines. On October 14, a large NVA Force attempted to cut the supply line from Dong Ha to the committed Marine regiment, this was prevented by the 2nd Battalion, 4th Marines, which again suffered heavy casualties. The last major action during Operation Kingfisher took place between 25–28 October. During this engagement the 2nd Battalion, 9th Marines, strength dropped to fewer than 300. The Marines classified the operation as a success and reported that 1,117 NVA were killed; 340 Marines were Killed In Action and 1,461 were wounded.

Kinnard, Harry William Osborn

In 1965, Major General Kinnard took the 1st Cavalry Division (Airmobile) to Vietnam, even though he originally lobbied to have it stationed in Thailand. He demonstrated the effectiveness of airmobile tactics during the Battle of the Ia Drang. When the NVA broke contact and began to withdraw, he made a request for permission to pursue them into Cambodia. His request was denied, which convinced him that the political leadership of the United States was not serious about winning the war.

Kissinger, Henry Alfred

Though he served as a consultant to both the Kennedy and Johnson administrations in the 1960s, Kissinger fully arrived on the political scene as a foreign policy aide to Governor Nelson Rockefeller of New York during his unsuccessful Presidential bid. Just prior to his inauguration in January 1969, President Nixon appointed Kissinger

Right: An ex-Viet Cong prepares to accompany a US patrol as a scout.

Special Assistant for National Security Affairs. Between 1969 and 1973 he made himself the central figure in the diplomatic effort to achieve a peaceful settlement in South Vietnam.

To this end, he held secret talks with officials from North Vietnam, the Viet Cong, the Soviet Union, and the People's Republic of China. In the summer of 1972, dealing head-to-head with Le Duc Tho, North Vietnam's negotiator, the peace talks began to move ahead. Due to major modifications in the US negotiating stance, they managed to reach agreement in October.

However, in November 1972, the North Vietnamese appeared to be stepping away from their October agreement. In response, Nixon ordered a massive bombing of Hanoi and Haiphong, as well as the mining of North Vietnam's ports and rivers.

In January 1973, the North Vietnamese agreed to abide by the October agreement and the Paris Peace Agreements were signed. In September 1973, Nixon named Kissinger as Secretary of State. Following President Nixon's resignation, Kissinger remained the Secretary of State for President Ford.

Below: US Presidential Advisor Henry Kissinger shares a lighter moment with Vietnamese Presidential Advisor Nguyen Phu Duc during a visit to Vietnam.

Kit Carson Scouts
The Kit Carson Scouts were former Viet Cong or NVA soldiers who had changed sides, often under the Chieu Hoi Program, and were willing to act as scouts, interpreters, or intelligence agents for the Allies. The program, initiated by the 9th Marines in I Corps, proved to be very effective and was rapidly used throughout all the US units in Vietnam.

Knowland, William F
Republican Senator William Knowland of California was the Senate majority leader from 1953 to 1955, and the minority leader from 1955 to 1959. As a member of the Senate Foreign Relations Committee, he succeeded in convincing Secretary of State Dulles to downgrade the US delegation at the Geneva Convention of 1954 to a simple observer status. He was a strong supporter of

Right: Robert Komer (left) was given the task by President Johnson of invigorating the pacification program in Vietnam.

South Vietnam President Ngo Dinh Diem, and labeled the Geneva Accords as a communist victory.

Komer, Robert W

In May 1967, President Johnson sent Komer, a Middle East expert for the CIA from 1947 to 1960, to Vietnam as the Deputy Commander of MACV. There, he established the Civil Operations and Revolutionary Development Support program, designed to speed up pacification and instituted the Hamlet Evaluation Survey (HES) in an attempt to determine the actual security status of the villages and hamlets. He also instituted the Phoenix Program to attack the Viet Cong infrastructure. Komer believed that the answer in Vietnam was not military, but his pacification program essentially failed.

Kong Le

The Laotian paratroop captain, Kong Le, led his battalion in a coup that overthrew the pro-Western government in Vientiane in 1960. He believed that his actions would result in the neutralization of Laos. Driven out of Vientiane by a CIA backed army under General Phoumi Nosavan, he retreated to the strategic Plain of Jars. Though he sometimes cooperated with the Vietnamese and Pathet Lao Communists in opposing the rightist government, he was a Neutralist at heart and continually backed Prince Souvanna Phouma's efforts to neutralize Laos. To that end, he fought against his former allies as the commander of the neutralist forces.

Korea, Democratic People's Republic of

When the Republic of Korea dispatched army units to Vietnam in 1965, Kim Il Sung, the communist leader of North Korea, informed Hanoi that he was willing to match the South Korean deployment. Hanoi politely refused the offer. However, a group of North Korean pilots did assist in training their North Vietnamese counterparts, and participated in some combat missions. The bulk of North Korean aid was technical and financial rather than directly military.

Korea, Republic of

The Johnson administration was adamant that other countries needed to support the American effort in Vietnam. To this end the Republic of Korea agreed to deploy troops there, and the advance party arrived on February 26, 1965. Eventually Korea sent more combat troops to South Vietnam than any other American ally, and as a percentage of their population they made a larger contribution of manpower than even the United States. Between 1965 and 1966 their Capital ("Tiger") Infantry Division, the elite division in all of the Korean armed forces, 9th ("White Horse") Infantry Division, second in quality only to the Capital Division, and 2nd Marine Brigade arrived. The two infantry division were assigned to operational areas between Cam Rahn Bay and Qui Nhon in II Corps on the central coast of South Vietnam. This remained their operational area throughout the war. Tough,

VIETNAM: A VISUAL ENCYCLOPEDIA

disciplined, and inured to hardship, the Koreans were meticulous in their planning and ruthless in carrying out their operations. Pacified villages in their area of responsibility stayed pacified, and they routinely achieved combat ratios of enemy killed and weapons captured that bettered almost every other unit in Vietnam. In a similar manner, the Marine Brigade deployed to an area of operations just south of Danang and habitually coordinated with or participated in operations of the US Marine Divisions deployed into I Corps. Like their Army counterparts they were tough, resourceful, and ruthless. The III MAF officially complemented their performance on numerous occasions. Korean troop strength peaked at just under 50,000 in 1968 and remained there until 1970, when the withdrawals began. The two Korean infantry divisions were among the last foreign troops withdrawn, finally leaving II Corps in March 1973.

Kosygin, Aleksei Nikolayevich

Initially, when he became Soviet Premier in 1964, Kosygin was reluctant to expand Soviet aid to North Vietnam, and supported a negotiated settlement. However, during a visit to Hanoi he observed a heavy US air raid on Dong Hoi (near Hanoi), which he characterized as "Hitlerite." Immediately upon his return to Moscow the Soviet Union begin shipping advance surface-to-air missiles, radars, MiG aircraft and anti-aircraft artillery to North Vietnam. He then informed Washington that the Soviet Union could not have normal relations with the United States unless they withdrew from Vietnam.

Above: General Westmoreland and Mr Vinh Tho of the Vietnamese Foreign Ministry welcome the first Korean troops to Vietnam in 1964.

Krulak, Victor H.

As a major general, Krulak served as Special Assistant for Counterinsurgency and Special Activities for the Joint Chiefs of Staff from February 1962 until January 1964. In that capacity he was responsible for the development of counterinsurgency doctrine. Awarded his third star, he was assigned as the Commander of Fleet Marine Force, Pacific until his retirement in 1968. Although he was not in the chain of command, his skill and forceful personality strongly influenced Marine strategy in I Corps. He was a powerful opponent of Westmoreland's search and destroy operations and Attrition Strategy.

L

La Vang Basilica

The La Vang Basilica is located approximately four miles outside of Quang Tri City in Quang Tri province. It was built in 1900 on the spot of an alleged appearance of the Virgin Mary to a group of persecuted Roman Catholics in 1798. It had a powerful emotional appeal to Vietnamese catholics, particularly those who had relocated from the north following the Geneva Accords of 1954, and was a favorite pilgrimage site. It was heavily damaged during the Easter Offensive in 1972.

Laird, Melvin R.

President Nixon selected Laird to be his Secretary of Defense based on the belief that Laird's reputation with Congress could be used to diminish criticism of Nixon's policies. Almost immediately Laird clashed with Henry Kissinger. He pushed the president hard for a precise timetable of troop reductions, and Kissinger believed such a timetable would damage his bargaining position. It was Laird who coined the term "Vietnamization," and informed critics it was the top priority of the Nixon administration. He opposed both the secret bombing of Cambodia and the Christmas bombing of North Vietnam. For that reason President Nixon bypassed the Secretary of Defense and issued the orders directly to the Joint Chiefs of Staff. Continually undercut and marginalized by Kissinger, and ignored by Nixon, he was eventually replaced by Elliot Richardson.

Lake, William Anthony Kirsopp

In 1963, Lake served in the Vietnamese Embassy and in 1964 and 1965 was the Vice Consul in Hue. While he was in Hue he noticed the wide disparity between the official pronouncements of MACV and what appeared to be happening on the ground.

He returned to the United States in 1965, and in 1969 he accepted a position as special assistant to Henry Kissinger. He accompanied Kissinger to the secret negotiations with North Vietnamese representatives in Paris. However, in 1970 he resigned in protest against the Cambodian Incursion.

Right: The La Vang Basilica outside Quang Tri, a blend of gothic and Oriental architectural styles, was an important pilgrimage site for Vietnamese catholics.

Opposite, top: Secretary of Defense Melvin Laird presents awards to the participants in the Son Tay Raid.

Opposite, bottom: Secretary of Defense Melvin Laird relaxes at a small reception held for him by General Creighton Abrams.

Above: Secretary of Defense Melvin Laird is shown with Joint Chiefs of Staff.

Above right: ARVN troops move deeper into Laos along the Ho Chi Minh Trail during Operation Lam Son 719.

Right: Badly outnumbered ARVN troops, faced with a heavy counterattack, begin to withdraw from Laos.

Lam Son

Le Loi, the Vietnamese nationalist who defeated an invading Chinese army in 1428, was born in Lam Son. ARVN forces routinely used the reference Lam Son, followed by a number, as a code-name for their military operations. They believed that it symbolically designated South Vietnam as the true descendants of Vietnamese nationalism.

Lam Son 719, Operation

On February 8, 1971 a task force of 15,000 ARVN troops invaded Laos with two objectives. The first was to capture Tchepone the key transshipment point on the Ho Chi Minh Trail 25 miles west of Khe Sanh. The second, and more problematic, was to sever the Ho Chi Minh Trail, which by 1971 had become North Vietnam's main logistical pipeline to the south. If the ARVN successfully cut the

Trail it would be a devastating blow to the North Vietnamese units operating inside South Vietnam. The invasion proved to be an unmitigated disaster. Planning was confined to a close circle in Washington and Saigon and the actual units to be involved in the invasion were told too late to develop a coordinated operation. Added to this, the South Vietnamese had never planned and conducted multiple-division operations. Outnumbered from the outset, the 15,000 ARVN initially engaged 22,000 logistical and security forces. However, by the second week of the invasion five NVA Divisions supported by armor and artillery had reinforced these troops.

By the third week of the invasion ARVN armor had been bottled up along Route 9, and the infantry spearhead was receiving intense 122mm and 130mm artillery fire. US planners had believed that American air power would be pivotal to the outcome of the invasion. As the North Vietnamese kicked off their counterattack the weather conditions

restricted the employment of both fixed-wing aircraft and helicopters. By the time the weather cleared, NVA antiaircraft systems covered virtually all potential helicopter landing zones, as well as providing a significant threat against ground attack fighters. Though the invasion had essentially ground to a halt, President Nguyen Van Thieu ordered the commander of Lam Son 719 to launch an airborne assault on Tchepone. On March 6, 120 US Army helicopters, escorted by Air Force fighter-bombers, lifted two battalions from the old Marine base at Khe Sanh into Tchepone. Two days later two other ARVN Battalions reached the city on foot, and one of the objectives of the operation was achieved, though the town had been evacuated by the NVA

some time previously. By the end of the operation, the ARVN Force had been ground down to less than 8,000 effectives and was faced by over 40,000 NVA regulars. Two of Saigon's premier units, the 1st Infantry Division and the ARVN Airborne Division, had been virtually destroyed. Lam Son 719 officially ended on April 6. On April 7, 1971 in a televised report to the nation, President Nixon announced that Lam Son 719 proved that Vietnamization had worked.

Land Reform

In modern Vietnamese history, Land Reform is the principle of forcible confiscation and redistribution of land. It was a central doctrine of the communist Viet Minh, the DRV, and was adopted in the RVN. The Viet Minh applied a limited land reform program to areas that fell under its control from the early 1950s, but after 1953 a more radical campaign was initiated. It spread across Vietnam and became increasingly brutal. Thousands of landlords were executed, some of whom barely met the description. In 1956, aware of the damage that was being done to their own power base by the land reform program, the Viet Minh revised the program, but it had already alienated the landlord class and allied it to the RVN. Diem's government reversed the redistribution program in the Mekong Delta, but after 1958 initiated its own land reforms. These were poorly implemented, far less generous to the peasantry than the communist reforms, and administered by corrupt officials. In 1970, Thieu made a belated bid to gain the allegiance of the tenant farmers in the RVN, and introduced radical legislation that redistributed almost all the remaining land owned by local landlords to the peasantry.

Landing Zone (LZ)

The US military term for the location where helicopters were to land, usually in remote areas, was known as the landing zone (LZ). In conversation it was simply referred to as an LZ. A "hot LZ" was one that was receiving enemy fire, and conversely, a "cold LZ" was not. When a landing zone was formed by dropping a 15,000lb bomb from a C-130 it was referred to as an "LZ cut."

Lansdale, Edward Geary

Just before the French signed the Geneva Accords in 1954, the CIA sent Lansdale to North Vietnam with a mission to

Above: Troops from the 25th Infantry Division run for cover in a hot landing zone.

undercut Ho Chi Minh, lay the groundwork for a stay behind intelligence network when the French withdrew, and bolster the Bao Dai southern State of Vietnam government. He quickly became a principal adviser to Ngo Dinh Diem who was Bao Dai's Premier, Defense Minister, and Commander of the Armed Forces. Partly as a result of his efforts, nearly a million North Vietnamese moved south. Diem accepted many of Lansdale's recommendations,

such as coopting the armed religious sects, and attacking the Binh Xuyen river pirates. Lansdale was one of the few people that President Diem listened to outside of his personal family. Lansdale, who was a staunch advocate of counterinsurgency and pacification, was resented and opposed by both the State

Above: An air guide brings a helicopter into a small landing zone in III Corps.

Department and Defense Department bureaucracies, which ultimately lessened his impact on the direction of the Vietnam War.

Lao Dong Party

The communist party, known as Lao Dong, was founded in 1951 and ruled the Democratic Republic of Vietnam from 1951 to the present day. From 1976, it became known as Dan Cong San Viet Nam (Vietnamese Communist Party). Lao Dong grew out of the Indochinese Communist Party (ICP), the coalition of Vietnamese Communist groups formed in the 1930s by Ho Chi Minh. Under Minh's leadership the Lao Dong increased its popular support in the immediate post war years and is currently the sole political party in Vietnam.

Lao Issara

Formed in 1945, Lao Issara (Free Laos) resisted any attempt to return to French colonial status. It established a provisional parliament, which declared the unification of the country and deposed the king in October 1945. After French troops began reoccupying the country in March 1946, the Lao Issara made a bid for unity by restoring Sisavang Vong as king of a united Laos.

The Lao Issara later fled to Thailand, but nevertheless, France was forced to accept the unified kingdom, a constitution, and parliament. The country was recognized as a self-governing unit within the French Union in 1949 by which time the Lao Issara had dissolved itself and returned to Laos. Some participants joined the Royal government and others the emergent Pathet Lao. Further French concessions towards independence were established under the Franco-Lao Treaty of Amity and Association in October 1953, but full independence was not granted until the following year.

Laos

Landlocked Laos is one of the most underdeveloped nations in the world. During the French Indochina War it was regarded as a backwater, but assumed far greater importance during the Vietnam War. In the late 1950s a civil war between the royal government and a communist

Above: Le Duc Tho arranges some papers before addressing Henry Kissinger as the Paris peace talks continue.

movement known as the Pathet Lao, bolstered by the North Vietnamese, pulled in both the United States and the Soviet Union. In 1962, another Geneva Agreement was signed, under which Laos became a neutral nation. However, the North Vietnamese violated the agreement by leaving their troops in place and eventually took control of a broad strip of eastern Laos within which they constructed the Ho Chi Minh Trail. During the subsequent war in Vietnam, this area became the most heavily bombed terrain on the face of the earth.

Lavelle, John D

In July 1971, Lavelle took command of the 7th Air Force in Vietnam. He very quickly became concerned about the complex rules of engagement his pilots were forced to observe. In 1972, he was charged with authorizing dozens of missions against North Vietnam in violation of the rules of engagement and forced to testify before both the Senate and House Armed Services Committees. He argued before the committees that he had been authorized to carry out the secret attacks by his superiors. He could not substantiate this assertion and was reduced two grades, to major general, and retired.

Le Duan

After Ho Chi Minh's death in 1969, Le Duan, the Secretary General of the Lao Dong Party, became the defacto leader of North Vietnam. A southerner, during the French Indochina War he conducted a brilliant war of attrition against the French in the Mekong Delta. He advocated a total war against the Diem regime almost from its inception. Following a secret trip to the south in 1959, he reported that if the Viet Cong did not launch an all-out effort they would be destroyed.

Based on his recommendation, Hanoi authorized war. When the United States intervened in 1965, Le Duan was the Politburo's strongest advocate of moving toward a conventional war similar to what it waged against the French. He noted that as the scale of combat increased, the French public's support for the war declined, and predicted that the same thing would happen in the United States. When South Vietnam fell, Le Duan, who was a devoted Marxist, was heavy handed when restructuring the reunited country and virtually destroyed the economy.

Le Duc Tho

In 1968, when the Paris peace negotiations convened, Xuan Thuy headed the first North Vietnamese delegation and Le Duc Tho was an advisor. He quickly became the real power in the North Vietnamese delegation. Believing that the United States was under pressure to resolve the war, he stonewalled for years by repeatedly demanding an unconditional US withdrawal and the dismantling of the Thieu government. In order to effect American withdrawal, he ultimately made concessions on both these points and he and Kissinger reached agreement in October 1972. This agreement was angrily rejected by South Vietnam. Renewed negotiations stalled in December 1972, and President Nixon unleashed the Christmas bombing in order to get the North Vietnamese back to the peace table. The final agreements were signed on January 27, 1973. Le Duc Tho and Henry Kissinger were awarded the Nobel Peace Prize, but Tho refused his, saying there was no peace.

Le Nguyen Khang

Khang was the first Vietnamese to graduate from the US Marine Corps' Amphibious Warfare School, and organized the South Vietnamese Marine Brigade. He refused to participate in the coup against Diem in 1963 and as a result he was posted abroad in order to minimize his influence. He was reinstated by General Nguyen Khan following his coup. Khang's competence and popularity with other senior ARVN officers and the troops led to his appointment as commander of the Capital Military District, Military Governor of Saigon, Commander of III Corps Tactical Zone, and a member of the National Leadership Committee.

Le Nguyen Vy

One of South Vietnam's few incorruptible generals, Le Nguyen Vy originally served with a battalion in the Mekong Delta. Promoted to Brigadier General,

he was the Deputy Commander of the ARVN 5th Infantry Division at the bloody battle of An Loc during the Easter Offensive. In 1973, he was appointed as the 5th Division Commander and was with them at Lai Khe in the spring of 1975. When faced with the possibility of having to surrender to the North Vietnamese, he shot himself instead.

Le Quang Tung

Under President Diem, Le Quang Tung was the commander of the Vietnamese Special Forces. He performed a number of missions for Diem, most notably the suppression of the buddhists. Intensely loyal, the generals plotting the coup against Diem believed he was extremely dangerous to their cause. On November 1, 1963, Tung met with a group of the generals at Tan Son Nhut Air Base. When he was told there was going to be a coup against Diem he castigated the plotters. A short time later he was executed.

Le Trong Tan

Colonel General Le Trong Tan infiltrated the South in the early 1960s and actively recruited and trained Viet Cong units. In 1968, he became the Deputy Commanding General of the People's Liberation Armed Forces, and moved to

assume control of operations in I Corps, and eastern Laos. He was the General Commander of the Campaign to Liberate Hue and Danang and the Deputy General Commander of the 1975 Ho Chi Minh Campaign. He was a special envoy to the Pathet Lao during the Plain of Jars campaign in the 1970s, and also took part in the invasion of Cambodia in 1979.

Le Van "Bay" Vien

During the French Indochina War Le Van Vien was the Deputy Commander of the Viet Minh in Cochin China. In 1947, he switched sides when the French agreed to recognize his river pirates as a religious sect. In 1954, Emperor Bao Dai gave him control of the National Police and he quickly seized control of all vice in Saigon. Upon becoming Prime Minister, Diem considered him to be the most immediate threat to his authority. In April 1955, encouraged by Edward Lansdale but urged to go slow by the US Embassy, Diem attacked and the National Army crushed the Binh Xuyen. Le Van Vien fled to France.

LeMay, Curtis Emerson

From 1957 to 1961, LeMay was the Commander of the Strategic Air Command and Chief of Staff of the Air Force from 1961 to 1965. He routinely stated that the United States should deploy its full military force, including nuclear weapons, against the North Vietnamese to end the war quickly. He said that the United States should bomb Vietnam " back to the Stone Age."

Leatherneck Square

Leatherneck Square was the nickname the US Marines applied to a heavily contested area in northern I Corps. Located just south of the Demilitarized Zone, the corners were roughly defined by the villages of Cam Lo, Gio Linh, Con Thien, and Dong Ha.

Lemnitzer, Lyman L

Lemnitzer was the Chairman of the Joint Chiefs Staff from 1960 to 1962. He toured South Vietnam in 1961 and returned convinced that the American public would not support fighting a guerrilla war. As the tension increased in Laos, he advised President Kennedy not

Left: General Lyman Lemnitzer, Chairman of the US Joint Chiefs of Staff, and Secretary of Defense Robert McNamara during their visit to Vietnam in 1962.

VIETNAM: A VISUAL ENCYCLOPEDIA

to get involved with less than 140,000 troops and a commitment to use nuclear weapons if necessary. His opinions did not square with Kennedy's fascination with counterinsurgency, and he was soon moved out of Washington.

Levy, Howard B

In May 1967, Levy was tried in one of the first antiwar court-martials. He was a US Army Medical Corps officer who refused to provide medical training for Special Forces personnel who were about to leave for Vietnam. His trial attracted wide attention when he invoked the so-called Nuremberg Defense, stating that his training would be used for criminal purposes.

The Army trial judge allowed the defense, but it failed because none of the decisions made at Nuremberg entitled a soldier to disobey an intrinsically legal order because other soldiers stationed in another country were given illegal orders. He received a dishonorable discharge and served 27 months in prison. He appealed his conviction but in 1974 the Supreme Court upheld it.

Lexington III, Operation

The US First Infantry Division conducted Operation Lexington III in the Rung Sat Special Zone from April 17–June 9, 1966. The Rung Sat, a thick mangrove swamp south of Saigon was a haven for Main Force Viet Cong units operating in the Capital Military District. The soldiers plowed through the swamp, often spending the entire day in mud to their hips and water to their chest.

Rifle companies were rotated every 48 hours in order to rest and reduce the incidence of trench foot. While there were no major engagements, there were a significant number of small actions as ambush patrols caught enemy sampans

Above: Soldiers carry a wounded comrade through waist-deep mud and water in the Rung Sat Swamp.

and small boats operating along the waterways in the swamp. After thrashing around for 45 days with little to show for it, the division called the operation off and withdrew.

Lifton, Robert J.

Robert Lifton was the psychiatrist who developed most of the definitions and treatment methods for post-traumatic stress disorder (PTSD). He based it on a number of group therapy sessions with Vietnam veterans. In 1972, he convinced the National Council of Churches to sponsor the first "National Conference on the Emotional Needs of Vietnam-era Veterans," and in 1976 he headed the

Above: A 1st Cavalry Division soldier carries a LAW into battle, as well as his M16A1, north of Bong Son on Operation Masher/White Wing.

American Psychiatric Association's Task Force on post-traumatic stress disorder.

Light Antitank Weapon (LAW)
The LAW was a single shot, 66mm rocket, specifically designed to provide the infantry with an antitank weapon that could be carried by an individual. In Vietnam it was routinely used against bunkers and was viewed as the equivalent to the NVA RPG, though not nearly as versatile a weapon. It was used against NVA Armor at both Lang Vei and An Loc with mixed success.

Lima Site 85 (Phou Pha Thi)
Located on Pha Thi Mountain, Lima Site 85 was a 5,800ft karst, 12 miles from the Laotian–North Vietnamese border. In October 1967, the US Air Force installed a ground control radar on top of the mountain, which allowed them to direct fighter-bomber strikes against Hanoi and its surrounding areas in all-weather conditions. Hanoi quickly recognized the importance of the site, and on January 12, 1968, launched a bombing attack against Site 85, the only one it staged against a US ground installation during the entire war. Four obsolete AN-2 Colt biplanes began the raid, but only two struck Site 85 at midday, wounding one, and knocking the tactical air navigation system temporarily offline. An Air America helicopter drove them off. The crew chief on the helicopter succeeded in shooting one down with an AK-47. On March 16, supported by heavy artillery, mortar, and rocket bombardment, sappers climbed the mountain in the dark and overran the site. It was the single largest ground combat loss of US Air Force personnel during the Vietnam War.

Linebacker I, Operation
Reacting with fury to the NVA 1972 Easter Offensive, President Nixon reportedly said, "The bastards have never been bombed like they're going to be bombed this time." On April 4, the President authorized a massive bombing campaign to include attacks against North Vietnam for the first time since October 1968. Operation Linebacker I had three objectives: to close the land and rail supply lines from China, destroy stockpiles of war matériel and food, and interdict NVA supply lines to the south. For the first time, Haiphong and other North Vietnamese harbors were mined. B-52s were first introduced, and thousands of strikes were flown against North Vietnamese troops in the south, while in the north all the bridges, tunnels, and highways were pounded around the clock.

At the same time, Navy surface action groups hammered the North Vietnamese coast with more than 110,000 rounds of naval gunfire. The Easter invasion was turned back, and the North Vietnamese re-entered peace negotiations.

Linebacker II, Operation
Following the breakdown of the Paris peace talks on December 13, 1972, President Nixon issued an ultimatum to

Above: The North Vietnamese fighter strip at Yen Bai was photographed by an F-4 enroute to a different target.

Left: A Corsair II pilot ducks flak as his bombs blanket the Hai Dong Railway Bridge.

the North Vietnamese to return to the conference table "or else," but the Vietnamese refused. Linebacker II began on December 18 with only one purpose, to force the Vietnamese to negotiate. The

differences between Linebacker I and II were in their objectives and in their intensity. Linebacker I was essentially an interdiction campaign designed to logistically starve units in the field. Linebacker II was a strategic bombing campaign to destroy the enemy's will. For the first time targets in and around Hanoi and Haiphong were allowed to be struck, and military planners rather than civilian bureaucrats determined the target lists. The attacks wreaked havoc on

North Vietnam's economic and military infrastructure. The Air Force flew 742 B-52 sorties and 640 fighter-bomber sorties against targets in Hanoi and Haiphong, dropping over 20,000 tons of bombs. Twenty-six aircraft were lost, including 15 B-52s, but the North Vietnamese were unable to replace their expended SAMs and their fighter force was virtually destroyed. On December 26, F-4 and F-105 fighter-bombers concentrated massive raids on antiaircraft

SAM sites throughout the day. At dusk F-111 fighter-bombers attacked the MiG bases and damaged all the runways. That night 120 B-52s struck ten targets in Hanoi within a 15-minute period. The combination and power of the attacks rendered North Vietnam defenseless against air attack and convinced the Politburo that they needed to take steps to stop the bombing They decided to return to the Paris peace talks. Though President Nixon subsequently restricted attacks against Hanoi and Haiphong, NVA troops in the field and logistical areas continued to be bombed until the peace agreement was signed.

Right: A swing-wing F-111 Aardvark extends its wings as it slows down and prepares to land.

Below right:A flight of F-105s refuels from a KC-135 tanker on their way to North Vietnam.

Below: A B-52 lands at U-Tapao during Linebacker II.

Above: An OH-6A Loach brings Major PC Gutzman, Senior Advisor to the Military Region 1 Ranger Command, to a meeting in Danang.

Loach

Loach was the name the troops used for the OH-6 Light Observation Helicopter, (LOH). Later it became common to call any observation helicopter a Loach.

Loc Ninh, Battle of (October 1967)

Loc Ninh was the capital of Binh Long province near the Cambodian border, 70 miles north of Saigon. As part of the strategic preparation for the Tet Offensive, General Giap launched two regiments of the VC 9th Division against the town in an attempt to draw elements of the US First Infantry Division away from Saigon. He succeeded, but the Viet Cong units were severely mauled and unable to take part in the Tet Offensive. The NVA struck Loc Ninh again during the Easter Offensive and on April 6, 1972 took the town. Subsequently it served as one of the NVA main headquarters, communications centers, and as a staging area for the final assault on Saigon in 1975.

Right: Ambassador Henry Cabot Lodge was appointed by President Kennedy as Ambassador to South Vietnam.

VIETNAM: A VISUAL ENCYCLOPEDIA

Lodge, Henry Cabot Jr

In 1963, Lodge, who spoke fluent French and had traveled widely in Vietnam, was appointed by President Kennedy to be Ambassador to South Vietnam. He arrived in Saigon in August 1963, at the height of the buddhist crisis precipitated by Diem's repression. In a very short time he determined that Diem's pride, arrogance, and the veniality of his family would never allow him to affect the reforms that would be necessary to prevent a Viet Cong victory. In 1963, Lodge notified Washington that a group of army generals were seeking US support for a coup and urged President Kennedy to support the conspiracy. During the six

months following the coup, as Vietnam was wracked with political instability, Lodge tired of his inability to accomplish anything and resigned in the spring of 1964.

Logistics (Allied)

As the French withdrew from Vietnam they took the bulk of the serviceable military equipment with them, leaving the fledgling South Vietnamese Army with a hodgepodge of broken and inferior matériel. They did not establish a logistical support structure for the Vietnamese either. As US troops poured into the country, the proportion of combat troops to logistical personnel was abnormally

Above: A Marine picks up a new pair of boots at a direct exchange point during Operation Harvest Moon.

high. The result was a logistical nightmare as thousands of tons of matériel poured into the country faster than it could be inventoried, stored, or delivered, overwhelming all available distribution networks.

The result was the buildup of a surplus estimated in 1967 to be in excess of two million tons. Though there were problems, there is no record of any operation ever being curtailed because of logistics,

Above: A CH-47 Chinook delivers ammunition to a 105mm firing battery.

and the advent of the cargo helicopter insured that consumable or expendable matériel could be rapidly deployed to the point of need. An inadvertent outcome of the US logistical operation was that the ARVN followed the US example of lavish consumption. When the US departed, the ARVN immediately began to experience problems in support, particularly with the supply and transportation of artillery ammunition.

Logistics (North Vietnamese and Viet Cong)

Initially the North Vietnamese and Viet Cong made use of weapons left over from World War II and captured from the French in the Indochina war. However, beginning in the late 1950s, increasing levels of aid from the Soviet Union and the People's Republic of China allowed them to standardize their small arms, mortars, and artillery. They were not successful, however, in restructuring their battlefield support system.

The overwhelming presence of American naval and air power precluded them from using a conventional method for supporting their deployed forces. They could not move large quantities of matériel forward to support an operation without significant loss. For this reason, they moved their supplies in small quantities, but with large numbers of carriers. This allowed them to buildup stockpiles in the sanctuary and secure areas where the Ho Chi Minh Trail debouched into South Vietnam. The same problem prevented them from rapidly reinforcing an operation or switching directions during a battle. This accounts for the pauses that followed each offensive until later stages of war. After the US withdrew, the North Vietnamese significantly improved the Ho Chi Minh Trail and adopted a conventional logistics structure for their final offensive.

Lon Nol

Actually born in Tay Ninh, Vietnam, Lon Nol was the Defense Minister in Prince

Above right: A truck can just be seen leaving a damaged road that crosses a river on the Ho Chi Minh Trail west of Kontum.

Right: The Cambodian President, General Lon Nol, waves to soldiers returning from a battle along Highway 1.

Norodom Sihanouk's government in Cambodia. He was pro-Western and opposed Sihanouk's neutrality, engineering a coup against him in March 1970. Sihanouk blamed the CIA for the coup, but there is no evidence that they were involved. Ill-prepared for war, Lon Nol attacked both the North Vietnamese sanctuaries in eastern Cambodia and the Khmer Rouge. His actions, including his support for the US Cambodian Incursion, precipitated a disaster. He alienated the population and they flocked to support the Khmer Rouge who destroyed his government in 1975.

Long Binh

Long Binh was a major United States Army headquarters and logistics installation constructed just outside the city of Bien Hoa, 20 miles north of Saigon. The US Field Force II, US Army Vietnam (USARV), and the ARVN III Corps Headquarters were all located there.

Long Binh Jail (LBJ)

The main US Army Vietnam stockade was known as the Long Binh Jail. It was derisively called the LBJ, a play on President Lyndon Baines Johnson's initials, by the troops. On August 29, 1968, several hundred African-American prisoners rioted there, the first widely reported incident of racial strife within the American military in Vietnam.

Long Tieng

Sometimes referred to as 20 Alternate, Long Tieng, was the headquarters of General Vang Pao's Hmong forces in Laos. Located in a valley in the southwest corner of Xieng Khouang province, the US Ambassador to Laos declared it off-limits to anyone except those few American forward air controllers, T-28 support personnel, Special Forces trainers, and CIA case officers who directly supported the Hmong.

Long Range Reconnaissance Patrols (LRRP)

Originally organized by the Special Forces to conduct reconnaissance deep

Right: A LRRP leader briefs his men on the mission.

Below: A Long Range Reconnaissance Patrol (LRRP) runs for a UH-1D during an extraction in III Corps.

within Viet Cong and North Vietnamese controlled areas, the success of the Long Range Reconnaissance Patrols (LRRP), called "Lurps" by the troops, prompted MACV to order all divisions and separate brigades to form their own LRRP units on a priority basis. Beginning in 1967, several separate LRRP companies were formed. The only National Guard rifle company to serve in Vietnam was a LRRP company, Company B, 151st Infantry, Indiana National Guard.

Recognizing the value of such formations, the US Army formalized the organization of these companies. They were converted to companies C through I and K through P, 75th Infantry (Ranger), and were the forerunner of today's US Army Ranger Battalions.

Lowenstein, Allard K.

Allard Lowenstein was a liberal antiwar activist who went to South Vietnam as a civilian observer of the 1967 elections.

Convinced that Johnson would not de-escalate the war, when he returned he organized the "Dump Johnson" campaign in 1967–1968, and helped entice Senator Eugene McCarthy to run against him in New Hampshire. He mobilized a corps of young campaign workers who nearly administered a stunning defeat to the President in the primary. At the Democratic National Convention he led the opposition to the nomination of Hubert H Humphrey.

Luc Luong Dac Biet (LLDB)

The Luc Luong Dac Biet (LLDB), the ARVN Special Forces, were initially established in 1960 by Ngo Dinh Nhu as a 2,000 man private army for him and his brother Ngo Dinh Diem. Their most notorious battle was the coordinated raids on the buddhist pagodas in 1963. Following the November 1963 overthrow of the Diem regime, the LLDB were reorganized along the lines of the US Special Forces and integrated into the ARVN. When the US Special Forces were withdrawn, the LLDB were disbanded and the units that operated with them were integrated into the ARVN Ranger Command.

Lynd, Staughton

A radical Quaker pacifist, Lynd was an assistant professor of history at Yale. He chaired the 1965 Students for a Democratic Society march on Washington and made a trip to North Vietnam with the antiwar activist Tom Hayden. While in Vietnam he described the war as immoral, illegal, and anti-democratic. Yale President Kingman Brewster accused him of "aiding the enemy." When Lynd left Yale, he was never able to find another teaching position and eventually became a lawyer.

Below: Troops congregate in the courtyard of the LLDB headquarters in Dong Tre.

Right: A Vietnamese Special Forces officer shows his adviser the position of a proposed ambush on a map.

Below right: A Special Forces NCO and an LLDB sergeant show a Montagnard crew how to fuze 105mm howitzer rounds.

M

MacArthur, Douglas
One of the most famous American Generals who fought in World War II and Korea, MacArthur was considered America's foremost military expert on Asia. He reportedly advised Presidents Kennedy and Johnson against involvement in a land war in Asia because of their large reserve of manpower.

MacArthur, Operation
Operation MacArthur officially lasted from October 13, 1967 to January 31, 1969 in the western central highlands of II Corps. The 1967 phase is more commonly known as the Battle of Dak To. Undetected, NVA forces had spent months fortifying the ridgelines and peaks around Dak To. During the first week of November, units from the 4th Infantry Division successfully cleared the hills to the south. But on November 6, Task Force Black of the 173rd Airborne Brigade took heavy casualties on Hill 823 south of Ben Het. On November 11, the 66th NVA Regiment caught them again in a U-shaped ambush under heavy triple canopy jungle, which reduced the effectiveness of air and artillery support. On November 14, two ARVN battalions engaged the 24th NVA Regiment northeast of Dak To in a bitter four-day battle. On November 19, the commander of the 173rd Airborne Brigade ordered an assault on Hill 875.

The 2nd Battalion, 503rd Infantry, was stopped cold. They were counterattacked by waves of NVA soldiers who enveloped and decimated the American unit, which hastily formed a tight perimeter and fought to hold on until reinforcements could arrive. NVA gunners shot down six helicopters attempting to resupply the trapped battalion, but some ammunition was delivered, and they held out for 50 hours before they were relieved. General Westmoreland proclaimed the Battle of Dak To "the beginning of a great defeat for the enemy." General Giap's perception of what had happened was probably markedly different.

Machineguns (Allied)
The allies used six different machineguns, four American and two Australian. Throughout the war the Vietnamese were equipped with the Browning model 1919A4 light machinegun, a belt-fed .30 caliber weapon. Later they were also issued the 7.62mm M60 general-purpose machinegun as well. The Australians used the L4 7.62mm Bren light

Right: An Air Force CH-3 approaches a landing zone.

Below right: A gunner stands by on his M2HB .50 caliber machinegun as his boat moves up the river.

Right: General Douglas MacArthur (center) at a conference in Manila just before the outbreak of World War II.

MACHINEGUNS (ALLIED)

Right: PFC Milton Cook of the 25th Infantry Division returns a sniper's fire with his M60 machinegun.

Below: A gunner links several ammunition belts together and readies his M60 machinegun.

Opposite, top: A Special Forces soldier cleans a mini-gun he salvaged from a downed helicopter and mounted on a jury-rigged mount to bolster his camp's defenses.

Opposite, bottom: A group of CIDG trainees fire a M1919A6 .30 caliber machinegun at the III Corps training center.

machinegun. Unlike the other weapons, the L4 was fed from a 30 round box magazine, which reduced its effectiveness in a sustained fire role. The Australians opted to trade in their L4s for American M60s. They also employed the L2A1 heavy barrel FN FAL. This was also a 30-round box magazine fed gun, however both Australia and New Zealand kept this gun in service. American SEAL teams used the Stoner Mark 23 Commando, a 5.56mm lightweight belt-fed machinegun. All of the allied forces also employed the Browning M2HB .50 caliber heavy machinegun.

Machineguns (North Vietnamese and Viet Cong)

North Vietnam and the Viet Cong used a variety of Soviet machineguns, and their Chinese copies, in calibers from 7.62mm to 14.5mm. The most commonly encountered light machineguns early in the war were the DPM and RPD, both in 7.62mm. Later the SG43 Goryunov and the Chinese Type 53 copy were also encountered in numbers. The DShK38, and the Type54 Chinese copy, a 12.7mm heavy machinegun, were encountered in large numbers in both the ground and antiaircraft role throughout war. The KPV 14.5mm Vladimirov heavy machinegun was frequently encountered as a twin-mount, the ZPU-2, in an anti-aircraft role along the Ho Chi Minh Trail and later inside South Vietnam.

Madam Ngo Dinh Nhu

The wife of Ngo Dinh Nhu, President Diem's younger brother and chief adviser, Madam Nhu was the defacto First Lady of South Vietnam and wielded enormous power. Aggressive, outspoken, and fervently anticommunist, she was prone to controversial pronouncements such as referring to the buddhist immolations as barbeques. Internally many Vietnamese referred to her as the "Dragon Lady." She was traveling in the United States when her husband and brother-in-law were assassinated and she went into exile in Rome.

Madman Strategy

President Richard M Nixon's attempt to fool the North Vietnamese leadership into accepting a negotiated settlement was known as the "madman" strategy. Following his re-election in 1972, Nixon temporarily abandoned diplomacy. For 12 days in December, the US unleashed a ferocious bombing attack on the North Vietnamese capital of Hanoi. Nixon gave no explanation for the bombing; he wanted to appear irrational, desperate, willing to do anything to get what he

Above, right: Master Sergeant James Cullen of the 9th Infantry Division looks over a 12.7mm Type 54 heavy machinegun captured south of Saigon.

Right: Early in the war the Soviet RPD-46 7.62mm machinegun with a flat magazine was often seen.

Opposite: President Richard Nixon surrounded by combat troops at the First Division base in Di An, ten miles northeast of Saigon.

wanted—even use nuclear weapons. Ostensibly, Nixon's "madman" strategy was successful. In January 1973, the United States and North Vietnam negotiated a peace settlement. However, the terms were little better than the ones proposed by North Vietnam in 1969, and more than 25,000 American lives were lost in the interim.

Malaysia

Malaysia provided only training and a limited number of specialized vehicles to Vietnam. However, because they had experienced an internal insurgency and, with the help of the British, successfully defeated it on the way to nationhood, the Vietnamese copied a number of seemingly successful innovations. One of these, the Strategic Hamlet Program, turned out to be a disaster.

Malheur I and II, Operations

In early 1967, Vietcong and NVA activity significantly increased in I Corps. To relieve some of the pressure on the Marines, MACV moved the 196th Light Infantry Brigade from Tay Ninh to Chu Lai and the 3rd Brigade of the First Cavalry Division from northern Binh Dinh province to southern Quang Ngai province. On April 22, MACV activated Task Force Oregon, a 15,000-man unit, in southern I Corps. On May 11, 1967 five battalions of Task Force Oregon launched Operation Malheur I in and among the fortified hamlets around Duc Pho south of Quang Ngai City. The object of the operation was to begin to clear Highway 1 from the southern Corps boundary to Danang. Many of the ensuing firefights took place inside the villages and hamlets. US forces employed artillery, tactical air, and heavy naval gunfire support. The destruction of civilian areas was massive. By early July the action had tapered off. Task Force Oregon then immediately launched Operation Malheur II, to push the Viet Cong and NVA units away from the coast and into the mountains to the west. Again, heavy fighting took place in densely populated areas.

When Malheur II ended in August, Task Force Oregon proclaimed it a success, though the VC 2nd Regiment and the 2nd NVA Division quickly reoccupied the area as US forces withdrew. While the heavy use of napalm, air strikes, artillery and naval gunfire reduced US casualties, the US Agency for International Development logged more than 6,400 civilian casualties and the large-scale destruction directly

Below: President Lyndon B Johnson (far right) met with world leaders at the Manila Conference. From left to right the leaders at the time were: Ky (S. Vietnam), Holt (Australia), Park (S. Korea), Marcos (Philippines), Holyoake (New Zealand), Thieu (S. Vietnam), and Thanon (Thailand).

resulted in a significant increase in the number of refugees.

Manila Conference

The Manila Conference convened on October 25, 1966, and was attended by President Johnson, and representatives of all the Allies, including Australia, the Philippines, Thailand, New Zealand, South Korea, and South Vietnam. It was staged partly in response to efforts by the international community and by the communist leadership of North Vietnam to seek a negotiated settlement to the escalating conflict in Southeast Asia. The most important result of the discussions at the Manila Conference was a pledge by the US to withdraw from Vietnam within six months if North Vietnam would withdraw completely from the South. However, the primary motive for the offer lay elsewhere. Most analysts recognize that it was largely a piece of political theater by a US government that wished to appear to the American and South Vietnamese public fully committed to peace in Southeast Asia. The conditions it attached to the withdrawal were deliberately harsh and therefore

unacceptable to the Democratic Republic of Vietnam.

Mansfield, Michael Joseph

Mike Mansfield, a Democratic Senator from Montana and Senate majority leader from 1961 to 1977, was an early supporter of Ngo Dinh Diem. He also initially supported increased US involvement in the war. However, after traveling in Vietnam and observing the war firsthand, in 1965 he counseled President Johnson not to introduce US troops. By 1967 he was a vocal critic of the war. In 1971, he introduced an amendment to the Selective Service bill that would require the withdrawal of US troops within nine months. His amendment passed the Senate, but was defeated in the House and instead a provision was substituted that urged President Nixon to establish a firm schedule for the withdrawal of US troops. This was the first time that Congress officially went on record in support of withdrawal.

Mao Tse Tung (Mao Zedong)

The leader of the People's Republic of China throughout the 1960s, Mao Tse

Left: Michael Mansfield initially supported Diem but eventually became a critic of the war.

Tung opposed the Soviet policy for ending the war in Vietnam through negotiation and counseled an armed struggle based on a protracted "people's war." Ho Chi Minh and General Giap made a number of changes to the Maoist doctrine in order to adapt it to the reality of the battlefield in Vietnam.

Because of the worsening schism between the People's Republic of China and the Soviet Union, in 1969 Mao turned to the United States as a counterweight. In February 1972, President Nixon went to China and the two nations signed the Shanghai Communiqué, which helped pave the way to the end of the US involvement in Vietnam.

Marble Mountain

A rocky outcrop south of Danang, Marble Mountain is honeycombed with caves, and was a major Viet Cong stronghold throughout the war. A trail led

Below: Chairman Mao Tse Tung of the People's Republic of China meets President Richard Nixon.

up the southeast side of the mountain to a buddhist shrine, where the interior could be accessed. A massive stone Buddha was located under a light shaft near the center of the mountain. There were numerous small buddhist and Cham stone carvings in the myriad of side caves and tunnels. The I Corps prisoner of war camp was located just north of the mountain.

March on the Pentagon

A major antiwar demonstration was staged from October 21–23, 1967. Organized by the Student Mobilization and National Mobilization Committees, the protest drew 100,000 people to the Lincoln Memorial in Washington, and 35,000 continued from there to march to the Pentagon. The 24-hour, sit-down protest in front of the building was punctuated by violence, but was almost universally condemned by the press and the public alike.

Below: Smoke partially obscures Marble Mountain south of Danang. The I Corps POW Camp is in the foreground.

Marigold, Operation

Operation Marigold was the code name for a failed peace initiative centered around US Ambassador Henry Cabot Lodge and the Polish representative on the International Control Commission, Janusz Lewandowski. Lewandowski's claim that he had a substantial peace offer from Hanoi prompted secret negotiations in the summer of 1966.

Although the talks initially seemed to hold great promise, Lewandowski's limitations as a diplomat and skepticism on the part of the US prevented any breakthrough and a planned December meeting between the US and the DRV in Hanoi never took place.

Market Time, Operation

In 1965, MACV estimated that the Viet Cong were receiving up to 70 percent of their supplies by sea. On March 11, 1965, Operation Market Time began. It was a joint effort by the US Navy and the South Vietnamese Navy to interdict the flow of supplies by patrolling all 1,200 miles of South Vietnam's coast. On July 31, 1965, Task Force 115, the Coastal Surveillance Force, was formed and had headquarters at Cam Rahn Bay. Three

Surveillance Zones, an outer barrier, an inner barrier, and an air barrier were formed. Initially the air barrier, 100 to 150 miles from shore, was patrolled by Skyraiders from carriers on Dixie Station, but by 1965, P-2 Neptune's, P-3 Orions, and P-5 Marlin amphibians, were performing the air screening mission. Closer to land was an Outer Surface Barrier patrolled by destroyers, minesweepers, radar picket ships and Coast Guard cutters. Between 1967 and 1971 the Royal Australian Navy provided three guided missile destroyers for this force. This barrier operated within 40 miles of the South Vietnamese coast from the 17th parallel to the Cambodian border in the Gulf of Thailand. In the inner or shallow water barrier, the US Navy deployed swift boats, shallow draft 50ft vessels armed with .50 caliber machineguns and 81mm mortars. The Vietnamese navy Junk Force also operated in the inner barrier. From January 1966 to July 1967 Market Time forces sank several North Vietnamese steel hulled trawlers and inspected or boarded more than 700,000 vessels in South Vietnamese waters. Except for five enemy ships that were intercepted trying

Above: An American officer and a Vietnamese sailor examine the manifest of a civilian junk.

to resupply their forces in the aftermath of the Tet Offensive, after Market Time was in place the North Vietnamese gave up trying to resupply over the beach. As part of Vietnamization, the Vietnamese Navy took control of all of the assets working in the inner barrier in September 1970. All of the Coast Guard cutters and some of the other ships patrolling the outer sea barrier were transferred to the Vietnamese between 1971 and 1972.

Martin, Graham A

Graham Martin was the last US ambassador to the Republic of South Vietnam. A staunch anticommunist, he replaced Ellsworth Bunker in 1973. He was emotionally engaged in the war because his stepson had been killed there earlier. He

Right: The press surrounds a grim faced Ambassador Graham Martin on the USS *Blue Ridge* the day after Saigon fell.

was also irascible, and difficult to approach, which soured his relationship with President Nguyen Van Thieu. He firmly believed that both the American and South Vietnamese position was stronger than it really was, and would not accept any contrary reports from his subordinates. Because of this, he delayed the order for the evacuation of the US Embassy until it was nearly too late, and could only be carried out by helicopter. The result of the delay to evacuate was that piles of classified documents and thousands of South Vietnamese supporters and employees of the US were left behind. Even after his return to the United States he refused to accept responsibility for what had happened.

Masher/White Wing, Operation
The 1st Cavalry Division launched Operation Masher on January 24, 1966, in northern Binh Dinh province in the II Corps Tactical Zone. It was the first search and destroy operation of the war. President Johnson insisted that the name of the operation be changed because Masher was too crude a title for a nation-building operation and would have an adverse effect on public opinion. This was indicative of the degree to which politics intruded into the conduct of the war. On February 4, it was officially renamed White Wing, even though it had nothing to do with nation-building.

During the fighting the Viet Cong 1st and 2nd regiments and the 18th and 98th NVA Regiments were forced away from the coast and into the An Lao Valley. Officially, by the time it ended on March 6, 1966, the operation returned 140,000 people to government control and ended the pressure on Bong Son, Quang Ngai, and Qui Nhon.

Critics of the operation charged that the lavish use of firepower simply converted the population into refugees. As virtually no pacification effort was associated with the operation, the enemy soon resumed control of the area.

Massachusetts Striker, Operation
In response to intelligence reports of increasing North Vietnamese logistical activity, on March 1, 1969, the 101st Airborne Division air assaulted into the A Shau Valley. Although there was little contact with the Viet Cong and North Vietnamese they began to uncover massive amounts of supplies.

Throughout April and May 1969, units of the 101st Airborne Division destroyed caches of weapons, ammunition, equipment, and food. On May 1, the 1/502nd, discovered a major supply base that contained a complete field hospital and a heavy machine repair facility. On May 8, the operation was terminated. Though Operation Massachusetts Striker did not produce any major battles, it severely disrupted NVA logistics in I Corps.

May Day Tribe
A protest group led by Rennie Davis (one of the Chicago Eight) came to be known as the May Day Tribe. Davis and his supporters staged a protest in Washington beginning on May 1, 1971 that attempted to completely shutdown the city. The attempt failed, and more than 12,000 were arrested during the course of the four-day demonstration.

Mayflower, Operation
The code name Operation Mayflower was given to the May 1965 diplomatic initiative by the Johnson administration to broker a peace in Vietnam, through cessation on the bombing campaign. Under increasing domestic and

international pressure to halt the aerial bombardment of the North (see Operation Rolling Thunder), Johnson developed the initiative firstly to deflect criticism and secondly to make it appear that the DRV was the real aggressor, allowing for a further escalation in the bombing. On May 12, bombing missions were halted, but attempts to establish diplomatic contact with the DRV by the US Ambassador in Moscow met with rebuff, and on May 18 the campaign resumed. By highlighting the DRV's failure to negotiate, Johnson was able to deflect criticism and justify the escalation of Operation Rolling Thunder.

Above: Members of the 101st Infantry Division take a break in the jungle during Operation Massachusetts Striker.

Left: 1st Cavalry Division troops skirt a small pond near Bong Son during Operation Masher/White Wing.

Right: Rennie Davis, leader of the May Day Tribe looks over the shoulder of Dr Ralph Abernathy at a press conference.

McCain, John Sydney Jr

A US admiral, McCain served as the Commander in Chief Pacific (CINCPAC) from July 1968 to September 1972. McCain was a strong supporter of President Nixon's Vietnamization program. He was also a consistent advocate of the heavy bombing of North Vietnam and the mining of its ports, harbors, and rivers. Though he was not directly responsible for either making or implementing policy in Vietnam, during the Easter Offensive of 1972 he successfully advocated the mining of North Vietnamese harbors and the strategic bombing of the area around Hanoi and Haiphong, even though his son was a prisoner in Hanoi at the time.

McCarthy, Eugene Joseph

A Democratic Senator from Minnesota, and member of the influential Senate Foreign Relations Committee, McCarthy initially supported the Gulf of Tonkin Resolution. However, by 1967 he had become a leading critic of the war. On November 30, 1967 he challenged President Johnson for the Democratic presidential nomination. He attempted to merge his support for the antiwar movement with political office and ran as an avowed antiwar candidate.

When he won 42 percent of the vote in the New Hampshire primary on March 12, 1968, Robert Kennedy also decided to challenge the president. McCarthy's strong showing was also a major factor in President Johnson's decision not to seek a second term. McCarthy lost the nomination to Hubert Humphrey at the Chicago Democratic convention.

McCloy, John Jay

John McCloy was a member of the Senior Advisory Group on Vietnam, often referred to as the " wise men." He fully accepted the Domino Theory and told President Johnson in 1965 that Vietnam should be considered a test case of the Containment Policy. At the crucial meeting in March 1968 to discuss possible reactions to the Tet Offensive, he adopted the minority view that an additional 200,000 troops should be provided to MACV.

McCone, John Alex

McCone was a conservative Republican that President Kennedy appointed as the Director of the CIA in September 1961 to succeed Allen Dulles. Considered a hard liner, McCone nevertheless argued

against support for the South Vietnamese President, Ngo Dinh Diem. He was a vocal internal critic of President Johnson's escalation of the war, and was eased out of office by 1965.

McGovern, George S

Between 1968 and 1972, McGovern led an effort to restructure the Democratic Party. He de-emphasized the support of urban machines and the South, in favor of women and minorities. Campaigning on the theme of an immediate withdrawal from the Vietnam War, McGovern became the Democratic nominee for the 1972 presidential race. He was undoubtedly the most liberal presidential candidate in more than a century and, though

Above: Admiral John McCain was the Commander-in-Chief, Pacific Forces (CINCPAC) at the height of the war, while his son was a POW.

his antiwar stance struck a chord with many Americans, President Nixon buried him in a landslide.

McNamara, Robert Strange

McNamara, who held the office from 1961 to 1968, was the longest serving Secretary of Defense. He proved to be one of the most influential figures in the history of the Vietnam War. A firm believer in technology and statistical methodology for measurements of progress, McNamara surrounded himself with systems analysts and game theorists

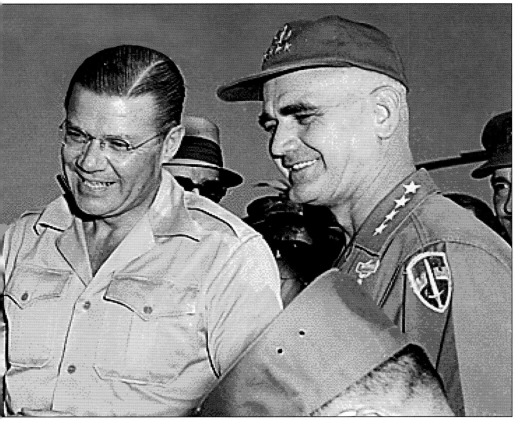

Above left: Senator Eugene McCarthy challenged President Johnson in the New Hampshire Presidential Primary in 1968, ultimately leading to Johnson's withdrawal.

Above: CIA Director John McCone repeatedly clashed with MACV over the number of enemy forces in South Vietnam.

Left: Secretary of Defense Robert McNamara with General William Westmoreland.

and routinely ignored the professional military advice offered by the Joint Chiefs of Staff. He was an advocate of intervention, bombing North Vietnam, and graduated response. He was puzzled by North Vietnam's resilience. He exercised both logistical and operational control over the war, frequently overriding military decisions made in the field. By 1967, he had become disillusioned and started offering contradictory advice to the president. In frustration President Johnson asked him to resign, which he did in November 1967. Later McNamara admitted that he "misunderstood the nature of the conflict."

Opposite: A Lieutenant guides medevac helicopter into a small landing zone to pick up
wounded after an ambush.

Left: A door gunner helps a wounded man into a
helicopter for medevac.

McNamara Line

Early in the war Secretary of Defense
Robert McNamara advocated the construction of an electronic barrier across
Southeast Asia. It would consist of a
large number of air and ground emplaced
sensors, which would transmit their readouts to both fixed geographical posts and
orbiting aircraft.

The purpose of the barrier was to fore-
warn US military units of NVA troop and
logistical operations down the Ho Chi
Minh Trail and across the Demilitarized
Zone. They could then attack the infiltrators at will. All it really did was demonstrate McNamara's naïve confidence in
American technology.

McNaughton, John T

McNaughton was a hard-line adviser to
Secretary of Defense Robert McNamara.
After passage of the Gulf of Tonkin
Resolution he argued that serious action
should be taken against North Vietnam,
and that only direct intervention by the
United States could save South Vietnam
from the communists. He recommended
that combat units be immediately introduced, airbases constructed, and naval
units stationed in the Gulf of Tonkin. By
1967 however, based on his participation
in the Jason Study, which found that US
actions in Vietnam had failed, he began
to question America's role. He was killed
in a plane crash in July 1967.

Meaney, George

From 1955 to 1979, George Meaney was
president of the American Federation of
Labor–Congress of Industrial Organizations (AFL–CIO). He was a strong supporter of both President Kennedy and
President Johnson's positions on
Vietnam. During the 1972 presidential
campaign he refused to endorse the pro-
labor but antiwar George McGovern.
Nor would he endorse President Nixon,
however, after the election he supported
his Vietnamization program.

Left: CBS News uses a jeep as a camera dolly
while interviewing the CO of the 1st Battalion
1st Marines during the Battle of Hue City.

Medal of Honor

See Congressional Medal of Honor.

Medevac

The term medevac was an abbreviation formed by combining the words, medical and evacuation. In Vietnam it was routinely associated with the movement of casualties by helicopter, however, it was also generally applied to the movement of casualties by any other means as well. The US Army initially deployed helicopter ambulance units to Vietnam in April 1962. Their numbers expanded rapidly as the troop deployments increased. At the height of the war no casualty was more than one hour's flying time from a hospital, and statistics indicate that 98 percent of the wounded that were evacuated lived. As a result, the rate of deaths as a percentage of hits fell to 19 percent in Vietnam compared with 29.3 percent in World War II and 26.3 percent in Korea.

Media and Vietnam

For many American veterans of the Vietnam War "media" is a word that evokes a strong, almost visceral, negative reaction. Even today they believe that journalists proved to be as much an enemy as the NVA or Viet Cong. Journalists believed that they were not accountable to government authority in the war zone, but instead to their corporate headquarters or to their international audience. As the war dragged on, more and more of the younger journalists adopted an antiwar tone in their writing and broadcasts. The troops became convinced that the media purposely portrayed them in the worst possible light, and rarely if ever filed a negative report concerning the actions of the Viet Cong or the NVA. They were particularly concerned that television coverage in effect, fueled the antiwar movement, and routinely cast them in a negative light. In this regard the military was in fact its own worst enemy. Official pronouncements rarely squared with what the reporters observed on the battlefield. This led to what became known as the "credibility gap." The conflict between the government and the media, which had festered during the Johnson administration, essentially became an open war during Nixon's. In the final analysis, it cannot be objectively shown that the media overtly affected the outcome of the war at all. Conversely, as older and more experienced journalists were replaced with younger ones, it is clear that the tone of the reporting became increasingly negative. In the search for why America failed to achieve her objectives in Vietnam, the media has become a popular target. Military–Media relations, strained during the Vietnam War, have never fully recovered and the press have only received minimal access to US military operations ever since.

Medics and Corpsmen

In Vietnam there were two medics or corpsmen authorized for each army or marine rifle platoon. However, as a result of casualties this was often reduced to one. They were responsible for initiating emergency care and evacuation from the battlefield. They stopped or restricted bleeding, secured airways for breathing, splinted fractures, relieved pain, and prepared the wounded for transport. Although under the terms of the Geneva Convention medical personnel are not supposed to carry weapons, in Vietnam virtually all medics were armed in order to protect both themselves and their patients. Their courage was legendary. Of 238 Medals of Honor awarded during the war, 12 went to Army medics and four to Navy corpsmen.

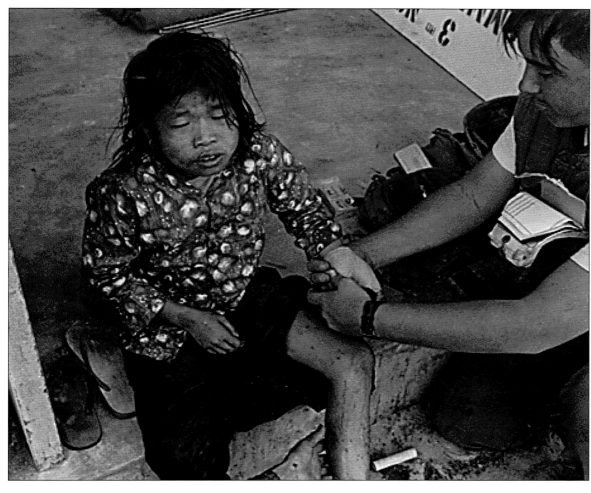

Opposite: A CBS reporter
captures the meeting
between Maxwell Taylor,
Ambassador to Vietnam,
and his son, a soldier in the
101st Airborne Division in
1965.

Left: A medic treats a
young girl wounded in an
NVA mortar attack during
the Battle of Namo Village.

Below: A Special Forces
medic, assisted by another
team member and a local
nurse he trained, debrides
the wound a CIDG Striker
suffered during a mortar
attack

Right: Captain Ernest Medina was Lieutenant William Calley's company commander at the time of the atrocity in My Lai.

Medina, Ernest L

Captain Ernest Medina commanded Company C, 1st Battalion 20th Infantry, of the 11th Infantry Brigade, Americal Division. On March 16, 1968, a platoon from his company committed the My Lai massacre. On March 10, 1970 he was charged with murder, manslaughter, and assault as a result of what happened at the My Lai 4 Hamlet. On September 22, 1970 a court-martial cleared him of all charges. He resigned from the Army on October 15, 1971.

Mekong Delta

The Mekong Delta contains more than 26,000 square miles. The most fertile and intensively farmed area of South Vietnam it was of great strategic importance. Formed by silt deposits, it is

Right: Captain Ernest Medina was Lieutenant William Calley's company commander at the time of the atrocity in My Lai.

Below: A French-designed river craft used by the Vietnamese Navy chugs up the Mekong in 1964.

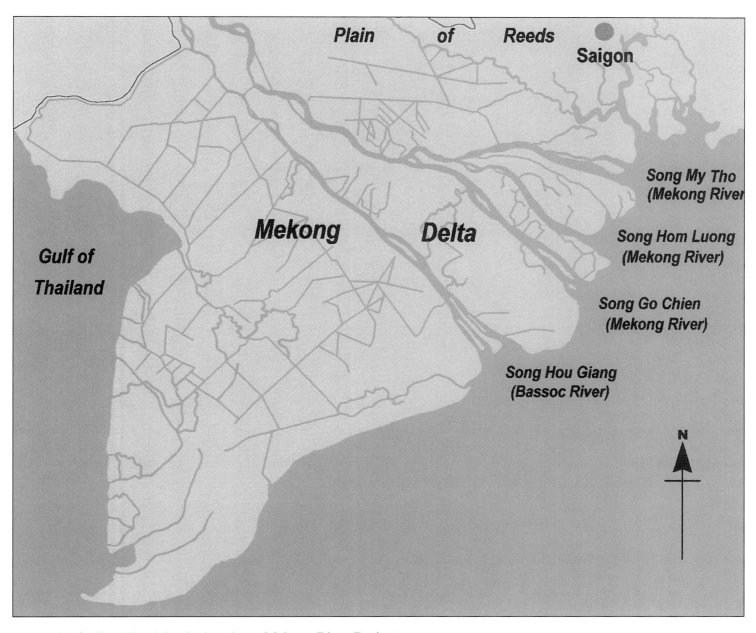

Above: A map showing the major outlets of the Mekong River to the South China Sea.

extremely fertile. The delta is largely inhabited by ethnic Vietnamese, however there are large concentrations of Khmer in the west and southwest. From 1962 to 1966 the Viet Cong controlled most of the northern Delta. A significant amount of the urban combat during the Tet Offensive occurred in the delta. Afterward an intensive pacification effort and the tremendous losses suffered by the Viet Cong during the Tet Offensive allowed the Saigon government to achieve control of the most important portions. IV Corps was the military command structure for the Mekong Delta. Athough of prime importance, very few North Vietnamese units served in the Mekong Delta because of its distance from North Vietnam and the fact that the Viet Cong managed to maintain a significant presence there throughout the war.

Mekong River Project

An ambitious project was fostered by the Economic Commission for Asia and the Far East, an office of the United Nations, to harness the potential of the Mekong Basin as a transport network, and as a source of agricultural irrigation and hydroelectric power. Funding for the project, which began in 1958, was supplied by 26 countries and numerous charitable foundations.

Mendenhall, Joseph A

Joseph Mendenhall served in the American embassy in Saigon between 1959 and 1962, and was director of the US Agency for International Development mission in Laos from 1965 to 1968. In 1963 President Kennedy sent Mendenhall and General Victor Krulak on a fact-finding mission to South Vietnam. On their return Krulak reported that the war was being aggressively fought and would be won. Mendenhall however, reported that there was a virtual breakdown in the civilian government and the Diem regime was fostering a religious war between the catholics and the buddhists, the results of which would be that the Viet Cong were going to win. After listening to the report President Kennedy remarked, "You two did visit the same country, didn't you?"

Menu, Operation

Operation Menu was the code name for President Nixon's secret B-52 raids into Cambodia from March 18, 1969 to May

Above: A flight of B-52s unloads a mix of 750lb and 1,000lb bombs on a target.

26, 1970. The first Arc Light raid was targeted against base area 353 just west of the border and was code-named Breakfast. Additional NVA and Viet Cong sanctuaries were targeted and given the code names of Supper, Lunch, Dessert, and Snack. After General Lon Nol deposed Prince Sihanouk, the need for secrecy disappeared when he appealed for US support against the Khmer Rouge and North Vietnamese units in Cambodia.

Meo
See Hmong.

MIA
See Missing in Action.

Michigan State University Advisory Group
Group of US political and sociological advisers that from 1951 worked with Diem's government to create an effective

Right: President Nixon with President Thieu during a 1969 visit to South Vietnam.

Above: The American Military Assistance Advisory Group–Indochina was later re-designated as the Military Assistance Advisory Group, Vietnam (MAAG–V).

infrastructure for the Republic of Vietnam. Although the US government hoped that the MSU could help the RVN to become a self-sustaining democracy, the group failed to overcome the inefficiencies, corruption and intrigue that characterized RVN politics. The criticism of Diem that came from within the group prompted him to cancel the contract in 1962.

Midway Island Conference

In June 1969, President Nixon met with the President Nguyen Van Thieu at Midway. The meeting, the first between the two men, was convened to avoid antiwar demonstrations in the US. Thieu's agenda was to stall the process of American withdrawal that he knew to

be inevitable and for which Nixon sought his approval. He was also interested in promoting a Korean-type solution to the conflict, where the North and South would be separated by a demilitarized zone policed by US soldiers. For his part, Nixon wanted approval for his plans to negotiate with the DRV, and to act as the representative of the RVN. Hailed as a success by Nixon, who ordered withdrawals to begin, Thieu left the conference feeling that he had a strong ally in Nixon, and guarantees of continued American support. In reality, Nixon and Kissinger had already agreed that the withdrawals would begin with or without the approval of the RVN.

Mike Force

See Mobile Strike Force Command.

Military Airlift Command (MAC)

Created in 1966 from the Military Air Transport Command, the Military Airlift Command (MAC) was responsible for

all strategic airlift in support of military operations in Southeast Asia until the collapse of South Vietnam in 1975. Though MAC began the war using propeller driven aircraft, in April 1965 the C-141 Starlifter became operational, and in December 1969 the C-5 Galaxy joined the fleet. These two jet aircraft became the mainstay of strategic airlift.

Military Assistance Advisory Group—Vietnam (MAAG—V)

In 1955, the Military Assistance Advisory Group (MAAG), Indochina, originally formed to assist in the transfer of American equipment to the French during the Indochina War, was re-designated as the Military Assistance Advisory Group, Vietnam, (MAAG—V). In 1955 and 1956, MAAG—V assumed the responsibility of training the Vietnamese National Army. It imposed standard American military doctrine and trained the Vietnamese to fight a conventional invasion across the Demilitarized

Zone. As part of President Kennedy's move to a counterinsurgency effort, he upgraded and replaced MAAG—V with the Military Assistance Command Vietnam (MACV) in 1962.

Military Assistance Command Vietnam (MACV)

Located on the Tan Son Nhut Air Base just outside of Saigon, MACV was a specified command reporting to the Commander in Chief Pacific. Although technically subordinate to CINCPAC, the MACV commander routinely dealt directly with the Joint Chiefs of Staff and the US Ambassador to South Vietnam. Even though it was a unified command, MACV military operations were geographically limited to within the borders of South Vietnam itself. Operations in Laos, North Vietnam, and at sea were directed through the Pacific Command and carried out by units and organizations not under MACV control. MACV did not command indigenous Vietnamese units, but had to coordinate US operations with Vietnamese operations through the Vietnamese Joint General Staff. This cumbersome arrangement frequently resulted in a less than optimal application of military power.

From its establishment in June 1962 to its disestablishment in March 1973, there were four commanders of MACV, including General Paul D Harkins, General William Westmoreland, General Creighton Abrams, and General Frederick Weyand.

Military Regions (MR)

The Vietnamese government divided South Vietnam militarily into four major geographical regions, known as Corps Tactical Zones, and a number of special zones, such as the Capital Military District around Saigon, and the Quang Da Special Zone around Danang. In July 1970, the Corps Tactical Zones were renamed Military Regions. The special zones essentially remained the same, however some urban centers were designated as autonomous cities.

Military Revolutionary Council

A council of generals was formed in the wake of the coup d'état against Diem,

Above: US Military Assistance Advisory Group H-21 helicopters ferry Vietnamese Rangers into battle on the Plain of Reeds.

which effectively ruled the RVN from November 1963 to mid-December 1964. Under the leadership of Duong van Minh, it proved no more politically adept than Diem, and rivalries among the 12 members soon came to the fore. In January 1964, General Kanh overthrew Minh, but proved equally inept. By the time that he resigned as head of state seven months later the country was in chaos. He was replaced by a triumvirate of generals who could do little to quell the unrest, and in December the MRC was itself overthrown by a faction of younger military officers that included Thieu and Ky.

Military Sealift Command

Called the Military Sea Transport Service (MSTS) until September 1970, MSC was the US Navy organization responsible for the transportation of the bulk of the war matériel used in Vietnam. At its peak it operated more than 500

Navy and leased ships. During the final North Vietnamese offensive, MSC transported troops and refugees from the northern provinces to the south, and later participated in the evacuation of more than 50,000 South Vietnamese when Saigon fell.

Mill Pond, Operation

In December 1960, as the Laotian crisis intensified and Soviet support began to enhance the Pathet Lao's effectiveness in operations on the Plain of Jars, the CIA clandestinely flew four black B-26 bombers from Taiwan to Takhli in Thailand. The fighting escalated in early 1961 and on March 9, President Kennedy approved an air strike against Pathet Lao forces under the code name Operation Mill Pond. In early April, 12 more B-26s and two RB-26Cs were flown from Okinawa and added to the strike force. The CIA recruited air force volunteer pilots to fly the strike. On April 16, the B-26s were armed with bombs, rockets, and napalm, however, the

Above: A forward observer with the Military Region II Mike Force unit crosses a small creek near Ban Me Thout.

Ambassador to Laos forbade the use of napalm, and it had to be taken off. The next morning, just prior to take off, the commander received word that President Kennedy had cancelled the mission. The pilots and aircraft remained at Takhli and flew armed reconnaissance over Laos for the next three months, after which Operation Mill Pond was abandoned.

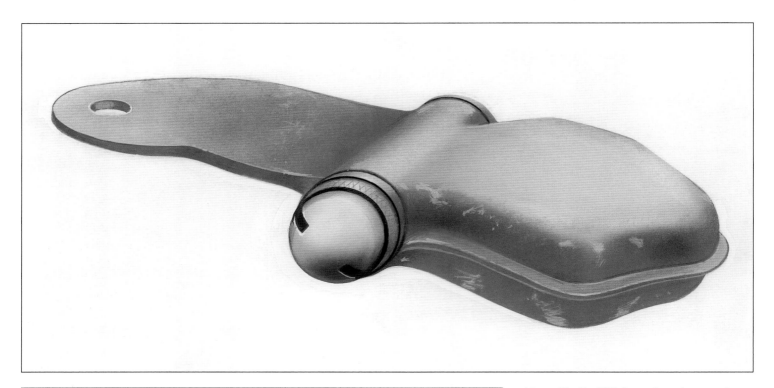

Above: The flat NVA butterfly antipersonnel mine was highly effective, but not frequently seen.

Left: A collection of Viet Cong mines and booby traps. The spiked ball is a trail mace, normally suspended in a tree and designed to sweep along a trail.

Mines

Both sides used mines and booby traps extensively. Approximately 10 percent of all US casualties were from mines and booby traps, while nearly 75 percent of all tank and armored vehicle losses could be attributed to that cause. Both sides made use of antitank, antipersonnel, and naval mines. The most commonly employed US mine was the 18A1 Claymore. Other mines used in quantity were small plastic M14 blast mines and M16A1 bounding mines, sometimes called Bouncing Bettys because when they were activated they ejected an explosive charge with a fragmentation jacket approximately one meter in the air where it detonated. Blast mines and Bouncing Bettys were routinely installed as minefields around firebases and base camps. The Claymore was also used around base camps as well as being carried on patrol and used to establish ambushes or protect night laagers. The US used the Captor naval mine to close Haiphong and the other North Vietnamese ports. Although they were available, US M7A2 antitank mines were rarely used.

The NVA and Viet Cong made extensive use of the DH-10 directional mine, which functioned similarly to the Claymore. They also sometimes deployed the Chinese No. 8 mine, which was a combination antipersonnel and antitank mine that weighed approximately 12lb. More frequently however, the mines and booby traps used by the VC and NVA were locally manufactured field expedient types. They ran the gamut from a large 83lb water mine to a small fabricated mine the troops referred to as a "toe popper." It was made with a homemade primer and a charge of black powder that was designed to detonate when it was stepped on, maiming the foot. Viet Cong and NVA mining operations were very effective. Not only did they create heavy casualties among the infantry, and destroy or damage a large number of armored vehicles, they also sank the USS *Card* (a small ferry aircraft carrier), rendered irreparable one destroyer, sank a number of patrol boats, and damaged a significant number of freighters as well.

Left: A crewman surveys his mine-damaged tank track in the Ho Bo Woods in III Corps.

Below: A CH-53 helicopter tows a magnetic mine clearance sled in Haiphong Harbor during Operation End Sweep.

Total Casualties by Race From All Causes

Race	Number	Percent
Black	7,273	12.36
East Asian	121	0.20
Malayo-Polynesian	254	0.43
Native American	225	0.38
Unknown	128	0.21
*Caucasian	50,478	86.31

* Hispanics were not treated as a separate minority but were included in Caucasian.

Above: The point man of a 173rd Airborne Brigade patrol moves out after a helicopter resupply.

Mine Clearance

The only large-scale mine clearance that took place during the Vietnam War was the removal of the sea mines from North Vietnamese ports and harbors under Operation End Sweep after the peace agreements were signed. Normal combat zone mine clearance was usually carried out by hand probing, digging, and deactivation, though occasionally tanks were run across antipersonnel mine fields to clear a trail, or mechanized equipment or armored trucks were run down a road to detonate mines that might be there.

Minorities in the American Military

One of the enduring myths of the Vietnam War is that minorities, particularly blacks, were more apt to be drafted and suffered a disproportionate number of casualties. In fact, during the period of the most intense combat, from 1968 through 1970, draftees did account for roughly 60 percent of all casualties, while at the same time they comprised only 40 percent of the Army. But taken as a whole, minorities, particularly blacks, did not contribute a higher number of casualties than their percentage of

Right: A Marine loads down with extra ammo in preparation for a mission.

the population would indicate they should. During the war years blacks made up approximately 12.55 percent of the US population.

Missing In Action (MIA)
Missing In Action (MIA) is a term used to describe a soldier whose fate is unknown. The January 1973 Paris Peace Agreement required the Democratic Republic of Vietnam and the National Liberation Front to return all US prisoners of war. Because of the low numbers of returnees, questions were immediately raised concerning over 2,000 MIAs. In 1977, the Pentagon reclassified all but one of the remaining MIAs as dead, body not recovered. Only Air Force Colonel Charles Shelton was still listed as MIA in order to keep the issue alive in negotiations with the North Vietnamese.

Mitchell, John Newton
The US Attorney General from 1969 to 1972, Mitchell labeled antiwar protesters as communists and advocated their prosecution under a number of legal theories. He also attempted to stop the publication of the Pentagon Papers, first by moral persuasion, and then by an injunction, and approved the indictment of Daniel Ellsberg for the release of classified documents. Later he was convicted for his role in the Watergate coverup, and became the first US Attorney General ever to serve a prison term.

Mobile Guerrilla Force (MGF)
Initiated in 1966, the Mobile Guerrilla Forces (MGF) evolved from the Special Forces Special Reconnaissance Projects, Delta, Omega, and Sigma. The MGF usually consisted of a Special Forces A-Team, a 150-man guerrilla rifle company, and a 34-man reconnaissance platoon. MGF operations carried the code name Blackjack and involved operating in remote Viet Cong controlled areas for up to 60 days.

Right: US Attorney General John Mitchell answers questions at a 1970 news conference.

Mobile Riverine Force

More than 50,000 Vietnamese Junks and small watercraft operated in the rivers and canals of the Mekong Delta, providing a ready logistics infrastructure for Viet Cong units operating there. Operation Game Warden was designed to interdict this logistics structure, however the problem of Viet Cong land forces remained. Drawing on the experience of the French, in 1967 the Navy activated Task Force 117, the Mekong Delta Mobile Riverine Force. The 2nd Brigade, 9th Infantry Division was attached to it. Using a variety of mechanized landing craft, minesweepers, and patrol boats, they conducted amphibious combat operations throughout all the waterways of the northern delta and in the Rung Sat Swamp southeast of Saigon.

Opposite, top: Troops keep a sharp lookout as they navigate a brush-lined stream in the Delta.

Opposite, bottom: A Monitor of the Mobile Riverine Force fires its flamethrowers at potential Viet Cong ambush sites.

Left: An armored troop carrier of Task Force 117 moves along a secondary waterway in the Mekong Delta.

Below: A member of the Mobile Strike Force Command indicates how many men are to board the next helicopter during an extraction.

Left: Captain Jerry Nills, 3rd Battalion, 2nd Mobile Strike Force Command, briefs Special Forces personnel at Ben Het on his operation around their camp in II Corps.

Mobile Strike Force Command

From 1961 to 1964 the Special Forces camps had to rely on Vietnamese units for reinforcement when they came under attack. In October 1964, a platoon of CIDG troops was formed at Pleiku for this purpose. Recognizing the problem, in June 1965, General Westmoreland authorized the creation of a small reserve force for each C detachment. Known as Mike Forces, eventually 47 companies were authorized and they were organized into battalions. Originally fully under US control, in 1966 they came under joint US Special Forces/Vietnamese Special Forces Command. In 1967, the Mobile Guerrilla Forces were folded into the Mike Force. Detachment B-55, later the 5th Mobile Strike Force Command, was

Below: A Mike Force company of II Corps Mobile Strike Force prepares to move out.

Right: The monsoon rains converted the roads and fields in the Highlands to a sea of mud.

under the 5th Special Forces Group Commander's control.

Momentum, Project

Project Momentum was the name the CIA gave the Hmong paramilitary guerrilla operations in northern Laos. It began when Bill Lair, the CIA operative who had organized the Police Aerial Reinforcement Units (PARU) in Thailand, and Lieutenant Colonel Pranet Ritilieuchai, the PARU Commanding Officer, met with Vang Pao at Muong Cha, a small hamlet in the highlands south of the Plain of Jars, in order to assess the military potential of the Hmong. Lair was impressed with Vang Pao and what he had learned about the Hmong activities against the Viet Minh in the earlier war, so he obtained permission from Desmond FitzGerald, head of the CIA Far East Division, to arm 2,000 of Vang Pao's people with small arms and a few mortars. As a part of the effort he also obtained concurrence from the Thai government for the PARU to assign teams to the Hmong to assist in both training and command and control. From this beginning Project Momentum eventually reached a troop strength of over 30,000, and ultimately tied down several North Vietnamese Divisions to support their Pathet Lao compatriots in Laos.

Momyer, William W.

In July 1966, General Momyer assumed command of the Seventh Air Force in Vietnam. He directed the Rolling Thunder bombing campaign against North Vietnam and the massive air operations in South Vietnam. He opposed target restrictions, and frequently complained that bombing halts signaled both a weakness and lack of resolve to Hanoi. He believed he should control all aircraft in the theater and frequently fought with the Marines over control of the Marine Air Wings. He staunchly advocated conversion of the Air Force to an all jet fleet, and clashed repeatedly with the Special Operations Squadron working over Laos on this point. He left South Vietnam in the summer of 1968.

Monsoon

Vietnam's climate is dominated by two monsoon periods. The southwest

Right: Troops try to catch a little rest under their ponchos during a downpour.

Above: Joint Chiefs of Staff in 1968: (from left) General C Westmoreland, General John P McConnell, Chairman General Earle G Wheeler, Admiral Thomas H Moorer, and General Leonard F Chapman.

Left: A group of Jarai Montagnards watch as a patrol moves through their hamlet near Plei Me in II Corps.

Below left: A group of Montagnard children in the highlands.

monsoon, from mid-May to mid-October, dumps heavy rain on all of Vietnam east of the Annamite Mountains except for the central coastal strip. It creates heavy flooding in the Mekong Delta before moving into the Tonkin highlands and the Red River Delta of North Vietnam. The northeast monsoon reverses the wet-dry cycle over the area and dumps heavy rain on the Red River Delta and the central coast of Vietnam as far south as Nha Trang from mid-September to late December. Military operations, particularly air operations, can be severely impacted by the monsoonal storms.

Montagnards

The Montagnards are the indigenous people of Vietnam's central highlands and mountains. Divided into approximately 30 separate tribes, they're scattered throughout Vietnam from the Chinese border south to a point where the central highlands gradually blends into the northern Mekong Delta. In North Vietnam the Montagnards formed a key military element of Ho Chi Minh's revolutionary movement, often like General

Chu Huy Man reaching very high rank. In South Vietnam, President Ngo Dinh Diem initiated a land development program to resettle refugees from the north by displacing Montagnard villages and seizing their land. In opposition to Diem, in 1955 the Montagnard began to organize, eventually forming the United Front for Oppressed Races (FULRO). In 1964 FULRO launched an armed revolt in an attempt to reclaim land seized from the Montagnards. US Special Forces teams working with the tribes defused the issue. In response to their grievances the Saigon government created a Ministry for the Development of Ethnic Minorities to address social and economic programs and improve Montagnard living conditions. During the war both sides heavily recruited Montagnards. The US Special Forces were particularly successful in obtaining tribal support. The Easter Offensive of 1972 again drove a wedge between the South Vietnamese government and the Montagnards. The tribes believed that the ARVN made little effort to prevent North Vietnamese attacks against them. By the time the US withdrew in 1975, many of the Montagnards battalions, trained by the Special Forces, were converted to ARVN Border Ranger units. After the fall of South Vietnam, the Montagnards continued armed resistance against the North Vietnamese, at least through 1993.

Moore, Robert Brevard

In June 1963, Admiral Moore assumed command of Carrier Division 5 in the

western Pacific and transferred his flag to the USS *Constellation*. Following the August 1964 Gulf of Tonkin Incident, he implemented Operation Pierce Arrow and directed the air strikes launched against the Democratic Republic of Vietnam from the aircraft carriers *Constellation* and *Ticonderoga*.

Moorer, Thomas H

Admiral Moorer was directly involved with the war in Vietnam longer than any other senior naval officer. He served first as the Commander of the 7th Fleet in 1962, and by 1965 as Commander in Chief of the Pacific Fleet, as the Chief of Naval Operations 1967 to 1970, and finally as chairman of Joint Chiefs of Staff from 1970 to 1974.

He strongly believed that the United States should have mined North Vietnam's ports and harbors at the outset and invaded North Vietnam as soon as forces were available. He was the architect of Operation Linebacker II, which dumped 36,000 tons of bombs on Hanoi in 12 days.

Moratorium to End the War in Vietnam

Peace demonstration held in Washington and several other US cities on October 15, 1969. Although a general strike was originally suggested, a more moderate position was adopted. The coordinated nationwide rallies attracted millions, and passed peacefully. Organizers of the Moratorium received praise from North Vietnam's Prime Minister Pham Van Dong, who stated in a letter to them "may your fall offensive succeed splendidly," marking the first time Hanoi publicly acknowledged the American antiwar movement. Dong's comments infuriated American conservatives including Vice President Spiro Agnew who lambasted the protesters as communist "dupes" comprising "an effete corps of impudent snobs who characterize themselves as intellectuals."

Morse, Wayne Lyman

Democratic Senator Wayne Morse of Oregon vigorously opposed the 1964 Gulf of Tonkin Resolution and charged that the Johnson administration was not providing Congress with all of the details surrounding the incident. He voted against the resolution, insisting that the matter should have been referred to the United Nations. In 1966, he introduced legislation to repeal the Gulf of Tonkin

Above: A Marine Corps 60mm mortar squad fires at a suspected enemy position near Ca Lu in I Corps.

Above right: An 81mm mortar crew at Khe Sanh fires in support of a patrol.

Resolution, but it failed. He lost a re-election bid in 1968.

Mortars (Allied)

The Allies used three different caliber mortars. The smallest was a 60mm that was commonly found among Vietnamese units, Marine elements, and was used by Army reconnaissance teams. It was light, accurate, and had a range of 800m. The standard Allied medium mortar was the American 81mm. It was found at all levels of the Allied combat forces, and provided a significant amount of readily available firepower to the maneuvering infantry. The Allies also utilized the 4.2in (107mm) heavy mortar. Although it was available to infantry units, because of its weight it was frequently left in the base camps or on the firebases. American armor and armored cavalry units made extensive use of the 4.2in mortar mounted in a modified M113 armored personnel carrier.

Mortars (North Vietnamese and Viet Cong)

Mortars were the basic artillery weapon utilized by the Viet Cong, and were of major importance to the NVA. The most common communist mortar was the 82mm. It was drop-fired and had a quite

sophisticated aiming device attached approximately halfway up the tube. The 82mm rate of fire was between 15rpm and 25rpm depending on the expertise of the crew.

The North Vietnamese developed a chemical delay impact fuze for this weapon that made it even more effective against dug-in infantry and bunkers. They also used the Chinese Type 55 120mm mortar, which was a version of the Soviet M43, though this was only infrequently encountered. The Viet Cong and NVA achieved spectacular success in the use of these weapons.

Moyers, Bill

Bill Moyers served as President Johnson's press secretary in 1965 and 1966 and worked hard to improve the President's relationship with the press. Publicly, Moyers was a strong advocate of Johnson's policies in Vietnam, however he began to believe that the war was absorbing more of the President's attention than it warranted, to the detriment of his domestic programs. He resigned in December 1966.

Mu Gia Pass

The Mu Gia Pass through the Truong Son Mountain Range was one of the critical chokepoints on the Ho Chi Minh Trail. A high percentage of NVA logistics traffic from Vinh to Tchepone transited the mountains there. Though the pass

Right: A 60mm mortar team sets up in front of a church in Quang Tri province.

VIETNAM: A VISUAL ENCYCLOPEDIA

Above: The 82mm mortar was the mainstay of NVA artillery support.

Above right: Helicopters do a quick bomb damage assessment, and rocket some survivors after a strike on Mu Gia Pass.

was routinely subjected to massive bombing, it was never closed for more than a short time. The CIA-backed Hmong guerrillas were repeatedly encouraged to attack the pass, however North Vietnamese defenses were simply too strong.

Munich Analogy

Term coined for an analogy that compared weakness in the face of communist expansion to the British and French foreign policy of appeasement of Hitler in the 1930s. Along with the Domino Theory and Containment Policy it was a pivotal influence on US policy makers and thus on US involvement in Vietnam.

Murphy, Robert D

A former Undersecretary of State for Political Affairs from 1953 to 1959, Murphy was selected by President Johnson to be one of the "wise men," a group of senior advisers the President consulted on Vietnam. Following the Tet Offensive of 1968, when the "wise men" reassessed US policy in Vietnam at the behest of President Johnson, Murphy strongly dissented from the group recommendation that the US should seek a negotiated peace. He argued that the United States should fight on to victory regardless of the cost.

Muste, Abraham J

A minister of the Dutch Reformed Church, Muste has sometimes been called a radical pacifist. He opposed US participation in World War I, World War II, and Vietnam. In the 1930s, he was the General Secretary of the Communist League of America and a member of the Fourth International (Trotskyite). He was one of the first critics of the Vietnam War and a keynote speaker at antiwar rallies from 1964 to 1966. He was expelled from South Vietnam for leading an antiwar demonstration in Saigon in early 1966 and in November 1966 he became chairman of the Spring Mobilization to End the War in Vietnam. He visited North Vietnam in January 1967, and died of a heart attack on February 11, 1967.

My Lai

Though dwarfed by the scale of the atrocity committed by the North Vietnamese in Hue during the Tet Offensive, My Lai has become the most notorious atrocity of the Vietnam War. On March 16, 1968, the 1st Platoon, Company C, 1st Battalion, 20th Infantry, of the Americal Division, commanded by Lieutenant William Calley, massacred several hundred men women and children in the hamlet of My Lai 4.

The incident was successfully concealed until Ronald Ridenhour, a former Americal Division public affairs office photographer, wrote a letter to President Nixon, a number of congressmen, and a number of Defense Department officials. Later investigation revealed that a significant number of high-ranking officers in the division had knowledge of the event. Subsequent investigations resulted in the indictment of 25 officers and enlisted men on numerous charges. War crimes charges were levied against Lieutenant Calley and 12 others. The Division Commander, Major General Samuel Koster, and 11 others were indicted for offenses connected with covering up the war crimes.

Only Lieutenant Calley, who was eventually charged with the deaths of 122 individuals, was convicted of murder by a military court martial and sentenced to life in prison. The charges against General Koster were dismissed, but he was administratively reduced in rank and forced from the service. All of the other charges resulted in acquittals or were dropped. After Lieutenant Calley was convicted on March 29, 1971, his defense appealed to both military and civilian courts. The dropping of the charges against all of the higher-ranking defendants resulted in a groundswell of support for Calley, and a belief that he was made a scapegoat by the Army. Eventually the Commanding General of Fort Benning, as the reviewing officer of the case, administratively reduced Calley's sentence to 20 years. The Secretary of the Army then further reduced it to 10 years. He was released on parole in November 1974.

Nam Dong, Battle of (July 1964)

Nam Dong was a Special Forces camp in the southwest corner of Thua Tien province in I Corps. At 2:30am on July 6, 1964, following a shattering mortar barrage and then three ground assaults by a reinforced battalion of Viet Cong, a major effort to seize the camp failed. The Viet Cong had crept undetected to the edge of the wire and cut lanes through it for their assault. Purely by chance the camp had been constructed around an old French installation that was too small to contain the CIDG Strike Force. Though the outer perimeter was quickly overrun, the Special Forces Team and the Nungs retreated to the inner, French-built perimeter, and beat off the attacks. Air cover arrived early the next morning, and reinforcements from a district headquarters, a three-hour march away up the valley, followed close behind. Captain Roger Donlon, the Special Forces commander of the camp, was awarded the Medal of Honor for his actions during the attack.

Nantucket Beach, Operation

On July 20, 1969, three battalions of the of Americal Division, and the 4th ARVN Regiment began Operation Nantucket Beach in the same area of the Batangan Peninsula in I Corps where the Marines had earlier carried out Operation Bold Mariner. The target was the Viet Cong 48th Battalion. Though there were numerous casualties from mines and booby traps, actual enemy contact was light. Americal engineers destroyed numerous bunkers, tunnels, and trenches. However, by January 1971 the VC 48th Battalion had reoccupied and rebuilt the area and was back in action on the Batangan Peninsula.

Napalm

Adding a thickener to gasoline makes napalm. It kills by burning or by asphyxiation; when it detonates it causes massive deoxygenation and produces lethal amounts of carbon monoxide. In Vietnam it was dropped from aircraft for close air support, and used in flamethrowers by both the Allied and the communist forces. The use of napalm was heavily criticized by the antiwar movement, particularly after the famous photograph of a young, naked, Vietnamese girl running down the road screaming following a napalm strike by Vietnamese aircraft was widely published in June 1972.

Nasty

The Nasty is a class of 80ft fast patrol boats displacing 85 tons. Powered by two Napier-Deltic diesels it is capable of 41 knots. It is armed with an 81mm mortar, a 40mm and two 20mm cannons, and one .50 Caliber machinegun. Crewed by Norwegian and German mercenaries, it was used to raid the North Vietnamese coast and land intelligence agents under OPLAN 34A early in the war.

National Assembly Law 10/59

Legislation was enacted in October 1959 by Diem's government that ordered the execution of Viet Cong, former Viet Minh, their friends, relatives and associates. Already, in May 1959, the National Assembly had introduced repressive legislation that legalized courts-martial and execution for those convicted of working

Opposite, top: Napalm engulfs a group of reportedly Viet Cong structures.

Opposite, bottom: A pair of Nasty Class patrol boats supporting a SEAL team maneuver in the shallow water close to shore.

Right: In Vietnam, napalm was dropped from aircraft and used in flamethrowers.

Above: A group of Revolutionary Development Support Cadremen graduate from the CORDS run school at Vung Tau.

with the Viet Cong. The repressive law was designed partly in response to communist violence in the countryside, but in effect it was used against any group or individual opposing the government. The courts were run by the military, and the penalties could be either death or life imprisonment. Both laws caused considerable resentment and catalyzed the popular uprisings in August 1959 and January 1960.

National Cadres Training Center

The National Cadres Training Center was established by the Civil Operations and Revolutionary Development Support (CORDS) organization at Vung Tau. The purpose of the center was to train Development Cadre Teams that would work in the hamlets and villages to raise their standard of living or obtain governmental support and assistance as an element of pacification.

National Committee for Peace and Freedom in Vietnam

An antiwar group that was an offshoot of the Peace and Freedom Party was formed in 1967 by a coalition of activists from the antiwar, civil rights and black liberation, farmworkers and labor movements. They collected the necessary voter registrations to place the Peace and Freedom Party on the California ballot in 1968. In response to the war in Vietnam, over 100,000 Californians registered to vote in this new political party of the Left in 1967.

During 1968, the Black Panther Party provided the leadership and Huey Newton, Bobby Seale and Eldridge Cleaver all ran for public office as representatives of the Peace and Freedom Party. Throughout its history, the Peace and Freedom Party has boldly taken on even the most liberal Democrats, such as Ron Dellums, Tom Hayden and Henry Waxman, in an unending struggle to move America's political dialogue further to the Left.

National Coordinating Committee to End the War in Vietnam (NCC)

The coalition of antiwar groups, known as the NCC, was initially created to coordinate the October 1965 International Days of Protest. The NCC later attempted to develop a cohesive antiwar program for its 33 affiliated groups. However, continuing internal disputes between more radical and moderate members hampered these plans. Instead, the NCC functioned primarily as a hub for information about antiwar activities, and individual groups continued to plan their own activities.

National Council of National Reconciliation and Concord (NCNRC)

The council charged with the responsibility for implementing the political stipulations of the 1973 Paris Peace Agreement within the Republic of Vietnam was the NCNRC. It was composed of representatives of the RVN, the Provisional Revolutionary Government and neutral representatives, and was to oversee free elections, the reunification process, and democratization. However, Thieu mistrusted the NCNRC, and it had achieved little before the war between the north and south recommenced.

National Front for the Liberation of South Vietnam (NFLSV)

The official name of the South Vietnamese revolutionary communist movement, commonly known as the Viet Cong, was NFLSV. In 1960, frustrated by its failure to unify the country through political means, the Hanoi-based ruling Lao Dong Party accepted that a new strategy was needed and formed the

Below: An officer of the National Police, South Vietnam's police force, directs traffic in Danang.

National Liberation Front for South Vietnam in Tay Ninh province. The NFLSV sought to mobilize anti-Diem sentiments in the south, both communist and non-communist, but communists dominated the organization hierarchy. Its military arm, the People's Liberation Armed Forces (PLAF) was armed by the North and carried out a sustained guerilla campaign against RVN and US targets.

In 1968, the NFLSV launched its biggest and arguably most successful operation against key southern cities, the Tet Offensive. In 1969, the NFLSV formed the Provisional Revolutionary Government, which hoped to assume power after the struggle, but after the fall of Saigon few of its officials were handed positions in the national government.

National Guard

The National Guard is a reserve branch of the US military. During the Vietnam War the military leadership pressed the political leadership to activate units of the National Guard. The President decided that potential economic and social disruption would make it politically inadvisable to do so, because the National Guard are part-time, citizen

soldiers. As a result, the National Guard became a haven for those who wished to avoid service in Vietnam. Only one National Guard ground combat unit served in the war.

National Leadership Council

A political body was established in June 1965 by Generals Ky, Thieu and Co in the wake of Phan Huy Quat's fall, and which governed the RVN until 1967. Its ten members were predominantly military men, and Ky held the key position. After the September 1967 national elections, a new government assumed power.

National Police

The National Police were South Vietnam's internal police force. They were organized and trained following the advice of the Michigan State University Advisory Group, led by professor Wesley Fishel. Michigan State had a contract with the Diem government between 1954 and 1961 to assist in establishing a nationwide civil administration. Sometimes they were derisively called the "white mice" because of the white hats, white shirts, and white gloves that made up their uniforms.

Above: The USS *Orleck*, DD-886, provides naval gunfire support to troops operating on the coast.

National Police Field Force
The National Police Field Force was a paramilitary arm of the National Police that operated in conjunction with the Republic of Vietnam armed forces. They worked in the villages and hamlets in an attempt to establish both a presence for the government and a modicum of security for the peasants. Over time they became one of the most corrupt organizations in Vietnam, because of their coercive power and the fact that they were not overseen by anyone.

National Security Council (NSC)
The US governmental council, the National Security Council, had the function of advising the president about the most effective way to integrate national domestic, foreign, and military policy, so as to enable the armed services and other departments of government to discharge their responsibilities with respect to national security. During the Vietnam conflict the NSC was frequently divided, notably over the decision to back the coup that toppled Diem.

Naval Gunfire
During the war two types of naval gunfire were employed in Vietnam; unobserved saturation bombardment of a

designated area, and observed fire called for either by ground or aerial observers. The first use of naval gunfire was during Operation Starlight in August 1965 when the heavy cruiser *USS Canberra* and five destroyers supported the Marines. The use of naval gunfire peaked during the Tet Offensive when there were 22 Navy ships providing gunfire support to the embattled ARVN and US forces.

Below: A naval gunfire support team plots a mission for the heavy cruiser USS *Canberra*.

Neutrality

A state of neutrality is non-affiliation with any party to a war or dispute. The Geneva Accords purportedly secured the neutrality of Laos and Cambodia but this was compromised by both the DRV, which from 1959 used both countries to infiltrate men and supplies into the south and the US, which sent Special Forces-trained interdiction teams into Laos. Later the DRV established permanent bases in Laos and Cambodia, and the US began a covert bombing campaign. In

1970, the neutrality of Cambodia, which had only ever been nominal, was completely compromised by the US invasion.

Neutralize

One of the most commonly used euphemisms for assassination is the term "neutralize," but its use in Vietnam was much broader. It could mean the destruction of an enemy target either by artillery or air strike, or in the pacification program, it frequently meant the destruction of an entire village or hamlet where

pacification had failed. The inhabitants were then relocated to a government-controlled area.

Nevada Eagle, Operation

Operation Nevada Eagle was designed to protect the rice harvest in Thua Tien province of I Corps immediately after the Tet Offensive. From May 1968 through February 1969, the 101st Airborne Division engaged in numerous sweeps along the mountains in Thua Tien. There were few contacts of any size. The major battle during the operation took place on May 21, 1968. While the bulk of the division was scattered throughout the province conducting sweeps, an NVA battalion attacked the division base camp. They succeeded in penetrating the perimeter and pushed the defending 3rd Brigade back to their final defensive lines. The assault was broken up by the artillery firing beehive rounds at point-blank range and a swarm of helicopter gunships.

Below: Specialist Leland Brooks, 101st Airborne Division, shares his water with a wounded buddy.

Left: An aged Vietnamese couple contemplate their future after they were evacuated to a New Life Hamlet.

Below: Vietnamese children peek at a patrol through the wire fence of a New Life Hamlet.

New Life Hamlets

The New Life Hamlets were a follow-on to the Strategic Hamlet Program. They were intended to separate the Viet Cong from the population by relocating the population into a secured and fortified area under government control. They ignored the deep-seated attachment the Vietnamese peasants had to their ancestral home. Under funded, under supported, and riddled with corruption, the New Life Hamlet Program failed for many of the same reasons the Strategic Hamlet Program had earlier.

New MOBE

The antiwar group, New MOBE, was formed in 1968, primarily to develop a strategy of protest at the Democratic National Convention in Chicago in August. The National Mobilization to

End the War in Vietnam (MOBE) held a planning meeting in Chicago in February 1968 to debate the various strategies for the upcoming Democratic Convention. The group of about 40, included Rennie Davis and Tom Hayden. In March 1968, MOBE sponsored another meeting, this one at Lake Villa, Chicago, to discuss plans for August. About 200 people, including the Chicago Seven defendants David Dellinger, Davis, Hayden, Abbie Hoffman, and Jerry Rubin, attended the meeting. A 21-page document, authored by Hayden and Davis, was distributed at the meeting. The document recommended non-violence.

Newport

The massive American troop buildup between 1965 and 1968 required enormous logistical support. Vietnam had few deepwater port facilities, and by late 1965 it was not uncommon for a freighter to wait 22 days to offload. To overcome this problem, the United States constructed additional deepwater port facilities at Cam Rahn Bay, Danang, Qui Nhon, and Newport near Saigon. Completed in 1967, and operated by the Army Transportation Corps, Newport routinely handled over 150,000 tons of supplies monthly.

New Zealand

Although New Zealand was a charter member of the South-east Asia Treaty Organization (SEATO), its internal political parties were sharply divided over the issue and were reluctant to become involved in the Vietnam War. However, because of New Zealand's desire to maintain close relations with the United States and Australia, it began sending military personnel to Vietnam in 1964, and by 1965 had formed a joint Australia/New Zealand (ANZAC) battalion that fought with the Australian Task Force. In concert with the American withdrawal, New Zealand began to withdraw its troops in 1970 and completed the withdrawal in 1971.

Ngo Dinh Can

The younger brother of President Diem, Ngo Dinh Can lived with the family matriarch in Hue where he maintained his own secret police force and controlled the shipping, and cinnamon trade in central Vietnam. He argued unsuccessfully for accommodation during the Buddhist Crisis. After Diem fell he was arrested and executed in a public square in Saigon.

Right: The Vietnamese Air Force pledges its loyalty to President Ngo Dinh Diem after two pilots bombed the Presidential Palace.

Below: Shipping backed up in Newport as the logistical distribution system struggled to keep up with deliveries.

in which he deposed the Emperor by receiving 98 percent of the vote. Acting quickly, he consolidated power by neutralizing the Cao Dai and Hoa Hao religious sects, while crushing the Binh Xuan pirates militarily. By the end of 1956, he had seriously damaged the Viet Minh cadres, who had stayed behind in the south, and the southern communist leadership began appealing to Hanoi for permission to launch an insurrection. Hanoi declined to authorize an armed struggle until late 1959. Always a recluse, and somewhat paranoid, Diem refused to delegate authority, relied almost entirely upon his family for advice, populated his emerging government with catholic refugees from North Vietnam, and did little to build a broad-based popular government. His repressive regime and refusal to implement any reforms severely damaged his relationship with the United States. The final straw was the suppression of the buddhist dissidents in 1963. Although not directly involved in the coup that removed him from power, the United States let it be known to the plotters that they would accept a change in government. A short time later the generals moved and Diem was dead.

Ngo Dinh Khoi

Ngo Dinh Khoi was a prominent political figure in central Vietnam and the eldest brother of Ngo Dinh Diem. He was killed by the communists because he was seen as a threat to their consolidation of power in 1945. His death caused Diem to reject a position in the government that was set up by Ho Chi Minh.

Ngo Dinh Nhu

The chief political adviser to Ngo Dinh Diem, Ngo Dinh Nhu was the head of the Can Lao political party, as well as the secret police and several paramilitary organizations. Devious and cynical, he became the regime's ideologue and was a constant impediment to better relations between the Americans and the Vietnamese. As Diem's power began to slip, Nhu looked to the regime in Hanoi and the National Liberation Front to explore whether a possibility of accommodation existed. In August 1963, he ordered elite US trained troops under his control to raid the pagodas throughout Vietnam and crack down on the activities of buddhist monks, infuriating nearly all of the political factions, as well as the Americans, and precipitating the final

Ngo Dinh Diem

An ardent nationalist and anticommunist, Ngo Dinh Diem's abhorrence of communism increased when the Viet Minh killed one of his brothers as they consolidated their hold on the Vietnamese nationalist movement. He refused an offer by Ho Chi Minh to join his government, denouncing him as a "criminal." In 1950, he traveled to the United States where, playing on his catholicism, he met Cardinal Spellman and senators Kennedy and Mansfield, contacts that later became important in his drive to obtain US support. In 1954, he became the Premier in Emperor Bao Dai's short-lived State of Vietnam. One of his first acts was to request American support. In 1955, he rejected the elections to reunify Vietnam as specified in the Geneva Accords. Instead, he organized a fraudulent National Referendum

crisis of the Diem presidency. During the November 2 coup, Nhu was executed along with his brother, Diem.

Ngo Dinh Thuc
The eldest male of the Ngo family, Thuc was a strongly anticommunist catholic priest in Hue. His relationship with American churchmen, particularly Cardinal Spellman of New York was instrumental in developing US support for his brother's regime. He was appointed Archbishop of Hue and served as a liaison to South Vietnam's 1.2 million catholics. He was in Rome when his brother was assassinated, and survived the coup. He was later excommunicated for investing priests without Rome's permission and died in the US in 1984.

Ngo Quang Truong
General Truong was widely held to be the most competent of all of the Vietnamese senior officers. Under his

Left: President Ngo Dinh Diem visits a Montagnard hamlet near Da Lat.

leadership the ARVN 1st Infantry Division achieved a reputation rivaling many American units. During the 1972 Easter Offensive, General Truong rallied the ARVN and retook most of the territory that was initially lost. He was sent to Hue during the final NVA Offensive to attempt to repeat his success, but constant meddling from Saigon prevented him from doing anything but running south. When South Vietnam fell General Truong escaped to the United States.

Nguyen Cao Ky

A Vietnamese Air Force officer, Nguyen Cao Ky first came to the attention of the United States when he supported the CIA by flying penetration agents and spies into North Vietnam in the early 1960s for William Colby. He played a key role in the coup against President Diem by securing air force support for the plotters. In 1964, he again supported the overthrow of the government. In 1965, he became the President. In 1966, the buddhists began agitating against the central government, but were crushed by tanks flown to Danang and Hue by Ky. In 1967, strongly influenced by the

Right: Seen here at a press conference at the Guam refugee camp in 1971, Nguyen Cao Ky was by this time no longer Vice President.

Below: General Ngo Quang Truong inspects a soldier's weapon as he takes command of I Corps during the Easter Offensive.

Above: Nguyen Cao Ky and Lieutenant General Ngo Quang Troung are escorted along the deck after they flew out of Saigon as it fell.

United States, he allowed General Nguyen Van Thieu to become the President of Vietnam and reverted to the Vice-President. Flamboyant and outspoken, he caused a worldwide stir when he informed reporters that his only hero was Hitler. Eased out between 1967 and 1975 as Thieu consolidated his own power, he filed to become a candidate for President in 1971, but was disqualified. Ky fled Vietnam at the outset of the North Vietnamese final offensive.

Nguyen Chan Thi

A devout buddhist, Colonel Thi assisted President Diem in crushing the Binh Xuyen gangsters in 1955. By 1960, his disillusionment with Diem caused him to lead a coup, which failed. In 1965, following Diem's fall, Thi was posted to I Corps where he quickly allied himself with the buddhist leader Thich Tri Quang and ruled the region as a virtual warlord. He refused to be replaced when Nguyen Cao Ky relieved him in March 1966, precipitating armed conflict between the buddhists and the central government. He was captured in May 1966, and exiled to the United States.

Nguyen Chi Than

General Nguyen Chi Than infiltrated into Tay Ninh province west of Saigon in 1965 and assumed control of all North Vietnamese and Viet Cong military operations in the south. Operating out of the Central Office for South Vietnam (COSVN), he favored conventional military operations to defeat the Allies. He was killed in a B-52 raid in June 1967, and the North Vietnamese switched back to guerrilla operations.

Nguyen Co Thach

Beginning his diplomatic career in 1954, Nguyen Co Thach was the Democratic

Republic of Vietnam's ambassador to India from 1956–1960. He headed the North Vietnamese delegation at the 1962 Geneva Convention, served as a contact during the Ronning Missions of 1966, and was a negotiator at the Paris peace talks. In 1975, he became Minister of Foreign Affairs for the Socialist Republic of Vietnam.

Nguyen Huu Tho
A French educated Saigon lawyer, Nguyen Huu Tho was not a member of the communist party, but opposed the Diem regime. He was imprisoned in 1961 for founding the Saigon-Cholon Peace Movement. Freed by a Viet Cong commando raid, he went to Tay Ninh province and became the Chairman of the National Liberation Front. In June

Left: General Nguyen Chan Thi, Commander of I Corps, greets Secretary of Defense Robert McNamara in 1965.

Below: Premier Nguyen Cao Ky (right) watches as President Johnson pins the Purple Heart on a wounded man in the Navy Hospital at Saigon.

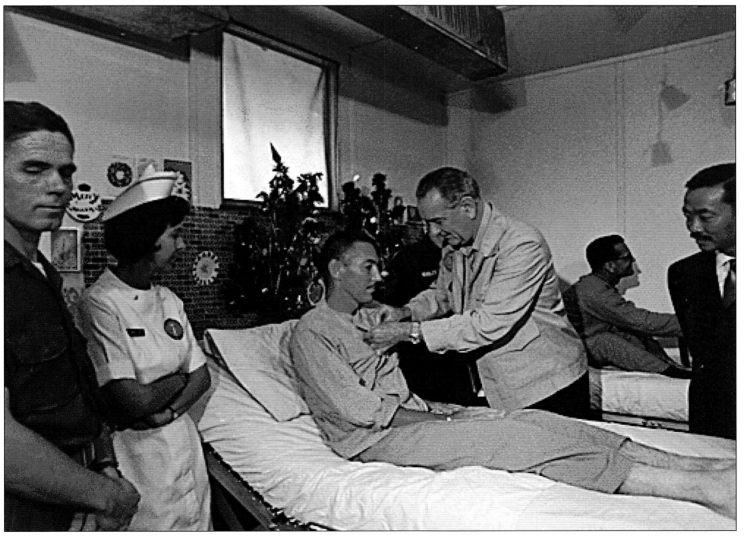

Above: Madam Nguyen Thi Binh, the People's Revolutionary Government Foreign Minister, signs a nine point peace plan for South Vietnam.

1970, he was Chairman of the Consultative Council of the Provisional Revolutionary Government of South Vietnam and he entered Saigon with the North Vietnamese forces in April 1975.

Nguyen Khanh
A French-trained officer of the Vietnamese National Army, by 1963 Khanh had become a general and participated in the coup against Diem. He followed that with a coup that put himself in power in 1964. In February 1965 Nguyen Cao Ky and Nguyen Van Thieu ousted Khanh and exiled him to the United States.

Nguyen Khoa Nam
General Nam, considered one of the few incorruptible senior officers of the ARVN, rose through the ranks of the South Vietnamese airborne, commanding first the 5th Airborne Battalion and then the 3rd Airborne Brigade. Promoted to Brigadier General, he commanded the 7th Infantry Division and finally IV Corps. When Saigon fell he committed suicide rather than surrender.

Nguyen Ngoc Loan
An Air Force Brigadier General and Director of the National Police, Loan will forever be remembered for his execution of a Viet Cong prisoner, caught on film by an Associated Press photographer during the Tet Offensive. This image contributed to the American public's increasing revulsion towards the war.

Nguyen Thi Binh
Madam Binh was the Minister of Foreign Affairs for the People's Revolutionary Government and Chief Delegate of the National Liberation Front to the Paris peace talks, ranking second only to Le Duc Tho. In 1975, she was appointed Minister of Education of the Socialist Republic of Vietnam, the highest position held by a woman.

Nguyen Thi Dinh
In 1960, Nguyen Thi Dinh founded a group of female communist sympathizers in Ben Tre called the "Long Haired Army," and led an uprising that allowed the Viet Cong to seize power in the province. This was the first organized resistance there. In 1965, she was appointed Deputy Commander of South Vietnam Liberation Armed Forces.

Nguyen Van Cu
Cu was a Vietnamese Air Force Skyraider pilot who bombed the Presidential Palace on February 27, 1962. Though one bomb penetrated a room in which Diem was located it failed to explode. He then flew his damaged plane to Phnom Penh, Cambodia, where he worked from then on as language teacher. Returning to Saigon after the fall of South Vietnam he was arrested and sent to a re-education camp, where he

was held until 1985. He emigrated to the United States in 1991.

Nguyen Van Binh

The catholic archbishop of Saigon from 1962 until his death in 1991, Nguyen Van Binh was considered a religious moderate. His artful diplomacy succeeded in maintaining relative peace between the Church and the new rulers after 1975.

Nguyen Van Hinh

Appointed by the French as the Commander of the Vietnamese National Army at its inception, General Hinh was despised by the bulk of his countrymen as a French puppet. He openly challenged Diem's authority in 1954 and plotted with the Bin Xuyen and the religious sects to overthrow the government. Ordered to France by emperor Bao Dai he reluctantly complied, defusing the situation. He later became Deputy Commander of the French Air Force.

Nguyen Van Linh

Born Nguyen Van Cuc, he was the Director of the Central Office for South Vietnam, 1961–1964, was an architect of the Tet Offensive, and was in charge of mass mobilization in the Saigon–Gia Dinh Special Zone. He was the Secretary of the Saigon City Party Committee, 1972–1973 and elected to the Politburo of the Vietnamese Communist Party Central Committee in 1976.

Nguyen Van Thieu

During the French Indochina War Nguyen Van Thieu fought the Viet Minh as an infantry lieutenant. He later graduated from the United States Army Command and General Staff College in 1957. Beginning in 1959, he held several senior ARVN commands. In 1963, he led one of the regiments of the ARVN 5th Division against President Diem's Presidential Guard during the coup. In 1964 he again took part in a coup that overthrew the government and, with Nguyen Cao Ky, became one of the "Young Turks" of the Vietnamese officer corps. Serving as the chief of state while Ky was the premier he outmaneuvered him to become the presidential candidate in the 1967 elections. The Ky–Thieu government was the longest lasting government in Vietnam. He bitterly opposed the 1972 draft peace agreement, calling it a sellout, and insisted on modifications which delayed its signing until 1973. To gain President Thieu's acceptance of the agreement, President Nixon provided him a series of secret promises of military support in the event the North Vietnamese violated the pact. When the North Vietnamese attacked, President Nixon was out of office and the War Powers Resolution prevented President Ford from coming to his aid. Thieu bitterly complained that America had abandoned Vietnam. He fled to Britain as Saigon fell.

Nguyen Van Toan

One of the most competent commanders in the ARVN, General Toan commanded the 4th Armor Squadron, the 1st Infantry Division, 2nd Infantry Division, and was appointed as Commander Military Region III (III Corps) in March 1975. Though this appointment was too late to be of much use, he did manage to hold up the NVA advance in Long Khan province in what was the last major battle of the war. When Saigon fell General Toan left Vietnam.

Below: President and Madam Nguyen Van Thieu depart the USS *Constellation* after a visit.

Above: President Nguyen Van Thieu welcomes President Lyndon B Johnson to Vietnam in 1966.

Nha Trang
Located 15 miles north of Cam Rahn Bay, the city, which was made an autonomous municipality in 1970, was a major command and control site. The headquarters of the 5th Special Forces Group and the US Army Field Force I, a Corps Headquarters responsible for all ground operations along the central coast and in the highlands, were located there.

Niagara, Operation
Operation Niagara was the code name for the massive artillery and air support provided to the US Marine Corps base at Khe Sanh from January 18–31, 1968. As the siege of the combat base tightened, General Westmoreland assigned it top priority for all available air strikes and artillery within range.

Nearly 100,000 tons of ordnance struck the encircling NVA units. Both the US command at the time, and the North Vietnamese leadership later, claimed that the NVA Divisions involved in the siege were shattered.

Right: Two crewmen hold their ears as a 175mm gun fires in support of Khe Sanh during Operation Niagara.

Above: Secretary of the Navy Paul Nitze visits the command post of the 1st Battalion, 7th Marines.

Nitze, Paul Henry
As President Kennedy's Assistant Secretary of Defense for International Security Affairs from 1961–1963, Nitze was the only senior dissenter on the decision to introduce ground troops into Vietnam. He was Secretary of the Navy from 1963–1967, and helped draft the San Antonio Formula in 1967. In 1968, he advised President Johnson not to commit additional forces, but to strengthen the Vietnamese forces instead and withdraw.

Nixon Doctrine
The Nixon foreign policy statement, known as the "Nixon Doctrine," was first made public on July 25, 1969. It advocated US military and economic assistance to nations around the world struggling against communism, but importantly sought to limit the direct involvement of American troops in future conflicts, and thus prevent the reoccurrence of a Vietnam-style ground war. The emphasis was placed firmly on local military self-sufficiency, backed by US air power and technical assistance to assure security. The adoption of the "Nixon Doctrine" led to the progressive withdrawal of American troops from Vietnam after 1969.

Nixon, Richard Milhous
As President Eisenhower's Vice President, Richard Nixon recommended a deeper involvement in Indochina to block what he considered to be a Chinese communist drive to the south. When he was out of office between 1961 and 1968 he supported military intervention, though he assailed President Johnson's failure to forcefully prosecute the war to victory. Though the Vietnam War could have been a defining issue in the 1968 presidential campaign, Nixon refused to

face a head-on confrontation. Instead, he flogged the Johnson administration on law-and-order issues while alluding to a "secret plan" for ending the war. Nixon viewed North Vietnam, South Vietnam, Laos, and Cambodia as a single theater of war rather than as four separate nations. In this regard he authorized the secret bombing of Cambodia under Operation Menu. Pressured to reveal his "secret plan," in 1969 he began the "Vietnamization" of the war and the withdrawal of US combat units. Vietnamization rested on several key assumptions: (1) the Thieu government was stable and willing to assume more responsibility for the war; (2) the withdrawal would be gradual, and South Vietnamese troops would replace American troops in combat operations; (3) the American withdrawal would be carried out in such a way that it could not be characterized as a defeat; (4) there would be no coalition government in the south; and (5) all prisoners of war would

be returned. However, North Vietnam never varied from the position that the US must unconditionally withdraw, and the government of President Thieu must be replaced with a coalition government. Between 1969 and 1972, Nixon withdrew all US combat forces. However, in 1970 he launched the Cambodian Incursion in order to destroy the NVA logistics infrastructure and prevent large-scale North Vietnamese attacks as the US phased down, and in 1971 he encouraged the ARVN to attempt to cut the Ho Chi Minh Trail with Operation Lam Son 719. The North Vietnamese reaction was to launch the Easter Offensive in March 1972. The situation deteriorated until on May 8, President Nixon authorized the largest air strikes against North Vietnam since 1968. He reportedly told the Chairman of the Joint Chiefs of Staff, "Those bastards are going to be bombed like they've never been bombed before." Operation Linebacker struck targets in and around Hanoi and Haiphong, mined the North Vietnamese ports, and hammered the NVA Army in the south. Negotiations picked up, and by October 1972 the outline of a settlement was in place. Two weeks before the 1972

presidential election, Henry Kissinger announced, "Peace is at hand," and Nixon won handily. President Thieu objected to several of the terms of the agreement, and Nixon secretly promised him that the US would once again intervene militarily if the North Vietnamese violated the agreement. The North Vietnamese began dragging their feet in negotiations, and Nixon responded by unleashing Linebacker II, the "Christmas Bombing." In 12 days, US planes dropped more bombs on North Vietnam than they had from 1969 to 1971 and the North Vietnamese returned to the peace talks. The peace agreement was signed on January 27, 1973, and the American prisoners of war returned in March 1973. A short time later, the details of the Watergate cover-up became known and Nixon was forced from office, resigning in August 1974.

Nolting, Fredrick Jr

Appointed as US Ambassador to Vietnam by President Kennedy, Nolting served in that capacity from 1961–1963. He had no knowledge of Asia, and became a staunch and unwavering supporter of Ngo Dinh Diem. Following his

Below: Rear Admiral Strean escorts Secretary of the Navy Paul Nitze down the flight deck of the USS *Enterprise*.

Above: President Richard Nixon presents awards for gallantry to members of the Son Tay Raid.

Right: President Richard Nixon congratulates Air Force Brigadier General Leroy Minor on the Son Tay Raid.

inadequate response to instruction during the Buddhist Crisis, Kennedy replaced him. After the American approved coup against Diem, he resigned from government service in disgust.

North Vietnamese Army (NVA)

NVA was an acronym American soldiers used for the North Vietnamese Army in South Vietnam instead of calling them the People's Army of Vietnam (PAVN).

Nuclear Weapons

The use of nuclear weapons in Vietnam was considered on several occasions. First, to support the French at Dien Bien Phu in 1954; second, for tactical purposes in the early 1960s (in an interview in 1965 Secretary McNamara stated they had not been ruled out); third, to defend Khe Sanh in 1968. When Congress found out that General Westmoreland was involved in nuclear strike planning at Khe Sanh, the uproar caused the Chief

Left: A US Army Caribou drops supplies to the Special Forces observation post on top of Nui Ba Dien, or Black Woman Mountain.

Below: A Special Forces sergeant and a group of South Vietnamese look out from the top of Nui Ba Dien in 1964.

of Staff of the Army to forbid nuclear planning for any purpose in the war. However, after the Tet Offensive began, both the Chairman of the House and Senate Armed Services Committees recommended that nuclear weapons be employed against North Vietnam.

Nui Ba Dien

Nui Ba Dien, Black Woman Mountain, was located just outside Tay Ninh, 50 miles northwest of Saigon. There was a US intelligence and radio relay site on the top, however the Viet Cong controlled the slopes. In one of the anomalies of the war there was generally a gentleman's truce at the only spring on the mountain, where both sides obtained water. Nui Ba Dien was commonly referred to as Black Virgin Mountain by US troops.

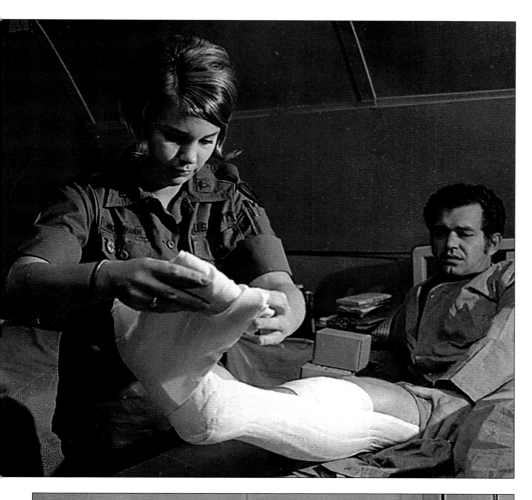

Left: A nurse changes the surgical dressing for a civilian contractor at the 24th Evacuation Hospital in 1971.

Below left: Lieutenant Francis Crumpton and Miss Nangoi Tongkin, a Thai nurse, talk to a patient at the Navy Hospital in Saigon.

Nung

In South Vietnam the Nung were a small Sino-Tibetan minority group, less than 20,000, who resided in the central highlands. There were also approximately 300,000 Nung living in North Vietnam. They were natural warriors, and became the most feared of all the native groups trained by the US Special Forces. Utterly fearless and scrupulously honest they were also recruited as guards by other US agencies.

Nur, Paul

Following the FULRO revolt in 1964, the South Vietnamese government set up a Ministry of Minority Affairs and appointed Paul Nur, a French-educated Rhade tribesman, as the first Minister. Unfortunately, Nur was extremely unpopular with the Montagnards, to include the Rhade, who referred to him derisively as the only Vietnamese Montagnard. His lack of real authority, coupled with his reputation with the tribes, crippled his ability to accomplish anything.

Nurses

Eighty percent of the approximately 10,000 women who served in Vietnam were military nurses. The first Army nurses were stationed at the 8th Field Hospital in Nha Trang in 1962, and the first Navy nurses arrived at the 3rd Field Hospital in Saigon at the same time. Air Force nurses came later. In 1969, at the peak of the war, 900 nurses were in Vietnam. One, 1st Lieutenant Sharon Lane, was killed by enemy fire in Chu Lai on June 8, 1969. Seven others died from other causes.

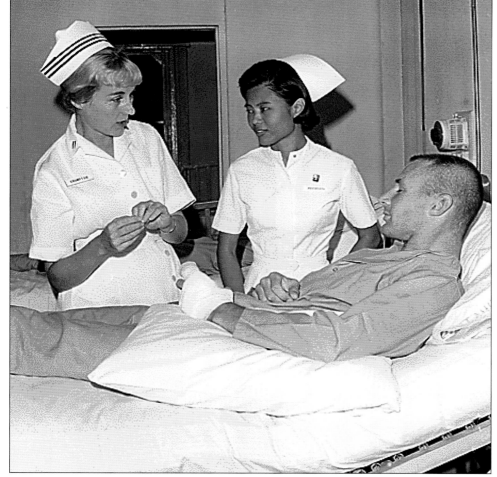

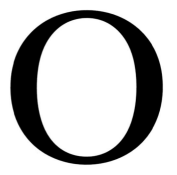

O'Daniel, John W

Lieutenant General John W O'Daniel was the chief of the US Army Military Assistance and Advisory Group (MAAG), Indochina, from March 1954 to October 1955. He developed a very close relationship with Ngo Dinh Diem, and became impressed with the military potential of the Vietnamese soldier. He retired from the US Army in 1955 and was a founder of the American Friends of Vietnam, which was an extremely effective lobby group.

Olds, Robin

Colonel Robin Olds was the commander of the 8th Tactical Fighter Wing in 1966 and 1967. In January 1967, capitalizing on an idea by Captain John B Stone, Colonel Olds launched Operation Bolo, which resulted in the shooting down of seven North Vietnamese MiG-21s, the greatest fighter success of the war. He flew more than 100 missions over North Vietnam in an F-4C Phantom II, and shot down two MiG-17s and two MiG-21s.

Olympic Torch

The code name, Olympic Torch, was given to the National Security Agency U-2 reconnaissance aircraft that orbited over the area where the borders of North Vietnam, Laos, and the People's

Above: Pilots of the 8th Tactical Fighter Wing carry Colonel Robin Olds away from his F-4B Phantom after his 100th mission over North Vietnam.

Republic of China meet. Its purpose was to monitor the electronic signatures, and report the location of NVA antiaircraft systems. The secondary purpose was to monitor the radio transmissions of units moving prisoners up the Ho Chi Minh Trail in an effort to organize a raid to rescue the POWs.

Omega Project

Project Omega was a specialized long-range reconnaissance and intelligence-gathering unit organized by the 5th Special Forces Group to respond to the requirements of Field Force I. It had 127 US Special Forces, and 894 CIDG troops. It was organized into a headquarters, a reconnaissance platoon with eight Roadrunner Teams and 16 Reconnaissance Teams, and a reaction force consisting of three rifle companies. It was US-led and did not contain Vietnamese elements.

OPLAN 34A

Approved by President Kennedy in November 1963, OPLAN 34 A included

Above left: The National Security Agency routinely orbited a U-2 surveillance aircraft, code-named Olympic Torch, over northeastern Laos to eavesdrop on NVA communications.

Above: The USS *Turner Joy* slides through the calm waters of the South China Sea off the Vietnamese coast.

Left: CIDG troops on patrol near the Cambodian border carry spare rounds for their mortar.

attack. In both instances carrier aircraft from the USS *Ticonderoga* attempted to support the destroyers. These two incidents, devolving directly from the raid launched under OPLAN 34A, led to the Gulf of Tonkin Resolution, which was in essence a defacto declaration of war against North Vietnam.

Order of Battle Controversy

The dispute between the CIA and Military Assistance Command Vietnam (MACV) concerning estimations of enemy combat strength was known as the "order of battle controversy." The problem arose because early estimates of the number of communist personnel active in South Vietnam were based on incomplete information and were too low. When more accurate information became available in 1967 the figures rose, creating a problem for military chiefs and government officials who were already facing growing domestic opposition to the war. The CIA argued for the higher estimates and their counterparts at MACV for lower estimates. In September 1967, they agreed to change the definitions by which the estimates were compiled, and a large section of the enemy forces was excluded from the final count.

raids by mercenaries and South Vietnamese commandos along the coast of North Vietnam. The raiders, usually at night, shelled coastal installations, landed and attacked communications posts and supply dumps, blew bridges, and mined roads. During the night of July 30, 1964, an OPLAN 34A raid was carried out against two small islands in the Gulf of Tonkin. The destroyer USS *Maddox*, conducting a DeSoto patrol, monitored the radar and radio transmissions during the raid. On August 2, the *Maddox* moved to within seven miles of the islands and was attacked by North Vietnamese PT boats. Joined by the USS *C Turner Joy*, on August 4, 1964 the two destroyers reported a second PT boat

P

Pacification

The term pacification is frequently defined as a process by which a government extends its influence into an area experiencing insurgency. In Vietnam the Viet Cong followed the Maoist model of guerrilla warfare. Beginning almost immediately after the Geneva Accords of 1954 communist guerrillas penetrated every level of rural hamlet and village life. By 1959, the Saigon government recognized the seriousness of the problem and attempted to blunt the expanding communist influence by separating the peasants from the Viet Cong. The Agrovilles program, launched that year, was designed to do that by concentrating the peasants in easily defended hamlets.

Left: A soldier from the 199th Infantry Brigade teaches English as part of the Brigade civic action program.

Below left: A group of visiting US Senators enjoy a drink of coconut milk at Huu Than, a show-place pacification hamlet.

Right: Although the higher authorities may not have approved, the Marines in the Arizona held their own "Miss Universe Contest."

Below: A medical team treats children's ailments as part of a pacification project.

Because the peasants were required to relocate from ancestral lands to the Agrovilles the program failed. In 1961, it was restructured as the Strategic Hamlet Program, and again failed, largely for the same reasons. In 1965, General Westmoreland decided that pacification was irrelevant, and attrition became MACV's main thrust. Until 1966, when President Johnson directed otherwise, the military essentially ignored pacification. In 1967, Robert Komer was put in charge of the pacification program known as Civil Operations and Revolutionary Development Support (CORDS), and made a deputy to General Westmoreland. Pacification efforts improved, but security remained a difficult issue. In August 1968, Komer received the full backing of the new Commanding General of MACV,

Right: Henry Kissinger and Le Duc Tho initial the Paris Peace Agreements as William Sullivan (lower right) and Xuan Thuy (upper left) look on.

General Creighton Abrams, and MACV began providing greater military support to the pacification effort. Recognizing that the Tet Offensive had devastated the Viet Cong, William Colby launched the Accelerated Pacification Program in November 1968. He significantly increased the strength and capabilities of the Regional and Popular Forces, and initiated the People's Self Defense Force, an informal militia designed to give the government an armed presence in virtually every hamlet and village. He also introduced the Phoenix Program in July 1968. One of the most controversial programs of the entire war, Phoenix was also one of the most effective, and resulted in the elimination of over 20,000 members of the Viet Cong infrastructure. Following the war, the North Vietnamese stated that they considered Phoenix one the most dangerous programs of the war. The Allies never really developed a comprehensive pacification strategy, and their lack of such a strategy resulted in the central government remaining unsupported by the population.

Palme, Olaf J

The Premier of Sweden, Olaf Palme, joined the North Vietnamese Ambassador to the Soviet Union in a demonstration against the US conduct of the war in 1968. In a speech, he compared Richard Nixon to Hitler. US-Swedish relations suffered for years as a result of it.

Palmer, Bruce C

Bruce Palmer served in Vietnam as the Commanding General, II Field Force, from 1967–1968, and later became Chief of Staff of the US Army, 1972–1974. Following his retirement he wrote a book castigating the civilian leadership for never establishing a clear combat goal to be achieved in Vietnam.

Paracel Islands

The Paracels are a group of 15 to 20 small islands in the South China Sea situated in a good position for monitoring naval traffic along the Indochinese coast. They were occupied by the South Vietnamese for over 20 years, and following rumors of oil deposits in the area were seized by force by the People's Republic of China in 1974.

Paris Negotiations

Attempts to arrive at a negotiated peace began in Paris on May 10, 1968 (the first formal meeting convened on May 13) but stalled after the US demanded that North Vietnamese troops withdraw from the South, while the North Vietnamese insisted on Viet Cong participation in a coalition government in South Vietnam. This was the beginning of five years of official talks between the US and North Vietnam in Paris.

The official talks began on January 25, 1969, with Henry Cabot Lodge, former American ambassador to South Vietnam, as senior US negotiator and representatives of South Vietnam, North Vietnam, and the Viet Cong all in attendance. Lodge quit his post in December, and in March 1972 the US staged a boycott with Nixon accusing Hanoi of refusing to "negotiate seriously." In late April, the talks resumed. By January 9, 1973, after a series of meetings between Henry Kissinger and Le Duc Tho in Paris, all remaining differences between the opposing factions had been satisfactorily resolved. This paved the way for the subsequent Paris Peace Agreement.

Paris Peace Agreement

Resulting from four years of peace talks in Paris, the Paris Peace Agreement was announced by Nixon on January 23, 1973 with the promise that it would "end the war [in Vietnam] and bring peace with honor."

The Paris Peace Accords were officially signed by the US, North Vietnam, South Vietnam and the Viet Cong on January 27, 1973. Under the terms, the US agreed to immediately halt all military activities and withdraw all remaining military personnel within 60 days. The North Vietnamese agreed to an immediate ceasefire and the release of all American POWs within 60 days. An estimated 150,000 North Vietnamese soldiers currently in South Vietnam were allowed to remain.

Vietnam was, however, still divided. South Vietnam was considered to be one country with two governments, one led by President Thieu, the other led by Viet Cong, pending future reconciliation.

Excerpt from the Paris Peace Accords, January 27, 1973:
Article 2
A ceasefire shall be observed throughout South Vietnam as of 24:00 hours GMT, on January 27, 1973. At the same hour, the United States will stop all its military activities against the territory of the Democratic Republic of Vietnam by ground, air, and naval forces, wherever they may be based, and end the mining of the territorial waters, ports, harbors, and waterways of the Democratic Republic of Vietnam. The United States will remove, permanently deactivate or destroy all the mines in the territorial waters, ports, harbors, and waterways of North Vietnam as soon as this Agreement goes into effect. The complete cessation of hostilities mentioned in this Article shall be durable and without limit of time...

Above: North Vietnamese captured by the ARVN in the Parrot's Beak wait evacuation to the rear.

Right: Members of the ARVN 10th Armored Cavalry and 46th Infantry Regiment move into the Parrot's Beak during the Cambodian Incursion.

Parrot's Beak

The Parrot's Beak is a sparsely populated, heavily jungled area of Cambodia that looks like a bird's beak and juts into South Vietnam 40 miles west of Saigon. The Cambodian ruler, Prince Sihanouk, allowed the North Vietnamese to establish base camps there in 1965. They were protected from attack until President Nixon authorized secret B-52 strikes against them under Operation Menu in March 1969. It was a key ARVN target during the Cambodian Incursion.

Pathet Lao

The Laotian resistance group, Pathet Lao (meaning "Land of the Lao"), was formed by Prince Souphanouvong in August 1950 to fight for independence from the French. Communists dominated

the leadership, and although the movement was careful to moderate its stance to appeal to non-communists, it never achieved the popularity of the Viet Minh.

Paul VI

Paul VI was the Pope, and leader of the Roman Catholic Church from 1963 to 1978. He constantly pressed the United States for a ceasefire and negotiations in Vietnam. Despite the fact that many of the early government hierarchy of South Vietnam were catholic, his influence there was minimal.

Paul Revere I–IV, Operations

Operations Paul Revere I–IV were a series of screening operations conducted along the Cambodian border in the Pleiku province of the central highlands from May 10–December 30, 1966. Encouraged by the success of the 1st Cavalry Division in the Battle of the Ia Drang, General Westmoreland was determined to concentrate US forces

Left: A mixed group of North Vietnamese and Pathet Lao prisoners captured on the Plain of Jars wait to be evacuated to a POW camp.

Below: A dozer tank takes up a position over-watching Highway 14 south of Pleiku during Operation Paul Revere II.

VIETNAM: A VISUAL ENCYCLOPEDIA

Left: Lieutenant General William Peers was specifically selected to lead the Army investigation of My Lai because he was not a West Point Graduate.

along the western edge of the province in an attempt to generate additional main force set piece battles against the 1st NVA Division. In both Operation Paul Revere I and II, units of the 1st Cavalry Division and 3rd Brigade of the 25th infantry Division had some success around the Chu Pong massif, and along the Ia Drang River. Operation Paul Revere III made only minimal contact, because the NVA units had withdrawn into Cambodia to regroup and refit. Operation Paul Revere IV, October 18– December 30, 1966, was the first major operation involving the newly arrived 4th Infantry Division. Again working in the area of the Chu Pong massif and the Ia Drang, the 4th Infantry Division, reinforced by elements of the 3rd Brigade of the 25th infantry Division and the 1st Cavalry Division, encountered a regiment of the 10th NVA Division. US forces suffered heavy casualties in a series of well-executed NVA ambushes. However, by the end of the operation the NVA Regiment, with a normal strength

Above: Howitzers of the 25th Infantry Division pound elements of the 66th NVA Regiment in the Battle of 10 Alpha on Operation Paul Revere.

of just under 3,000, had left 977 dead on the battlefield.

Peers, William B

Lieutenant General Peers, who had commanded both the 4th Infantry Division and Field Force I in Vietnam, was appointed by the Army Chief of Staff and the Secretary of the Army to head a commission to investigate the cover-up of the My Lai massacre. His exhaustive 255-page report fixed responsibility at several levels, and led to court martial charges against 12 Army participants.

Later, after only Lieutenant Calley was convicted of wrongdoing, and disgusted with what he considered the Army's failure to bring those responsible to justice, he wrote a book which explicitly laid out both the findings of his commission and his concerns.

Peers Inquiry

On November 26, 1969, General William C Westmoreland, then the US Army Chief of Staff, and Secretary of the

Above: A CH-54 maneuvers a new section of a bridge on Highway 9 into place and the Marines secure it during Operation Pegasus.

Army, Stanley C Resor, appointed Lieutenant General William Peers to head up a special inquiry into the alleged cover-up of the My Lai massacre by the Army chain of command. Four months later the inquiry panel recommended court-martial charges against 12 officers for covering up what happened at My Lai and two others for war crimes. While the cases against those recommended for charges were extensively documented, senior commanders in the Army administratively dismissed the charges against the most senior officers, as well as those against several of their subordinates. In the end the Army determined that no one was guilty of any criminal wrongdoing. Lieutenant Calley, who was not one of

those involved in the Peers Inquiry because he had already been charged with murder, was the only one of those involved at My Lai who was court-martialed and convicted.

Pegasus, Operation

Operation Pegasus, April 1–15, 1968, was launched to relieve the Marines under siege at Khe Sanh. Under the command of Major General John Tolson, the 1st Air Cavalry Division, reinforced by two battalions of the 1st Marines, an ARVN Airborne Task Force, and an ARVN Ranger Battalion, made up the relieving force of approximately 30,000 men. To confuse the NVA divisions surrounding Khe Sanh, on March 31 other

Marine units attacked north toward the Demilitarized Zone. On April 1, the task force Marines and the 1st Cavalry Division attacked west along Highway 9. NVA units along Route 9 were pounded by tactical air, B-52s, and 1st Cavalry Division gunships. By executing a series of battalion-sized leapfrog combat assaults, the task force rapidly overran the NVA who opposed them. On April 8, the 1st Cavalry linked up with the Marines in Khe Sanh and on April 11 the

1st Marines completed the opening of Route 9. Operation Pegasus was the first full division-sized airmobile assault.

Pennsylvania, Operation

Operation Pennsylvania was the code name for a secret diplomatic attempt to end the Vietnam War in the summer and fall of 1967. Operating through two French citizens, one a socialist member of the World Health Organization who knew Ho Chi Minh, and the other a French biologist, Henry Kissinger established a communication channel with the highest levels of the North Vietnamese government. North Vietnamese Premier Pham Van Dong insisted on an unconditional stop to the bombing over the north but said that it did not have to be publicized. After much discussion, on August 8, 1967 Secretary of Defense Robert McNamara obtained concurrence from President Johnson and Secretary of State Dean Rusk to go ahead, and agreement was communicated to the North Vietnamese, with a start date of August 24. Unfortunately, bad weather, which had been slowing the raids against the North, cleared, and on August 20 the US launched the most intense air strikes of the war up to that point against North Vietnam. The North Vietnamese believed that they had been duped. By October 20, 1967 they terminated the communications link.

Pentagon Papers

The Pentagon Papers was a 7,000-page, 47-volume, classified document prepared by a task force created by Secretary of Defense Robert McNamara to document the history of US involvement in Vietnam. Compiled between 1967 and 1969, it details the history of that involvement from 1945 through 1968. It is based solely on internal documentation generated within the US government, mostly from the files of the departments of Defense and State, and the CIA. It also included some White House documentation and informal memoranda from within the Department of Defense, though no formal White House documentation is contained in the study. Dr Daniel Ellsberg, who had been a participant in the study, secretly copied portions of it and delivered them to *The New York Times*. Attorney General John Mitchell informed *The New York Times* that publication of the study would be a violation of the espionage laws. *The New York Times* refused to stop publication and the government took them to court. Eventually the Supreme Court ruled six to three against the government's claim that publication would harm the nation and in agreement that the First Amendment to the Constitution took precedence over the administration claim to secrecy. The papers were published.

People's Army of Vietnam (PAVN)

The People's Army of Vietnam (PAVN) began life as a small guerrilla force under the control of Ho Chi Minh and commanded by Vo Nguyen Giap during World War II. It grew and expanded in the late 1940s during the French-Indochina War. By 1950, though still simply called the Viet Minh, it consisted of three infantry divisions with around 35,000 troops. While sometimes overlooked, it was the regular units, rather than guerrillas, that defeated the French at Dinh Bien Phu. Emerging from the French war equipped with a hodgepodge of captured and communist supplied weapons, the PAVN began a modernization program in 1957. In 1960, the

Below: A 1st Cavalry Division Loach flies over a Marine column headed for Khe Sanh during Operation Pegasus.

Democratic Republic of Vietnam instituted a three-year compulsory military service law. By 1960, the ground combat forces had been organized into infantry, air defense, artillery, engineering, and communications branches. With support from the People's Republic of China and the Soviet Union, an Air Force, Navy, and small armored, transportation, and chemical units were also organized. The 1960 army consisted of approximately 160,000 troops, 93,000 of whom were infantry. With the introduction of US combat forces to Vietnam in 1965, the PAVN underwent another transformation. Generously provided with modern weapons by the Soviet Union and the People's Republic of China, the army's capability significantly expanded. The air defense units, in particular, were increased in size and the sophistication of their weapons systems made Hanoi and Haiphong the most heavily defended locales in the world. Although overwhelming US fire support during the American phase of the war repeatedly decimated PAVN units, their courage and tenacity earned the American soldiers' respect. By 1975, the PAVN had become a highly skilled, experienced, and modern light infantry army consisting of 24 divisions, 10 artillery regiments, 10 independent infantry regiments, 15 surface-to-air missile (SAM) regiments, and 40 antiaircraft artillery regiments. They also had three training divisions. The Air Force contained one light bomber squadron, four MiG-21 and two MiG-19 fighter squadrons, six MiG-17 fighter-bomber squadrons, and associated support troops. A militia numbering approximately 1.5 million backed them up. The Navy, which was routinely hammered by the US Navy and Air Force, only had about 3,000 men and a number of small coastal craft. In the final offensive the PAVN committed all but one division to the destruction of South Vietnam.

People's Liberation Armed Forces (PLAF)

The People's Liberation Armed Forces (PLAF) the military arm of the National Front for the Liberation of South Vietnam (NFLSV) was commonly referred to as the Viet Cong. It was formally established in early 1961, and consisted of regular forces, guerrillas, and a part-time guerrilla militia. As the Viet Cong's control of the countryside increased, the size of the PLAF increased as well. The introduction of US ground forces in 1965, and their subsequent release for offensive operations, resulted in several significant battles with the PLAF and the increased infiltration of combat units of the North Vietnamese Army into the South. The PLAF spearheaded the attacks against towns and cities during the Tet Offensive. They suffered horrendous casualties. After Tet, the NVA shouldered more and more of the burden of directly engaging US troops, while the PLAF rebuilt its village and hamlet infrastructure.

By 1975, they had rebuilt their units to the point that General Van Tien Dung, Chief of Staff of the North Vietnamese Army, credited them with significant accomplishments during the final offensive that resulted in the fall of South Vietnam. After the war most PLAF units were disbanded, though a few were integrated into the NVA.

People's Self Defense Force (PSDF)

Influenced by the recommendations of William Colby and the CIA, one element

Right: A Marine closely guards a North Vietnamese prisoner as they move to the POW collection point.

and in some places functioned as People's Liberation Armed Forces support troops.

Pershing, Operation

Operation Pershing was the largest continuous operation conducted by the 1st Air Cavalry Division during the war. Pershing I ran from February 11, 1967 to January 21, 1968. Pershing II began on January 22, 1968 and ran through February 29. The purpose of the operation was to drive the North Vietnamese Yellow Star Division away from the coast and pacify Binh Dinh province. In the end, the 1st Air Cavalry Division reported that they had succeeded. In reality, what they had done is chase the North Vietnamese units back into the mountains, forcibly relocating over 100,000 inhabitants, and then literally drenching the now depopulated cropland with the defoliant Agent Orange. However, they did achieve victories over large NVA forces at Tam Quan, and at Dam Tra-O Lake in March 1967.

The last major battle of Operation Pershing was fought from December 6

of the Republic of Vietnam's General Mobilization Law (June 1968) was created to form the People's Self Defense Force (PSDF). All male citizens that were 16 or 17 and between the ages of 39 and 54 were required to join the PSDF. A four-week training course was established at national training centers for team and section leaders, however few attended. Armed with a mish-mash of obsolescent weapons, the PSDF rarely engaged the Viet Cong or NVA directly. However, in many villages and hamlets, they did undertake low-level guerrilla actions against them.

By 1972, it was claimed that the PSDF had over 1 million members, most of whom had received some combat training. Their performance was sporadic, but in some localities security appeared to increase. On the other hand, the PSDF was heavily infiltrated by the Viet Cong

Right: A 12-year-old member of the People's Self Defense Force with a grenade launcher stands among the devastated houses following an attack on Tan Son Nhut.

to December 20, 1967 when the 1st Brigade and units of the 22nd ARVN Division encountered two battalions of the 22nd NVA Regiment near Tam Quan, killing over 600 of them.

Pham Hung

A protégé of Pham Van Dong, in 1956 Pham Hung became the highest-ranking Party official from South Vietnam elected to the Politburo. In 1965, he assumed command of the Central Office of South Vietnam (COSVN) and took charge of the Viet Cong insurgency.

As the COSVN Commander and Political Commissar for communist forces in the south, he oversaw the Tet Offensive in 1968. In 1975, he served as General Van Tien Dung's Political Commissar in the final offensive.

Pham Ngoc Thao

A Viet Cong intelligence agent, Pham Ngoc Thao penetrated the highest levels of the South Vietnamese government and military. In 1963, he had been promoted to Colonel and placed in charge of the Strategic Hamlet Program. He was active in the coup against President Ngo Dinh Diem, and was assigned to the Vietnamese Embassy in Washington DC in 1964. In 1965, he returned to Vietnam and disappeared. The speculation was that the South Vietnamese had discovered his true allegiance and eliminated him. After the fall of Saigon the Socialist Republic of Vietnam promoted him posthumously to Brigadier General and proclaimed him a hero.

Below: A platoon takes a break and drinks some coconut milk during Operation Pershing in Binh Dinh Province.

Above: An infantryman searches a Viet Cong supply cache in the An Lao Valley during Operation Pershing.

Pham Van Dong

Along with Ho Chi Minh and Vo Nguyen Giap, Pham Van Dong was one of the founders of the Lao Dong Party, and for over 40 years was one of the three men who dominated North Vietnamese politics. He was active in the Viet Minh and fought against both the Japanese in World War II and the French in the Indochina War. In 1954, he led the Viet Minh delegation to the Geneva Conference. From 1950 to 1975 he served as the Democratic Republic of Vietnam's Premier. After Ho Chi Minh died in 1969, he consolidated his power, and played a key role in both the war and the Paris negotiations. After the fall of the south in 1975, he was appointed as the Prime Minister of the Socialist Republic of Vietnam.

Pham Van Phu

In 1954, Pham Van Phu served in the 5th Parachute Battalion of the Army of the State of Vietnam and fought for the French at Dien Bien Phu. He later commanded the South Vietnamese Special Forces and by 1975 had become the commander of II Corps. In March 1975, his troops suffered heavy losses as he led

the disastrous retreat from the central highlands to the coast during the first phase of the NVA Final Offensive. On April 30, 1975, as Saigon fell, he committed suicide.

Phan Huy Quat

In February 1965, Phan Huy Quat, who had been one of the leaders of the "Caravel Group" in April 1960 and had urged President Diem to implement political reforms, became the last civilian Premier of the Republic of Vietnam. He was caught by surprise by the initial deployment of US combat troops because no one in either the embassy or the military had informed him it was going to happen. Nguyen Cao Ky overthrew his government in a coup. The communists executed him after South Vietnam fell.

Phan Khac Suu

President Diem's first Minister of Agriculture, Phan Khac Suu, was a devout member of the Cao Dai religion. He strongly opposed Diem's suppression of the sect. He participated in an abortive coup against Diem in 1960 and was imprisoned. Released after Diem's death, he became the Chief of State of South Vietnam in 1964, but Nguyen Cao Ky overthrew his government in 1965. He served as the President of the Constituent

Assembly in 1966 and 1967 and was an opponent of Generals Nguyen Cao Ky and Nguyen Van Thieu. He died in 1970.

Phay Dang

Phay Dang was a prominent Hmong leader in northeastern Laos. He fought against the Japanese in World War II, and with the Viet Minh against the French in the Indochina War. He opposed US intervention in Laos and became a leader of the Pathet Lao. He was a bitter enemy of Vang Pao.

Philippines

The Philippines was a member of the South-east Asia Treaty Organization, and extended diplomatic recognition to South Vietnam in 1955. It staunchly supported the US position in South Vietnam and served throughout the war as a strategic rear area for both the US Navy and Air Force. In 1966, the Philippines deployed 2,000 combat engineers to South Vietnam to work on pacification projects. However, as internal opposition to the war grew, they were withdrawn in October 1969, and a troop commitment was never again considered.

Phnom Penh

Phnom Penh, the capital of Cambodia, essentially remained at peace until Lon Nol overthrew Prince Sihanouk in

Left: A CH-54 starts the relocation of a 155mm artillery battery near Phu Bai to support Operation Niagara.

1970. That, coupled with the US bombing of the border areas with Vietnam, resulted in a flow of refugees into the city and an expansion of the Khmer Rouge. By 1973, the civil war in Cambodia had spread to the environs of Phnom Penh. The city fell to the Khmer Rouge in 1975 and their draconian rule essentially depopulated it. The 1979 Vietnamese invasion brought some life back to the capital, and the final decline of the Khmer Rouge by 1991 initiated reconstruction.

Phoenix (Phung Huong) Program

Easily one of the most controversial programs of the Vietnam War, Phoenix was begun by Robert Komer, the civilian head of the US Civil Operations and Revolutionary Development Support (CORDS). Financially supported and directed by the CIA, CORDS instituted a new Intelligence Coordination and Exploitation (ICEX) program. Its purpose was to collect, analyze, and disseminate information about the Viet Cong infrastructure to field units. As the CIA were involved in running it, there were

concerns that it violated the sovereignty of South Vietnam.

In early 1968, William Colby, Chief of the CIA Far East Division, obtained a signed decree from President Nguyen Van Thieu establishing an organization named Phung Huong (Phoenix) to assume the running of the ICEX operation. Working from lists of communist personnel gleaned from numerous sources of intelligence, the organizers of Phoenix or Phung Huong Program gave orders to the Regional Forces/ Popular Forces, Provincial Reconnaissance Units, or the National Police Field Force to either apprehend or kill specific individuals that were identified with the Viet Cong infrastructure.

Despite the controversial nature of the program in the United States, top-ranking Viet Cong and North Vietnamese leaders agreed that the Phoenix Program was a success, and severely eroded the communist infrastructure in those provinces where it was active. By the end of the war over 20,000 VCI operatives had been neutralized, either captured or killed.

Phoumi Nosavan

A Laotian general and political leader, Phoumi Nosavan continually intrigued against the government in power. In 1960, while he was the Minister of Defense, a paratroop captain named Kong Le staged a coup d'état and overthrew the government in August. With Thai and CIA support, in December Phoumi staged a rightist countercoup under the nominal leadership of Prince Boun Oum. He served as the Deputy Premier of an internationally brokered coalition government that took office in June 1962. Caught up in a 1965 rightist coup plot that failed, he fled to Thailand and never returned to Laos.

Phu Bai

A small town 45 miles north of Danang and five miles south of Hue, Phu Bai was an important American military installation from 1965 to 1972. It served first as the headquarters of the 9th Marine Expeditionary Brigade, then the headquarters of Marine Air Group 39, and finally after the construction of Camp Eagle in 1968, as the headquarters of the 101st Airborne Division.

Phuc, Kim

Kim Phuc was the subject of one of the most widely distributed photographs of the Vietnam War. She was the little girl who, following a South Vietnamese Air Force napalm strike on a village near Trang Bang northwest of Saigon, was photographed running screaming down a road with a group of panicked refugees, having torn her burning clothes off. The photograph was used by many antiwar groups to decry the inhumanity of US Air Force operations, even though no Americans were involved.

Phuoc Binh

Approximately 80 miles north of Saigon, Phuoc Binh was the capital of Phuoc Long province. Almost due east of Snuol, Cambodia, a major NVA base area, it was frequently attacked. Heavy fighting took place there in May 1965, and again in October 1967 as a prelude to the Tet Offensive. Phuoc Binh was the first provincial capital to fall during the NVA's Final Offensive.

Pierce Arrow, Operation

The initial retaliatory strikes against North Vietnam ordered in response to the Gulf of Tonkin Incident were code-named Operation Pierce Arrow. Aircraft from the US aircraft carriers *Ticonderoga* and *Constellation* struck North Vietnamese naval vessels along the coast and a petroleum storage facility at Vinh. Sixty-four sorties were flown and four aircraft were lost. The petroleum storage facility was destroyed, and at least one coastal patrol vessel was sunk. One pilot was killed, and Lieutenant Everett Alvarez was captured and became America's first, and longest held, prisoner of war. Both sides claimed victory and significantly exaggerated the outcome of the raid. Pierce Arrow was a precursor to Operation Rolling Thunder.

Pike, Douglas

Douglas Pike was a State Department Foreign Service officer from 1958 to 1982. He is an expert on Vietnamese communism and their development of politico-military strategy. He stated that "there is no proven counterstrategy," for the Vietnamese concept of revolutionary war. He also credited the success of North Vietnamese propaganda and political activity for the sustainment of the antiwar movement in the United States.

Piranha, Operation

Operation Piranha was the first large-scale combined military operation run by the US Marines and the ARVN. Begun on September 7, 1965, it was a follow on from Operation Starlight on the Batangan Peninsula in Quang Ngai province. It was designed to mop up the remnants of the 1st VC Regiment, which had been severely mauled by the Marines during Operation Starlight. Contact was only light and sporadic, and by the end of the month it was terminated. As a result of the back-to-back operations however, the commanders of the Viet Cong regiment recognized that they could not face the Marines in a stand-up fight and expect to win. By reverting to a lower level of combat, the 1st VC Regiment remained active on the Batangan Peninsula and in Quang Ngai province throughout the war.

Pistols (Allied)

The most widely available pistol in Vietnam was the American M1911A1 .45 caliber semiautomatic. They were standard issue to those US personnel authorized a sidearm, and large quantities were provided to the South Vietnamese, South Koreans, Thais, and Filipinos. There were some 9mm Browning High-Powers used by the Australian and New Zealand contingents as well. The Browning 9mm Mark 1 and the suppressed 9mm Smith and Wesson Military Mark 22 Model O, "Hush Puppy" were sometimes used by SOG and the SEALs. Clandestine units frequently carried a suppressed High Standard .22 caliber semiautomatic. Some 38-caliber revolvers, Smith and Wesson Military, or Colt Police Positive Specials, were issued to military police units and aircrews.

Pistols (North Vietnamese and Viet Cong)

There were not many communist design pistols in use in Vietnam. In the Viet Cong and North Vietnamese forces a pistol was a status symbol for the officers, and was only rarely issued to enlisted men. The most common pistols in the

Below: Viet Cong prisoners are evacuated to the regimental collection point for interrogation.

Tuong provinces west of Saigon, it is sparsely populated. The Viet Cong and NVA normally used it as a transit area from War Zone C and Cambodia to the more heavily populated regions of the Delta to the south. The US Navy, as part of Operation Barrier Reef, effectively interdicted this route.

Pleiku

The capital of Pleiku province located in the central highlands, Pleiku City was the headquarters of the II Corps Tactical Zone. Located at the junction of north-south National Route 14 and east-west National Route 19, it was an important regional market for the Montagnards. On February 7, 1965 the Viet Cong attacked a US helicopter base, Camp Holloway, and Pleiku's airfield, killing nine and wounding 128 Americans. This served as one element of President Johnson's justification for launching Operation Flaming Dart, the retaliatory air strikes against North Vietnam that quickly became Operation Rolling Thunder.

VC and NVA, other than captured US weapons, were the 7.62mm Soviet Tokarev TT 33, and Chinese copies of it designated types 51 and 54. There were also a few 9mm Makarov PMs and the Chinese Type 59 copy.

Plain of Jars

A large rolling plain located in Xieng Khouang province of northern Laos near the border of North Vietnam, the Plain of Jars is named for a large number of big stone urns of unknown origin scattered across it.

Its strategic location, abutting and transited by the Ho Chi Minh Trail, as well as its importance to both the Hmong and the Pathet Lao, made it the most heavily fought over area in Laos. Without control of the Plain of Jars it is virtually impossible to control Laos.

Plain of Reeds

The Plain of Reeds is a marshy and brush-covered region formed by a depression in the Mekong River Delta. Located mainly in Kien Phong and Kien

Right: A PACV crew sets their air cushion vehicle down on the Plain of Reeds.

Right: Bob Hope arrives in Pleiku for a Christmas show at the 4th Infantry Division base camp.

Point

The point is a man or group of men advancing ahead of the main body of troops in a column formation. The purpose of the point is to either discover the presence of the enemy by observation or by drawing enemy fire, as well as to search out and clear or mark mines and booby traps so that the movement of the main body is not impeded. The point was the least desirable position in a patrol.

Pol Pot

Born Saloth Sar, Pol Pot was the leader of the communist Khmer Rouge and the

Below: The point carefully searches the flanks of the trail for any indication of the enemy's presence.

Below right: A point moves through a deserted rice paddy in I Corps.

architect of the Cambodian genocide. Achieving power in 1975 with the defeat of the US-backed Lon Nol government, his intent was to return Cambodia to its pro-buddhist glory by rebuilding the medieval economy of the Angkor Kingdom and regaining ancient territory from Vietnam and Thailand. In 1977, he launched guerrilla raids on Laos, Thailand, and Vietnam. The Vietnamese invaded Cambodia in 1979 and drove him from power, though he continued guerrilla warfare from the jungle. Finally captured in 1997 he died April 15, 1998 of a heart attack.

Poland

Along with India and Canada, Poland was a member of the International Commission for Supervision and Control. It was set up by the 1954 Geneva Accords to supervise the cease-fire that ended the French-Indochina War and the political reunification of Vietnam following the 1956 elections. Polish support for communist positions hamstrung the Commission, because Commission actions required a unanimous agreement among the parties.

Police Aerial Reinforcement Unit (PARU)

The Police Aerial Reinforcement Units were the equivalent of a Special Forces structure in Thailand. PARU units both trained and commanded Laotian troops and Hmong guerrillas fighting in Laos. They also recruited and commanded several battalions of Thai mercenaries raised for combat in Laos. At the peak of the war there was the equivalent of a Thai Division engaged in Laos.

Popular Forces

The Popular Forces were paramilitary units charged with the security and protection of their own villages and hamlets. They were first formed in 1955, and operated under the control of the province chiefs. In 1964, they were integrated into the Vietnamese armed forces as a part of the territorial forces along with the Regional Forces, and the Joint General Staff assumed control of their operations and support. As the United States began to withdraw from Vietnam, a great deal of attention was paid to upgrading the weapons and training of all of the territorial forces. The improved territorial forces assumed greater combat duties as American withdrawal progressed and the ARVN began integrating

Above: Pol Pot, the leader of the Khmer Rouge, talks to a Japanese journalist near the Thai-Cambodian border.

the Popular Forces into Army operations and deploying them away from their home villages. Still charged with the local defense task, because they were lightly armed they were also a frequent target of NVA attacks and during the final offensive they were overwhelmed. They were generally looked down upon by the ARVN, who considered them second-rate units.

Porter, William James

In 1965, William Porter was assigned as the Deputy Ambassador to South Vietnam. His function was to create order out of the chaotic pacification program that was being established, however, within 18 months the program had been transferred to MACV and Porter was reassigned to Korea. His broad experience in dealing with an insurgency, gained while assigned to Morocco and Algeria, qualified him for his most

significant role in the Vietnam War as an advisor to Lyndon Johnson.

Positive Identification and Radar Advisory Zone (PIRAZ)

In 1965, Navy surface warships established themselves between the coast of North Vietnam and the American aircraft carriers at Yankee Station. In July 1966, these patrols were named PIRAZ for "Positive Identification Radar Advisory Zone." The ships conducted early

Above right: A Popular Forces squad advances cautiously down a road in Thua Tien province.

Right: Much like the cavalry forts in the old American west, a wooden stockade surrounds a small Popular Forces camp.

Right: Three troops take a smoke break in the rain in the Demilitarized Zone during Operation Prairie.

warning and fighter control duties, provided a navigational reference point for US aircraft, tracked all planes flying over the Gulf of Tonkin and eastern North Vietnam, directed search and rescue helicopters, and insured that American fighters did not intrude into communist Chinese air space.

Poulo Condore
See Con Son.

Powell, Colin L
Colin Powell was the first African-American to serve as Chairman of the Joint Chiefs of Staff. He served two tours in Vietnam, the first as an ARVN advisor in 1962 and 1963, and the second as an assistant operations officer in the Americal Division in 1968 and 1969. He wrote the Americal Division's first official response concerning the My Lai massacre, and reported that the rumors of its occurrence were unfounded. Later, some investigators came to consider Powell's report as part of the cover-up, but he staunchly maintained that he knew nothing about it until it became public in November 1969.

Practice Nine Project
In 1966, Secretary of Defense Robert McNamara ordered the implementation of a proposal by a Harvard professor named Roger Fisher to create a high-technology barrier against North Vietnamese infiltration from the South China Sea to the Laotian border along the Demilitarized Zone. The concept depended heavily on sensors, which would monitor, detect, and report the location of movement electronically. These reports would then be acted upon by aircraft, which would attack the areas within which the movements were reported. MACV modified the original proposal, and in the summer of 1967 began implementation of a cleared linear barrier along the Demilitarized Zone 600–1,000m wide, containing barbwire, mine fields, sensors, and strong points which would be backed by artillery bases that provided an interlocking pattern of

Right: A North Vietnamese militia fighter escorts an American pilot shot down over the north to prison.

320

Left: A captured Air Force pilot is paraded through a North Vietnamese village in the back of a truck.

he grudgingly approved a small operating area along the eastern Laos panhandle south of Tchepone, where small Special Forces teams would be allowed to conduct limited reconnaissance. The MACV Studies and Observations Group (SOG) initially named the area and the operation Shining Brass. In 1967, the name was changed to Prairie Fire. Prairie Fire was also the code words used in a radio call for emergency extraction of a reconnaissance team.

Prisoners of War (POWs), Allied

American POWs were held in 11 prisons in North Vietnam. There were four prisons in Hanoi, six others within a 50-mile radius of the city, and one at Cao Bang near the Chinese border. Additional prisoners were held by the Pathet Lao in Laos and by the Viet Cong in South Vietnam. The treatment of prisoners varied greatly depending on where they were held. In South Vietnam they were caged, poorly fed, and forced to work on agricultural or other projects, but were rarely tortured or mistreated. Of the hundreds of men missing in Laos, only ten were released at the end the war. In

fire from the South China Sea inland for 30km. The original code name for this barrier was Practice Nine. It was later renamed Dye Marker.

Prairie, Operation

Operation Prairie was a series of recurring actions designed to prevent the NVA 324B Division from moving across the Demilitarized Zone into Quang Tri province and establishing an operating base. During Prairie I, August 3, 1966–January 31, 1967, the US 3rd Marine Division fought the NVA in a number of savage encounters around Con Thien, Gio Linh, and Cam Lo, in northern I Corps, an area that later became known as Leatherneck Square. They drove the North Vietnamese back across the DMZ, killing over 2,000 NVA soldiers, but suffered 200 dead, and well over 1,000 wounded in the process. In Prairie II, January 31, 1967–March 18, 1967, the 3rd Marines fought a series of running engagements with the 812th Regiment of the NVA 324B Division between Cam Lo and Khe Sanh, killing 483 NVA and losing 93 Marines. In Operation Prairie III, the 3rd Marine Division engaged units from the NVA 324B and 341st Divisions around Gio Linh, Cam Lo, Con Thien, and Mai Loc, March 18, 1967–April 19, 1967. Once again the NVA were pushed back across

the Demilitarized Zone with heavy losses on both sides.

Prairie Fire

Ambassador William Sullivan adamantly refused to allow any US military ground operations inside Laos. However, after increasingly acrimonious negotiations between the MACV and the ambassador,

Below: POWs, returning after the Paris Agreements, cheer as they debark from the C-130 that brought them home.

Far left: A 1969 North Vietnamese propaganda photograph that purportedly shows a POW tending his garden at the Hanoi Hilton.

Left: Two American POWs are shown ostensibly reading magazines in a prison library festooned with slogans.

Below left: Inside South Vietnam the Viet Cong frequently confined their prisoners to bamboo cages similar to this one.

North Vietnam, from 1965 to 1969, prisoners were isolated, moved from camp to camp, malnourished, and brutally tortured. Although the Democratic Republic of Vietnam agreed to abide by the 1949 Geneva Convention on the treatment of prisoners of war, they steadfastly contended that the captive Americans were not prisoners of war but were "air pirates" and criminals, and therefore the Geneva Convention did not apply to them. After the death of Ho Chi Minh in September 1969, the torture stopped and conditions improved. After the Son Tay Raid in 1970, all of the prisoners in North Vietnam were moved into a single prison in Hanoi. Following the Paris Peace Agreements in 1973, the North Vietnamese released 565 US military, and 26 civilian prisoners of war. Because the number was so low, and many confirmed to have been prisoners were not released, the issue became extremely controversial, and colored US–Vietnamese relations for nearly 30 years. There was never an accounting of the number of South Vietnamese prisoners who were held.

Prisoners of War (POWs), North Vietnamese and Viet Cong

The South Vietnamese government operated four prisoner of war camps, one in each Corps Tactical Zone. They were Phu Qouc Island, which was the largest, Tan Hiep, Can Tho, and Danang. US forces did not operate any prisoner of war camps. After initial interrogation all prisoners were turned over to Republic of Vietnam control. A prisoner census taken in 1973 indicated that there were slightly more than 40,000 enemy soldiers in POW camps throughout South Vietnam. These totals did not include political prisoners from the Viet Cong infrastructure who were not members of the Viet Cong and North Vietnamese armed forces. Civilian detainees were not covered by the Geneva Convention and several thousand of them were interred at the infamous French-built correction center at Con Son (Poulo Condre Island) known for its "tiger cages," where recalcitrant prisoners were held incommunicado. There were no NVA prisoners at Con Son.

Programs Evaluation Office (PEO)

The Programs Evaluation Office (PEO) was a device utilized by the US government to circumvent the prohibition against a foreign military presence in Laos. Organized in 1955, it was attached to the US operations mission. It was headed by a US Army General and staffed by US military personnel, all of whom had been removed from the active duty lists of their services and detailed to Laos, ostensibly as civilians. The PEO had sole jurisdiction over the expenditure of funds provided to Laos by the US Congress under the Mutual Security Program. Additionally, although attached to the US operational mission, the PEO also possessed an exclusive communication channel to Washington through the Commander in Chief Pacific and the Defense Department. It was the PEO that brought in Special Forces troops to assume the Royal Lao Army training mission from the French, and provided much of the support for General Phoumi Nosavan and the rightist elements in Laotian politics.

Project 22-101

A contingency plan, known as Project 22-101, was constructed for the forward defense of Thailand along the Mekong Valley inside Laos in the event that the People's Republic of China entered the war. It was coordinated with the Thai government as a part of the negotiations for Thai support of the ground war in Laos, and also for the use of airbases and other installations to prosecute the war in Vietnam.

Left: Two blindfolded North Vietnamese infantrymen wait to be turned over to the ARVN for interrogation.

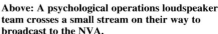

Above: A psychological operations loudspeaker team crosses a small stream on their way to broadcast to the NVA.

Above right: A US Air Force C-47 scatters psychological warfare leaflets west of Nha Trang in II Corps.

Project 404

As the war in Laos grew, Project 404 was initiated in order to provide uniformed US military advisers to both the Royal Lao Army and the Royal Laotian Air Force. The expansion of the Royal Lao Forces, coupled with French reluctance to increase and enhance their training, meant that the training mission was eventually absorbed by the United States. However, to maintain a facade that the United States was still abiding by the Geneva Accords for Laos to remain neutral, the troop deployments were carefully monitored and attempts were made to conceal the numbers.

Project 100,000

On August 23, 1966, Project 100,000, a social engineering program, was initiated by Secretary of Defense Robert McNamara. Its purpose was to induct 100,000 individuals each year with poor academic or mental skills that would normally not be qualified for service in the armed forces. McNamara declared when he announced the program that the military would salvage, "tens of thousands of these men each year, first to

productive military careers and later for productive roles in society." The armed forces accepted about 354,000 men under Project 100,000 guidelines. Approximately 37 percent were African-American, and 75 percent of those accepted served in either the army or the Marines. Just over 30 percent were sent to direct ground combat assignments and nearly 2,100 died during the war.

Protective Reaction Strikes

On October 31, 1968, President Johnson ordered all naval and air offensive strikes against North Vietnam to be stopped. However, reconnaissance flights over the north were continued. There had been a tacit agreement between American and North Vietnamese negotiators in Paris that reconnaissance flights would not be engaged. The North Vietnamese routinely violated the agreement and soon armed escorts accompanied most reconnaissance flights. When a reconnaissance flight was fired on, the escorts were allowed to engage the antiaircraft systems attacking the reconnaissance planes. These retaliatory attacks were called Protective Reaction Strikes.

Provincial Reconnaissance Units (PRU)

The Provincial Reconnaissance Units were a specialized branch of the National Police Field Force. As such they were not under the command and control of the ARVN, and were not subject to military discipline. Organized into 18-man

units consisting of three Strike Teams they were armed and trained by the US CIA. Urged by the CIA, in 1969 MACV provided 100 military advisors to these units, most of which were commanded by either former or present ARVN officers. In 1970, General Creighton Abrams, frustrated by the lack of military control, directed MACV to withdraw its support from the PRUs, though he left the advisors in place, albeit with orders not to go on field operations or participate in interrogation through torture. While castigated by the American press and antiwar movements as assassins and murderers, after the war both the Viet Cong and the North Vietnamese confirmed that the PRUs were extremely effective in rooting out and eliminating the Viet Cong infrastructure.

Provisional Revolutionary Government of South Vietnam (PRG)

The unofficial shadow government, known as the PRG, was the communist alternative or administration-in-waiting established in 1969 by the National Liberation Front (Viet Cong) and the Alliance of National Democratic and Peace Forces. Led first by Huyn Tan Phat, the legitimacy of the PRG was recognized by fellow communist governments and it sent a delegation headed by Madame Nguyen Thi Binh to all rounds of the Paris peace talks. After the reunification of the country, the PRG was integrated into the Socialist Republic of Vietnam, but the PRG leadership was

Right: An AC-47 "Dragonship," mini-guns ready, heads for its operational area in 1967.

Right: An AC-47 "Dragonship," mini-guns ready, heads for its operational area in 1967.

largely sidelined. The only significant appointment was Madame Nguyen Thi Binh as minister of education.

Psychological Warfare Operations (PSYOPS)

The United States Information Agency and MACV invested enormous amounts of energy in the conduct of psychological operations aimed at the North Vietnamese, Viet Cong, and uncommitted South Vietnamese. The US Army deployed a psychological operations battalion in each Corps Tactical Zone. Between 1965 and 1972 more than 50 billion psywar leaflets were dropped on North and South Vietnam, on the Ho Chi Minh Trail, and in Laos. Loudspeakers on board aircraft broadcast thousands of hours of tapes made by prisoners and Chieu Hois in an attempt to encourage others to defect. In the final analysis however, the only truly effective psychological operation conducted by the Americans was the Special Forces campaign among the Montagnards. On the other hand, the North Vietnamese, working through the international press and American antiwar groups were highly effective in generating opposition to the American presence in Vietnam.

Public Opinion

American public opinion about the war in Vietnam followed a predictable pattern. Prior to US intervention very few citizens knew anything about Vietnam. Immediately following the Gulf of Tonkin Incident most Americans rallied around the flag and supported President Johnson's actions. Following the initial deployment of US ground forces a majority of Americans believed that the Viet Cong and North Vietnamese were a tool of the People's Republic of China and that it was necessary to oppose them in Vietnam. As the war ground on with no clear strategy to achieve victory, and it appeared that the government was not being forthright with the American public, support for the

war waned. Following the shock of the Tet Offensive a majority of Americans favored withdrawal, however not retreat or surrender. President Nixon defused the issue of Vietnam by implementing the Vietnamization program. However, he created a further erosion of support when he invaded Cambodia. By the time the Paris Peace Agreements were signed, the only concern the American public had was retrieval of American prisoners of war. Once this was accomplished, Vietnam simply vanished from the public ken.

Puff the Magic Dragon

The AC-47 gunship, a propeller-driven World War II cargo plane armed with three side-firing SUU-11 7.62mm mini-guns, each capable of firing up to 6,000rpm, was referred to by the troops as "Puff the Magic Dragon." The name was drawn from a popular song.

Punji Stakes

Punji stakes were made by cutting bamboo into strips, sharpening the strips to a point, then fire hardening them and embedding them in the bottoms of shallow holes or around fighting positions. A punji stake could generally penetrate a combat boot and they were frequently coated with feces or some other substance to cause infection. The Viet Cong were especially adept at using them in both offensive and defensive roles.

Left: Punji Stakes protrude above the water in a moat around a Popular Forces outpost.

Q

Quach Tom

As part of OPLAN 34A, Quach Tom was a survivor of a commando group parachuted into North Vietnam by the CIA. When the CIA suspended commando operations they knowingly lied to the dependents of those Vietnamese troops who had been parachuted into the north by telling them that they were all dead. Following 19 years of imprisonment by the North Vietnamese, Quach Tom was released and came to the United States. He sued the United States government in 1996 on behalf of 360 surviving commandos, seeking compensation. He also lobbied the president and Congress in an attempt to get compensatory legislation passed. Senators John Kerry and Bob Kerrey introduced legislation on his behalf, but he died in August 1997, just before it passed.

Quang Ngai

The southernmost province of I Corps, Quang Ngai was a Viet Minh stronghold during the French Indochina War. During the Vietnam War the population was heavily communist. My Lai was located in Quang Ngai province.

Quang Tri, Battle of (March–May 1972)

On March 30, 1972, under supporting fire from North Vietnamese 130mm and 152mm heavy artillery, and spearheaded by T-54 and PT-76 tanks, four NVA Divisions attacked out of the Demilitarized Zone into Quang Tri province. This powerful force hit the newly formed ARVN 3rd Infantry Division head on. By April 1, the ARVN had been driven from their initial defensive positions and were attempting to regroup around the city of Quang Tri that was defended by a Vietnamese Marine Corps brigade. As they attempted to reestablish a defensive line, the Division's 57th Regiment broke, and the

Below: General Westmoreland watches the ceremonies welcoming the Thai Queen's Cobra Regiment to Vietnam.

56th Regiment, defending the fire support base at Camp Caroll west of the city, surrendered en-masse. Though President Nixon ordered immediate air support for the beleaguered ARVN, cloud cover during the first two weeks of April limited close air support. When the weather cleared in mid-April, B-52s and tactical air hammered the oncoming NVA. Ignoring their losses, the NVA crossed the Cam Lo-Cua Viet River barrier and struck Quang Tri from three sides. Dong Ha fell on April 28, and by May 1, the South Vietnamese defenders had been compressed into Quang Tri City itself, which then began receiving heavy artillery fire.

Mass panic set in, many ARVN soldiers gathered their families and began running towards Hue to the South. The 3rd Infantry Division had ceased to exist, and though the Marines fought on and retired in good order, they could not stem the tide. As huge numbers of South Vietnamese refugees fled south on Highway 1, the NVA targeted the road with heavy artillery fire killing thousands. NVA forces took the city that day, and the rest of the province two days later. Their forces savaged by naval gunfire, B-52s, and tactical air, the NVA ran into stubborn resistance by the Vietnamese Marine Brigade and their offensive stalled north of Hue. Late in the summer the ARVN launched a counterattack, and following weeks of intense combat recaptured the city on September 15, 1972. Much of the remainder of the province however, remained in the hands of the North Vietnamese.

Queen's Cobra Regiment

The Queen's Cobra Regiment was the first Thai combat unit deployed to Vietnam. It arrived in September 1967 and was attached to the US 9th Infantry Division in the Delta. As it was withdrawn to Thailand in August 1968, the Black Panther Division replaced it.

Qui Nhon

Qui Nhon was one of the first US air bases and a major supply base and transportation terminal in II Corps where east-west National Route 19 intersected north-south National Route 1 on the seacoast. It was one of five coastal surveillance centers supporting Operation Market Time, the naval interdiction operation along the South Vietnamese coast. A major logistics installation was also located there.

Above: An LST waits to unload C Company, 1/69th Armor, at Qui Nhon after it moved from Cu Chi.

VIETNAM: A VISUAL ENCYCLOPEDIA

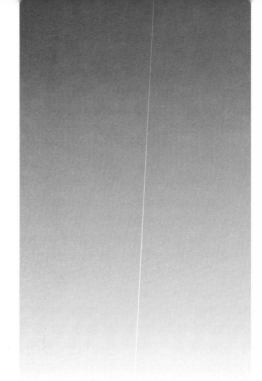

Radar

As well as interdicting North Vietnamese seaborne logistics traffic, radar played a pivotal role in the ability of the United States to launch effective air strikes over North Vietnam. Air search radars mounted on surface warships and both ground-based and carrier-launched surveillance aircraft provided a constant real-time look at the location of both friendly and enemy aircraft. This allowed air planners and commanders to either engage or avoid the enemy as the situation required. A modified bomb-scoring radar emplaced on a limestone karst, known as Site 85, in Laos significantly improved the accuracy of raids against the north and allowed the strikes to be conducted in all weather conditions. Surface search radar on American warships and Coast Guard cutters, as well as maritime patrol aircraft, effectively eliminated the sea as a logistics pipeline to the south by making it virtually impossible for all but very small supply vessels to evade interception. Army units made extensive use of ground surveillance radar around major base camps, with limited success, in order to detect Vietcong or North Vietnamese sapper probes. Occasionally, ground surveillance radars were teamed with artillery or armor to establish ambushes by fire on trails that had been detected by other means. As the war progressed mortar and artillery locating radars, designed to detect weapons being fired and calculate their location for counter-battery purposes, were added to the mix. The North Vietnamese made wide use of air surveillance and ground controlled intercept radars to counter the American air raids. In addition, the fire control radars associated with the surface-to-air missile systems and anti-aircraft guns operated in a variety of frequencies, complicating the electronic warfare mission for the United States, and resulting in a great deal of difficulty in jamming them to the point where the fighter-bombers could expect to operate with impunity.

Radio Research Units (RRU)

The specialized electronic intelligence activities of the Army Security Agency were known as Radio Research Units. They both monitored enemy communications traffic for intelligence purposes and carried out radio direction finding for the targeting of possible enemy headquarters and command elements.

Ranch Hand, Operation

Operation Ranch Hand was the code name for the aerial spraying of herbicides to defoliate key areas of the jungle and deny the Viet Cong concealment as they moved. A secondary purpose was to kill food crops that were grown by the Viet Cong in their base areas. Initially the spraying was done by South Vietnamese helicopters. However, on November 28, 1961, six UC-123 Provider cargo planes equipped with spray bars were deployed under the Farm Gate Program and Americans flew the

Right: Marine Corps counter-mortar radar at Khe Sanh significantly increased the effectiveness of counter-battery fire.

328

missions. Eventually there were 33 spray aircraft assigned to Operation Ranch Hand. By the time the operation was terminated on January 7, 1971, over 19 million gallons of herbicide had been sprayed on six million acres in South Vietnam, and 400,000 gallons had been dumped on 163,000 acres along the Ho Chi Minh Trail in Laos. Although the defoliants used in the program were considered to be non-toxic to humans, it has been determined that dioxin, an impurity in Agent Orange, named for the color of the band painted around its shipping container, can cause debilitating illnesses, rashes, tumors, and birth defects.

RAND Corporation

The RAND Corporation (Research and Development) is a US government think tank that began as an outgrowth of operations research groups used during World War II. Founded in 1948, it was the first private, nonprofit, federally funded think tank. During the Vietnam War it produced hundreds of both classified and unclassified reports on every aspect of the war. Its most famous researcher was Dr Daniel Ellsberg, who leaked the Pentagon Papers to *The New York Times* in 1971.

Rangers

The US Special Forces began training South Vietnamese Ranger units in 1960, and the first Ranger Company was activated in 1961. In 1963, companies were combined into Ranger Battalions, and in 1967 Ranger Groups consisting of a

small headquarters, three Ranger Battalions, reconnaissance, transportation, and an engineer company were formed. Nicknamed "The Black Tigers," the Vietnamese Rangers were an elite volunteer unit, and were among South Vietnam's most reliable troops. Recruited largely from ethnic minorities or enemy Hoi Chanh, 20 Ranger Battalions were formed. Eventually the

Above left: A Ranch Hand C-123 sprays defoliant along a road east of Saigon.

Above: A 75th Rangers scout, armed with an AK-47, keeps watch along the Dong Ngai River northeast of Xuan Loc.

Below: A squad of ARVN Rangers fights its way down a side street in Cholon during the Tet Offensive.

Above:An exhausted refugee woman and her three small children rest on the deck of the USS *Wabash*.

Above right: A Vietnamese refugee, with his belongings clutched in his teeth, climbs a cargo net to the deck of the USS *White Plains*.

US also consolidated the American Long Range Reconnaissance Patrol units into Ranger Companies, and officially designated them as elements of the 75th Infantry Regiment, (Ranger). After the war the US Rangers expanded into a multi-battalion force tailored for raids, infiltration, and reconnaissance.

Refugees

Refugees were a problem in Vietnam throughout, and even after the war. Following the defeat of the French in 1954, nearly 100,000 Viet Minh moved from the south to the north across the 17th parallel, and almost 1,000,000 northerners, mostly Roman Catholics, came south.

Between 1955 and 1963, the Diem government forcibly displaced over a million peasants under various resettlement programs such as the Agrovilles

Right: Refugees stream past ARVN M-113s outside My Tho during the Tet Offensive.

Left: A Vietnamese officer fires an M79 grenade launcher at the Thua Tien Regional Forces training center.

and Strategic Hamlets, creating a large body of internal refugees. With the entry of the United States into the war in 1965, the refugee problem accelerated. By 1975, widespread combat, and the American penchant for the utilization of overwhelming firepower, coupled with forcible relocation and the creation of Free Fire Zones, resulted in more than 12 million refugees in South Vietnam, nearly half the population. The communist oppression of the ethnic Chinese minority, and the specter of the re-education camps for South Vietnamese who had any dealings with Americans during the war, resulted in nearly two million refugees fleeing from Vietnam after Saigon fell.

Regiment

Larger than a battalion but smaller than a brigade, a regiment is a basic military organizational unit. In the American armed forces only the US Marine Corps and US Army armored cavalry units are organized into regiments, which normally consist of a headquarters plus three battalions, or squadrons in the case of the armored cavalry. In the case of Vietnam all of the belligerent forces, except the US Army and the Korean army, used the regiment as a basic building block of their force structure.

Regional Forces

Initially called the Civil Guard and responsible only to President Diem, the Regional Forces (RF) were first activated in 1955 within the Interior Department of South Vietnam to protect critical locations in the Delta. All of the commanders were Diem loyalists. By 1960, they were defending or occupying 9,000 posts, more than half of which were in the Delta, and they were transferred to the Defense Department. In 1964, the Civil Guard was renamed the Regional Forces, taken out from under the command of the province chief, and placed under the control of the ARVN. The Regional Forces were a popular alternative to service in the regular South Vietnamese military because they were employed in and around the villages and hamlets where the troops lived. The

Left: A Regional Forces patrol moves through a Montagnard village in the highlands.

Above: The troops relax and swim at China Beach, just outside of Danang.

basic combat unit in the Regional Forces was the company, and by 1973 there were more than 1,800 RF companies. Throughout the war, in the main, the RF companies fought well, even though they were ill-equipped and poorly supported.

Reinhardt, George Fredrick

President Eisenhower appointed George F Reinhardt Ambassador to the Republic of Vietnam in 1955. Reinhardt became an ardent supporter of Ngo Dinh Diem and his chief objective became solidifying the relationship between the new Republic of Vietnam and the United States. By the time he departed Saigon in 1957 he had succeeded.

Reserve Components

In July 1965, President Johnson made the decision not to activate units of the US Military Reserve Components for the Vietnam War. As a result, the Reserve Components became a haven for draft dodgers and, as the active services expanded to accommodate the increased manpower demands of the war, the experience and maturity levels of the force, particularly in the mid-grades, declined precipitously. The military leadership repeatedly requested activation of specific units within the reserves. Their requests were routinely denied.

Rest and Recuperation (R&R)

All of the troops assigned to Vietnam were authorized a five day leave for rest and recuperation (R&R) during their one-year tour. The program provided service personnel with transportation to any one of a number of friendly nations around the Pacific Rim. Additionally, three in-country sites were established, China Beach in Danang, Nha Trang, and Vung Tau, where a soldier could go to relax as a reward for performance. The troops sometimes referred to R&R as L&L (Liquor and Lovin') or I&I, (Intoxication and Intercourse). Everyone eagerly anticipated it.

Rheault, Robert B

Colonel Robert Rheault was the commander of the US 5th Special Forces Group from May to July 1969. During this time a Viet Cong double agent was apprehended and executed. This occurred after coordinating their action with the CIA, which controlled the American operation the agent was engaged in. Though he had full knowledge of what had happened, when questioned about the incident by General Creighton Abrams, Colonel Rheault lied. General Abrams filed court martial charges against Rheault and six of his officers for executing the double agent. The CIA refused to cooperate in the court martial and the charges had to be dropped for lack of evidence.

Rhee Dai Yong

Brigadier General Rhee Dai Yong was the former Deputy Commander of the Korean Forces in Vietnam, and the former Deputy Head of the Korean CIA. In April 1975, he was the Charge d'Affaires at the Korean Embassy in Saigon.

Left: General Matthew Ridgway just prior to the Normandy Invasion in World War II.

Promised evacuation by the Americans, he reported to the US Embassy on April 29, 1975. Though his presence was known, he was among those abandoned when the US ended their evacuation flights. Captured by the communists he died in prison two years later.

Richardson, John H

John H Richardson was the CIA Saigon station chief in 1962 and 1963. He had a close working relationship with both President Ngo Dinh Diem and his powerful brother Ngo Dinh Nhu. Because of his close ties with Nhu, the generals organizing the coup against President Diem did not trust him. They made this fact known to Ambassador Henry Cabot Lodge, who wanted more control over CIA activities in Vietnam anyway, and on October 5, 1963, Lodge had Richardson recalled to the United States.

Ridgway, Mathew B

General Matthew B Ridgway was a US Army Chief of Staff in 1953 and 1955. He opposed US intervention in support of the French at Dien Bien Phu, and the later introduction of US forces into South Vietnam. As one of the "wise men" in 1968 he was instrumental in convincing President Johnson to deescalate the war.

Rifles

Early in the war a number of older French and Japanese weapons, as well as World War II era US models, were widely used by the Viet Cong and the South Vietnamese Territorial Forces. As the American presence grew, modern US equipment was issued to all of the Allied forces, and the Russians and the Chinese almost completely re-equipped the NVA and VC with the SKS and AK-47. However, the Australians and New Zealanders opted to keep their own UK designed battle rifles, though they did use the US M16 for some purposes.

Ripcord, Battle of Fire Support Base (July, 1970)

By the summer of 1970, US units were under orders to minimize American casualties. As a precursor to their

Left: A sniper takes careful aim with his Remington 700 as his side-man prepares to spot for him.

VIETNAM: A VISUAL ENCYCLOPEDIA

Above: An instructor watches a Vietnamese Navy student assemble a M16 at the Small Boat School.

Above right: A Marine cradles his M14 rifle as he prepares for a mission with the Reconnaissance Battalion.

Right: Sergeant Harry Mayer braces himself as he demonstrates firing an M60 machinegun from the hip.

Rifles/Carbines

Make/Model	Type	Caliber	Feed	Range	Operation
Soviet M1944 Chicom Type 53	Carbine	7.62mm	5rd Integral Magazine	400m	Bolt Action
Soviet Model SKS Chicom Type 56	Carbine	7.62mm	10rd Integral Magazine	400m	Gas, Semi-Auto.
US M1/M2	Carbine	.30 Cal.	15/30rd Box Magazine	300m	Gas, Semi/ Full Auto.
French MAS-36	Rifle	7.5mm	5rd Integral Magazine	500m	Bolt Action
Soviet M1891/30	Rifle	7.62mm	5rd Integral Magazine	500m	Bolt Action
US M1 Garand	Rifle	.30 Cal.	8rd Clip	500m	Gas, Semi-Auto
US M14	Rifle	7.62mm	20rd Box Magazine	500m	Gas, Semi-Auto
US Springfield M1903	Rifle	.30 Cal.	5rd Integral Magazine	500m	Bolt Action
Australian L1A1 SLR	Assault Rifle	7.62mm	20rd Box Magazine	500m	Gas, Select-Fire
German G-3	Assault Rifle	7.62mm	20rd Box Magazine	500m	Blowback, Select-Fire
Soviet AK-47 Chicom Type 56	Assault Rifle	7.62mm	30rd Box Magazine	400m	Gas, Select-Fire
US M16	Assault Rifle	5.56mm	20rd Box Magazine	300m	Gas, Select-Fire
Mosin Nagant M1891/30	Sniper Rifle	7.62mm	5rd Integral Magazine	800m	Bolt Action
Remington M-700	Sniper Rifle	7.62mm	5rd Integral Magazine	1,000m	Bolt Action
Soviet Dragunov SVD	Sniper Rifle	7.62mm	10rd Box Magazine	1,000m	Gas, Single-Shot
UK L42A1	Sniper Rifle	7.62mm	10rd Box Magazine	800m	Bolt Action
US M1D Garand	Sniper Rifle	.30 Cal.	8rd Clip	800m	Gas, Semi-Auto
US M14 (21) National Match	Sniper Rifle	7.62mm	20rd Box Magazine	800m	Gas, Semi-Auto
US Springfield M1903A4	Sniper Rifle	.30 Cal.	5rd Integral Box Magazine	1,000m	Bolt Action

withdrawal, the 101st Airborne Division launched an operation in an effort to regain the initiative in and around the Ashau Valley. To do so they opened a number of fire support bases in western Thua Tien province. At the same time, the NVA 304th and 320th Infantry Divisions began probing eastward from the A Shau and south from the vicinity of Khe Sanh. Fires Support Base Ripcord came under attack on July 1, 1970. The ensuing battle was the costliest of the year. The NVA opened the battle with a mortar and artillery attack against the Fire Support Base. This was quickly followed by ambushes of reconnaissance patrols operating outward from the base. By the end of the first week the base was clearly under siege. The US command found itself hamstrung by political considerations. After the disastrous battle at Hamburger Hill two years prior, taking large numbers of American casualties was unacceptable. The NVA constantly reinforced their units operating around Ripcord, as well as intensifying the shelling, and American casualties increased. On July 18, a Chinook helicopter was shot down and crashed into the main ammunition dump on the fire support base. The resulting explosions destroyed the heart of the defenses. On July 20, reconnaissance patrols operating around the base reported that there were between 9,000 and 11,000 NVA poised for a final assault. On July 23, 1970, having suffered heavy losses, the remaining 300 defenders executed a fighting withdrawal and B-52 strikes were called in to destroy what was left of Ripcord. While the US military mantra is that "we won every battle but lost the war," at Ripcord the NVA were left in control of the battlefield, and it was clearly a North Vietnamese victory.

Riverine Operations

The Mobile Riverine Force (MRF) consisted of sufficient afloat facilities to accommodate two US Army infantry battalions, approximately 100 specialized shallow draft assault craft organized into two rivers assault squadrons, and several maintenance and supply ships. The Mobile River Base (MRB) was designed to be anchored as much as 50km from an operational area, however it was usually much closer. Heavily armed river monitors and assault patrol boats, coupled with shore-based infantry platoons, secured the MRB. Riverine operations were designed to encircle an enemy area. Infantry units were moved by both watercraft and helicopter to assault positions, while reserve elements were normally held afloat. Fire support was provided by helicopter gunships, fixed wing tactical aircraft, or artillery that was either mounted on a barge or air-emplaced ashore. The MRB was frequently shifted, because it was determined that the infantry was incapable of sustaining tactical operations lasting more than two or three days. Therefore, frequent movement was used to compensate for the inability to move far from the operational landing area.

Riverine Vessels

There were a number of different classes of vessels involved in riverine operations. Two types of fast patrol boats, the Nasty class, and the Swift class operated extensively both along the coast and in the small waterways of the Mekong Delta. The heavily armed Nasty class carried one 81mm mortar, one 40mm and two 20mm cannons, and was capable of 41 knots. The smaller swift class was employed in far larger numbers and was

Right: A Swift Boat gunner returns fire when the Viet Cong open an ambush at the mouth of the Saigon River.

Below right: A monitor of the Mobile Riverine Force leads a group of troop landing craft on an operation in the Delta.

armed with an 81mm mortar and three .50 caliber machine guns. Although it was slower than the Nasty class, only capable of 28 knots, because of its shallow one meter draft it was frequently used both as a river patrol boat and to ferry troops into operational areas. A large number of landing ships armed with one 75mm, four 40mm, four 20mm cannons, and four machine guns were also used. Eighteen LSTs were adapted as either fleet support or mother ships for smaller craft. More than 150 LCM type landing craft, modified into various configurations as either troop carriers or fire support vessels, were also available, and about 200 other small armored vessels rounded out the riverine force.

The heavyweights of the riverine fleet were the so-called monitors (ex-LCM6s) harking back to the American Civil War. Armed with 40mm Bofors and M10–8 flamethrowers forward, heavy machine-guns and 20mm cannon at the stern, they were formidable.

Rivers, L Mendel

L Mendel Rivers was the chairman of the House Armed Services Committee through most of the Vietnam War, and was one of President Johnson's staunchest supporters. His only serious criticism was that the war was not prosecuted vigorously enough. Following the Tet Offensive, he advocated the use of nuclear weapons against North Vietnam.

Road Watch Teams (RWT)

US ground combat forces, other than Studies and Observations Group (SOG) reconnaissance elements, were barred from conducting operations in Laos. SOG teams were allowed to operate in a strip 20km wide from Tchepone to the Cambodian border. In order to monitor the traffic on the Ho Chi Minh Trail outside of this narrow zone, the CIA

Opposite, top: A flotilla of River Patrol Boats, PBR, sets out for their operational area in 1969.

Opposite, bottom: An LST anchored in the Bassac River serves as a base for the "Seawolves" Light Helicopter Attack Squadron.

Left: The crew rearms an Aerial Rocket Artillery "Hog" with 2.75in folding-fin rockets.

soft. After Nixon was elected, Rockefeller steadfastly supported his policies on the war. Following Nixon's resignation, Gerald Ford selected Rockefeller as his Vice President.

Rockets (Allied)

The Allies employed six separate rocket weapons systems. The 3.5in rocket launcher, commonly called a bazooka, which had been developed during World War II and refined in Korea as an anti-tank system, was frequently used by the Marines and the Vietnamese to attack bunkers and enemy troops in buildings. The M66 LAW, a lightweight antitank rocket in a throwaway launch tube, was frequently carried for the same purpose and essentially replaced the bazooka later in the war. Helicopters were equipped with 2.75in folding-fin rockets that had an HE, WP, or flechette warhead. These were the staple of rotary wing close air support. Some Navy and Marine aircraft were armed with 5in Zuni rockets, a high explosive air to ground system. The Navy also employed 5in spin stabilize rockets fired from a vessel they called an inshore fire support

organized teams made up of eight to 12 Laotian or Hmong troops, known as Road Watch Teams, to reconnoiter the rest of the Trail. They were designed purely for reconnaissance, and were not encouraged to engage in combat.

Rockefeller, Nelson A

Nelson Rockefeller, a presidential candidate in the 1968 elections, was a strong supporter of the US commitment to Vietnam and attacked the Johnson administration's policies as being too

Below: A fire rages on the outskirts of Danang as NVA rockets slam into the airbase there.

Above: The troops hunker down in their bunkers and fighting holes as NVA rockets shower Khe Sanh.

Right: People search through the remains of their homes following a VC rocket attack.

ship. These were frequently used along the coast to provide area fire. Toward the end of the American involvement the TOW (Tube-launched Optically-tracked Wire-guided) antitank missile was deployed in small numbers.

Rockets (North Vietnamese and Viet Cong)

The North Vietnamese made wide use of a variety of artillery rocket systems. The two most common calibers were 107mm and 122mm, both of which were employed throughout South Vietnam. They also used the 140mm rocket launcher, although these only appeared in small numbers and were essentially confined to I Corps. Simple to operate, possessing a fairly long range, reasonably accurate in an area fire mode, and with relatively large high explosive warheads, they could be set up and fired by small teams. They effectively supplemented the widespread use of mortars in an artillery role. It was not uncommon

VIETNAM: A VISUAL ENCYCLOPEDIA

Left: Replacements on the Rockpile had to exit while the chopper hovered because there was no room to land.

Below left: This aerial view of the Rockpile clearly shows its ruggedness and outstanding field of observation.

for the North Vietnamese or Viet Cong to utilize rockets against South Vietnamese villages, towns, and cities. During the Easter Offensive in 1972, the North Vietnamese introduced the Sagger, a command-to-line-of-sight wire-guided antitank missile, into South Vietnam. Initially it was effective against South Vietnamese armored units in Quang Tri province, but they quickly learned how to either avoid or counter the system.

Rockpile, The

The Rockpile was a 700ft high peak with sheer sides and a flat top located at a fork in the Cam Lo River 16 miles west of Dong Ha and 1,000m south of National Route 9. It dominated the landscape between Camp Caroll to the east and Khe Sanh to the southwest. The Marines routinely stationed a rifle squad on top of the Rockpile as an observation post and resupplied it by helicopter.

Rogers, William Pierce

In 1969, President Nixon appointed William Rogers as the Secretary of State. At the same time, he named Henry Kissinger as the Special White House Assistant for Foreign Affairs. Nixon distrusted many in the State Department and routinely failed to include Rogers in the development of foreign policy, but instead leaned heavily on Henry Kissinger. Rogers was often put in a position of defending policies that had been developed without any input from the Department of State. However, he continued in his position until after the Paris Peace Agreements in 1973, when he resigned.

Rolling Thunder, Operation

On March 2, 1965, Operation Rolling Thunder began. It continued until President Lyndon Johnson announced a halt to the bombing of North Vietnam on October 31, 1968. Instead of a coordinated air campaign to destroy the enemy's ability to wage war, Rolling Thunder was designed to meet a diplomatic rather than a military purpose. Essentially, it was the primary tool to be used for gradual escalation in an attempt to cause the North Vietnamese to cease supporting the southern insurgency. Secretary of Defense McNamara defined its purpose on February 3, 1966 when he said: "US objectives are not to destroy or to overthrow the communist government in North Vietnam. They are limited to the destruction of the insurrection and aggression directed by North Vietnam against the political institutions of South Vietnam." The command relationships for Rolling Thunder exemplified the lack of planning and coordination that went

Below: Secretary of State William Rogers, accompanied by William Sullivan (right) arrives in Paris to sign the Peace Agreement.

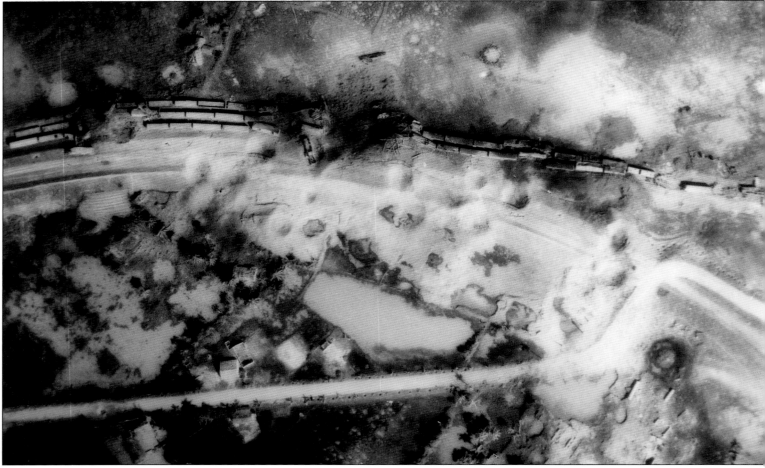

POST-STRIKE   DONG PHONG THUONG RR BR

DESTROYED SPAN

4 APRIL 1965

Left: Pilots blew a gap in the railroad and then raked a trapped train with cannon fire during Operation Rolling Thunder.

Below left: A large amount of rolling stock was destroyed when a marshalling yard was struck during Operation Rolling Thunder.

Above: An aerial photo of the wreckage of a bridge struck during Operation Rolling Thunder clearly shows it is down.

Above right: A thermal power plant lies in ruins after an Operation Rolling Thunder attack by planes from the USS *Constellation*.

into the campaign. Targets were divided into Air Force and Navy geographical packages. Route Package I, immediately north of the Demilitarized Zone, was seen as a part of the war in South Vietnam and was controlled by the US Military Assistance Command in Saigon. All of the remaining target packages were under the control of Pacific Command in Honolulu. Route Packages II, III, IV, and VIB were the responsibility of the US Navy's 7th Fleet Task Force 77, flying from Yankee Station. Route Package V and VIA were the responsibility of the US Air Force headquartered in Thailand. B-52 bomber operations remained under the control of the Strategic Air Command in Omaha, Nebraska. Seven separate bombing halts were proposed during Rolling Thunder. Each was intended to signal a US willingness to negotiate, however, the only result was that the North Vietnamese were granted a respite to rebuild their defenses and increase the flow of equipment to the south. The signal they were

actually receiving from the bombing halts was that the US was not serious about pressing the war to a conclusion. From 1964 to 1968 the United States lost 922 aircraft to enemy action and the CIA characterized Rolling Thunder as, "the most ambitious, wasteful, and ineffective campaign ever mounted."

Rome Plow

A Rome Plow was a specially designed bulldozer blade fitted to crawler tractors for the purpose of clearing jungle. It got its name from Rome, Georgia, where it was originally designed. The blade had a sharp point for splitting large trees and cutting edges for clearing brush. It was widely used in the Iron Triangle and several areas around Saigon.

Romeos

See Rules of Engagement.

Romney, George W

Romney was a liberal Republican who ran for the presidential nomination in 1968. Initially the front-runner, he became an object of derision during the New Hampshire primary when he claimed that he had originally supported the war because he had been brainwashed by the Pentagon. He later served as the Secretary of Housing and Urban Development in the Nixon Cabinet.

Ronning Missions

A series of secret and ultimately unsuccessful peace initiatives fostered and led by retired Canadian diplomat Chester A Ronning, which opened negotiations

with North Vietnamese politicians Nguyen Co Thach, Nguyen Duy Trinh, and Pham Van Dong. In March 1966, Ronning met with the three men in Hanoi and went to Washington with assurances that the DRV was prepared to enter negotiations conditional on a halt in the bombing campaign. Johnson and his advisers rejected this proposal outright, but left some room for negotiation by demanding a reciprocal deescalation in the North Vietnamese military effort. Ronning returned to Hanoi in June with this offer and met again with Thach, but little of note resulted.

Rostow, Eugene Victor

President Johnson appointed Eugene Rostow as the Undersecretary of State for Political Affairs in 1966. Along with his brother, Walt Rostow, the National Security Adviser, he was among the policy making elite at the height of the war. He frequently argued that the Gulf of Tonkin Resolution was the legal equivalent of a declaration of war. He supervised the "Marigold" initiative and other secret peace initiatives, but counseled the president that they could be interpreted as a sign of weakness.

Rostow, Walt Whitman

Walt Rostow was a key member of President Kennedy's "brain trust" who believed that Southeast Asia would be the final confrontation between communism and democracy. Following Kennedy's death, President Johnson appointed Rostow as his National Security Adviser. He was the most

VIETNAM: A VISUAL ENCYCLOPEDIA

Above: An A-6 Intruder returns to its carrier after striking targets in Route Package VI.

Above right: An A-7 Corsair II prepares to launch from the USS *Constellation* on its way to Route Package IV.

Below: A Ruff-Puff sentry guards the gate to his hamlet.

steadfast believer in American military action and, as American public opinion turned against the war, President Johnson leaned heavily on Rostow's advice. He was a member of the "wise men" and usually recommended deescalation of the war. However in March 1968, after the Tet Offensive, his recommendation was to intensify the bombing, mobilize the reserves, and invade North Vietnam. Following Johnson's decision to deescalate, Rostow left office in 1969.

Route Packages

As more and more assets were committed to the air war over North Vietnam, in order to simplify navigation and planning, the country was divided into sections known as Route Packages, or RPs. The Navy and Air Force were each given specific packages as their responsibility.

Route Package I, from the DMZ north to approximately the 18th parallel, was seen as an extension of the ground war in South Vietnam and was controlled by MACV. Packages II, III, and IV, each consisting of a horizontal slice of the narrow tail of North Vietnam and extending to just south of Hanoi, were assigned to the US Navy. Route Package V, which contained the area from the Chinese border to just south of Hanoi and west of the Red River was assigned to the Air Force.

Route Package VI was divided into two parts, VIA and VIB. Route Package VIA, which stretched from the Red River east to the rail line running northeast from Hanoi into China, and north from Hanoi to the Chinese border was assigned to the Air Force. The Navy was responsible for Route Package VIB, stretching from the Hanoi and Haiphong corridor north to the Chinese border and west to the northeast railroad.

Route Package VI became the most heavily defended piece of air space in Southeast Asia, and newly arrived Air Force pilots were not allowed to fly into

Above: Marine CH-34s on the USS *Princeton* prepare to lift troops into the Rung Sat during Operation Jackstay.

Above right: A Navy "Swift" boat searches a Vietnamese ship in the Rung Sat Special Zone.

Route Package VI before they had completed ten missions in Route Package I.

Rowe, James N

On October 29, 1963, Lieutenant Nick Rowe, a Special Forces advisor in the Mekong Delta, accompanied his unit on a raid against a Viet Cong village. In the ensuing battle the South Vietnamese unit was decimated and Lieutenant Rowe, along with two other Americans, was taken prisoner. Five years later, on December 31, 1968, he escaped and was fortunately picked up by an American helicopter, making him one of the few prisoners to ever escape the Viet Cong. In 1989, he was killed by Philippine rebels in an ambush.

Rubin, Jerry

Jerry Rubin was a radical antiwar activist who often attracted media attention. In August 1965, he attempted to stop troop trains outside San Francisco by having his followers lie on the tracks. In January 1968, he was one of the founders of the Youth International Party (Yippies). He helped organize the demonstations at the Chicago Democratic Convention in 1968 and as one of the "Chicago 8" was tried on charges of conspiracy and intent to riot in 1969.

Ruff-Puffs

The Regional Forces and Popular Forces were known as Ruff-Puffs, a slang term almost universally used by American and Australian troops in Vietnam.

Rules of Engagement (ROE)

Officially, rules of engagement are "directives issued by competent military authority which delineate the circumstances and limitations under which United States forces will initiate and/or continue combat engagement with other forces encountered." During the Vietnam War, rules of engagement were issued at every level of command from the White House to the committed combat company. They frequently changed, and even differed between divisions and organizations fighting side by side. Sometimes they were ludicrously restrictive. For instance, in early 1966, there were areas around Cu Chi in III Corps, where armored units could only engage the enemy firing at them with .45 caliber pistols and submachine guns. They were barred from using tank mounted machineguns and cannon.

Rung Sat

The Rung Sat was an extensive mangrove swamp formed by the deltas of the Saigon and Dong Nai Rivers

Left: Marines in small outboard motor boats scoured the Rung Sat swamp during Operation Jackstay.

Above: Secretary of State Dean Rusk addresses students at Emory University in Atlanta, Georgia.

approximately seven miles south of Saigon. Sappers operating out of the Rung Sat frequently mined the shipping lanes from Saigon to the South China Sea. To alleviate this problem the SEALs operated extensively in the Rung Sat.

Rusk, Dean

Dean Rusk served as the Secretary of State for both Presidents Kennedy and Johnson. He consistently argued that US global interests would be vitally damaged if the United States did not support South Vietnam. He refused to accept that the war was a nationalist rebellion. He was convinced it was, in fact, a clear example of communist aggression. He

consistently supported MACV requests for increased troop commitments and urged President Johnson to continue to prosecute the war despite the growth in the antiwar movement and the decline in public confidence. Dean Rusk is as closely associated with the Vietnam War in the public's mind as Lyndon Johnson.

Russell, Richard B.

Richard Russell was a Democratic Senator from Georgia who served as the Chairman of the Senate Armed Services Committee from 1951 to 1969, and the Chairman of the Senate Appropriations Committee from 1969 to 1971. Initially he recommended to the president that the United States not get involved in Vietnam because he did not believe that there were any vital interests involved

there. Following the commitment of US forces however, he supported the President. After the Tet Offensive he recommended an all-out attack on North Vietnam, to include nuclear weapons.

Russo, Anthony J Jr

Anthony Russo was an antiwar RAND researcher who helped Daniel Ellsberg copy the classified Pentagon Papers by renting a Xerox machine from an advertising agency. He and Ellsberg were indicted for this action in 1972, but the charges were dismissed in 1973. In October 1972 he testified at the third annual session of the Commission of Enquiry into US War Crimes in Indochina, and in 1973 he tried to organize a nationwide campaign to impeach President Nixon.

Saigon

In 1956, Ngo Dinh Diem named Saigon the capital of South Vietnam. Located on the Saigon River, 45 miles inland from the coast of the South China Sea, Saigon was the largest city in Indochina and was the hub of the US war effort.

Several huge logistical installations were located in Saigon and its environs, as well as the headquarters of the Military Assistance Command–Vietnam (MACV), US Army Vietnam (USARV), and the Republic of Vietnam Armed Forces (RVNAF). The massive influx of US troops and money turned Saigon into a storied example of Western decadence and beggars, thieves, prostitutes, drug dealers, and black marketeers were everywhere. Heavily damaged during the Tet Offensive, the North Vietnamese and Viet Cong finally overran Saigon in 1975 and renamed it Ho Chi Minh City.

Above: A scratch unit of MPs engages Viet Cong infiltrators at Bachelor Officer Quarters 3 in Saigon during the Tet Offensive.

Right: MPs provide security for an Explosive Ordnance Disposal team while they defuse a booby trap.

Above: A line of "cyclo" drivers, the Saigon equivalent of a taxi, wait to pick up a touring USO troup.

Above right: The wreckage from a Viet Cong terrorist bomb was a common sight in Saigon.

Saigon Military Mission (SMM)

A CIA-funded group organized in Saigon in 1954 to try and destabilize the DRV while simultaneously stabilizing the State of Vietnam was known as the Saigon Military Mission (SMM). Headed by Edward Lansdale, who became a close confidant and influential adviser of Prime Minister Diem, the SMM sent agents into the north on sabotage missions and bought the support of South Vietnamese warlords. The mission ended after the October 1955 elections, which it helped to win for Diem.

Salisbury, Harrison E

Harrison Salisbury was the assistant managing editor of *The New York Times*. In 1966, he became the first US correspondent to travel to North Vietnam. His dispatches from there became controversial when he claimed that the United States was bombing civilian areas, a charge vigorously denied by the Johnson administration. Many of his journalistic colleagues strongly criticized him for giving aid and comfort to the enemy.

San Antonio Formula

President Lyndon B Johnson's proposed solution to the stalemate in peace negoti- ations between the DRV and US, known as the San Antonio formula, was delivered in a speech at San Antonio, Texas. Johnson's offer, which promised a halt in the bombing, was conditional on a reciprocal agreement that the DRV would enter peace negotiations and cease its efforts to infiltrate men and matériel into the south. Kissinger traveled to Hanoi to deliver the offer but the DRV made no official response.

Sanctuaries

A sanctuary is normally defined as a place of safety and refuge. During the Vietnam War, Laos and Cambodia were both proclaimed neutral nations. Even though international law allows a belligerent to use force on neutral territory when the neutral nation is not preventing another belligerent from using it, for political reasons, the United States essentially observed their neutrality. Viet Cong and NVA units routinely retreated to Laos and Cambodia following combat in South Vietnam to rest and refit. Because the US only clandestinely operated against them there, they were considered sanctuaries.

Sanitize

"Sanitize" was a slang term for the assassination of a member of the Viet Cong Infrastructure (VCI), by someone associated with the Phoenix Program. Though the term was widely used before the initiation of the Phoenix Program, the American antiwar movement inextricably linked the two together.

Sappers

Sappers were highly trained Viet Cong and NVA troops who specialized in the penetration of secured areas, mining roads and waterways, clearing minefields, and sudden violent attack, normally with satchel charges. They were the most feared of all the enemy soldiers. By 1973 there were four regiments, 35 Battalions, and two special groups of Sappers in the communist order of battle.

Schlesinger, James R

President Nixon appointed Schlesinger Secretary of Defense in 1973. He remained in that position through the Watergate crisis and the fall of South Vietnam. Nixon and Henry Kissinger routinely ignored him in matters of Vietnam policy. He supported President Ford's plan to grant limited amnesty to draft evaders, but Ford disliked his imperious attitude and replaced him on November 2, 1975.

Scotland, Operation

Operation Scotland was fought around the Khe Sanh combat base from November 1, 1967 through March 30, 1968. Three NVA divisions, backed by artillery and rockets, repeatedly attacked the hill positions around Khe Sanh. Though artillery and rockets showered the Marines throughout the entire period, the actual ground battle started on January 20, 1968, when a unit of the 26th Marines engaged an NVA battalion between Hills 881 North and 881 South. In the ensuing battle the NVA managed

Right: Company B, 1st Battalion, 4th Marine Regiment crosses a small stream during Operation Scotland.

Below: Two troops probe the opposite bank of a river in the Demilitarized Zone.

to take Hill 881 North, which they then used as an artillery observation post. The next morning, an NVA attack on Hill 861 was repulsed but the ammunition dump at Khe Sanh was hit and blew up. On February 5, 1968, the NVA 325C Division attacked Hill 861A, breaching the wire but being thrown back in hand-to-hand fighting. On February 6, 1968, an NVA regiment, backed by tanks, over-ran the Lang Vei Special Forces Camp and continued east toward Khe Sanh. Artillery, B-52s, and tactical air, guided and controlled from the outposts on the surrounding hills, savaged the NVA units as they moved down the valleys.

On February 25, 1968, Company B, 1st Battalion 26th Marines, was ambushed and lost two-thirds of its men. By mid-March the NVA, who suffered incredibly high losses, had begun to withdraw back across the Demilitarized Zone to North Vietnam. Operation Scotland officially ended on March 30, 1968 with another engagement fought by a reconstituted Company B, 1/26th Marine south of Khe Sanh.

Sea Dragon, Operation

Operation Sea Dragon, from October 1966 to October 1968, was a US Navy campaign designed to cut the seaborne logistics flow from North Vietnam to its committed units and the Viet Cong in the south. The ships involved were usually older, gun armed cruisers and destroyers, which could make high-speed raids on logistics' chokepoints, radar and communications sites, antiaircraft and SAM sites within range, and coastal shipping. At its peak, Operation Sea Dragon employed two cruisers and 12 destroyers. To counter these raids the NVA installed a significant number of 130mm shore batteries, which engaged US warships 10 to 15 times a month. NVA gunners hit 29 Sea Dragon ships, killing five sailors and wounding 26. When President Johnson announced the bombing halt over North Vietnam in October 1968, Operation Sea Dragon ended and the ships withdrew south of the DMZ.

Seabees

Naval construction units, nicknamed Seabees, were active in Vietnam from June 1954 until November 1971. Initially, they constructed camps for refugees fleeing North Vietnam after the

Below: The heavy cruiser USS *Canberra* fires an 8in gun salvo at a North Vietnamese target.

Geneva Accords, but by 1962 they had begun building camps for the Special Forces, and in 1965, as part of the 30th Naval Construction Regiment, they began supporting the deployment of major US combat units to Vietnam. One of their most notable projects was the sprawling port of Cam Rahn Bay.

SEAL (Sea Air Land) Teams

The SEALs are a US Navy special operations force that evolved from the underwater demolition teams of World War II. From 1962 to 1964 SEAL detachments trained Republic of Vietnam naval commandos. They also carried out hydro-

Above: A SEAL clutches his Stoner light machinegun and watches for movement in a wooded area by a stream.

graphic surveys along the coast and supported raids into North Vietnam. In 1965, MACV requested that the SEALs operate in the Rung Sat Special Zone, a large mangrove swamp seven miles south of Saigon. The Rung Sat had long been a VC stronghold. The SEALs, operating in three to seven-man, hunter-killer teams, virtually eradicated the Viet Cong in the swamp. From 1968 to 1970 they engaged in covert operations along the entire

Above: A Strike Assault Boat moves in at high-speed to pick up a SEAL team near the Cambodian border.

Left: Members of SEAL Team One move down the Bassac River in a Seal Team Assault Boat (STAB).

coast of South Vietnam. Between 1970 and 1972, they again worked with the South Vietnamese naval commandos and accompanied them on forays into North Vietnam. They were withdrawn in 1972.

Seale, Bobby

Bobby Seale was a political activist and co-founder of the Black Panther Party. One of the key tenets of the party platform was the exemption of all blacks from the requirement for military service. Arrested as one of the "Chicago 8" for disrupting the 1968 Democratic Convention, his case attracted national attention when Judge Julius Hoffman ordered that he be bound and gagged while in the courtroom because of his disruptive behavior.

Left: The crews ready a flotilla of patrol boats for operations on the Bassac River.

Below left: A River Patrol Boat loaded with Marines moves up the Saigon River near Dau Tieng.

SEALORDS

The largest naval operation of the war was SEALORDS (Southeast Asia Lake, Ocean, River, Delta Strategy). Designated Task Force 194, it combined 586 naval vessels and the gunboats of the River Patrol Force and the Mobile Riverine Assault Force with 655 Vietnamese Navy warships and gunboats to cut enemy supply lines from Cambodia and disrupt Viet Cong base areas in the Mekong Delta. Beginning in October 1968, it involved a two-year effort to create barriers that formed an interdiction line stretching from the Gulf of Thailand through the Mekong Delta to Saigon. The first involved the opening of two canals between Rach Gia on the Gulf of Thailand and Long Xuyen on the Bassac River. The second barrier was created when gunboats began operating between Ha Tien on the Gulf and Chau Duc on the upper Bassac River. The third barrier was established after hard fighting when the Vam Co Dong and Vam Co Tay rivers on both sides of the Parrot's Beak were secured. The Barrier system was completed in January 1969 when patrol sectors were established westward from the Vam Co Tay River to the Mekong River, extending the waterway interdiction barrier from Tay Ninh all the way to the Gulf of Thailand. The effectiveness of the operation was proven by the fact that during the Easter Offensive the only area of the country that was not struck was the upper Mekong Delta.

Search and Destroy

Search and Destroy was an ad-hoc tactical innovation created to implement the Attrition Strategy in Vietnam. It relied on the premise that American technology,

Above right: A flaming arrow is used to set fire to a Viet Cong structure in the Delta during Operation SEALORDS.

Right: A recoilless rifle gunner passes a burning hooch during a search and destroy operation in the Mekong Delta.

Above: A unit of the 1st Cavalry Division crosses a group of rice paddies on line during a search and destroy mission.

Left: Marines destroy Viet Cong bunkers and tunnels with explosives in An Hoa village.

Above right: Troops from the Mobile Riverine Force slog through waist deep mud and water during a search and destroy operation in IV Corps.

coupled with aggressive ground patrolling, would be able to find the Viet Cong and NVA main force units. Then American firepower would be able to inflict such severe casualties that the enemy would be unable to sustain the war. Those assumptions however, were flawed, because the Viet Cong and the North Vietnamese retained the strategic initiative and could pick the timing, location, and intensity of a given engagement. Additionally, more than 200,000 men reached draft age in North Vietnam every year, far more than the number of casualties the US was capable of inflicting. Because of its negative connotation in the press, search and destroy was later called reconnaissance in force.

Left: The CG of the 101st Airborne Division addresses a unit that are going on a search and destroy mission.

VIETNAM: A VISUAL ENCYCLOPEDIA

Above: An HH-3E Jolly Green Giant is escorted
by two A1-Hs as it heads toward a downed
airman in North Vietnam.

Right: A helicopter plucks an F-8 Crusader pilot
from deep within Haiphong Harbor as North
Vietnamese junks close in.

Search and Rescue (SAR)

The first US Air Force rescue team
arrived in South Vietnam on January 10,
1962. Originally it did not have its own
aircraft and had to rely on either the
Army or the Marines for support. This
very quickly proved to be an unworkable
situation. As a result, in March 1964, the
first dedicated air force helicopters
arrived. In January 1966, the Air Force
activated the 3rd Aerospace Rescue and
Recovery Group at Tan Son Nhut with
the mission to be the primary rescue
agency in Southeast Asia. Between
March 1964 and August 1973, search
and rescue crews picked up 3,883
American fliers, 555 Allied military
fliers, 476 civilians, and 45 others.
Search and rescue (SAR) operations
retrieved nearly one-third of all downed
airmen during the war.

Sharp, Ulysses Simpson Grant

Admiral Sharp was Commander in Chief
Pacific (CINCPAC) from 1964 to 1968.

Right: Marine CH-34 helicopters of Operation Shufly loaded with Vietnamese soldiers approach a Landing Zone.

He was one of the most consistently hard-line supporters of the war in Vietnam, which he saw as necessary to halt communist aggression in Asia. He oversaw the air strikes against North Vietnam and was responsible for Operation Rolling Thunder. He continually argued with President Johnson and Secretary of Defense Robert McNamara that gradual escalation was a strategy for defeat. In a 1978 book he bluntly stated that: "The war was lost in Washington, not on the battlefield."

Sheehan, Cornelius Mahoney "Neil"

As the Saigon Bureau Chief for United Press International from 1962 to 1964, Neil Sheehan was one of the first correspondents of the Vietnam War. He angered the government establishment by reporting that the Battle of Ap Bac was an utter disaster. He also discovered that the CIA and the embassy were backing the generals' coup against President Diem, but was moved out of the country to Tokyo before he could break the story. In June 1968, it was Sheehan that published the Pentagon Papers, supplied to him by Daniel Ellsberg. In March 1971, he wrote a lengthy article questioning whether the US leaders had committed war crimes in Vietnam.

Shining Brass, Operation

Operation Shining Brass, begun in October 1965 and later renamed Prairie Fire in 1968, was the largest and most important Special Forces strategic reconnaissance campaign in Southeast Asia. Carried out by 12-man teams consisting of three US Special Forces and nine Montagnard or Nung CIDG troops, Shining Brass operations were designed to monitor, and later interdict, the Ho Chi Minh Trail in Laos. The teams operated under severe restrictions imposed by William Sullivan, the US Ambassador to Laos. Originally the teams were not allowed to operate more than 20km inside Laos or use helicopters for insertion, but could use them for emergency evacuation if necessary. After months of wrangling, permission was eventually obtained to use helicopters for both purposes. Because of the results achieved in these operations the North Vietnamese eventually committed nearly 20,000 men to prevent them.

Shufly, Operation

On April 15, 1962, Marine medium helicopter squadron 362 (HMM-362) was deployed to Soc Trang, South Vietnam to supplement US Army helicopters supporting the ARVN. Their deployment and operations were code-named Shufly. Operation Shufly continued until December 31, 1964, though the squadron was repeatedly relocated within Vietnam and it finally ended up in Danang.

Initially the Marine helicopters, unlike their Army counterparts, did not have machineguns mounted in the cargo hatch because Marine commanders reasoned that the weapon would hinder loading and unloading during critical periods. Eventually, however, the Marines not only added door gunners, but also experimented with converting an H-34D into an armed escort in 1963. Because the Marine Corps helicopters were more rugged and had a greater operating range than the Army H-21, HMM-362 became the unit of choice to support larger operations. Though Shufly officially ended on December 31, 1964, the helicopters remained in Vietnam and joined the Marine ground units that landed in 1965.

Sigma I and II

The name of two major war games conducted by the US in 1963 and 1964 was Sigma I and II. Sigma I was staged to assess the ability of the US military to achieve victory over the Viet Cong; analysts concluded that it would take at least 500,000 men to achieve this objective. Sigma II assessed the potential effects of a dramatically increased air offensive against the North. The conclusions were that such an offensive stood little chance of success.

Sigma Project

In August 1966, General Westmoreland ordered the 5th Special Forces Group to organize a long-range reconnaissance unit for III Corps patterned after the successful Project Delta unit that operated in II Corps. Sigma was controlled by Special Forces Detachment B56, and located at Thu Duc between Saigon and Long Binh. With a strength of approximately 900 CIDG troops and 125 Special Forces personnel, Sigma was capable of conducting saturation patrolling over wide areas. The reconnaissance elements had eight Roadrunner Teams and eight Reconnaissance Teams. Three airborne qualified Mike Force companies with 150 CIDG and 25 Special Forces each backed up the reconnaissance elements. Sigma conducted its initial combat operation on September 11, 1966 and performed 14 more in War Zones C and D before it was folded into SOG on November 1, 1967.

Left: A Special Forces soldier watches as a CIDG commander deploys his troops in an ambush position.

Below: North Vietnamese Premier Pham Van Dong follows Prince Norodom Sihanouk of Cambodia as he waves to the crowd during a visit to Hanoi.

Above: Prince Norodom Sihanouk answers questions at a news conference in New York after the fall of Cambodia to the Khmer Rouge.

Above right: Lieutenant Colonel Hal Moore approaches a wounded trooper during the Battle of the Ia Drang (Operation Silver Bayonet).

Sihanouk, Prince Norodom

French officials installed Prince Norodom Sihanouk as the King of Cambodia in 1941. After the French defeat at Dien Bien Phu in 1954, Sihanouk declared Cambodia an independent nation. Immensely popular with his people, he organized a referendum in 1955 and they voted him in as Prime Minister. Between 1954 and 1970 he walked a very delicate line, attempting to keep Cambodia neutral in the new American war in Vietnam. However, the North Vietnamese established an extensive base camp system in eastern Cambodia and in 1969 he acquiesced to the secret bombing of that area. He was deposed by General Lon Nol in 1970 and participated in a number of attempts to regain power. All failed. During the Vietnamese invasion of Cambodia in 1978 he tried without success to form a coalition government. When the Vietnamese withdrew in 1989 he returned briefly as head of state in 1993, but was again overthrown and left Cambodia in 1997.

Sihanouk Trail

In 1966, the North Vietnamese reached an understanding with Prince Norodom Sihanouk of Cambodia that allowed them to use the port of Sihanoukville as a logistics terminal for supplies shipped to their southern front by sea. Commercial cargo ships moved the war matériel directly to Sihanoukville, where it was offloaded and transported to established NVA base areas in eastern Cambodia. Two Cambodian trucking companies, chartered by Prince Sihanouk for that purpose, performed transportation within Cambodia. The road net from Sihanoukville to the North Vietnamese supply points was christened the Sihanouk Trail. By 1969, the increasing number of North Vietnamese in eastern Cambodia created tension with the Cambodians and right wing elements of the Cambodian government insisted on the closure of the Sihanouk Trail. At the same time American B-52s were beginning to launch raids into eastern Cambodia. This combination of circumstances resulted in the closure of the trail in late 1969.

Silent Majority

The epithet "silent majority" was given by Nixon to his middle-class supporters during a speech on November 3, 1969. Written in response to the nationwide antiwar protests (Moratorium Against the War) in autumn 1969, the speech was a direct appeal for support from what Nixon dubbed the "great, silent majority," meaning the group of pro-Nixon, pro-war Americans whom he suggested had thus far not spoken out in support of his policies.

Silver Bayonet, Operation

Operation Silver Bayonet, November

10–20, 1965, was a 1st Cavalry Division search and destroy operation in II Corps designed to intercept the North Vietnamese forces that had attacked the Plei Me Special Forces Camp before they could retreat into Cambodia. From November 14–16, three battalions of the division engaged the 66th NVA Regiment near the base of the Chu Pong Massif, and only murderous artillery fire and tactical air support prevented the NVA from overrunning the American positions. On November 17, the 2nd Battalion, 7th Cavalry, was ambushed by the 8th Battalion, 66th NVA Regiment, and in a short battle 151 were killed, 121 wounded, and four were missing. Silver Bayonet was the first significant engagement between American and North Vietnamese forces. It would later be known as the Battle of the Ia Drang.

Simons, Arthur D "Bull"

Arthur "Bull" Simons was a US Army Special Forces officer who commanded the covert Hotfoot/White Star teams that operated in Laos in the early 1960s. In 1970, he was selected to command the strike force that attacked the Son Tay prisoner of war camp in North Vietnam in an attempt to rescue a group of American prisoners. On the night of November 20, 1970, he led 56 men on a bold assault of the prison 23 miles from Hanoi. Unfortunately, due to local flooding in the area earlier, the prisoners had been moved and the camp was empty. Nevertheless, he and his team inflicted heavy casualties on a North Vietnamese unit that was bivouacked nearby. They then escaped back to South Vietnam without suffering any casualties, other than one individual who broke his leg in the initial landings of the helicopters at the prison. He retired from the Army in 1971. Later, during the hostage crisis in Iran, he organized and led a rescue team that retrieved a number of EDS employees from the Ayatollah Khomeini's supporters for Ross Perot.

Sit-Ins

The occupation of a building as a means of protest came to be known as a sit-in. Popularized by the civil rights movement in the 1950s, sit-ins were adopted by antiwar groups. The most popular targets for sit-ins were college administration buildings. Because they were relatively peaceful, sit-ins were popular among moderate antiwar groups but were abandoned by radicals in favor of more violent means of protest.

SLAM (Search, Locate, Annihilate, Monitor)

In September 1967, the press had begun to refer to the battle at Con Thien as another Dinh Bien Phu. To counter their assertions General William Momyer, Commander of the US Seventh Air Force, devised SLAM, a program that integrated the entire spectrum of Allied fire support. Naval gunfire, tactical air, B-52 bombers, artillery, and other ground weapons were orchestrated into an overwhelming concentration of

Below: Colonel Arthur "Bull" Simons at a press conference in San Francisco concerning the Son Tay Raid.

firepower. For 49 days the NVA units around Con Thien were subjected to an unprecedented bombardment that turned the surrounding terrain into a virtual moonscape. When the North Vietnamese retreated back across the DMZ, General Westmoreland commented, "It was a Dien Bien Phu in reverse."

Slick

Slick was the term applied by the troops to any transport helicopter armed only with door guns and specifically employed to land troops. It was most commonly applied to the UH-1 Huey. However, it eventually came to mean any helicopter other than a cargo, medevac, or gunship.

Right: Troops form up in "lifts" on a landing zone and wait their turn to board an incoming flight of slicks.

Below: A 101st Airborne Division UH1-D slick lands at the Ta Bat airstrip in the A Shau during Somerset Plain.

Right: A patrol fords a small stream in the A Shau Valley during Operation Somerset Plain.

Somerset Plain, Operation

Operation Somerset Plain was a search and destroy operation in the A Shau Valley from August 4–20, 1968. It was aimed at destroying NVA troops that were trying to re-enter the valley following Operation Delaware earlier. A task-force composed of units from the 1st Cavalry Division, 101st Airborne Division, 3rd Brigade, 82nd Airborne Division, and ARVN 1st Infantry Division, were to attempt to bring the NVA to a decisive battle. During the initial air assault a US F-4 fighter-bomber was shot down, and 17 helicopters were either shot down or damaged beyond repair. Once landing zones had been secured, and the ARVN and American units had linked up, the North Vietnamese broke contact and evaded toward Laos. On August 10, an F-100 Super Sabre accidentally strafed troops of the 101st Airborne, killing seven and wounding 54. The operation degenerated into a series of small patrolling actions with no serious enemy contact. Allied losses were 34 killed, 161 wounded, and four missing. The North Vietnamese lost 171 men and four prisoners were taken. Because the NVA had "been driven out of the A Shau Valley," MACV classed Operation Somerset Plain as a victory.

Song Be

The capital of Phuoc Long province, Song Be, was located 50 miles north of Saigon near the Cambodian border. It was overrun by the Viet Cong on May 11, 1965. The communists inflicted heavy casualties on South Vietnamese troops, and then withdrew after holding the city overnight. It was attacked again by the NVA on October 27, 1967. In the second attack, the defenders were stiffened by US air power, and turned the enemy back with heavy losses.

Song Be, Battle of (October 1967)

The ARVN base at Song Be was one of only five small South Vietnamese enclaves in communist dominated Phuoc Long province. Its position, close to the Cambodian border and between the North Vietnamese supply caches in Cambodia and War Zone D, made it a constant thorn in the enemy's side. During the fall of 1967, in preparation for the Tet Offensive, General Giap

initiated a series of small battles along the Cambodian border in an attempt to draw US and Allied units away from Saigon and other key cities. Just after midnight on October 27, 1967, the 88th NVA Regiment launched an attack against an ARVN battalion just south of Song Be. The small, 200 man, ARVN unit, outnumbered approximately four to one, fought back and immediately called for American air support.

Before dawn the NVA launched three human wave attacks at their small outpost. All three attacks reached the inner wire at the edge of the perimeter and were broken up by US Air Force Shadow and Stinger gunships. The NVA withdrew back into Cambodia at first light.

Son Tay Raid

In the summer of 1970, President Richard Nixon was presented a plan for a daring raid on the Son Tay prisoner of war camp located 23 miles west of Hanoi. The President, under fire in the press for the Cambodian Incursion, quickly approved the plan, believing that American prisoners were being tortured and killed by the North Vietnamese and also that an effort to free the prisoners would give him credit with the American public. Though the brainchild of Army Brigadier General Donald Blackburn, Air Force Major General LeRoy Manor was chosen as the overall task force commander, and Special Forces Colonel Arthur "Bull" Simons was selected to

Above: An ARVN squad calls in its location while on patrol near Song Be.

lead the raid. After three months of training in Florida, 56 handpicked Special Forces volunteers launched from Takhli Royal Thai Air Force Base on November 20, 1970. The plan called for the raiders to fly to Son Tay in one HH-3 and four HH-53 helicopters, supported by five A-1E Skyraiders and two SOF "Combat Talon" C-130Es. The HH-3 was to crash-land inside the compound and the troops inside were to eliminate the guards. The remainder of the ground forces would land from two of the other helicopters and ensure that the guard force at Son

Above: Following the abortive Son Tay Raid, Special Forces Colonel Arthur, "Bull", Simons responds to a question during a press conference.

Tay could not be reinforced from elsewhere. The fixed-wing aircraft would provide air cover and navigational support, while the empty helicopters would serve as transports for any prisoners rescued. In reality, the HH-3 crashed into the compound and the startled guards were quickly eliminated. One of the other troop carrying helicopters inadvertently landed at the wrong compound. It turned out to be a training center, and the raiders decimated the troops and cadre, who came out to investigate what was going on. A short time before the raid the prisoners had all been relocated and none were rescued. Within 27 minutes of the initial landing, the raiders had cleared the compound and were on their way back to Thailand, with no casualties. Though no prisoners were rescued, the assault caused Hanoi to consolidate their prisoners within Hanoi itself in order to prevent another raid from being successful. It was later learned that the attack significantly buoyed prisoner morale and created great consternation among the North Vietnamese leadership.

Right: An aerial photograph of the Son Tay POW Camp taken by a "Buffalo Hunter" drone aircraft.

Above: Prince Souphanouvong (left), the leader of the Pathet Lao meets with his half-brother Prince Souvanna Phouma on the Plain of Jars.

Son Thang

On February 19, 1970, a Marine patrol entered the small hamlet of Son Thang 20 miles south of Danang. They killed 16 women and children in the village. When the incident in the village was reported, there was an immediate investigation and four of the five Marines involved in the patrol were charged with premeditated murder. Two were convicted; and two were acquitted in what many called a war crime and a mini-My Lai massacre.

Souphanouvong, Prince

Prince Souphanouvong was a member of the Laotian Royal Family. Following World War II, he became a supporter of the Viet Minh in their war against the French. Married to a Vietnamese woman, he also became a close associate of Ho Chi Minh and the leader of the Laotian communist movement, the Pathet Lao. In 1957 and 1962, he served as a minister in a coalition government designed to neutralize Laos. Strongly opposed by rightist politicians supported by the United States, both governments were short-lived. Throughout the war in Vietnam the Prince and the Pathet Lao fought the Lao Army and the CIA supported Hmong guerrillas, led by General Vang Pao, on and around the Plain of Jars. His forces were heavily reinforced with regular North Vietnamese troops. Following the US withdrawal and the subsequent collapse of the Laotian government, he became the first President of the Lao People's Democratic Republic.

Southeast Asia Treaty Organization (SEATO)

A US-sponsored organization for the collective defense of member nations was known as SEATO. The Southeast Asia Collective Defense Treaty admitted the States of Cambodia and Laos and the free territory under the jurisdiction of the State of Vietnam under a protocol dated September 8, 1954. This made those states and territory eligible for the economic benefits contemplated by Article III of the Treaty.

Souvanna Phouma, Prince

Prince Souvanna Phouma was a member of the Laotian Royal Family, and the half-brother of Prince Souphanouvong, the leader of the communist Pathet Lao. A dedicated neutralist, Souvanna Phouma repeatedly attempted to form coalition governments to keep Laos out of the Southeast Asian war.

After 1962, his governments publicly declared their neutrality, but were unable to resist either North Vietnamese use of eastern Laos for the Ho Chi Minh Trail, or American bombing of the area and support of the Hmong guerrillas fighting the Pathet Lao on the Plain of Jars.

Following the American withdrawal in 1973, the Pathet Lao and the North Vietnamese increased their pressure on Souvanna Phouma's government. On December 2, 1975, they seized control of the government and announced the formation of the Lao People's Democratic Republic. Souvanna Phouma was appointed as an advisor to the government, an honorary post he held until his death in 1984.

Below: The neutralist Premier of Laos, Prince Souvanna Phouma, attends a meeting designed to attempt to create a coalition government.

Left: Captain Philip C Gutzman leaves a 4th Infantry Division briefing on Operation Paul Revere.

Special Forces

The US Army Special Forces were originally organized in 1952. Specifically trained to wage guerrilla warfare and raise resistance forces behind enemy lines, President Kennedy believed that they were uniquely qualified to carry out his new counterinsurgency strategy. They initially deployed a series of temporary duty training teams to Vietnam from Okinawa in 1957.

In 1959, specialized teams, code-named Project Hotfoot, were deployed to Laos. These were later renamed White Star Mobile Training Teams in 1960. Also in 1960, teams began rotating in and out of Vietnam under the control of the Central Intelligence Agency's Combined Studies Group. In 1961, they began training the ethnic minorities in the central highlands.

This program became the basis of the Civilian Irregular Defense Group (CIDG) and by 1965 more than 80 fortified CIDG camps had been established among the Montagnards and minorities. In 1962, Secretary of Defense McNamara directed that the CIA operation be transferred to MACV and that the US Army assume control of Special Forces units operating in the central highlands. This transfer was code-named Operation Switchback.

Due to the rapid expansion of the CIDG program, the 5th Special Forces Group was officially established in Vietnam on October 1, 1964. Over time, the Special Forces trained more than 54,000 CIDG troops.

On August 27, 1969, General Creighton Abrams, who was a staunch opponent of the Special Forces, or any other elite unit, ordered the phaseout of the CIDG program and the withdrawal of the 5th Special Forces Group. The Special Forces CIDG camps were turned over to the ARVN Ranger Command, and on March 1, 1971 the 5th Special Forces Group ceased all operations in Vietnam and withdrew.

Above right: A Special Forces communications NCO operates the team's single side-band radio.

Right: Gia Vuc, in I Corps, was a typical Special Forces Camp.

Left: A Special Forces Sergeant checks a 106mm recoilless rifle at Camp Bu Prang in II Corps.

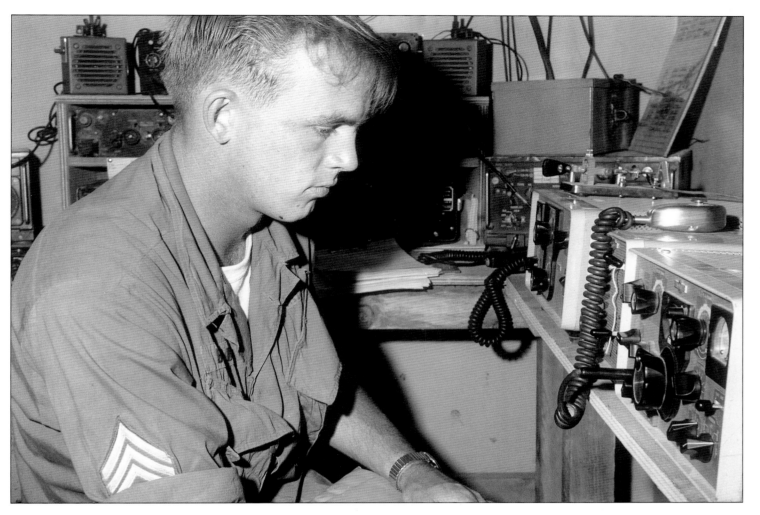

Special Services

The Special Services is an organization that provides recreational opportunities for military personnel. The US Navy originally organized their activities in Vietnam. On July 1, 1966, responsibility for Special Services activities was transferred to the US Army and subsequently assigned to the 1st Logistical Command of US Army Vietnam (USARV).

Special Services operated over 250 libraries, arranged USO tours by name entertainers, and established in country recreational and Rand R facilities. Approximately 300 civilians, 75 percent women, served in Vietnam in Special Services organizations.

Spellman, Francis Joseph

The Roman Catholic Archbishop of New York, Cardinal Spellman was an articulate supporter of Ngo Dinh Diem. One of the most politically influential religious leaders in America, he organized a pro-Vietnam lobby in Washington DC. As Pope John Paul VI pushed for a

Above: Thousands of troops listen to Ann Margaret sing during a USO show in 1966.

Right: Actress Carol Baker throws open her arms to the men of the USS *Ticonderoga* during a USO show in 1965.

Above: John Wayne signs a young Marines helmet during a USO tour.

Right: The well-known pediatrician, Benjamin Spock, addresses an antiwar rally in Washington DC.

negotiated settlement to the Vietnam War, Cardinal Spellman proclaimed the struggle in Vietnam a holy war against the godless communists, triggering a split with the Vatican. Even as American public opinion turned against the war he consistently supported the American military intervention.

Spock, Benjamin M

A prominent pediatrician who also held a commission in the Naval Reserve as a psychiatrist, Dr Benjamin Spock frequently spoke out against nuclear weapons testing in the early 1960s. By 1963, he had become a vocal opponent of the escalating war in Vietnam. A prominent supporter of President Johnson as the "peace" candidate running for President in 1964, Spock felt betrayed by Johnson's introduction of combat troops into Vietnam in 1965. In 1967, he began to devote all his time to opposing the war. He was active in encouraging draft age men to resist induction. In 1968, he was indicted for

Left: A squad interrogates a NVA prisoner during Operation Badger Catch.

Below left: A squad leader from the Americal Division shouts orders to his troops during a 1971 fire fight south of Chu Lai.

conspiring to violate Selective Service Laws. He was convicted, fined $5,000, and sentenced to two years in prison. His conviction was overturned on appeal. In 1972, he ran for president on the People's Party ticket.

Spring Mobilization to End the War in Vietnam

The first coherent demonstration by the US antiwar movement was held on April 15, 1967 in New York and San Francisco. The organizing committee called for support from right across the spectrum of antiwar groups, and was rewarded by a turnout of over 200,000 in Central Park, New York, and 50,000 in Kezar Stadium, San Francisco.

Squad

A squad is the basic organizational building block of the United States Army and Marine Corps. It is usually commanded by a sergeant E-6, and normally contains from 9 to 13 men. Internally it is made up of two fire teams comprising four to six men, usually led by corporals or sergeants E-5. In the artillery a single howitzer or gun and its crew is considered a squad.

Staley, Eugene

Eugene Staley was an economist who went on a fact-finding mission to South Vietnam for President Kennedy. He reported that Vietnam needed a self-sustaining economy and believed that the economy could not be improved without both social and political reforms. He believed that this could be achieved by providing greater protection to the civilian population. To do this, he recommended the construction of a network of strategic hamlets. Although this concept was academically and theoretically

sound, given the Vietnamese peasants' deep attachment to their ancestral land it was completely impractical. Instituted in 1962, the Strategic Hamlet Program became a disaster within its first year and was rapidly abandoned.

Starlight, Operation

A Viet Cong deserter revealed that the 1st VC Regiment was concentrating in the village of An Cuong and planning to attack the airfield at Chu Lai. General Lewis W Walt, commander of the 3rd Marine Amphibious Force, launched a spoiling attack of his own. On August 18, 1965, the 3rd Battalion, 3rd Marines (less M Company) plus three flame-thrower tanks and a platoon of M48 medium tanks made an amphibious landing to the south of the village to block any VC escape in that direction. M Company moved overland from Chu Lai

Below: Marines unload from a CH-46 during the initial airlift in Operation Starlight.

to a ridge four miles northwest of the landing area and established a blocking position. Meanwhile 2nd Battalion, 4th Marines, landed at zones about 2,000m apart and one mile inland from the coast. The plan was that all of the forces would converge at the hamlet of An Cuong. H Company, 2/4 Marines, inadvertently landed almost on top of the 60th Viet Cong Battalion, entrenched on a nearby hill. After a bitter fight the hill was over-run. As the 2/4 Marines moved to link up with the 3/3 Marines, they came under heavy fire from the hamlet of Nam Yen, and were forced to withdraw. Meanwhile a marine supply convoy was ambushed near An Cuong and a company from 3rd Battalion, 7th Marines was landed to relieve them. After hard fighting the Viet Cong broke contact. Despite stiff resistance from VC forces, the Marines succeeded in pushing the insurgents to the coast were close air support, tanks, and naval gunfire inflicted heavy casualties. Operation Starlight, the first major US

Above: A pair of Marines carefully observe an area they took sniper fire from on the Van Truong peninsula.

Left: A company cordons a small village and searches it for Viet Cong.

Right: A Skyraider peels off to strike a target on the Ho Chi Minh Trail.

ground combat operation of the Vietnam War, ended August 24, 1965. The 1st VC Regiment had been severely mauled, the 60th Battalion destroyed, and the 80th Battalion suffering heavy losses.

Steel Tiger, Operation

Operation Steel Tiger was a US air interdiction campaign over the Ho Chi Minh Trail in the northern panhandle of Laos from April 1965 to December 1968. It proved to be a textbook case of the unsuccessful use of limited air power. Rather than allow the application of air power to targets generated by the military forces in Southeast Asia, civilians in Washington selected them and then sent them to planners in Saigon for implementation. The time lag in the planning loop was such that time sensitive targets could never be engaged. The development of target lists for the Steel Tiger area by civilians in Washington DC hopelessly confused the command and control of air operations over the Ho Chi Minh Trail. Air Force, Navy, and Marine air commanders were loath to divert aircraft from higher priority missions to strike the targets that were generated. Finally, in 1968, Operation Steel Tiger was merged with Operation Tiger Hound, which was focused on interdiction of communist supply routes in the southern Laotian panhandle, and the new operation, code-named Commando Hunt, controlled interdiction of the entire Ho Chi Minh Trail network.

Stennis, John Cornelius

John Stennis was a powerful Democratic Senator from Mississippi. He was a member of the Senate Armed Services Committee, and served as its chairman from 1969 to 1989. Initially he did not favor US intervention in Vietnam. However, following the Gulf of Tonkin Incident he became a consistent hardliner. He constantly chided the Johnson administration for not unleashing the full military power of the United States. The Tet Offensive, however, convinced him that the US could not win with the strategy they were following. He also came to believe that the President's war making power needed be curbed, and in 1971 he was a co-sponsor, with Senator Jacob Javits, of the War Powers Act.

Stillwell, Richard G

General Stillwell was a military intellectual with years of service with the CIA when he was assigned to Vietnam in 1961 as the Chief of Operations for MACV. In 1963, he became the Chief of Staff of MACV. As the Chief of Operations he opposed the use of helicopters for medical evacuation purposes, stating that they were too important to waste on that mission. He fully supported the conversion of the ARVN from a territorial based military involved in local security to a structure patterned after the US Army and designed to repel a conventional invasion of the country. He never did believe that a guerrilla war could topple a nation.

Stockdale, James B

Commander Stockdale was the carrier air-group commander of the *USS Oriskany* when he was shot down over North Vietnam on September 9, 1965. The North Vietnamese repeatedly attempted to use Stockdale as a propaganda tool. His resistance through eight years of torture and solitary confinement was an inspiration to the other POWs. He was the leader of what became known as the Alcatraz Gang, a POW hall of fame made up of the most hard-line resisters. His wife, Sybil, organized the National League of Families of American Prisoners and Missing in Southeast Asia, and became an articulate spokesperson for the POW wives and families. While a prisoner, Stockdale was promoted to Vice-Admiral, and in 1976 he was awarded the Medal of Honor for his conduct as a prisoner.

Strategic Hamlet Program

The Strategic Hamlet Program was inaugurated in 1961. It was an attempt to separate the Viet Cong from the peasants. It was an ambitious program to construct new fortified hamlets and relocate the peasants into them. Under the concept the countryside would be pacified and the peasants won over to the government by providing security, fair elections, land reform, good schools, and improved medical services. While intellectually sound, the program required the peasants to relocate from their ancestral homelands into fortified camps established in less desirable locales. The promised land reform was never carried out, and millions of dollars in US aid earmarked for construction of schools and the improvement of medical facilities was diverted by corrupt government officials into their own pockets. The failure

Below: An aerial photo of one of the main POW compounds in North Vietnam, nicknamed Alcatraz, where Stockdale was imprisoned.

Right: South Vietnamese peasants dig a combination moat and punji pit around the Hoai My Strategic Hamlet.

Below right: A group of villagers is evacuated from their Viet Cong contested village to a Strategic Hamlet near Saigon.

ALCATRAZ

of the program encouraged the Viet Cong to expand their military efforts and widen the war. They exploited peasant discontent with the program and significantly increased their penetration of local governments where the forced relocation of the populace was attempted. By 1964, the program was in such disarray that it was cancelled. As a result of the failure of the Strategic Hamlet Program, pacification was relegated to secondary importance and the military dimension became the venue for winning the war.

Strategy (Allied)

The American political and military leadership never did arrive at a comprehensive strategy for fighting the Vietnam War. Instead, they adopted a number of approaches, none of which could really be considered an integrated strategy. At national level, the closest thing to an actual strategy was the policy of graduated response. The premise of this approach was that the US could inflict increasing levels of damage on North Vietnam and eventually, as the pain increased, the North Vietnamese would discontinue the war rather than face the next increment. The North Vietnamese, however, looked upon the incremental use of force as a sign of timidity. The result was that they became convinced that the US did not have the will to successfully prosecute the war. Initially, on the battlefield, the US tried counterinsurgency. However, they quickly disregarded the critical political and economic element that makes this an actual strategy and concentrated almost exclusively on the military dimension. This allowed the Viet Cong and North Vietnamese to infiltrate a significant number of villages and hamlets and established a shadow government. As it became apparent that counterinsurgency was failing, the military moved to Attrition Strategy. Actually an ad-hoc tactical ploy, it was based on the belief that American military power could kill a sufficient number of the Viet Cong and NVA that the enemy would simply run out of troops and have to stop fighting. None of the adopted "strategies" worked.

Strategy (North Vietnamese and Viet Cong)

The North Vietnamese strategy was one of total war. They did not believe there was a distinction between the military and civilians. They had no concept of a noncombatant, but viewed the people as a weapon to be employed and expended as necessary.

Their strategy visualized two elements as the jaws of a pincer. There was a political jaw, and a military jaw, and to be successful the two must work in concert. The political arm of the strategy consisted of any activity that involved motivation, social organization, propaganda, manpower mobilization, and support. The military arm encompassed both ordinary military and quasi-military actions, such as assassinations, kidnapping, and terror. Under their concept of protracted warfare it was axiomatic that the two must be simultaneously employed to be successful. While much of their strategy was devolved from the Chinese three-stage guerrilla war concept, General Giap and Ho Chi Minh specifically adapted it to the realities of

Below left: Troops from the 1st Cavalry Division await orders during a search and destroy mission in 1968.

Below: A prisoner caught on the "Street Without Joy" is guarded until someone can escort him to the rear for interrogation.

American high-technology warfare. Strategically they had a significant advantage over the United States in that there were well-defined objectives to be achieved and a road map to do so.

Street Without Joy

The Street Without Joy was a name given by French soldiers to a section of Vietnamese National Highway 1 between Quang Tri and Tan My north of Hue. A major Viet Minh stronghold during the French-Indochina War, it was heavily infested by the Viet Cong during the Vietnam War. The US Marines were routinely ambushed and fought a number of heavy engagements along this stretch of the road. It was here that Dr Bernard Fall, a noted expert on Vietnam, was killed by a Viet Cong mine while on patrol with the Marines.

Students for a Democratic Society (SDS)

The antiwar organization SDS was formed in 1960 as the collegiate arm of the League for Industrial Democracy. Within a single year, SDS was taken over by student radicals Al Haber and Tom Hayden, both of the University of Michigan. In June 1962, SDS members met at Port Huron, Michigan, and from this meeting materialized a manifesto, the Port Huron Statement, which expressed disillusionment with the establishment. Throughout the first years of its existence, SDS focused on domestic concerns. The students actively supported Lyndon Johnson in his 1964 campaign against Barry Goldwater and following Johnson's victory, they refrained from antiwar rhetoric. However, the SDS took on a firm antiwar stance later on and organized against the government.

Studies and Observations Group (SOG)

The MACV Studies and Operations Group (SOG) was organized in January 1964. Closely associated with the Vietnam War, it was actually a cover for a number of highly classified clandestine operations in Cambodia, Laos, North Vietnam, and the southern provinces of the People's Republic of China. SOG did not report to the Commanding General of MACV, but directly to an agency of the Joint Chiefs of Staff. By 1966, SOG strength had reached nearly 10,000 men, roughly 2,000 Americans and 8,000 Montagnard, Nung, and Vietnamese. It was divided into a number of specialized

Above: A Koho Montagnard team cooks a meal of rice and beans early in the morning to hide the smoke.

groups. The Psychological Studies Group, working from Hue and Tay Ninh, broadcast propaganda over powerful radio transmitters and carried out psychological warfare operations throughout the theater. The Air Studies Group, which included the Air Force 90th Special Operations Wing, specialized in the insertion and retrieval of clandestine intelligence teams in Laos, Cambodia, North Vietnam, and the People's Republic of China. The Maritime Studies Group was made up of a number of specialized fast patrol boats and SEAL platoons. They carried out commando raids all along the North and South Vietnamese seacoast from the People's Republic of China all the way to the Gulf of Thailand, however, they operated most frequently in the Mekong Delta. The Ground Studies Group was by far the largest, and carried out the greatest number of missions. In 1967, the Ground Studies Group was organized into three operational field units called Command-and-Control North (CCN) located in Danang, Command-and-Control Central

VIETNAM: A VISUAL ENCYCLOPEDIA

Above: A Special Forces Sergeant, armed with an M3A1 .45 caliber "grease gun," accompanies Vietnamese troops on a combat patrol in 1965.

Above right: A crewman of the Junk Force stands guard with a Thompson submachine gun while a boat is searched.

(CCC), stationed in Kontum, and Command-and-Control South (CCS), headquartered in Ban Me Thout. Primarily constituted from Special Forces, Nung, and Montagnard troops, the Ground Studies Group also included teams drawn from Marine Force Reconnaissance. They worked extensively in Laos and Cambodia, as well as North Vietnam, and carried out a number of missions that ranged from reconnaissance through ambush and interdiction to the capture of enemy POWs, planting mines and booby traps, recovery of downed pilots, and attempts to retrieve Allied prisoners of war. SOG teams suffered a high percentage of casualties, and Command and Control Central (CCC) was the most highly decorated small unit of the war.

Submachine Guns (Allied)

There were a number of submachine guns used by Allied forces during the war. However, the advent of the M16 rifle with its selective fire capability gave every infantrymen an automatic weapon and, except for armor crewman and some Special Forces uses, submachine guns were essentially phased out by the end of 1968, though the Popular Forces and People's Self Defense Forces kept some. The most commonly issued Allied submachine gun was the M3A1 "grease gun," a .45 caliber, blowback operated weapon that was part of the basic equipment on a tank, and also had been issued in significant numbers to the South Vietnamese. The Special Forces and CIA occasionally used the 9mm "Swedish K," and there were a few World War II Thompson .45 caliber models in the hands of the South Vietnamese. Many classified the 5.56mm CAR-15, which was issued to SOG and some reconnaissance units, as a submachine gun, however, the original US Army designation categorized it as a carbine.

Submachine Guns (North Vietnamese and Viet Cong)

The Viet Cong and North Vietnamese sometimes used captured Allied submachine guns. Early in the war they were occasionally equipped with a Soviet PPSh41 7.62mm weapon designed in World War II, or the People's Republic of China copy known as the Type50.

They also had a North Vietnamese adaptation of the same weapon they called the K50, though very few of these were seen. All of the guns of this design were blowback operated and had an effective range of about 150m. The most common submachine gun used by the North Vietnamese and the Viet Cong was the French MAT 49. A large number of these were captured during the French Indochina War and they were quite popular with the Vietcong. Originally a 9mm Parabellum, the Vietnamese rechambered the weapon for the Soviet 7.62mm by a 25P cartridge. It had a very high cyclic rate of fire, nearly 900rpm. As the war progressed and the AK-47 assault rifle became widely available, the sub machineguns were rarely issued or used.

Sullivan, William Healy

A protégé of Averill Harriman's, Sullivan served as the Deputy US Representative to the Geneva Conference on the Neutralization of Laos in 1961 and 1962. In December 1964, President Johnson appointed him the Ambassador to Laos. For the next four years he directed the secret war in that nation. He barred all regular US military ground operations from Laos, except in very narrow defined areas along the Ho Chi Minh

Right: A Supplemental Recreation Activities Office volunteer judges a surfing contest at China Beach.

Trail. He retained approval of all air operations within Laos until late in his tour of duty, and frequently clashed with the military over what they considered his unwarranted meddling in the war. He left Laos in 1969 and became an adviser to Henry Kissinger in Paris, where he played an important part in negotiating the 1973 Paris Peace Agreements that ended the war in Vietnam.

Summers, Harry G

Colonel Harry Summers served as the Chief of the Negotiations Division of the Four Party Joint Military Commission in 1974 and 1975. Following the war he was on the faculty of the US Army War College Strategic Studies Institute where he wrote "On Strategy," the most widely quoted analysis of America's failure in Vietnam. He pointed out that the United States had no defined goal or strategic objective in Vietnam, and that General Westmoreland's Attrition Strategy was not really a strategy, but rather an ad-hoc tactical approach to the war in the absence of definitive guidance from Washington. He postulated that the United States should have cut the Ho Chi Minh Trail in Laos, while the South Vietnamese dealt with the Viet Cong political insurgency.

Sunflower, Operation

A January 1967 US peace initiative, spurred by the failure of Operation Marigold, was code-named Operation Sunflower. It consisted of a direct approach to the government of the DRV through its Moscow embassy and a parallel effort through the offices of the British Prime Minister, Harold Wilson, and the Soviet Ambassador to Britain, Alexsei Kosygin. In essence "Sunflower" was a restatement of previous US demands, notably mutual deescalation, and Hanoi's response was much the same—an unconditional halt in US acts of war in the North as a precondition to talks. Again, neither side was willing to concede, and diplomatic relations became hardened as a result of the diplomatic misunderstandings.

Sunrise, Operation

Operation Sunrise was one of the first attempts to establish a Strategic Hamlet Program in an area that was not secure.

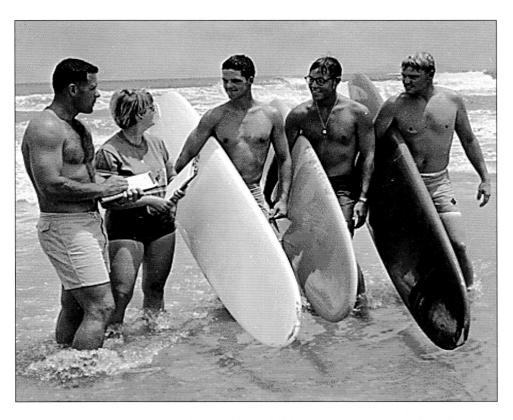

Responding to a recommendation by Sir Robert Thompson, who had run a similar program during the Malayan Emergency, from March 1962 to August 1963 the ARVN attempted to establish 14 hamlets north of Saigon in War Zone D. By November 1962, only four had been partially constructed, and the peasants refused to live in them. The National Liberation Front cited the strategic hamlets as proof in their propaganda that the South Vietnamese government intended to imprison all of the peasants. Ben Tuong, the main hamlet was routinely used by President Diem as a showpiece for visiting congressmen and American delegations to prove that American aid was being wisely spent. In August 1963, the Viet Cong overran Ben Tuong and essentially dismantled it, effectively ending a very costly experiment.

Supplemental Recreation Activities Overseas (SRAO)

The Supplemental Recreation Activities Overseas Program (SRAO), a service offered by the American Red Cross, operated in Vietnam from October 1965 to May 1972. Initially established in Danang in October 1965, the program eventually encompassed 28 sites. Mainly staffed with female college graduates who receive two weeks' training in Washington DC, the SRAO provided refreshments and recreational activities, visited hospitals, and periodically visited field units. Most commonly referred to as "Donut Dollies" their presence was really appreciated by the troops. Three SRAO women were killed in Vietnam.

Supreme Court

The Supreme Court was the highest federal court in the US. During the Vietnam War it intervened on several occasions to block the passage of legislation and made several important decisions regarding the antiwar movement. In 1965, in one of the first anti-Vietnam War decisions, the Court extended conscientious objector status to those who did not necessarily believe in a supreme being, but who opposed war based on sincere beliefs that are equivalent to religious faith. In the 1969 Tinker v. Des Moines case the Court invalidated the suspension of public school students for wearing black armbands to protest the Vietnam War, writing that students did not "shed their constitutional rights to freedom of speech or expression at the schoolhouse gate." It also gave permission for the Pentagon Papers to be published in 1971.

Surface-to-Air-Missiles (SAMs)

The Vietnam War saw the first large-scale utilization of surface-to-air missiles for air defense. The North Vietnamese employed the Soviet SA-2 "Guideline," a radio controlled medium to high-altitude missile, in large numbers. Later in the war they also introduced the SA-7

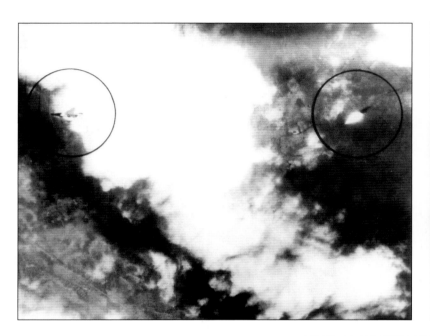

BAMBOO MATTING

Above: A reconnaissance pilot took a picture of a SAM that missed his wingman on a mission over North Vietnam.

Above right: A North Vietnamese SAM site was caught napping by a low-flying reconnaissance plane.

Right: A photo-interpreter found ten SAMs hidden under camouflage netting 50 miles south of Hanoi.

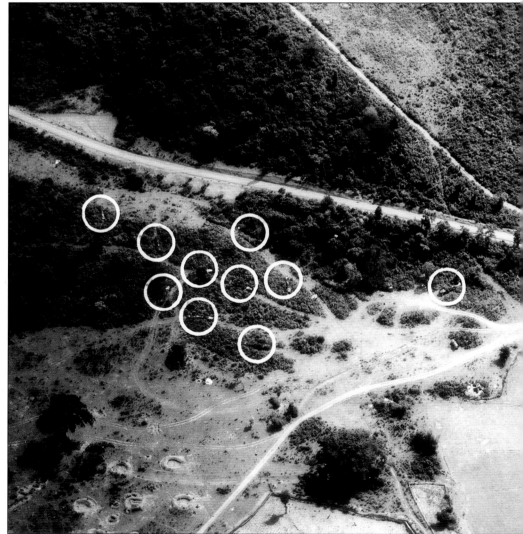

"Grail/Strela," an infrared guided shoulder-fired short range system, into both Laos and South Vietnam to counter the helicopter and engage low-flying forward air control aircraft and fighter-bombers. Over 10,000 missiles were launched during the war, but only 196 aircraft were shot down by NVA or Viet Cong missiles. Their greatest effectiveness was in forcing American strike aircraft to fly at lower altitudes where antiaircraft guns and automatic weapons accounted for over 86 percent of all planes shot down. Allied forces deployed the Hawk, a low to medium altitude air defense missile system, in South Vietnam, but no enemy aircraft came within range prior to the withdrawal of American forces. When they were deployed in response to the Tet Offensive, a brigade of the 82nd Airborne Division also brought the American Redeye shoulder-fired infrared antiaircraft missile with them. However, it was maintained under Brigade control in the base camp and never taken to the field, because there was no enemy air threat. Fleet air defense is the responsibility of naval aviation, however, on several occasions North Vietnamese aircraft engaged naval units. US warships were armed with Talos, Tartar, or Terrier surface-to-air missiles. During the war US ships launched surface-to-air missiles at North Vietnamese MiGs on numerous occasions. The first aircraft shot down by a ship-launched surface-to-air missile was a North Vietnamese MiG brought down by the cruiser USS *Long Beach* on May 23, 1968. By the end of the war American warships had destroyed seven enemy aircraft by missile fire.

Tactical Area of Responsibility (TAOR)

As there were no "front lines" in the Vietnam War, Corps, Division, or other unit boundaries could not be devised by simply drawing lines on a map. Additionally, South Vietnamese forces did not come under US command. It was therefore necessary to devise a different method to assign responsibility for security and military operations within a geographical area to a specific maneuver unit or command.

This was accomplished by generating non-contiguous geographical designations called Tactical Areas of Responsibility (TAOR). The boundaries of these areas periodically changed, based on negotiations between the US and Vietnamese commands. Within an assigned TAOR, a military unit was responsible for all tactical operations, and most logistics functions. Pacification activities, which later fell under the purview of CORDS, frequently crossed over multiple TAOR boundaries.

Taiwan

See China, People's Republic of.

Tan Son Nhut

Located on the outskirts of the city, Tan Son Nhut, was both an Air Force Base and the major civilian air terminal for Saigon. Throughout the war it housed the headquarters of the Vietnamese Air Force and after 1967 MACV. The US Air Force began operations there in October 1961. By 1969, more than 70,000 sorties per month were flying from Tan Son Nhut, and it was the busiest airport in the world. Though well defended it was constantly attacked by Viet Cong and NVA ground forces throughout the war. The Americans destroyed the MACV headquarters installations on April 29, 1975, as they withdrew. The North Vietnamese seized it the next day. After the war it was repaired and now serves as the air terminal for Ho Chi Minh City, formerly known as Saigon.

Task Force 78

Under the provisions of the Paris Peace Agreements the United States agreed to remove the naval mines that had been dropped to choke off the North Vietnamese seaborne logistics effort as part of the Linebacker Operations against the north. To do this CINCPAC activated Task Force 78, a specially configured mine countermeasures task force under the command of Rear Admiral Brian McCauley. It deployed from the Philippines to the coast of North Vietnam in early February 1973 and initiated Operation End Sweep, the code name for the mine clearance activity. Using sophisticated mine hunting gear aboard sleds towed behind Marine Corps CH-53 helicopters, as well as other more traditional methods, the task force cleared the ports and harbors at Haiphong, Cam Pha, and Hon Gai by early April. Following a short suspension due to political squabbling between the North Vietnamese and the Americans, the Task Force completed its mission on July 18, 1973 and departed.

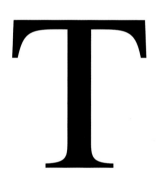

Below: A squadron of Vietnamese Air Force CH-34s sits on the ramp at Tan Son Nhut.

Left: A pair of Navy Inshore Patrol Craft transit a narrow canal.

Below left: A UH-1B gunship provides air cover for two River Patrol Boats during a Game Warden patrol.

Right: An armored troop carrier provides security for a medevac helicopter on the Vam Co Tay river.

Below: The USS *Benewah*, APE-35, acts as the mother ship for part of Task Force 117.

Task Force 116

The riverine assault force that conducted Operation Game Warden was officially designated Task Force 116. It was organized by the US Navy in December 1965 to interdict Viet Cong logistics operations on the inter-coastal and interior waterways of South Vietnam. It was especially active in the Mekong Delta.

Task Force 117

In early 1967, MACV assigned two brigades of the US Army 9th Infantry Division to work with US Navy riverine elements in the upper Mekong Delta. This joint Mobile Riverine Force was designated Task Force 117. MACV withdrew the Army elements and abolished this force in August 1969.

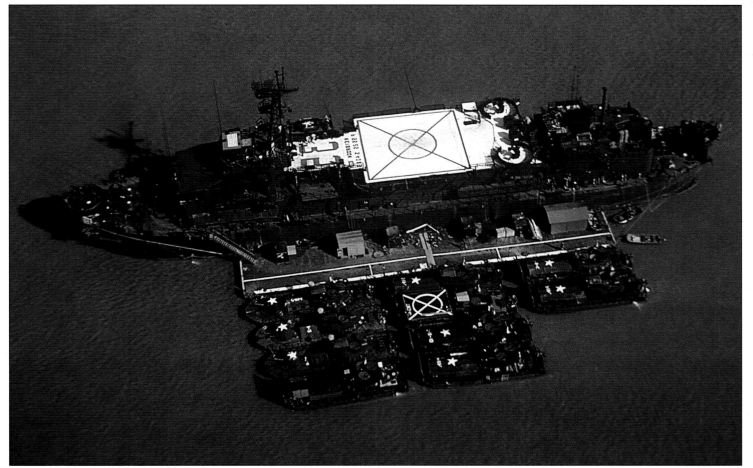

Above: The crew of an M110 8in howitzer responds to a call for fire.

Task Force Oregon

In February 1967, combat pressure in I Corps had stressed the 3rd Marine Amphibious Force to the limit. To bolster American combat power and allow the Marines to concentrate in the northern part of the Corps, MACV formed an ad-hoc division sized unit in southern I Corps known as Task Force Oregon. Support troops were drawn from various units, and the combat elements consisted of one brigade from the 101st Airborne Division, one brigade of the 25th Infantry Division, plus the independent 196th Light Infantry Brigade. In September 1967, the two divisional brigades returned to their parent units and were replaced by the 11th Infantry Brigade and the 198th Infantry Brigade. At that point in time Task Force Oregon was renamed the Americal Division and assigned responsibility for the southern provinces of I Corps.

Taylor, Maxwell Davenport

Maxwell Taylor was the chief architect of the theory of "flexible response" in US military planning. It called for a diversified military capability and a reduction in the reliance on nuclear weapons. One of the key elements of his theory was the doctrine of counterinsurgency and limited war. President Kennedy was impressed with Taylor's concepts and appointed him a Special Military Advisor to the President. He was appointed Chairman of the Joint Chiefs of Staff in 1962 and then as the Ambassador to South Vietnam in 1964. He worked hard to return Vietnam to civilian rule after the assassination of Ngo Dinh Diem, until he left Vietnam in 1965. As a special adviser to president Lyndon B Johnson, Taylor was a strong advocate of the American military presence in South Vietnam.

Taylor–McNamara Report

A report on the military and political situation in South Vietnam was authored by Secretary of Defense Robert McNamara and Chairman of the Joint Chiefs of Staff, Maxwell Taylor, based on a fact-finding mission to the country in September 1963. The twin goals were to assess the progress of the war and investigate the prospects of a coup d'état against Diem. The authors were upbeat about the prospects for military success but warned that the instability of Diem's regime presented a threat.

Taylor-Rostow Mission

In October 1961, President Kennedy sent his Special Military Advisor, General Maxwell Taylor, and the Deputy Special Assistant to the President for National Security Affairs, Walt Rostow, on a fact-finding mission to South Vietnam. They arrived in Saigon the day President Diem declared a national emergency following a Viet Cong attack.

Their visit reinforced their belief in the Domino Theory and on their return they recommended the expansion of MAAG—V to MACV, and the immediate dispatch of 8,000 US troops to reassure President Diem. As a result of the recommendations Kennedy increased the strength of US forces in Vietnam from 600 to 15,000 within one year.

Tchepone

A town in Laos approximately 25 miles from the border with South Vietnam called Tchepone was located where the north-south Ho Chi Minh Trail crossed Route 9, the major east-west route from the Vietnamese seacoast to the banks of

Above: General Maxwell Taylor visits the
II Corps Montagnard Training Center before
becoming Chairman of the Joint Chiefs of Staff.

the Mekong River in Laos. It was a major NVA logistical center.

At numerous times CIA-sponsored Hmong guerrillas unsuccessfully attempted to attack Tchepone from the west. It was the major objective of the South Vietnamese raid code-named Operation Lam Son 719. Heavily defended both on the ground and by anti-aircraft guns, it fell to the South Vietnamese during Lam Son 719, but an immediate counterattack by the North Vietnamese retook it within two weeks. In preparation for the final assault against South Vietnam, the North Vietnamese used the town as a division staging area.

Teach–Ins

An early non-violent manifestation of antiwar protest, known as a teach-in, was modeled after earlier Civil Rights seminars, which sought to educate large

Right: Professor Eric Wolf of the University of
Michigan speaks at the first teach-in against the
Vietnam War in 1965.

Right: A rocket man helps a woman and small child through a window during the Tet Offensive.

Below right: A group of Marines take a break after securing a battle-scarred building in Hue.

segments of the student population about both the moral and political foundations of US involvement. The first teach-in—featuring seminars, rallies, speeches, and a debate between protesters and administrators of the government —took place at the University of Michigan at Ann Arbor in March 1965. In May, a nationally broadcast teach-in reached students and faculty at over 100 campuses, and eventually the format spread to campuses around the country and brought faculty members into active antiwar participation. The strong impact of the national teach-in contributed to the resignations of several government officials, including McGeorge Bundy in early 1966. Indeed, the level of exposure given to this well-publicized debate made the antiwar effort both more respectable and more widespread.

Tet

The most important holiday of the Vietnamese year is known as Tet. Normally celebrated during the first week of the first month of the lunar calendar, if falls between the dates January 19 and February 20. The Vietnamese believe that the first week of the New Year will determine the family fortunes for the remainder of the year. The first night of the new moon is the most important night during Tet. It is celebrated by feasting, fireworks, and veneration of one's ancestors.

Tet Offensive

The 1968 Tet Offensive was the decisive battle of the Vietnam War. On January 30 and 31, 1968, a combined total of approximately 84,000 Viet Cong and NVA troops assaulted 36 of the 44 provincial capitals, five of the six autonomous cities, and 64 of the 242 district capitals in South Vietnam. The countrywide attacks were scheduled to begin on January 31, however confusion over the lunar calendar resulted in some units in I Corps and II Corps kicking off

Opposite, top: Troops from the 40th Signal Battalion attempt to repair a cable while under fire during the Tet Offensive.

Opposite, bottom: A squad lays down a base of fire while another one tries to flank the Viet Cong during the Battle of Namo Village.

Above: A grenadier helps a sick woman caught in the cross fire at a hospital down the street to safety.

early. At 12:15am on 30 January, Danang, Pleiku, Nha Trang, Kontum, and eight other cities were assaulted. During the night of January 31 the remainder of the attacks began. Almost all of the attacks caught the Allied forces by surprise. As many of the ARVN units had released a large number of their soldiers to go home for the Tet holiday, the offensive enjoyed a number of initial successes. However, the North Vietnamese and Viet Cong high command had counted on an uprising of the South Vietnamese people to bolster their attack. The uprising did not materialize and the units of the South Vietnamese army, particularly the Regional Forces and Popular Forces, fought with a greater tenacity than was anticipated. While fighting was bloody, within a few days the NVA and VC had been turned back nearly everywhere except Hue. The North Vietnamese who had overrun the fortified citadel in the center of Hue managed to hold out until March 2. Militarily the Tet Offensive was a disaster for the communists. The Viet Cong, who spearheaded the attacks into Saigon and several other major cities, were shattered. Additionally many of their political operatives, who had been anonymous up to this point, had surfaced and were hunted down. In all, the communists lost over 50,000 men either killed or captured. Paradoxically, though a crushing tactical disaster, the Tet Offensive was an overwhelming strategic victory. Throughout 1966 and 1967, the American public had been repeatedly told that the communists were losing and the war would soon be over. The television images of the intense combat and the shattered cities in Vietnam caused them to increasingly question what the government was telling them. The sight of General Westmoreland walking among dead Viet Cong inside of the US Embassy compound, proclaiming that the battle had been an American victory, and the picture of the execution of a Viet Cong suspect by ARVN General Loan, demoralized the American public. The sense of disaster was further heightened by the general tone of reporting by the media in Vietnam. Reacting to only what they could see, a significant number of reporters pronounced Tet as a major American defeat. They continued to do so well after it was clear that they were wrong. On March 31, 1968, during a national television address in which he announced the unilateral halt of the bombing of North Vietnam and that he would not seek reelection, President Johnson turned what had been a potential major military victory into a disastrous psychological defeat, and set the stage for the American withdrawal. General Giap, recognizing the import of President Johnson's speech, ordered his units to regroup and then concentrate on inflicting the maximum number of American casualties possible; a reversal of the Attrition Strategy. This time the Attrition Strategy worked.

Texas, Operation
On March 20, 1966, a combined United States Marine and ARVN reaction force launched Operation Texas to relieve a trapped Regional Forces company 25 miles northwest of Quang Ngai City at An Hoa. On March 20 the 3rd Battalion, 7th Marines, and 5th ARVN Airborne Battalion succeeded in relieving the surrounded RF company. As the Viet Cong withdrew to the south the 2nd Battalion, 4th Marines, quickly combat-assaulted into an area ahead of them, blocking

Right: A 101st Airborne Division UH-1D flies in to evacuate a casualty north of Fire Support Base Ripcord.

Below: The commander of the 7th Marine Regiment confers with his logistics officer during Operation Texas.

their escape. The relieving force and the RF Company then attacked south, trapping the 1st Viet Cong Regiment between the two forces. In heavy fighting they killed 623 Viet Cong of an estimated regimental strength of 1,050. Though reconstituted later, the 1st VC Regiment never did achieve the same level of military competence they had before the battle of An Hoa.

Texas Star, Operation

Operation Texas Star was a joint operation between the 101st Airborne Division and the ARVN 1st Infantry Division. Its purpose was to regain the initiative in the mountains east of the A Shau Valley in the Quang Tri and Thua Thien provinces. The operation lasted from April 1, to September 5, 1970. The fighting was heavy throughout the entire period, but the intensity steadily increased during late June and early July. It culminated in

Above: As part of Operation Texas Star, 101st Airborne troops work with a group of children as a pacification effort.

Above right: US aircraft are lined up in their revetments at Udorn Royal Thai Air Force Base.

Right: An honor guard passes in review as III MAF welcomes the 1st Marine Division to Vietnam.

the Battle of Fire Support Base Ripcord. The 101st Airborne Division was forced to abandon this on July 23 when intelligence indicated that an entire 9,000 to 11,000 man NVA Division was moving into position to attack the 300 US troops defending the firebase.

Thailand

As a member of the Southeast Asian Treaty Organization (SEATO), Thailand was a staunch ally of the United States during the Vietnam War and the first Asian nation to contribute troops. By 1967, Thailand had 11,000 troops in Vietnam and another 16,500 assisting the Hmong guerrillas and Royal Lao forces in Laos. The US Air Force utilized seven Thai Air Force bases, and by 1969 there were 49,000 US servicemen serving there. Thailand was flooded with refugees following the fall of South Vietnam and the Khmer Rouge takeover of Cambodia.

Thich Quang Duc

On June 11, 1963, 66-year-old Thich Quang Duc was the first buddhist monk to immolate himself in public as a political protest against the Diem regime. While self-immolation is not uncommon in many parts of Asia, the media coverage of the event profoundly affected the attitude of the Kennedy administration toward the South Vietnamese regime. Although eventually over 30 buddhist monks and nuns burned themselves to death, Thich Quang Duc, as the first one, served as the catalyst for the events that eventually led to the downfall of President Diem.

Thich Tri Quang

Thich Tri Quang was both a charismatic buddhist leader and a profound nationalist. He organized buddhist opposition to Ngo Dinh Diem, and also opposed the US presence in South Vietnam. He believed that if the Diem government was overthrown and the Americans withdrew, a return to traditional ways and an end to Catholic domination of the government could lead to peace talks, and the country could be reunited. In 1966, he organized buddhist opposition to Premier Nguyen Cao Ky in I Corps. Ky dispatched military forces to Danang and crushed the buddhist opposition. Thich Tri Quang was placed under house arrest and kept there to the end the war. The North Vietnamese exiled him to a monastery in 1975

Third Marine Amphibious Force (III MAF)

Established at Danang in May 1965, the 3rd Marine Amphibious Force (III MAF) grew to become the largest combat organization ever commanded by a Marine in

wartime. By 1968, it included two reinforced Marine Divisions, a Marine Air Wing, a US Army Corps, a Korean Marine Brigade, and an assortment of logistical and support organizations. Its tactical area of responsibility (TAOR) was a 30 to 70-mile wide zone stretching from the DMZ 225 miles south to Sa Huynh, where a spur of the Annamite mountain chain pushed out to the sea. The commanders of III MAF were continually at odds with the commanders of MACV over the conduct of the war, favoring counterinsurgency and pacification to search and destroy operations. Though most of the heavy combat during the war took place in I Corps, III MAF was one of the first units phased out during the withdrawal.

Thompson, Sir Robert Grainger Ker
Sir Robert Thompson gained prominence as a recognized expert in counterinsurgency based on his experience in communist terrorist action in Malaya. In 1961, at the request of the United States, he came to South Vietnam as the head of the British mission there. As an adviser to President Diem, he recommended the development and implementation of the Strategic Hamlet Program, which was patterned after a population control effort that had been successful in Malaya. In Vietnam it was a miserable failure, and he and his advice were marginalized by the American military. In 1969, as Vietnamization became the US policy; he spent some time as a consultant to the Nixon administration.

Thunderhead, Operation
Operation Thunderhead was a highly classified search and rescue mission conducted from May 29–June 19, 1972. Based on an intelligence report of a pending prisoner of war escape attempt, Navy SEALs, reconnaissance aircraft, and search and rescue helicopters methodically searched the reported escape route for POWs attempting to exfiltrate from North Vietnam. Though it was later determined that no escape took place, following their release in 1973 the POWs reported that one had been planned, but heightened security following a breakdown in the peace talks in Paris caused them to abort their effort. Officially classified as a failure, many believe that the operation, during which only one man was lost, provided a successful template should the future opportunity to retrieve POWs, who had escaped, present itself.

Ticket Punching
As the war in Vietnam ground on, it became clear to the officer corps of the US armed forces that the only path to a promotion was to have an outstanding officer fitness report for their time in Vietnam. Even minor aberrations, which in the past would have been noted as a tool for counseling subordinates, were the death knell for an officers' career. Careerism, and the achievement of statistical indicators, such as body count or volunteer missions accepted, became far more important than the leadership intrinsic to their position. Officers became more interested in doing the minimum necessary to be promoted, getting their "ticket punched," than they were in leading their troops.

Tiger Cages
Epithet given to the notorious confinement cells at the RVN prison on Con Son island. Built during the French colonial administration to hold prisoners of war and political prisoners, the "Tiger Cage" was a windowless 5ft by 9ft concrete box with a ceiling so low that it was impossible to stand upright. Prisoners were poorly fed and kept in constant confinement. In 1970, revelations about Con Son led the Red Cross to charge the RVN with violations of the Geneva Convention.

Tiger Hound, Operation
Operation Tiger Hound was the code name for the allied air interdiction of the Ho Chi Minh Trail in the southern Laotian panhandle from Tchepone, near the 17th parallel, south to the Cambodian border. In 1965, the US Embassy and Laotian government recognized the Laotian panhandle as an extension of the war in Vietnam and, though they still barred regular US ground forces, ceded control of air operations over this part of Laos to MACV. Tiger Hound struck North Vietnamese elements operating along the Trail both day and night until April 1973. More than a million tons of bombs were dropped in the southern Laotian panhandle in an attempt to impede North Vietnamese infiltration.

Toan Thang, Operation
Operation Toan Thang (Complete Victory) was a code name applied to a number of joint ARVN–US operations, the most important lasting from April 8, to May 25, 1968. All were part of the Allied counter-attack in response to the Tet Offensive, and were designed to push the Viet Cong and NVA units away from Saigon and the Capital Military District. They overlapped and countered the second phase of the Tet Offensive, sometimes referred to as the mini-Tet. The fighting was very heavy around Tan Son Nhut Air Base, the Binh Thien Bridge, and the Y Bridge that links Saigon with the industrial area of Nha Be. Although the heaviest combat ended on June 25, 1968, it took the 5th ARVN Ranger Group until the end of June to clear the

Below: A group of F4-D Phantoms and A7 Corsair IIs drop their ordnance on an Operation Tiger Hound LORAN strike mission.

Right: A 9th Infantry Division machinegun team lays down suppressive fire at the "Y" bridge in Saigon during the Tet Offensive.

Above: A 25th Division medic paddles down a canal toward a casualty collection point during Operation Toan Thang.

Viet Cong from Cholon. The ARVN subsequently named another series of operations, including their portion of the incursion into Cambodia, Toan Thang.

Ton That Dinh

Ton That Dinh was the youngest general in the ARVN. He was considered loyal to President Ngo Dinh Diem, however the plotters against Diem needed his support because he commanded the troops in and around Saigon. They convinced him to side with them. Following the coup he was appointed as the Minister of the Interior. Dinh was later arrested with several other key politicians for allegedly plotting to negotiate a peace settlement with Hanoi, and imprisoned. Freed by Nguyen Cao Ky, he was given command of a Corps but was relieved for supporting the buddhists in the Buddhist Crisis. He entered the Vietnamese Senate in 1967 and fled Vietnam in April 1975 as the communists took over.

Tonkin

Under the French, Vietnam was divided into three separate administrative entities: Tonkin in the north, Annam in the center, and Cochin China in the South. Drained by the Red, Clear, Black, and Thai Binh Rivers, much of Tonkin is a fertile delta that supports a dense population. Hanoi, located at a major fork in the Red River, was the adminis-

Above right: A North Vietnamese torpedo boat sheers away after making a firing run on the USS Maddox.

Right: Weary sailors mop up the accidental fire aboard the carrier USS Forrestal that killed 134 men and injured 161 more.

trative capital of French Indochina and became the capital of the Democratic Republic of Vietnam. Haiphong, the major seaport of North Vietnam, is located downstream from Hanoi.

Tonkin Gulf Incident

On the night of 30–31, July 1964, South Vietnamese fast attack craft, crewed by CIA-recruited mercenaries, shelled two small islands in the Tonkin Gulf under OPLAN 34A. On the night of August 1,

the destroyer USS *Maddox* approached Hon Me Island, one of those that had been attacked the day before. On August 2, three patrol boats from the North Vietnamese navy base on the island attacked the Maddox with torpedoes. All the torpedoes missed their target and Maddox returned fire, claiming hits on one boat. As the North Vietnamese attacked, the American destroyer requested assistance from the aircraft carrier USS *Ticonderoga*, which was also in the area. F-8 Crusaders from the Ticonderoga attacked the PT boats with Zuni rockets and 20mm cannon fire. They also claimed that they had damaged at least one boat before the North Vietnamese fled for their harbor on the island. On August 3, the destroyer USS *C Turner Joy* joined the USS *Maddox*, and they resumed the patrol, farther out to sea. On the night of August 4, the two destroyers reported they were again under attack. The *C Turner Joy* fired at radar targets that could not be detected by the *Maddox*, while the *Maddox* sonar reported the sound of torpedoes in the water, a sonar indication that was not heard on the *C Turner Joy*. The two destroyers maneuvered at high speed and continued the engagement, again calling for air support from the USS *Ticonderoga*. The reported second attack led directly to US air strikes against North Vietnam and the passage of the Gulf of Tonkin Resolution. It was later determined that no second attack had taken place.

Tonkin, Gulf of, Resolution

Legislation was introduced in the aftermath of the Gulf of Tonkin incident that involved the US Naval vessels USS *Maddox* and USS *C Turner Joy*. On August 7, 1964 the US Congress, at the behest of President Johnson, passed the Gulf of Tonkin Resolution put forward by the White House, allowing the President "to take all necessary steps, including the use of armed force" to prevent further attacks against US forces. The Resolution, passed unanimously in the House and 98 to 2 in the Senate, granted enormous power to President Johnson to wage an undeclared war in Vietnam from the White House. On March 1, 1966, an attempt to repeal the Gulf of Tonkin Resolution led by Senator Wayne Morse failed in the US Senate by a vote of 92 to 5. Finally, on June 24, 1970, it was repealed by Senate.

Tran Buu Kiem

The foreign relations specialist of the National Front for the Liberation of South Vietnam (NFLSV) was Tran Buu Kiem who was the architect of the propaganda thrust among non-aligned nations and in Europe for the neutralization of Vietnam. He later served with Madam Nguyen Thi Binh as a representative of the NFLSV to the Paris peace talks in 1968.

Below: A French-built Vietnamese Navy command boat moves down a canal in a Viet Cong controlled area.

Tran Kim Tuyen

Dr Tran Kim Tuyen was a catholic physician who fled North Vietnam in 1954. A confidant of Ngo Dinh Diem, he became the head of the Office of Political and Social Studies, a powerful secret police organization established by the CIA that was loyal to Diem. He became disaffected with Diem in the late 1950s, and in 1962 began plotting his overthrow. Diem discovered the plot and exiled Tuyen by naming him a diplomatic counsel to Egypt. Tuyen fled to Hong Kong, from where he continued to oppose Diem. Though he returned to Vietnam after Diem's death, he was never again prominent in South Vietnamese politics.

Tran Hung Dao, Operation

Operation Tran Hung Dao was part of the Southeast Asia Lake, Ocean, River, Delta Strategy (SEALORDS). The operation began on November 1, 1968 when a riverine screen was established along the Cambodian border and connected the waterborne combat patrols into a continuous barrier from the Gulf of Thailand to the Saigon River. By January 1969, the barrier had proven effective in reducing Viet Cong and NVA logistics operations throughout the northern and western Mekong Delta. It also assisted in reducing infiltration from the NVA base camps through War Zone C into Hau Nghia province and the area around Saigon.

Tran Van Don

Born in France, Tran Van Don became a career soldier in the French army during World War II. During the French Indochina War, when the French decided to create the Vietnamese National Army, Don, who was a colonel, was appointed as the chief of staff.

He was one of the senior officers Ngo Dinh Diem counted on during his wars against the Binh Xuyen and the religious sects in 1955. He was also one of the principal conspirators in the coup against Diem. Later, under Nguyen Van Thieu, he served as the Deputy Prime Minister, Army Chief of Staff, and as a roving ambassador. In 1975 he escaped to the United States.

Tran Van Hai

During the Tet Offensive, Tran Van Hai commanded the ARVN Ranger Command, and led the Ranger force that ejected the NVA and Viet Cong from Cholon. He was then assigned as the chief of the National Police and was largely regarded as incorruptible. During the NVA Final Offensive he commanded the ARVN 7th Infantry Division at Dong Tam near My Tho. When Saigon fell, he committed suicide rather than surrender.

Tran Van Huong

A former Viet Minh who served as mayor of Saigon, Tran Van Huong became the Prime Minister of a civilian government orchestrated by General Nguyen Khanh in 1964. Following bitter opposition from the buddhists, his government fell after only three months. He became the Vice President of South Vietnam in 1971. When Nguyen Van Thieu abdicated the presidency on April 21, 1975, Huong became the President. Nine days later he transferred authority to General Duong Van Minh, who surrendered to the North Vietnamese the following day.

Tran Van Tra

During the French Indochina War, Tran Van Tra was a zone commander in central Vietnam. Following the Geneva Accords of 1954 he regrouped to the North. In 1958, he commanded the NVA 330th Division and was promoted to major general and elected to the Party Central Committee. In 1963, he returned to the South and assumed command of the People's Liberation Armed Forces. In 1964, he was promoted to Colonel General and became the Chairman of the

Above: The reconnaissance platoon of Troop A, 1/9th Cavalry investigates a tunnel in Quang Ngai province.

Military Affairs Committee of the Central Office of South Vietnam, COSVN. He planned and orchestrated the assault on Saigon during the Tet Offensive, and also advocated a national military campaign in 1974–1975 to disrupt the ARVN. He served as a Deputy Commander of the NVA Final Offensive in 1975. From May 1975 to January 1976, he commanded the military occupation force for Saigon. Following the publication of a book in which he criticized the NVA performance and admitted that the Tet Offensive was both poorly planned and executed, he was purged from the Communist Party in 1982.

Trang Sup, Battle of (January 1960)

Most Vietnamese consider the Battle of Trang Sup on January 26, 1960, as the first major engagement launched by the Viet Cong and the actual start of the ground war. The village, in Tay Ninh province, was attacked and overrun by 200 Vietcong guerrillas. The ARVN infantry regiment headquartered in the village disintegrated and ran away. Lieutenant General Samuel Williams, the commander of MAAG-V, reported to Washington that, even though the Viet Cong had proven capable of launching large-scale attacks, some military reforms might be needed but that US troops were not.

Transportation Group 559

The NVA Logistical Command in charge of transportation along the Ho Chi Minh Trail was Transportation Group 559. Formed in May 1959, the group originally worked to improve the roads through the passes in the Annamite Cordillera between Laos and North Vietnam. In short order, building from the established Laotian road net, by 1962 a modest quantity of supplies was moving down the trail. As the Ho Chi Minh Trail expanded and the quantities of matériel that was being moved increased by several orders of magnitude, the Group 559 headquarters was established just west of the end of the Demilitarized Zone in an area of operations code-named Nickel Steel. Though it was repeatedly attacked by air, and SOG ground operations occasionally came close, it was never really threatened. By the end of the war, Transportation Group 559 was moving several thousand tons of matériel and thousands of soldiers per month down the Trail.

Troop

A troop is an armored cavalry or air cavalry unit equivalent to a company. It is usually commanded by a captain and consists of two or more platoons. The term "troop" was also used as a slang reference meaning soldier, which is simply the shortening of the full term "troops."

Truong Chinh

During the French Indochina War, Truong Chinh was the Director of Viet Minh intelligence and propaganda. By 1953, he had risen to power second only to Ho Chi Minh. He was the chief North Vietnamese Marxist theorist, and a leader of the Red Chinese faction in the North Vietnamese government. He strongly advocated reunifying Vietnam by supporting guerrillas in the south, and routinely opposed the movement to conventional warfare. He frequently clashed with General Vo Nguyen Giap on military matters and was sometimes viewed as a moderate advocate of negotiations to settle the war.

After the fall of South Vietnam, though staunchly opposed to capitalism, he encouraged the reintroduction of private enterprise in order to re-energize the Vietnamese economy.

Truong Dinh Dzu

An obscure buddhist lawyer, Truong Dinh Dzu was encouraged by the CIA to run against President Nguyen Van Thieu in the 1967 South Vietnamese elections in order to counter the argument that they were rigged. He became the token peace candidate, and rallied an eclectic segment of the electorate that ranged from militant buddhists to neutralists, taking 17 percent of the vote.

President Nguyen Van Thieu only received 35 percent of the vote, and Dzu's strong showing weakened Thieu's legitimacy. He was immediately jailed following the election. After the fall of South Vietnam, Dzu was sentenced to a re-education camp.

Truong Nhu Tang

In the late 1950s and early 1960s, Truong Nhu Tang headed the Vietnam Bank for Industry and Commerce and the Vietnam Sugar Company in Saigon. He became disillusioned with the corruption of the Diem regime, and strongly opposed the American presence in Vietnam. In 1964, he helped found the People's Movement for Self-Determination, an organization opposed to the central government. Following imprisonment in 1967 and 1968 for advocating negotiations with the Viet Cong, in 1968 he joined the National Liberation Front.

In 1969 he became the Minister of Justice for the Provisional Revolutionary Government. Following the conquest of South Vietnam, in 1975 he was appointed the Minister of Justice for the southern part of the Socialist Republic of Vietnam.

Below: Truong Chinh (left) representing the Democratic Republic of North Vietnam, and Pham Hung (right) representing the People's Revolutionary Government of South Vietnam, sign the documents officially uniting the nation.

Opposite: A "tunnel rat" examines the remains of a Viet Cong cooking fire in a tunnel near Cu Chi in III Corps.

Left: An open approach trench/tunnel the Viet Cong dug nearly up to the perimeter of a Special Forces Camp.

Below: The entrance to a Viet Cong tunnel found in II Corps.

Tunnel Rats

The small infantry soldiers armed only with a knife, pistol, and a flashlight, that entered Viet Cong and North Vietnamese tunnels to flush out the enemy, were christened tunnel rats. While almost all division-sized units employed tunnel rats at one time or another, only the 1st and 25th Infantry Divisions had squads specifically organized and trained for this mission. The others simply employed volunteers.

Tunnels

Once characterized by General William Westmoreland as "an army of moles," the Viet Cong made extensive use of an elaborate tunnel system first constructed in various areas of South Vietnam by the Viet Minh in the 1940s. The most extensive was around Cu Chi, located approximately 25 miles northeast of Saigon.

Left: General Nathan Twining just before his return to Washington from a Far East tour in 1946.

This complex extended for over 125 miles, and contained barracks, storage areas, headquarters, and hospitals. Defying repeated attempts to destroy it, this complex is now a major tourist attraction on the outskirts of Ho Chi Minh City, formerly Saigon.

Twining, Nathan Farragut
General Nathan Twining was the Chief of Staff of the US Air Force from 1953 to 1957 and was appointed Chairman of the Joint Chiefs of Staff by President Eisenhower in 1957. A devoted advocate of airpower, and a firm believer that wars should not be limited, in 1954 he recommended that the US drop "one to three tactical nuclear weapons" in support of the French at Dien Bien Phu. His position as an advisor to Barry Goldwater's 1964 presidential campaign was used to convince the public that Goldwater would take the nation into war in Southeast Asia.

U Minh

The U Minh is a huge forest area at the southern tip of Vietnam. Encompassing large parts of An Xuyen and Kien Giang provinces, it was a well-fortified refuge of the Viet Cong. Though the United States never operated extensively in the U Minh, the waterways throughout it were heavily mined and it was repeatedly sprayed with Agent Orange and other defoliants. Coastal patrols sometimes fought skirmishes with the Viet Cong units in the U Minh as they were being resupplied by sea or moving along the narrow coastal interface.

U Thant

Immediately following the 1964 Gulf of Tonkin Incident, U Thant, Secretary-General of the United Nations from 1962 to 1967, attempted to arrange a diplomatic meeting with both sides. Ho Chi Minh agreed, but the Johnson administration rejected his efforts. In January 1965, working through the US Ambassador to the United Nations, he developed preliminary plans for a meeting in Burma. This became known as the "Rangoon Initiative." On January 30, the Johnson administration also rejected that

Above: UN Secretary General U Thant responds to questions on Vietnam during a 1964 press conference.

plan. The Secretary-General then recommended that another Geneva Conference be held. President Johnson also rejected this. U Thant then took the unprecedented step of holding a news conference and making public Washington's refusal to negotiate.

Right: A gunner peppers a Viet Cong position on a riverbank on the lower Ca Mau peninsula with machinegun fire.

Above: Secretary General U Thant of the United Nations holds a press conference following his return from the meetings on Vietnam in Burma in 1967.

Union I and II, Operations

Operations Union I and II were search and clear operations in Quang Nam and Quang Tin provinces of southern I Corps. They were designed to force the 2nd NVA Division out of the Phuoc Hoa/Que Son valley. Up to that point the ARVN had been unable to establish a presence outside of the district capitals. It was initiated following a sharp engagement between the 2nd Battalion, 1st Marines, and the 3rd NVA Regiment on April 20, 1967. On April 21, 1967 the 3rd Battalion, 5th Marines, 1st Battalion 1st Marines, and 1st ARVN Ranger Group were inserted and engaged in heavy fighting in the Que Son Valley. By April 25, the NVA had started to withdraw westward and combat tailed off. As contact diminished, elements were withdrawn until by the end of the month only the 5th Marines were still in the valley. On May 10, heavy combat broke out

Right: Marines move over a hill covered with terraced rice fields near Tam Ky.

around Hill 110 and for the next five days, supported by heavy artillery fire and air strikes, the 5th Marines slugged it out with the NVA on the valley floor. They finally overran the communist defenses and the NVA withdrew. Union I ended on May 17, 1967. Union II kicked off on May 26, 1967 when two battalions of the fifth Marines and the 6th ARVN Regiment attempted to prevent the escape of the 3rd and 21st NVA Regiments spotted withdrawing up a valley north of Tin Phuoc. The Marines quickly closed with the NVA and at times the fighting became hand to hand combat. Supported by artillery fire and air strikes, the Marines overran the 21st NVA Regiment, scattering it. Operation Union II ended on June 5. Though the combined operations did not last long, they were the bloodiest the Marines had fought up to that point in the war. The 5th Marine Regiment was awarded the Presidential Unit Citation for their performance in Operations Union I and II.

Union of Soviet Socialist Republics (USSR)

The USSR under Joseph Stalin retained an arm's length relationship with the Democratic Republic of North Vietnam. However, during the French-Indochina War the Soviet Union forwarded a significant amount of military aid to the Viet Minh through the People's Republic of China. At the Geneva Conference of 1954, the USSR pressured the Viet Minh to accept the partition of Vietnam. The leadership of the Democratic Republic of Vietnam considered this action a betrayal. When Nikita Khrushchev achieved power in the Soviet Union he began looking for ways to counter the rising People's Republic of China's influence in Southeast Asia. One of his initial steps was to begin the airlift of weapons and matériel to the Pathet Lao, who had initiated an insurgency in Laos. Soviet transports routinely landed on the Plain of jars with equipment and North Vietnamese "volunteers." However, as the war expanded, he became increasingly reluctant to provoke a confrontation with the United States.

Soviet Premier Alexei Kosygin visited Hanoi in February 1965 and was present during a US bombing raid. He immediately pledged full support for the North Vietnamese war effort. Upon his return home he initiated a propaganda war against the United States in the United Nations and other world forums, while

simultaneously dramatically increasing the shipment of high-technology surface-to-air missiles, planes, artillery, tanks, fuel, ammunition, and infantry weapons to the Vietnamese.

By 1968 Soviet aid amounted to over 80 percent of all supplies reaching North Vietnam. Following the fall of South Vietnam in 1975, the Soviet Union provided economic assistance to the stricken Vietnamese economy in return for basing rights at Cam Rahn Bay and other military installations.

Uniontown, Operation

Operation Uniontown was conducted by the 199th Light Infantry Brigade in War Zone D from December 17, 1967 to March 8, 1968. The purpose of the operation was to prevent the Viet Cong Dong

Above: Members of the 199th Infantry Brigade carry a wounded man away from a fire fight.

Nai Regiment from launching mortar, rocket, and ground attacks on the Bien Hoa-Long Binh complex. Just after the operation kicked off the Viet Cong and NVA launched the Tet Offensive. The 199th adjusted their operational plan and conducted the defense of Long Binh, screening operations around Bien Hoa, and fought infiltrators in the streets of Saigon until relieved by the ARVN 5th Ranger Group. As American forces pushed the enemy out of Saigon and away from the Bien Hoa-Long Binh complex, the 199th Light Infantry Brigade successfully prevented the Dong Nai Regiment from consolidating their initial gains, then forced them away from

Above: A pair of loaded F-105 Thunderchiefs set out to strike a target on the Ho Chi Minh Trail in Laos.

the cities and back into northern War Zone D, inflicting extremely heavy casualties on the Viet Cong unit.

United Front

A unified effort by disparate groups to achieve a common political objective was a common strategy used by Vietnamese communist groups. The first example was Ho's Viet Minh, organized in 1941 to mobilize all Vietnamese nationalists against the French.

Only later did the Viet Minh become communist dominated. The NLF (Viet Cong) and Pathet Lao also called for a broad-based effort under a common flag, and attracted many non-communists to their cause.

United Nations

International body established in 1945. The UN played only a limited role in Vietnam, despite the efforts of Secretary-General U Thant to broker a peace in 1964, 1968, and 1970.

As both the Soviet Union and US were permanent members of the Security Council, with the right to block resolutions, little could be achieved. Neither the DRV nor RVN was a member, and the major UN contribution came through its work in banning the use of biological weapons after 1972 and rehabilitating refugees after the war.

United States Air Force

In November 1961 President Kennedy ordered the United States Air Force to provide support to the Republic of Vietnam under the code name Operation Farm Gate. From that time until August 1973, when Congress ordered an end to the bombing of Cambodia, more than eight million tons of bombs were dropped on Southeast Asia. During the same time the Air Force lost 2,257 aircraft, most of them in South Vietnam. Of the 1,349 planes that were lost in combat, 1,173 fell to light automatic weapons and antiaircraft guns, 112 were accounted for by surface-to-air missiles, and 64 were shot down by North Vietnamese MiGs. The Air Force fought under severe political restrictions almost from the outset to the end the war. Sanctuary areas, bombing halts, and weapons restrictions all served to reduce their effectiveness.

Airpower enthusiasts point out, with some justification, that the heavy strategic raids against Hanoi and Haiphong during the Linebacker campaigns in 1972 and 1973, brought the communists to the negotiating table and resulted in an agreement to end the war. Others, also with some justification, contend that by 1972 the character of the war had changed to the point that airpower could have a greater effect. During its earlier phases there were no high-value targets that could be struck, the loss of which would have adversely impacted the North Vietnamese capability to maintain

their forces in the south, and the armor, artillery, and mass troop formations that were savaged in Linebacker I were not present on the battlefield during the earlier parts of the war. One thing is clear, the absolute domination of the air by the US Air Force significantly reduced US casualties and increased those of the Viet Cong and North Vietnamese.

United States Army

As the largest component of the American armed forces, the majority of the troops who fought in Vietnam were in the Army. US Army involvement in Vietnam began with the establishment of MAAG–Indochina on September 17, 1950. It continued at a low level until President Kennedy began introducing significant numbers of advisers in 1961. Between 1961 and 1975, 30,868 Army troops died as a result of hostile action in Vietnam, and over 201,000 more were wounded. On balance, the US Army utterly devastated the Viet Cong, and created an environment wherein North Vietnamese Army units could only operate at the risk of their destruction. On the other hand, the US Army's performance, poor morale, and the lack of professionalism among its officer corps have been widely criticized. Much of that criticism is justified, but some has been overstated. Careerism and "ticket punching" by the officers, coupled with the fact that they only served six months in the field as opposed to the 12 months an enlisted man could expect, eroded the soldiers' confidence in their officer's leadership. Additionally, the overwhelming dependence on statistical indicators such as the body count to measure success fostered cynicism and a sense of separation between the soldier and the civilian leadership. This was further exacerbated by refusal to activate the reserves, which became a haven for draft dodgers. Vietnam was the only war for which the reserves were not called up. The Army's replacement system, which focused on the individual rather than unit replacement served to further damage unit cohesion. Although the average soldier had no real idea why he was fighting in Vietnam, morale, particularly in the combat units, tended to be high until quite late in war.

Following the Tet Offensive in 1968, antiwar sentiment and the public's unwillingness to continue to support their effort in Southeast Asia grew. This, coupled with the attitudes experienced by professional soldiers who returned to the United States and then were again reassigned to Vietnam, was reflected in the general attitude of what had become a largely draftee Army. Morale declined, discipline eroded, and combat performance suffered. By the time the last units withdrew in 1972, even the elite forces were a mere shadow of what they had been at the outset.

United States Army Vietnam (USARV)

The United States Army Vietnam (USARV) was organized as a logistical and administrative command headquarters in July 1965. Originally established in Saigon, it was later transferred to Long Binh, were it remained until it was deactivated in March 1973. The Deputy Commander of the Military Assistance Command, Vietnam (MACV) headed USARV.

Below: A 9th Infantry Division medic holds a plasma bottle for a soldier wounded near the Kinh Doi Canal south of Saigon.

United States Coast Guard

On February 16, 1965, a North Vietnamese trawler was spotted unloading weapons and equipment for the Viet Cong at Vung Ro Bay south of Qui Nhon in II Corps. It took nine days to get a sufficient number of ARVN troops to the beach to destroy the trawler and capture any offloaded cargo that remained. The US Navy, which is organized to operate in deep water, was il-equipped to patrol the extensive coastline of Vietnam. It was clear that some action had to be taken to prevent seaborne supplies being transferred from North Vietnam to the South. While it took up to 170 days for matériel to transit the Ho Chi Minh Trail, far more could be shipped within two or three days by sea. On April 29, 1965, President Johnson authorized the use of US Coast Guard cutters to conduct inshore patrols in an attempt to interdict this logistics traffic. The first squadron of patrol boats arrived in Danang on July 20, 1965. This deployment was later reinforced to the point that the Coast Guard maintained patrols from the

Demilitarized Zone all along the Vietnamese coast to the Gulf of Thailand. In December 1965, the Defense Department requested that the Coast Guard install an electronic navigation system to assist the US Air Force in flying precision strikes over both North and South Vietnam. On August 8, 1966, a LORAN-C chain, code-named Operation Tight Rein, went on the air. In addition to supporting navigation and Operation Market Time, on June 5, 1966 the Coast Guard provided the Army First Logistical Command with a number of explosives loading detachments. Experience had shown that the Vietnamese stevedores lacked the experience to safely handle ammunition ships and there was a great deal of concern about the potential for explosion in the crowded ports. These detachments both trained and supervised the crews that were used to offload ammunition and ordnance. As the tempo of combat operations increased, in April 1968 Coast Guard helicopters began supplementing Navy and Air Force search and rescue

operations along the coast line. As Vietnamization began, on May 16, 1969, the first two Coast Guard cutters, the Point League and Point Garnet, were turned over to the Vietnamese Navy. On March 19, 1975, the Tan My LORAN station 42 miles south of the DMZ was evacuated as North Vietnamese troops neared. On April 29, 1975 the Con Son Island LORAN station was evacuated. On April 30, 1975, South Vietnam surrendered, and on October 3, 1975, the US Coast Guard Southeast Asia LORAN-C Network was disestablished. Between 1965 and 1975, 8,000 Coast Guardsmen served in Southeast Asia, where seven were killed in action and 63 wounded.

United States Information Agency (USIA)

The United States Information Agency was a government agency, based in Saigon. The USIA was part of the original US advisory team in Vietnam, and was responsible for actively promoting US interests and policies and those of its Vietnamese allies. It was led from 1963 by John Mecklin, a former Time reporter and veteran of the French war. Initially, the USIA actively supported the Diem regime but Mecklin became increasingly disillusioned and lobbied the Kennedy administration to put pressure on the regime to change.

United States Marine Corps

The Vietnam War was the bloodiest war the US Marine Corps ever fought. By

1970, 14,836 marines had been killed in action and an additional 88,542 were wounded, more casualties than the Marine Corps suffered in all of World War II. Marine Corps involvement began in April 1962 when Marine helicopter units deployed to the Mekong Delta in Operation Shufly to lift ARVN elements into battle. On March 8, 1965, the 9th Marine Expeditionary Brigade (MEB) landed two battalions at Danang and the buildup began. In May 1965, 3rd Marine

Above: A Marine tank commander grips a .30 caliber machinegun he has added to his tanks armament.

Above left: A fire team gets ready to sprint through a breech in a wall on the grounds of the Imperial Palace in Hue.

Below: Marines prepare to engage a group of snipers forted up in a building with a 106mm recoilless rifle.

Left: Smoke rises over a burning petroleum barge that Navy pilots struck in Haiphong Harbor.

Amphibious Force (III MAF) was organized in Danang. It became the largest combat force ever commanded by a Marine, including at one time a full Army Corps, two Marine divisions, a Marine air wing, and numerous logistical, support, and artillery units. The Marines emphasized pacification and clashed repeatedly with MACV over the proper strategy for the war. Eventually they gave in and shifted to the search and destroy form of the Attrition Strategy. In I Corps the Marines fought two distinct wars. The northern provinces featured both small and large unit combat against elements of the North Vietnamese Army, supported by artillery and later tanks. In the southern provinces the Viet Cong were stronger and, until the Tet Offensive, most engagements were with them rather than the NVA.

During the Tet Offensive the Marines held off a multi-division NVA force at Khe Sanh, engaged NVA forces around the periphery of Danang, and three battalions fought with ARVN troops to recapture the ancient citadel of the city of Hue. In the summer of 1969, the Marines began to withdraw from Vietnam under President Nixon's Vietnamization program. In March 1970, the XXIV Corps replaced the 3rd Marine Amphibious Force (III MAF) as the command headquarters for I Corps and the Marine Tactical Area of Responsibility was reduced to simply Quang Nam province and the city of Danang. In April 1971, III MAF headquarters was withdrawn to Okinawa and the only Marines, other than the embassy guards, remaining in Vietnam were assigned as advisers to the Vietnamese Marine Corps.

United States Navy

At the time of the August 1964 Gulf of Tonkin Incident the United States Navy was designed and trained to take part in a nuclear war. Gun-armed ships had been steadily withdrawn from service, and most amphibious transports and fleet support ships were World War II veterans

Below: An A-7 Corsair II is poised to launch for a strike against North Vietnam.

that had been slated for retirement or replacement. In order to carry out the missions assigned to the Navy, a number of gun-armed cruisers and the battleship USS *New Jersey* were returned to service. The small Essex Class aircraft carriers that had been slated for retirement were retained, and provided much needed air support early in the war when the US Air Force involvement was limited. While the most visible operations the Navy carried out were air strikes launched from Yankee Station against North Vietnam, surface warships gave fire support to friendly troops ashore and, as part of Operation Sea Dragon, they mounted raids along North Vietnam's coast. Under Operation Market Time they established a three zone series of patrols designed to interdict the maritime infiltration from the north. In the outer zone, long-range patrol aircraft and destroyers watched for infiltrators. Closer inshore, destroyers, destroyer escorts, and high endurance Coast Guard cutters maintained a close watch on fishing fleets and the numerous

merchant ships transiting the area. Along the coast shallow-draft Coast Guard cutters and fast patrol boats called "swift boats" intercepted sampans, junks, and small boats that ducked in and out of estuaries. In the Mekong Delta the Navy organized a riverine fleet of shallow-draft landing craft, patrol boats, and fire support monitors to interdict Viet Cong traffic on the numerous rivers and small waterways. In the final stages of the war, naval gunfire and air strikes helped break up the North Vietnamese Easter Offensive. When President Nixon launched Operation Linebacker I, the Navy carried out an aerial mining campaign of North Vietnamese harbors that was especially effective. They also extricated the last Americans as South Vietnam fell in 1975. The Navy suffered 2,551 killed in action and 14 Navy men won the Medal of Honor.

Unity Project

In June 1970, the 46th Special Forces Company in Thailand began organizing and training Thai "volunteer" Battalions at Nam Phong for use in Laos. The code name for this effort was the Unity Project. By the time the cease-fire was achieved in Laos in February 1973, there

were 30 infantry battalions, six heavy weapons companies, six groupment mobile staffs, and three task force headquarters with a total strength of 17,808 Thai troops trained by Unity fighting in Laos. At that point, the US Embassy and Royal Lao Government decided to phase out the Unity formations in 1974, and this was accomplished.

University of Wisconsin Bombing

In 1970 an attack was made by the Weathermen on the University of Wisconsin campus. The attack was the fifth carried out by the radical student group, and targeted the Army Mathematics Research Center at the college. The bombing was planned and executed by Karl and Dwight Armstrong, David Fine and Leo Burt on August 24, 1970. The explosion killed graduate student Robert Fussnach, injured three others and caused $6 million in damage. It also had the effect of polarizing many supporters of the antiwar movement.

USS *C Turner Joy* (DD-951)

The USS *C Turner Joy* was a Forrest Sherman Class destroyer that was patrolling an area 100 miles off the North Vietnamese coast when the USS *Maddox*

Below: US Air Force Master Sergeant Jack Cheek gives a Thai Captain some pointers on the M60 machinegun.

Right: The USS *C Turner Joy* (DD-951) underway in the South China Sea.

reported she was under attack by North Vietnamese torpedo boats on August 2, 1964. She quickly joined the other destroyer and on August 4, 1964, both ships picked up what they believed to be five small surface craft approaching in bad weather. With reports of torpedoes in the water, the two destroyers opened fire on the radar images and requested air support from the carrier USS *Ticonderoga*. While the two American ships maneuvered and fired furiously, it was later determined that there were no torpedo boats in the area. This phantom engagement, coupled with the actual attack on the USS *Maddox* two days earlier, triggered President Johnson's retaliatory air strikes against North Vietnam, and the authorization by US Congress of the Gulf of Tonkin Resolution.

USS *Maddox* (DD-731)

The USS *Maddox* was an Allen M Sumner Class destroyer engaged in a

Below: The USS *New Jersey* (BB-62) fires all nine of her 16in guns at a target in North Vietnam.

Right: Gun crews on the *USS Maddox*, DD-731, service the guns during a gunfire support mission.

DeSoto Mission in the Gulf of Tonkin on August 2, 1964. North Vietnamese patrol boats, reacting to an OPLAN 34A attack by the South Vietnamese on a small island off the coast of North Vietnam, attacked the USS *Maddox* with torpedoes. The USS *Maddox*, armed with six 5in guns, responded and also received air support from the aircraft carrier USS *Ticonderoga*, driving the torpedo boats off. Two days later, on August 4, 1964, the USS *Maddox* had been joined by the USS *C Turner Joy* and reported they were again under attack. This became the Gulf of Tonkin Incident, triggering the Vietnam War.

USS *New Jersey* (BB-62)
On September 29, 1968, the USS *New Jersey*, the only active battleship in the world, weighing 58,000 tons and belonging to the Iowa Class, joined the gun line off the coast of Vietnam and added her nine 16in guns to the naval gunfire support available for use along the northern coast. By the time she departed on March 31, 1969, she had delivered more than 6,000 tons of high explosive, either against targets in North Vietnam or in support of the troops ashore.

Below: The "grunts" hug the ground and swap steel during a heavy fire fight with dug in Viet Cong.

Utah, Operation
Operation Utah was a joint US Marine Corps, ARVN action against the 21st NVA Regiment northwest of Quang Ngai in I Corps from March 4–7, 1966. On the morning of March 4, a battalion of ARVN and three companies of the 2nd Battalion, 7th Marines, landed in a hot landing zone southwest of the village of Chau Nhai. Despite heavy NVA fire, landings were successful and the Allied units promptly moved to take hills 50, 85, and 97, which were the major terrain features in the area. They met heavy opposition on Hill 50 and pounded it with 1,900 rounds of artillery in a two-hour period. On March 5, a joint assault by the ARVN and Company L, 3rd Battalion, 1st Marines, took the hill. By the end of the day on March 6, the NVA and VC were withdrawing and contact became light and scattered. The operation ended on March 7 and the Marines claimed 358 NVA had been killed as opposed to a loss of 98 Marines.

V

Van Cao

Van Cao was a Vietnamese musician who composed the national anthem of both the Democratic Republic of Vietnam and, following the fall of South Vietnam in 1975, the Socialist Republic of Vietnam. Although periodically in trouble for his open opposition to the limited freedom of expression granted to writers, poets, and musicians by the communist government, in 1993 he was awarded the Medal of Independence by the Socialist Republic of Vietnam in recognition of his works.

Van Tien Dung

The number two man in the North Vietnamese army, General Dung handled northern air defense, logistics operations, chiefly the Ho Chi Minh Trail, sea infiltration, and the war in Laos, while General Giap concentrated on the war in the south. He assumed a field command

Above: General Van Tien Dung directed the 1972 Easter Offensive and was the architect of the Final Offensive in 1975.

in 1971 and largely directed the 1972 Easter Campaign. He is generally credited with being the architect of the final battle of the war in 1975.

Vance, Cyrus Robert

In 1962, President John F Kennedy named Cyrus Vance the Secretary of the Army. Vance was a key player in the development of airmobile concepts. Appointed as a Deputy Secretary of Defense in 1964 by President Johnson, he was assigned the responsibility of approving all covert raids against the Democratic Republic of Vietnam. In 1967, he resigned for health reasons, but functioned as one of Johnson's "wise men." In 1968 he was a deputy negotiator at the Paris peace talks, but resigned

Above: Secretary of the Army Cyrus Vance talks to General William Westmoreland and a group of French officers.

in 1969. In 1977, President Carter named him the Secretary of State, and he tried to negotiate normalized relations with North Vietnam, but the attempt fell apart over the issue of war reparations demanded by the Vietnamese.

Vang Pao

Until 1954, Vang Pao fought for the French against the Viet Minh. He then organized opposition to the Pathet Lao and their North Vietnamese sponsors by Hmong villagers on and along the borders of the Plain of Jars in Laos. In 1961, working with both the CIA and the Thai military, Vang Pao obtained weapons, training, transportation, and logistic support in return for conducting a guerrilla war against the North Vietnamese and Pathet Lao on the Plain of Jars, and along the North Vietnamese border with central Laos. Eventually his Hmong forces exceeded 30,000 men, and he also had nearly 18,000 Thai troops at his disposal. His guerrilla operations were highly successful against the North Vietnamese and Pathet Lao until the CIA insisted that he engaged in a more conventional war. After 10 years of fighting, the Hmong casualties had reached the point that many families only had one male member left, usually under the age of 15. As the war in Vietnam moved to its conclusion and the Americans withdrew, the North Vietnamese devoted more troops to crushing the Hmong. Vang Pao withdrew his people from around the Plain of Jars and concentrated them near the Thai border. When the ceasefire was announced in Laos, Vang Pao and thousands of Hmong crossed into Thailand. He and thousands of his followers were further evacuated to the United States, but thousands more remain refugees.

Vann, John Paul

In 1963, John Paul Vann was the senior advisor to an ARVN unit that was decimated by the Viet Cong at the Battle of Ap Bac. When his reports of what had happened were sanitized by his higher headquarters and forwarded to the Pentagon indicating that the battle had been a victory, he leaked contrary information to the press. He was reassigned to the Pentagon where he was also unsuccessful in getting the US military to realistically assess what was happening on the battlefield in Vietnam. As a result, on July 31, 1963, he retired and became a vocal critic of the war. He returned to Vietnam as a pacification specialist in the Agency for International Development. By 1966, he became chief of the civilian pacification program for the provinces around Saigon. In 1967, he denounced Westmoreland's strategy, and the Tet Offensive in 1968 gave credibility to his critique. In May 1971, in an unprecedented move, he became the Senior Adviser to II Corps in the central highlands and was given command of US military forces and civilians in the pacification program. In fact, he held the equivalent rank of Major General in the US Army. Indirectly he commanded the bulk of the Vietnamese forces assigned to II Corps, and on July 9, 1972, while he was on his way to inspect the battlefield at Kontum during the aftermath of the Easter Offensive, he was killed in a helicopter crash.

Vientiane

The Kingdom of Laos had both a Royal and an Administrative Capital. Vientiane, located on the east bank of the Mekong River in central Laos, was the Administrative Capital. It was here that all of the normal arms of the government met and the foreign diplomatic representations were established.

Vientiane Agreement

The peace agreement that brought a halt to the war in Laos, signed by representatives of the Royal Lao government and the Pathet Lao on February 21st, 1973, after nearly four months of negotiations. Ceasefire was implemented at noon the following day. The 14 articles of the agreement detailed the processes for establishing a democratic government, repatriating prisoners of war, and the withdrawal of all foreign military personnel and equipment from the country. The resulting Provisional Government of National Union was headed by Prince Souvanna Phouma, and the National Political Consultative Council by Prince Souphanouvong.

Vientiane Protocol

The formal record of the Vientiane Agreement gave effect to the decisions made during the 1972–73 winter negotiations. Effective from September 14, 1973, the protocol consisted of 21 articles that expanded and modified those of the Vientiane Agreement, adding stipulations on the creation of a police force, the demarcation of ceasefire lines, disbandment of special forces, and the formation of the new government. The implementation of procedures for releasing prisoners of war and locating others reported as missing proved difficult, and ceasefire violations provoked fresh hostility between the rival factions.

Below: General Vang Pao calls in an air strike against communist forces attacking his air base at Long Tieng in Laos.

Right: A Viet Cong soldier armed with an SKS crouches in a bunker.

Viet Cong

Following the 1954 Geneva Conference, Ngo Dinh Diem consolidated his power in South Vietnam. Between 1955 and 1960 southern remnants of the Viet Minh revolutionary struggle against the French began to organize an insurgency with the goal of toppling the Diem regime and reuniting North and South Vietnam. On December 20, 1960, they formally organized the National Liberation Front of South Vietnam. In discussions with the Kennedy administration, President Diem derisively referred to them as the Viet Cong, which was short for Vietnamese Communists. The name stuck.

Viet Minh

Viet Minh is the shortened common name for the Vietnam Doc Lap Dong Minh Hoi, (League for the Independence of Vietnam), an umbrella nationalist organization created by Ho Chi Minh in May 1941 to mobilize nationalism in Vietnam. Vietnamese patriots of all political persuasions fought against first the Japanese, and then the French, as part of the Viet Minh. Though controlled by the communists from the outset, the Viet Minh emphasized anti-imperialism until the fall of Dinh Bien Phu, when the communists formally seized control and eliminated other contenders for power.

Vietnam, Climate of

The climate of Vietnam is characterized as tropical monsoon. Located in the belt between the equator and the Tropic of Cancer, seasonal change is marked more by a variation in rainfall than a variation in temperature. The rainy season in the lowlands south of Cape Dinh and in the central highlands begins in early May and extends through November. Average rainfall during this period is approximately 80in. North of Cape Dinh, the rainy season begins and ends approximately one month earlier, with Hanoi receiving around 69in of rain, and the mountains around 160in. Typhoons are not uncommon along the central coast from July through November. Daily temperatures from the tip of the Mekong

Right: A Viet Cong suspect is led out of a village west of Danang.

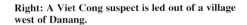

Delta to the edge of the central highlands range between 64°F and 91°F . The highlands are somewhat cooler, and the temperatures in North Vietnam are subject to greater variation, with lows sometimes around 50°F and daily temperature variations of as much as 45°F.

Vietnam, Democratic Republic of

In August 1945, following the Japanese surrender at the end of World War II, the Viet Minh seized power in Hanoi, Hue, and Saigon. On September 2, they declared Vietnam an independent state, the Democratic Republic of Vietnam (DRV). At the same time the French, with British Assistance, were moving back into the south as the first step in reasserting control of Indochina. In 1946, the Democratic Republic of Vietnam promulgated a constitution based on a combined US and French parliamentary model. In November 1946, the French attempted to reassert control of Tonkin and war broke out. Following the French defeat at Dien Bien Phu, Vietnam was divided at the 17th parallel by the 1954 Geneva Accords. Ho Chi Minh re-assumed power in the north and again promulgated the Democratic

Republic of Vietnam. In the late 1950s, the DRV began supporting the communist insurgencies in South Vietnam and Laos. In 1965 they began a ground war against the United States and the South Vietnamese. The North Vietnamese leadership never lost sight of the fact that their purpose was to reunite the entire country under their control. Following the conquest of South Vietnam in 1975, the Democratic Republic of Vietnam was renamed the Socialist Republic of Vietnam.

Vietnam Information Group

Public relations body organized by the Johnson administration to counteract negative publicity about the war. Known from August 1965 to 1967 as the Public Affairs Committee for Vietnam, the principal tasks of the group were to disseminate positive information about the war, discredit Johnson's opponents, and monitor public opinion.

Viet Nam Quoc Dan Dang (Vietnam National Party)

Vietnamese political party; the first socialist organization in Vietnam. Founded by Nguyen Thai Hoc in 1927,

Above: Troops fight their way through 5ft high elephant grass, common in the climate of Vietnam.

the clandestine movement launched surprise attacks against French personnel and property in February 1930, but was quickly crushed and brutally repressed. The survivors fled to China where they reorganized and formed a loose alliance with the Viet Minh, but upon returning to Vietnam after the war thousands of VNQDD were massacred by the Viet Minh. Another migration ensued, to China and the south. More followed after the 1954 Geneva Accords, but the party had by this time become deeply divided.

Vietnam, Republic of

The final agreements of the 1954 Geneva Accords divided Vietnam into two parts at the 17th parallel. The communists controlled the north and the Emperor Bao Dai, who had been the titular head of the State of Vietnam under the French, controlled the south. The Republic of Vietnam was created on October 26, 1955 with its capital at Saigon. It came into being when Prime Minister Ngo

VIETNAM: A VISUAL ENCYCLOPEDIA

417

Above: The South Vietnamese Presidential Palace in Saigon.

Left: President Johnson meets with President Thieu and the other leaders of the Republic of Vietnam.

Dien Diem, reacting to an attempt by the Emperor to remove him from office, organized a referendum between himself and Bao Dai. Diem received nearly 95 percent of the vote. A National Assembly of 123 members was created in March 1956, and on October 26, 1956, a national constitution, based roughly on the US Constitution, was promulgated. From 1955 to 1959, President Diem consolidated his power by crushing the Binh Xuyen river pirates and the Cao Dai and Hoa Hao religious sects. At the same time, the government made significant progress in reducing the presence of former Viet Minh, particularly in the Delta.

This led to a decision by the communists to shift from political action to an armed insurgency. The Republic of Vietnam also received significant backing from the United States, though in 1963 the United States tacitly approved of a coup to remove President Diem from power. Diem's fall led to a period of political instability. This in turn encouraged President Johnson to intervene with ground forces. The rise of Nguyen Van Thieu brought stability to the political situation, but increased the level of corruption. When the US withdrew in 1973, the Republic of Vietnam proved incapable of defending itself and was absorbed by the Democratic Republic of Vietnam in April 1975.

Vietnam, Republic of, Army (ARVN)

The Army of the Republic of Vietnam was created by the United States in 1955, out of the remnants of what was known as the Vietnam National Army—a French construct organized to provide

Above: ARVN troops and their advisers prepare to assault a Viet Cong position during the Tet Offensive.

Right: Civil Guards and regular ARVN troops board US Army H-21 helicopters on their way to a battle in the Delta.

manpower for their losing fight in the Indochina War. Patterned by the United States in accordance with American military doctrine, the ARVN was never organized to fight a guerrilla war. Instead it was constructed to repel an all-out invasion across the Demilitarized Zone. In the early 1960s ARVN units were routinely mauled by the Viet Cong. Therefore, in order to preserve a non-communist South Vietnam, the United States essentially took over the ground war and relegated the ARVN to the secondary duty of pacification. The Viet Cong and North Vietnamese looked on the ARVN with disdain, and the Tet Offensive of 1968 was specifically designed to humble them. Much to the surprise of the Viet Cong and North Vietnamese, though some ARVN units crumbled, the bulk of them fought well. During the Cambodian Incursion of 1970, ARVN units plowed deeper into Cambodia than the US units did. However, most of the North Vietnamese

and Viet Cong forces the ARVN faced chose to withdraw rather than stand and fight. Though in many cases the ARVN did well, the campaign clearly showed they were still reliant upon US logistical networks and tactical air support. In 1971, the ARVN launched an invasion of Laos to cut the Ho Chi Minh Trail at

Tchepone. Political decisions in the United States prevented US troops from accompanying them. Though they succeeded in taking the city, North Vietnamese counterattacks quickly created an untenable situation. Their subsequent retreat rapidly developed into a rout, and many US commentators, who

VIETNAM: A VISUAL ENCYCLOPEDIA

419

Above: Vietnam Veterans Against the War (VVAW) march outside the Democratic National Convention Hall in Miami Beach.

failed to recognize that the ARVN were seriously outnumbered, ridiculed their performance. As the United States withdrawal progressed, the North Vietnamese decided to test the ARVN again and launched an all-out invasion of South Vietnam in 1972, expecting that they would collapse. Instead, in spite of reverses, backed by US air power the ARVN fought well and the North Vietnamese were roughly handled. In July 1973, the US Congress ended funding for American military activity in Cambodia, Laos, North Vietnam, and South Vietnam, effectively depriving the ARVN of the air support they so critically required. When the North Vietnamese launched their final offensive, the ARVN had neither the logistical underpinnings nor direct air support to defend the entire nation. Confronted by a breakdown in command and control and the flight of a lot of senior officers, many units disintegrated. When well led, such as the 18th Division at Xuan Loc outside Saigon, the ARVN fought with skill and determination. However, that was the exception and not the rule.

Vietnam, State of

The State of Vietnam was formally recognized by the Elysee Agreements on March 8, 1949, (ratified by the National Assembly on January 29, 1950) as an Associated State within the French Union, with Bao Dai as head of state. The Republic of Cochin China, which was established by France in 1946 in response to the declaration of the Democratic Republic of Vietnam, was incorporated. Although the new state was to some degree autonomous, French economic domination continued.

Vietnam Veterans Against the War (VVAW)

The VVAW was an organization of ex-servicemen opposed to the Vietnam War. In 1966, veterans from World Wars I and II, along with veterans from the Korean and Vietnam wars staged a protest rally in New York City where discharge and separation papers were burned in protest of US involvement in Vietnam. The VVAW was formally established in April of the following year, and took a major role in subsequent actions, most notably in the April 1971 demonstrations.

Vietnamese Air Force (VNAF)

The Vietnamese Air Force (VNAF) was

created in the summer of 1955 when the French turned over 28 F-8F Bearcat fighter-bombers, 35 C-47 transports, and 60 L-19 spotter aircraft to the newly organized Republic of Vietnam. In 1958, the United States supplemented the Bearcats with the T-28, a trainer modified to carry guns and bombs. They also began the introduction of the A-1. While ostensibly organized to provide ground support, interdiction, and reconnaissance, in reality the VNAF was incapable of performing any of these missions. In 1961, President Kennedy began supporting their efforts with training, helicopters to ferry troops, and ill concealed close air support. The increasing tempo of combat operations led to a significant expansion of the VNAF. By 1965 the ineffectual T-28s and Bearcats had all been replaced by the A-1E, which became the backbone of the Republic of Vietnam Air Force. By mid 1968, they were flying more than 25 percent of all combat sorties in South Vietnam. The same year saw the introduction of the A-37 Dragonfly and the F-5A Freedom Fighter as their first jet aircraft. With Vietnamization, equipment was dumped on the VNAF under Project Enhance faster than they could absorb it. By the time the US withdrew, it was numerically one of the largest air forces in the

Above: A Vietnamese Air Force A1E bombs a Viet Cong position at the edge of a rice paddy.

Left: A South Vietnamese Air Force UH-1H descends toward a landing zone.

to achieve reunification through political means, it took up armed struggle against the US-backed Saigon regime, and organized the NLFSV (Viet Cong) in the South.

Vietnamese Marine Corps (VNMC)

The Vietnamese Marine Corps (VNMC) was sometimes referred to by their former American comrades as the Spartans of Vietnam. The VNMC was organized on October 13, 1954, as a corps of infantry within the naval establishment. Almost from its inception, US Marine Corps advisory elements permeated every level and function of the VNMC. Eventually the VNMC grew to nine infantry battalions, three artillery battalions, and supporting units. The VNMC, Ranger, and Airborne units became the Republic of Vietnam's strategic reserve and fought in every region of the nation, from the Ca Mau Peninsula to the Demilitarized Zone. The VNMC participated in the recapture of Hue following the Tet Offensive, and the 1970 invasion of Cambodia. During Lam Son 719 it

world. However, the supply system was chaotic and unreliable, and its maintenance and support structures were laughable. When the North Vietnamese final offensive struck South Vietnam in 1975, the VNAF simply melted away.

Vietnamese Communist Party

The Vietnamese Communist Party, or Dang Cong San Viet Nam, grew out of Ho Chi Minh's Vietnam Revolutionary Youth League in the late 1920s, and adopted a modified version of Marxism that suited Vietnam, with its predominantly rural agrarian proletariat. It distanced itself from other anti-colonial groups, but in 1941 formed the Viet Minh to embrace all nationalist forces and unite them against the occupier. After 1954 the VCP once again returned to its goal of socialist revolution in Vietnam, but having failed by 1960

Right: A Vietnamese Navy crew opens fire with their 81mm mortar.

Below right: Vietnamese Navy divers work at salvaging a sunken boat in Vinh Binh.

was the VNMC that blunted the North Vietnamese counterattack and assisted the ARVN retreat from Tchepone. During the Easter Offensive of 1972, the VNMC, though vastly outnumbered, prevented the NVA from moving south out of Quang Tri and attacking Hue by staging a series of counterattacks and even making an amphibious landing from US ships behind the attackers at one point. Their steadfast defense cost them over 20 percent of their organized strength in casualties. During the North Vietnamese Final Offensive the VNMC was split into two forces. One engaged the NVA north of Danang and was submerged by two NVA divisions, and the other fought near the Presidential Palace in Saigon. When South Vietnam fell, fewer than 250 Vietnamese Marines escaped.

Vietnamese National Army (VNA)
This army was organized, trained, and equipped by the French to fight alongside its own forces against the Viet Minh. The right of the State of Vietnam to maintain its own army was recognized by the Elysees Agreement, but although Bao Dai was its notional commander, the VNA was in reality under the French High Command. At its peak the VNA numbered some 95,000 troops, but it was hampered by a disorganized conscription program, inadequate and inexperienced officer corps, no general staff, and poor training, and also suffered from a conflict of command between the French and Bao Dai. The VNA formed the basis for the ARVN under Diem.

Vietnamese Navy (VNN)
During the 1950s and 1960s the United States supplemented the few vessels turned over to the Vietnamese Navy, (VNN), by the French. Eventually they built it into one of the world's largest navies with over 1,000 vessels of one kind or another. Originally organized into a Sea Force, a River Force, and the Marine Corps, the different missions of the Navy's combat units determined their

Right: A Vietnamese Navy Armored Landing Craft moves in toward the docks at Nha Be.

422

command structure. Operationally the Sea Force, renamed the Fleet Command in 1966, were involved in open sea and coastal patrol missions in coastal zones that corresponded with the Army's numbered Corps areas. The River Force was modeled after the French Dinassaut, (Naval Assault Divisions), and originally was concentrated in the Mekong River Delta. The River Force operated under the control of the Army units in the Delta. Reorganized and partially re-equipped in line with suggestions from the US Navy, the VNN was an important element of both Operation Game Warden and Operation Market Time. They intercepted and destroyed hundreds of small craft ferrying munitions and personnel along the coast and inland waterways. The also conducted raids and escorted merchant shipping up the Mekong as far as Phnom Penh. During the Cambodian Incursion the VNN secured control of the Mekong River and prevented the North Vietnamese and Viet Cong from using it either to reinforce or escape. As Vietnamization progressed, the VNN received additional equipment transfers from the US Navy and US Coast Guard, and by August 1972 they took responsibility for the entire coastal patrol and river interdiction missions. A serious logistics shortfall created by the US Congress' reduction in financial support forced the Vietnamese Navy to reduce its overall operations by 50 percent in 1974 and reduce its combat and river patrol activities by 70 percent. During the North Vietnamese Final Offensive, the VNN organized a flotilla of vessels with 30,000 sailors, their families, and other key civilians aboard and fled to the Philippines.

Vietnamization

Shortly after taking command of MACV, General Creighton Abrams stated that he was training the Vietnamese army in order to "Vietnamize" the war. At the Midway Island Conference on June 8, 1969, President Nixon officially initiated the Vietnamization policy. It involved the phasing out of US forces, and included strengthening South Vietnam by intensifying the ongoing pacification programs, dramatically increasing the amount of US material assistance, and expanding and reorganizing the Vietnamese Army, Navy, and Air Force. From that point forward American policy concentrated more on extracting the US from the Vietnam War "with honor" than

Above: A group of patrol boats are transferred to the Vietnamese Navy under the Accelerated Turnover to Vietnam (ACTOV) Program.

it did on winning. The Vietnamese referred to Vietnamization as the "three selves:" self-defense, self-government, and self-development. The Vietnamese invasion of Laos during Operation Lam Son 719 was touted as proof that Vietnamization was working. However, most objective observers viewed it as a nearly complete failure. Similarly, when the North Vietnamese Easter Offensive failed, it was again proclaimed as proof that Vietnamization was working. Unfortunately, scant attention was paid to the fact that US air power and naval gunfire support were the cornerstones of South Vietnam's successful defense. Once American air power was not made available to blunt North Vietnam's probing attacks in 1974, it became clear to Hanoi that America would not reenter the war. The rapid collapse of the Republic of Vietnam's armed forces during the North Vietnamese Final Offensive in 1975 clearly proved that Vietnamization had not worked.

Vinh Tap, Operation

In mid-1971 the CIA discovered an elevated multiplex telephone trunk line 15 miles southwest of Vinh in North Vietnam. They determined to put two taps on the phone line. Earlier, on April 8, 1971, Hughes Aircraft Company had

unveiled a helicopter they dubbed the "Quiet One." At a press demonstration a standard OH6A had flown by and was detected over a mile away. The "Quiet One" could not be detected at 300m. Three weeks later, the CIA contracted for its use and Air America hired three experienced US Army pilots. Due to a series of training accidents, the Vinh Tap mission was not flown until December 6, 1972. That night a group of Hmong Raiders, flying nap-of-the-earth from Thakhek in Laos, landed in a bomb crater that had been created specifically as a landing zone for the mission. They quickly climbed a telephone pole and inserted the taps, inadvertently setting both taps on the same phone line. Twenty minutes later the helicopter returned and retrieved the Raiders who flew back to Thakhek. On December 7, the day after the taps went on-line, the North Vietnamese negotiators at the Paris peace talks caused a break in negotiations. Eleven days later President Nixon launched Linebacker II against North Vietnam and the North Vietnamese quickly returned to the negotiations. By that time, Henry Kissinger was receiving

Above: General Vo Nguyen Giap, who led the Vietnamese to victory against both the French and the Americans.

near real-time intelligence information from the Vinh Tap, significantly affecting his ability to deal with Le Duc Tho in reaching a final agreement.

Vo Nguyen Giap

In 1941, Vo Nguyen Giap helped Ho Chi Minh organize the Viet Minh. During the latter stages of World War II, assisted by American OSS teams, he led a guerrilla war against the Japanese in North Vietnam. In 1946, Ho Chi Minh appointed him as the Commander in Chief of the People's Army of Vietnam, PAVN. Giap adapted the guerrilla warfare teachings of Mao Tse-Tung to the peculiarities of the Vietnamese anti-colonial struggle against the French. He developed the Dau Tranh strategy of total war, in which the political dimension is co-equal with the military. During the French Indochina War, Giap was cautious and so meticulous in his planning that operations were frequently delayed because he felt that either the time was not propitious, or all of the elements were not yet in place. His real expertise, most convincingly demonstrated at Dien Bien Phu, was moving men and matériel around the battlefield far faster than his enemies anticipated. He was a genius of logistics, organization, and planning. Tactically, he was not particularly innovative and his operations were predictable. He never did believe that the North Vietnamese Army could not

achieve victory against the Americans by moving to the third stage, full-scale conventional war, of his three-phase construct of guerrilla warfare. This led him into a number of clashes such as the Tet Offensive, and the Easter Offensive, wherein his army was severely mauled by superior American firepower and mobility. As a result of this tactical rigidity, following the Easter Offensive wherein the North Vietnamese suffered more than 100,000 casualties, he was effectively demoted when he was appointed Minister of Defense rather than retaining the overall command of the North Vietnamese military. General Van Tien Dung, who led the final assault on South Vietnam in 1975, replaced him. However, as the only widely known North Vietnamese military figure, he has been credited with the victory. In 1980, Giap retired as the Minister of Defense of the Socialist Republic of Vietnam.

Vogt, John W Jr

From 1965 to 1968 General John W. Vogt was the Deputy for Plans and Operations of Pacific Air Force headquarters in Honolulu, where he was deeply involved in planning the conduct of air operations in Vietnam. In 1972, he took command of the 7th Air Force in Vietnam. During 1972 and 1973 the 7th Air Force carried out some of the heaviest bombing raids of the Vietnam War. He oversaw Operation Freedom Train, the massive air interven-

tion that blunted the NVA Easter Offensive in 1972, and Operations Linebacker I and Linebacker II, during which the first strategic raids by B-52s were carried out against North Vietnam. In 1973, he transferred his command to Nakhon Phanom Royal Thai Air Base in Thailand and supervised the Air Force withdrawal from South Vietnam.

Vu Quoc Thuc

Vu Quoc Thuc was a Vietnamese intellectual who was a special adviser to President Ngo Dinh Diem and was placed in charge of reconstruction and development. He was a close associate of Eugene Staley and co-authored many of the reports on reconstruction and development programs that were submitted to Presidents Kennedy and Johnson.

Vung Tau

Vung Tau was the fifth largest city of South Vietnam and is located in Phuoc Tuy province in III Corps. Formerly known as Cap Saint Jacques when the French controlled Vietnam, it is located at the entrance to the portion of the Mekong River system leading to Saigon, and is the southernmost port in Vietnam. The Revolutionary Development Cadre School, and the Mobile Riverine Force support area were both located in Vung Tau. It also served as an in-country rest and recuperation (R&R) site for American forces.

Right: Elements of the advanced party of the 1st Cavalry Division (Airmobile) disembark from a landing craft at Vung Tau in 1965.

Wahiawa, Operation

Operation Wahiawa was a search and destroy operation conducted by the 1st and 2nd Brigades of the 25th infantry Division from May 15, 1966, to May 27, 1966, in the Filhol Rubber Plantation and Boi Loi Woods of Hau Nghia province, 35 miles northwest of Saigon. It was one

Above: A gun crew from the 7th Battalion, 11th Artillery, responds to a request for fire during Operation Wahiawa.

of a series of operations conducted to clear elements of the Viet Cong 272nd Regiment from the area immediately surrounding the division's base camp at Cu Chi. The division found a large number of well constructed log bunkers with up to 3ft thick mud walls throughout the area of operations. They also captured several hundred tons of rice and other supplies. Though the Viet Cong evaded heavy contact, they employed a large number of mines and booby traps. A combination of pressure-activated and command-detonated mines damaged 11 armored personnel carriers and four other vehicles. This area of Hau Nghia province remained an active operational area throughout the war.

Walk in the Woods

Troops who were selected to go on either a combat or reconnaissance patrol in an area where they expected contact were said to be going for a "walk in the woods."

Left: PFC Russell Widdifield takes a break during a "walk in the woods" in the Arizona.

Above: General Lewis Walt confers with a company commander during Operation Harvest Moon.

Wallace, George Corley Jr

George Wallace, the governor of Alabama, was a populist candidate for president in 1968. He ran on the Independent Party ticket with retired Air Force General Curtis LeMay as his running mate. He called for more vigorous prosecution of the war to include bombing the transportation links to China and mining Haiphong Harbor. After General LeMay refused to rule out using nuclear weapons during a press conference, Wallace sent him on a tour of Vietnam to keep him out of the country until after the election.

Walt, Lewis K

Lieutenant General Lewis K Walt commanded the 3rd Marine Amphibious Force from June 1965 until June 1967. Walt's strategy for prosecuting the war in I Corps emphasized the balance of small unit patrols, large unit operations, and a pacification program. This led to clashes with General Westmoreland who insisted on large search and destroy operations aimed at Main Force Viet Cong units and large NVA formations.

Right: General Lewis Walt, center, listens as a Marine platoon leader briefs a group of visiting politicians in 1965.

War Powers Act

Legislation passed by Congress in November 1973 that limited the powers of the US President over the military. Under the act, the president is required to consult with Congress before committing troops abroad, and any deployment longer than 90 days must also be authorized. Introduced in the aftermath to the invasion of Cambodia in 1970, the act is seen by some as a direct reaction to the Vietnam experience and others as the product of decades of debate over the respective powers of Congress and the president. Nixon tried to block the act, stating that it violated the Constitutional authorities of the president and would weaken the executive branch at a crucial time. Others see the act as a necessary rein on presidential powers, and encouragement for greater dialogue between the legislature and chief executive in times of emergency.

War Resisters League

Pacifist group, established in 1932, that promoted a non-violent stance against the war and conscription during the Vietnam War. Under the leadership of Chicago Eight defendant David Dellinger and David McReynolds, the most public of its activities were public draft card burnings (declared illegal by Senate in 1965). Between 1964 and 1973 membership grew from 3,000 to 15,000.

War Zone C

The border of War Zone C ran from Ben Cat up Route 13 to the Cambodian border, then southwest along the Cambodian

access to Saigon from the central part of the country. Numerous major operations were carried out to clear War Zone D but all failed.

Ware, Keith L

Major General Ware was the Deputy Commander of Field Force II from December 1967 to March 1968. He was then assigned as the Commanding General of the 1st Infantry Division, where he was killed in action when his helicopter was downed by enemy ground fire southeast of Loc Ninh on September 13, 1968. He was considered one of the best American combat leaders of the war.

Warnke, Paul C

Warnke was Assistant Secretary of Defense for International Security Affairs from 1967 to 1969. He was a vigorous opponent, within the Defense Department, of the Vietnam War. When General Westmoreland requested an additional 206,000 troops in 1968, Warnke convinced Secretary of Defense Clark Clifford that increased troop deployment would only increase casualties, and that the United States still would not prevail. General Westmoreland later blamed Warnke for converting Clifford from a hawk to a dove about Vietnam.

Wars of National Liberation

In January 1961, Soviet Premier Nikita Khrushchev pledged support for "wars of national liberation" throughout the world—an armed conflict from within a state against the governing power which seeks to achieve political, social, and economic change. His statement greatly encouraged communists in North Vietnam to escalate their armed struggle to unify Vietnam under Ho Chi Minh. The war in Vietnam, some argue, was a war of liberation. However, the US government took the view that the war was sponsored primarily by the Democratic Republic of Vietnam and was thus an invasion of an independent country, and that the NLFSV and COSVN were simply communist tools. While it is true that the NLFSV and COSVN received considerable backing from the north, this viewpoint fails to fully take into account the popular support for the revolution in the south.

Above: A squad carefully moves through heavy secondary growth in War Zone D.

War Zone D

War Zone D shared a border with War Zone C along Route 13 north from Ben Cat to the junction of Routes 13 and 14. It then followed Route 14 to Bu Nard, swung east and south to Than Son, then west to the Dong Ngai River and south to Route 20. From there the border swung due west to Route 1, then followed Route 1 through Bien Hoa and northeast to rejoin Route 13 and back to Ben Cat. This was an area of heavy jungle, rainforest, and elephant grass, and provided

border to Tapang Raboa, and finally back through Tay Ninh City to Ben Cat. It had been under Viet Minh control during the French-Indochina War and contained numerous Viet Cong supply dumps, command posts, and hospitals. It also served as the primary infiltration route from the Cambodian border towards Saigon.

Surface Warships Used In Vietnam

Type	Class	Displacement	Speed	Armament	Crew	Notes
BB	Iowa	57,500 tons	33kts	9x16in/50 12x5in/38	1,500	1
CA	Newport News	20,434 tons	33kts	9x8in/55 12x5in/38	1,800	2
CAG	Boston	17,947 tons	32kts	6x8"/55 2 x Terrier 10x5in/38	1,550	3
CLG	Oklahoma City	15,152 tons	32kts	6x6"/47 2 x Terrier 2x5in/38	1,380	4
DD	Gearing	3,493 tons	34kts	4x5in/38	274	5
DD	Forrest Sherman	4,050 tons	33kts	3x5in/54	292	6
DDG	Charles F Adams	4,576 tons	35kts	2x5in/54 1 x Tartar/Terrier	354	7

Notes:

1. The only active battleship, the USS *New Jersey* was deployed with a reduced compliment in order to meet Navy manpower requirements.
2. The Newport News was originally a unit of the Des Moines Class. These cruisers were fitted with a new, fully automated 8in gun that significantly enhanced the rate of fire. She was retired in 1975.
3. Originally built as Baltimore Class heavy cruisers during World War II, the *Boston* and her sister ship, the *Canberra*, were fitted with a Terrier double antiaircraft launcher in place of the aft turret in the 1950s. They were scrapped in the 1970s.
4. Like the *Boston*, a number of Cleveland Class light cruisers, such as the *Oklahoma City*, were fitted with Talos or Terrier antiaircraft missiles in the 1950s. All of them were scrapped in the 1970s.
5. The World War II Gearing Class destroyers were all disposed of in the 1970s. The USS *Higbee*, DD-806, the only major US warship named for a woman, was heavily damaged when bombed by a MiG-17 in 1972.
6. The Forrest Sherman Class destroyers were the last American warships built with only a gun armament. Entering service from 1953–1959, they were all disposed of in the 1990s.
7. The Charles F Adams Class destroyers carried the Terrier missile as primary armament, though their guns were their primary weapons in Vietnam. Three Australian Charles F Adams Class ships, the *Perth*, *Hobart*, and *Brisbane*, were equipped with the Tartar missile and served on the gun-line in Vietnam.

Left: A destroyer searches for North Vietnamese seaborne infiltrators off the coast of North Vietnam.

Warships

At the start of the Vietnam War the US. Navy was moving toward a fleet of missile armed surface ships, designed to provide support to the carrier battlegoup, and away from the gun armed ships that could support either an amphibious landing or troops ashore. The battleships had all been either scrapped or put in mothballs, and the gun armed cruisers were being retired or, in a few cases, converted to guided missile cruisers by reducing their gun armament and adding missiles, while also adding the necessary accoutrements to convert them to flagships. Missiles had even become the primary armament on destroyers. In Vietnam, however, missiles were of little use except to protect the carriers from the remote likelihood of air attack. The Marines, who normally received a significant portion of their fire support from

the Navy agitated to have at least one battleship reactivated and the *USS New Jersey* was. A few remaining heavy and light cruisers, armed with 8in and 6in guns respectively, were deployed in fire support and to attack targets along the North Vietnamese coast in an attempt to reduce aircraft losses. A significant number of the remaining gun armed destroyers, as well as a number of missile types that retained some guns, were deployed on what was called "the gun line" to provide naval gunfire support. Usually there were somewhere around 20 to 24 ships on the gun line. The US Navy eventually utilized almost every warship type in their inventory, except submarines, in combat in Southeast Asia.

Washington Special Actions Group (WSAG)

High-powered group organized in 1969 by Henry Kissinger for the purpose of developing contingency plans and crisis management. Its most important decisions were to increase support for the beleaguered government of Lon Nol in

Cambodia, and back the US invasion in 1970 of that country and the mining of Hai Phong Harbor in 1972. On balance, the WSAG can be seen as a key influence on Nixon on matters of national security.

Water Pump, Operation

In June 1963, President Kennedy reassessed his policy toward Laos. One of the recommendations made by his advisers, and concurred in by the Ambassador to Vientiane, was to provide some sort of air support to the Royal Lao Government. At the time he demurred. In December 1963, the recommendation surfaced again. It was approved, and on March 9, 1964, Operation Water Pump was initiated. Its purpose was to train Laotian and Hmong pilots to fly the T-28, a propeller driven trainer converted to a ground attack aircraft. However,

Below: The USS *New Jersey* fires a 16-inch gun in support of ground operations along the coast of II Corps in 1969.

immediately after the American training team arrived at Udorn Royal Thai Air Force Base, the Pathet Lao opened a major offensive on the Plain of Jars. Having not yet trained any pilots, the American trainers flew ground strikes in support of Laotian and Hmong forces. Later, Water Pump achieved significant success in training Laotian and Hmong pilots for close air support and interdiction operations along the Ho Chi Minh Trail. The Water Pump Detachment remained active in one form or another until 1974.

Watergate

Name of the Washington hotel building where on June 17, 1972, five burglars were arrested while attempting to plant hidden microphones in the Democratic National Committee offices. Subsequent investigations revealed they had ties to the Nixon administration, leading to the resignation of top Nixon aides HR Haldeman and John Ehrlichman, and the 1974 impeachment proceedings against President Nixon.

Weapons

During the Vietnam War the United States used virtually every conventional weapon in its arsenal except submarines. Extensive research and development, and weapons trials were also carried out throughout the war. Likewise, the Soviet Union and the People's Republic of China equipped the North Vietnamese with modern infantry and air defense combat systems. However, unlike the United States, most of these were at least one generation old.

Weather War

Beginning in 1963, specially configured WC-130s flew cloud seeding missions over eastern Laos, western North Vietnam and the Ho Chi Minh Trail. The purpose was to increase the amount of rainfall during the monsoon season in an effort to washout or otherwise damage the road and trail net, restricting the flow of supplies and men from North Vietnam. The program was nicknamed "Weather War."

Weathermen

The radical antiwar group, the Weathermen, was created at the March 1969 "war council" of the Students for Democratic Society. Drawing on principles of Marxist philosophy, the Weathermen promoted armed struggle as necessary to bring about a radical restructuring change in American society. It carried out violent attacks on federal government institutions in the 1970s, including the University of Wisconsin bombing, but such tactics polarized the group from other protest groups and most of American society.

Westmoreland, William Childs

General William Westmoreland was commissioned in artillery and served during World War II. Before being assigned as the Deputy Commander of the US Military Assistance Command Vietnam in January 1964, he had commanded the 101st Airborne Division, and been the Superintendent of West Point. Assuming command of MACV in June 1964, he began to lay the groundwork for an expanded US role in Vietnam. In August 1964, he was promoted to full general, and proceeded to put his stamp on the war.

Initially, this thrust was to carry out a series of spoiling attacks until the

Below: A Special Forces sergeant teaches a CIDG crew how to fire the 4.2in mortar.

logistics infrastructure for a larger force could be put in place. With the arrival of US units in 1965, he initiated what became called "search and destroy" missions, the chief tactical underpinnings of the Attrition Strategy. Westmoreland was convinced that he could win the war by inflicting such heavy casualties on the North Vietnamese and Viet Cong that they would simply stop fighting. He also essentially ignored the political ramifications of the war in Vietnam and only paid limited attention to pacification. By late 1967, he was convinced his strategy was working and reported so to the political powers in Washington DC. His most famous pronouncement was that we were now seeing "the light at the end of the tunnel." In January 1968, the communist Tet Offensive proved to be his downfall. Caught by surprise, he reacted quickly and inflicted a stinging military defeat on the enemy. However, the Communists proved that the rosy picture he had been reporting was false and achieved a psychological victory. When he then asked for over 200,000 additional troops, President Johnson recalled him, appointed him Chief of Staff of the

Army, and replaced him with General Creighton Abrams. He retired in 1972, but once again ended up in the spotlight in 1982 when the CBS News documentary "The Uncounted Enemy: A Vietnam Deception" charged him with misleading the government and the nation by manipulating the data on enemy troop strength in 1967. He sued CBS for libel, but failed to prove his case.

Weyand, Frederick C

General Frederick Weyand initially served in Vietnam as the Commander of the 25th Infantry Division in 1966. He then commanded Field Force II from July 1967 to August 1968. In January 1968, based on his evaluation of radio intercepts, he convinced General Westmoreland to let him pull additional combat battalions in around Saigon. This action, more than any other, prevented the VC and NVA from taking the city during the Tet Offensive. In 1969 and 1970, he was the chief military advisor to the Paris peace talks. He returned to Vietnam in April 1970 as the Deputy Commander of MACV. He became the final Commander of MACV in July 1972

and presided over the military withdrawal. In 1973, following the disestablishment of MACV, he was assigned to Washington DC, where he became Chief of Staff of the Army in October 1974.

Wheeler, Earle G

Though General Wheeler graduated from West Point in 1932, when President Kennedy appointed him as the US Army Chief of Staff in 1962, he had no combat experience. In 1964 President Johnson appointed him Chairman of the Joint Chiefs of Staff. Following the Gulf of Tonkin Incident he constantly pushed the President for even more drastic measures and deeper involvement in the war in southeast Asia. In 1967, President Johnson asked Wheeler what would be required for the United States to win the war and when it would happen. General Wheeler pressed for a full mobilization, to include a call up of the reserves, and could not establish an end date for the war. When the Nixon administration

took over and began the process of Vietnamization, he lobbied to have it carried out as slowly as possible. He retired in 1970, having served longer as the JCS Chairman than any other officer.

Wheeler/Wallowa, Operation

Operation Wheeler/ Wallowa lasted from November 1967 to November 1968. Begun by a multi-brigade taskforce, Task Force Oregon, which had deployed to southern I Corps in mid-1967 to blunt an offensive by the reinforced 2nd NVA Division, it later became the first division-sized operation of the Americal Division. It consisted of a series of sweeping operations in the Que Son and Hiep Duc Valleys, two areas that had been under communist control since the middle of the French-Indochina War. Faced with determined resistance that resulted in the loss of dozens of helicopters in the Hiep Duc Valley, and regi-

mental sized attacks against three key firebases in the Que Son Valley, the task force was reinforced by a brigade of the 1st Cavalry Division just prior to the Tet Offensive. Following intense combat around the Quang Tin Provincial Capital of Tam Ky, the 3rd Brigade of the 82nd Airborne Division was added to the task force.

When the operation ended, on November 11, 1968, the US claimed that over 10,000 VC and NVA, the equivalent of a full division, had been killed. Nevertheless, fighting against the 2nd NVA Division continued in the Que Son and Hiep Duc Valleys for as long as American forces were in I Corps. The area never was considered pacified.

White Horse Division

"White Horse" was the nickname of the Republic of Korea 9th Infantry Division. Headquartered at Ninh Hoa in II Corps.

Above: A gun crew sets the fuze on a smoke round. The infantry will use it to plot their defensive fire from.

It served in Vietnam from September 27, 1966 to March 16, 1973.

White Star, Operation

In July 1959, President Eisenhower authorized the use of US Army Special Forces to assist in the training of the Royal Laotian Army. Under the terms of the Geneva Accords of 1954, the French were responsible for the development of the Laotian armed forces. Headquartered at Seno, they resisted any encroachment into this activity by the Americans, and the mission had to be carried out semi-clandestinely. Reduced strength Special Forces teams, initially code-named Hotfoot, were covertly inserted into Laos, and eventually over 500 personnel were assigned there. By 1960 the

Russians and the North Vietnamese had significantly reinforced the Pathet Lao capabilities, and the Royal Laotian forces had come to rely heavily on CIA trained Hmong guerrillas. Operation White Star, formerly known as Hotfoot, was made public in 1961 when President Kennedy ordered that all US military in Laos don their uniforms. Redesignated as White Star Mobile Training Teams, the Special Forces essentially replaced the French. With the agreement to neutralize Laos in 1962, the White Star teams were withdrawn and the operation came to a close on October 7, 1962.

White Star Mobile Training Team

In April 1961, President Kennedy converted the Program Evaluation Office in Laos into a full-scale Military Assistance Advisory Group. At that time, a number of US Army Special Forces training teams that had clandestinely been working with the Royal Laotian Army and elements of the Hmong guerrilla force, were officially designated White Star

Left: A Laotian light machinegun team practices on a range built for them by their White Star Training Team.

Below: A member of a White Star Team works with Laotian soldiers on squad tactics.

Mobile Training Teams. After the Neutralization of Laos, which formed part of the Geneva Agreements in 1962, they were withdrawn.

Wild Weasel

On November 26, 1965, four F-100F Super Sabres, modified to carry the new radar homing and warning system, (RHAWS), code named Wild Weasel, arrived at Korat in Thailand. The mission assigned to these new aircraft was to attack any SAM site that threatened the strike force they accompanied. The attack mission was code-named Iron Hand, and generally consisted of four aircraft; two Wild Weasels carrying air to ground missiles, and two more loaded with conventional bombs or cluster bomb units. While this innovation showed great promise, the F-100F proved to be the wrong platform. In very short order all of the modified Super Sabres had been shot down or damaged beyond repair. They were replaced with F-105Fs, F-105Gs, and finally F-4Cs. Additionally, the antiradiation missiles, such as the Shrike and the Standard ARM, became much more effective. During attacks over heavily defended areas, such as Hanoi and Haiphong, the Wild Weasels significantly decreased the effectiveness of the surface-to-air missile threat. While the anti-SAM mission continued to be named Iron Hand, as the word about it spread, the public began referring to it as a Wild Weasel mission and that nickname stuck.

Williams, Samuel T.

In 1955, General Samuel "Hanging Sam" Williams was appointed as the first commander of the Military Assistance Advisory Group for Vietnam. He dismissed the Viet Cong guerrilla operations as inconsequential and shifted the structure of the Vietnamese army from one of territorial regiments and light units engaged in local security, to a conventional force patterned after US divisions and designed to repel a Korean style attack across the demilitarized zone. He had a close relationship with President Ngo Dinh Diem, but fought bitterly with the US Ambassador Elbridge Durbrow. He left Vietnam in 1960. He was nicknamed "Hanging Sam" because in World War II he had ordered troops that he believed were cowards to be hung.

Wilson, Harold

Harold Wilson was the British Prime Minister from 1964 to 1970. A public supporter of the US bombing North Vietnam after the 1964 Gulf of Tonkin Incident, privately he encouraged President Johnson to end the bombing and negotiate an end to the war. He played a key part in the Operation Sunflower contacts with the Soviet Union in 1967. However, he later stated that he did not believe the Soviet Union had a great deal of leverage over the actions of North Vietnam.

Wing

A Wing is an organizational entity in the Air Force, Navy, and Marines. An Air Force Wing is generally commanded by a Colonel and consists of three squadrons of 25 aircraft each, as well as a headquarters, supply, and engineering units. A Naval Air Wing is commanded by a Captain and contains approximately 75 aircraft, two fighter squadrons, four attack squadrons, and some reconnaissance aircraft. A Marine Corps Air Wing is a much larger organization, sometimes

Above: The fourth officer, and the first five enlisted Air Force women to be assigned arrive in Vietnam.

containing as many as 500 aircraft of different types. A Major General commands it.

Winter Soldier Investigation

An unofficial inquiry by the Vietnam Veterans Against the War group was made into alleged war crimes and atrocities committed by US/Allied troops in Vietnam. The investigation was staged in Detroit in February 1971, primarily as a media event, and was funded for the most part by actress Jane Fonda and Mark Lane. Over 100 former servicemen testified about "crimes" they had witnessed, but the validity of some of these claims has been questioned.

Wise Men

An advisory group was created by President Lyndon Johnson, composed of 12 distinguished elder US statesmen and soldiers, which first met in July 1965. The group included former Secretary of State Dean Acheson and World War II

General Omar Bradley. On 25 March, 1968, Clark Clifford held a dinner for the "wise men," at the State Department. They were given a blunt assessment of the situation in Vietnam, including the widespread corruption of the Saigon government and the unlikely prospect for military victory "under the present circumstances." The next day the group gathered at the White House for lunch with the president, and eight of the group advocated US withdrawal from Vietnam.

Withdrawal

The process of detaching US armed forces from involvement in South Vietnam was begun in April 1970 under the Nixon administration, which promised and succeeded in withdrawing 150,000 by April of the following year. By November, a further 100,000 were home, and by the time that the 1972 Easter Offensive was launched the US presence stood at 69,000 men. During this time the process of "Vietnamisation" was undertaken, to make the RVN able to continue fighting independently of the US. At the opening of the 1973 Paris Conference, only a token force

remained. With the advance on Saigon of DRV forces in 1975, the remaining American troops and embassy staff were evacuated amid some chaos on 29–30 April.

Women in the War (Allied)

American women were exempt from the draft and the vast majority of those who served in Vietnam were both volunteers and officers. Different methods of compiling the total number of women who served in the war resulted in a range that varies from 7,000 to 21,000. By restricting the number to those that actually were physically located inside the borders of Vietnam or aboard the ships assigned to the engaged task forces, the Pentagon claims that 7,465 women served in the war. Of these, 6,254 were Army nurses and medical specialists. There were also 734 members of the Women's Army Corps (WAC), 432 Women in the Air Force (WAF), 36 Women Marines (WM), and nine Women Accepted for Voluntary Emergency Service (WAVES). Lieutenant Sharon Lane, an Army nurse at Chu Lai, became the only American

Right: A North Vietnamese medic treats Captain Wilmer Grubb's injuries while he is guarded by his captors.

Below right: A group of female anitwar protesters clash with police after they crashed a barricade in front of the White House in 1967.

woman killed in action when she died during a rocket attack in 1969. In the ARVN the Women's Armed Forces Corps was established in 1964.

It never numbered more than a few thousand, and was mainly relegated to clerical duties. However, there were also women assigned to the paramilitary National Police Field Force. In the National Police the women were very active in organizing and running intelligence nets, and later were a key element of the Phoenix Program.

Women in the War (North Vietnamese and Viet Cong)

Women were a far more important element of the Viet Cong and North Vietnamese military than they were on the Allied side. Madam Nguyen Thi Dinh was the Deputy Commander of the People's Liberation Armed Forces, and nearly 40 percent of the Viet Cong regimental commanders were women. They also contributed greatly to the logistics and engineering efforts of the Viet Cong. In North Vietnam women comprised a significant percentage of the militia unit strength. They became particularly proficient with light and medium antiaircraft weapons, and were a critical component of the forces that maintained the logistical lines of communication within North Vietnam and along the northern part of the Ho Chi Minh Trail. Some, usually younger women without children, joined the North Vietnamese Army and served in artillery units. It has been estimated that nearly 2 million women served in one capacity or another in the North Vietnamese military effort.

Women Strike for Peace (WSP)

The prominent US antiwar organization, WSP, was founded in 1961 as a nuclear disarmament group. The WSP's moderate stance and appeals to the nation's mothers attracted a great deal of support in middle America,. It was among the most active of protest groups, lobbying Congress, staging demonstrations, establishing communications with POWs in North Vietnam, and counseling draftees.

Xenon

In Vietnam some tanks were equipped with a 1.5 million candlepower xenon searchlight that could operate in either the visual light or infrared spectrum. Using the lights, at night a good crew could engage targets out to 2,000m in "white light" mode, and to 1,000m firing infrared. The same lights were mounted on helicopters and aircraft for use in both illuminating targets and firing on them. In addition, they were sometimes either mounted on the back of a Jeep or on a pedestal, and used in perimeter defense to illuminate enemy attackers. The troop shorthand for referring to the searchlights was Xenon.

X-Ray Operations

The US Air Force 21st Special Operations Squadron stationed at Nakhon Phanom Royal Thai Air Force Base inserted and exfiltrated CIA and SOG reconnaissance and road watch teams, along the Ho Chi Minh Trail in the eastern panhandle of Laos using

Above: A gunner provides suppressive fire with his mini-gun as they approach the Landing Zone during an X-Ray Operation.

CH-53C Helicopters. These activities were code-named X-ray Operations.

Xuan Loc, Battle of (April 1975)

Xuan Loc, the capital of Long Khan Province, is located on National Route 1 near the junction with National Route 20, 37 miles northeast of Saigon. It was the site of the last stand of the ARVN during the North Vietnamese Final Offensive. From April 9 to April 23, 1975, the ARVN 18th Infantry Division, commanded by Brigadier General Le Minh Dao, reinforced by some Regional and Popular Forces battalions, repulsed the NVA 6th, 7th, and 341st Divisions' attack on the city. For nearly two weeks the battle raged, with North Vietnamese artillery pounding the defenders unrelentingly, and intense ground assaults both day and night. With their timetable disrupted, the North Vietnamese threw

Above: Panicked refugees fleeing the advancing North Vietnamese Army try to get aboard a CH-47 Chinook that had dropped off supplies along Highway 1, 38 miles north of Saigon.

Left: Refugees running from the fighting at Xuan Loc pass the body of a young boy killed by NVA artillery fire.

Right: Two CH-47s pick up refugees from Highway 1 after dropping off ammunition at Xuan Loc.

another division at the few remaining defenders and, after having destroyed 37 NVA tanks, killing over 5000 enemy soldiers, and delaying the North Vietnamese offensive for two weeks, the 18th Infantry Division was finally overwhelmed. On April 22, 1975, Xuan Loc fell. Though always considered mediocre by US advisors throughout the war, in the end the 18th Division proved to be one of South Vietnam's finest.

Xuan Thuy

Xuan Thuy was the foreign minister of the Democratic Republic of Vietnam from 1963 to 1965, and their chief delegate to attend the Paris peace talks from 1968 to 1970. In 1970, Le Duc Tho replaced him. Averill Harriman, the chief American negotiator, described him as:

"A dreadful fellow to face across the table day after day."

XXIV Corps

During the Tet Offensive in 1968, General Westmoreland established a MACV-Forward headquarters in I Corps to control the large number of army units transferred there to support the Marines. Immediately following the Tet Offensive, MACV-Forward was re-designated as the US Army Provisional Corps, Vietnam. It was again renamed as the XXIV Corps on August 15, 1968, and placed under the command of the 3rd Marine Amphibious Force. The XXIV Corps conducted operations along the Laotian border and the southern edge of the Demilitarized Zone in conjunction with Marine units. By March 1970,

Army maneuver elements in I Corps outnumbered Marine elements by more than three to one. Therefore, as plans went forward for the withdrawal of the Marines, XXIV Corps replaced 3rd Marine Amphibious Force as the command headquarters in I Corps. It was withdrawn from Vietnam and deactivated on June 20, 1972.

Below: Xuan Thuy (center) waits for the first session of the peace talks to begin in 1968.

Right: A XXIV Corps Artillery 155mm howitzer parks in a maintenance area and waits for a mechanic.

Yankee Station

The Yankee Station was a fixed point in international waters located at 17 degrees 30 minutes north, 108 degrees 30 minutes east, in the South China Sea. It was the staging area for the US Navy's Task Force 77 aircraft carriers assigned to attack targets in North Vietnam. Along with the Dixie Station, located further south, it was part of what was sometimes referred to as the Tonkin Gulf Yacht Club.

Below: An RA5C Vigilante is launched from a carrier on Yankee Station for a reconnaissance mission.

Above: The USS *Coral Sea*, background, and the USS *Ranger* rendezvous on Yankee Station.

Right: A machine-gunner keeps an eye peeled as he cautiously advances through a coconut grove near Bong Son.

Yellow Star

The North Vietnamese 3rd Infantry Division was named the Yellow Star Division. Throughout the war it operated in II Corps, particularly in Binh Dinh province. It was frequently engaged by the 1st Air Cavalry Division and reported to have been routed or driven out of the province and away from the coast. However, any operation run in Binh

Above: Troops gather around a guitar player at a 25th Infantry Division fire base stand-down during Operation Yellowstone.

Below: Three members of the YouthInternational Party (Yippies) hold a press conference after they return from a propaganda trip to Algeria.

Dinh province throughout the war encountered units of the Yellow Star Division, and during the final offensive in 1975 it launched its attack from Binh Dinh province.

Yellowstone, Operation

Operation Yellowstone, in War Zone C in the northern half of Tay Ninh province from December 8, 1967, to February 24, 1968, involved a series of heavy engagements between the 271st and 272nd VC Regiments and the 3rd Brigade of the 25th Infantry Division. The biggest battle took place on January 1, 1968, when the two VC Regiments assaulted Fire Support Base Burt, the 3rd Brigade's key fire support base. Following heavy machine gun, recoilless rifle, and rocket grenade fire, the Viet Cong launched a furious ground assault and cut their way into the perimeter. In the resulting savage conflict, the Americans managed to repel the attack by having the artillery fire beehive and calling napalm strikes along the edges of their perimeter. Simultaneously, they reinforced the units trying to contain the Viet Cong by stripping men from other locations along the perimeter and rushing them to the point of penetration. The Viet Cong withdrew as dawn approached. The 25th Division continued to engage VC units in heavy fighting along the Cambodian border throughout the rest of the month of January. As a result, General Giap succeeded in luring more than half of the 25th Division's maneuver battalions into a position where there were not available to reinforce Saigon during the Tet Offensive.

Youth International Party (Yippies)

The "Yippy" party was created in Chicago in January 1968 by antiwar activists Jerry Rubin and Abi Hoffman. Rubin maintained that the antiwar movement was a conflict between youth and older generations, and his group emphasized this through its promotion of an uninhibited lifestyle which excluded the over-30s. The group planned an outlandish "Festival of Life" involving music and theater in Chicago to coincide with the 1968 Democratic Convention. Authorities took a dim view of the Yippie activities, charged Hoffman and Rubin with incitement to riot, and put them on trial.

Zap

"Zap" was a slang term for kill used by American troops of all services. While there were others such as grease and waste, that meant the same thing, zap was the most common. It also meant "shoot" in some contexts.

Zhou Enlai (See Chou En Lai)

Zip

"Zip" was a derisive term applied to the South Vietnamese civilians and military by American troops. It was never used to describe the North Vietnamese or Viet Cong, who were normally referred to as dinks, (by the Army), gooks, (by the Marines and Navy), or Gomers, (by the Air Force.)

Zippo

During the Vietnam War, Zippo, which was the brand name of a windproof cigarette lighter popular with the troops, was also applied to all of the various flamethrower weapons. Backpack flamethrowers, most frequently used by the Marines, were called Zippos, as were the M67A1 tank-mounted flamethrowers organic to the Marine tank battalions. Army M-132 mechanized flame throwers, mounted on the M-113 armored personnel carrier chassis, and Navy riverine LCM-Monitors, which mounted two M10-8 flamethrowers were referred to as Zippos as well.

Zippo Squad

"Zippo Squad" was the slang term used to denote a flamethrower team. It was also frequently used to describe those soldiers who sometimes set fire to peasant houses following a search and destroy mission.

Zorinthian, Barry

Zorinthian was the Director of the Joint US Public Affairs Office, (JUSPAO), from 1964 to 1968. He was the initiator of the " 5 o'clock Follies, " and was also responsible for all psychological operations carried out by MACV. Most members of the press believe that under Zorinthian the JUSPAO functioned well and provided them what they needed.

Zulu Time

Because military forces operate in all of the world's time zones, it is essential to have a standard frame of reference when issuing orders or logging reports. Zulu Time, an expression indicating Greenwich Mean Time, is generally used for that purpose.

Zumwalt, Elmo R. Jr.

In September 1968, Admiral Zumwalt assumed command of US riverine

Below: An M-132 "Zippo" fires at a concealed bunker during Operation Circle Pines.

Above: A "Zippo squad" with an M67A1 flame tank burns No-Name Village in Quang Ngai province.

Right: A flame gunner fires his "Zippo" at a concealed bunker.

warfare units in South Vietnam. He was tasked with interdicting Vietcong logistics operations in the Delta, supporting allied ground troops in the area, and turning over the riverine war to the Vietnamese. To accomplish the first he supplemented existing Market Time patrols by operating on small secondary waterways that cross the Vietnamese border from Cambodia. He used shallow draft landing craft to provide the Army 9th Infantry Division with greater mobility and more rapid logistical support. To implement Vietnamization he organized Project ACTOV. ACTOV was an acronym for the Accelerated Turn Over to the Vietnamese. On July 1, 1970, Zumwalt became the youngest officer ever appointed as the Chief of Naval Operations.

ACKNOWLEDGMENTS

The publisher wishes to thank all those who kindly supplied the illustrations for this book, as follows:

Pages 19, 27 (bottom), 40, 46 (top), 48 (top and bottom), 57, 62 (top and bottom), 67 (bottom left and bottom right), 71, 82 (bottom), 96 (top), 114 (bottom), 117 (bottom), 127 (bottom), 178 (bottom), 179 (top), 180, 189, 197 (bottom), 198 (top), 217 (bottom), 246 (bottom), 262 (bottom), 263, 266, 268, 270 (top and bottom), 322 (top, middle and bottom), 334 (top left), 346, 354 (top), 355 (top), 374, 395 (bottom), 436 (bottom), 448,
supplied by Chrysalis Images;

Pages 20 (top and bottom), 21 (top), 22 (top and bottom), 23 (top), 23 (bottom), 24 (top and bottom), 25 (bottom), 26 (top and bottom), 28, 29 (top and bottom), 33 (bottom), 34, 35 (bottom left), 38 (middle), 42 (top), 45 (top), 53, 56 (top), 58 (bottom), 59, 61, 64 (bottom), 66 (top and bottom), 68 (bottom right), 69 (bottom), 70, 73 (top and bottom), 74 (bottom), 75 (top), 76, 77 (bottom), 79 (top, middle left and middle right and bottom), 80 (bottom), 81, 87 (top and bottom), 88 (top and bottom), 90 (top and bottom), 93 (top), 95, 99 (top), 103 (bottom), 104 (top and bottom), 108 (top and bottom), 111 (bottom left and bottom right), 113 (top), 115 (top and bottom), 116 (bottom), 117 (top), 118 (top and bottom), 120 (top and bottom), 121 (bottom), 122, 123 (top and bottom), 126, 127 (top), 131 (bottom), 132, 133 (top), 134 (bottom), 135 (bottom), 137 (top and bottom), 139, 140 (top), 141 (top), 144, 145 (top and bottom), 146, 147, 148, 149 (top), 150, 151, 155 (bottom), 156 (top and bottom), 157, 158, 159 (top and bottom), 163 (top), 164 (bottom), 165 (bottom), 166 (top left, top right and bottom), 167, 168 (top and bottom), 170 (bottom), 171 (top and bottom), 172 (top and bottom), 173 (top and bottom), 174, 175 (top and bottom), 176 (top), 177 (top), 178 (top), 179 (bottom), 181 (top right, top left and bottom), 182, 184, 187 (top), 192 (top), 193, 194, 195, 196 (top and bottom), 197 (top), 199, 200, 204 (top and bottom), 206, 207 (top), 208, 209, 210, 211, 212 (top and bottom), 214-215 (top), 215 (bottom), 219, 221 (top and bottom), 223 (top and bottom), 224, 225, 226, 227, 229, 230, 231, 233 (bottom right), 236 (top left), 238, 240, 241 (top and bottom), 244 (bottom), 245 (top and bottom), 249 (bottom), 251 (top), 252, 256, 257(top) 258 (bottom), 259 (bottom), 260 (bottom), 262 (top), 264, 265, 267 (bottom), 271 (top and bottom), 272 (top and bottom), 274 (bottom), 276 (top left and top right), 277 (top right), 279 (top and bottom), 282, 283,284, 288, 290, 291 (top), 294 (top and bottom), 296, 297 (top and bottom), 298 (top and bottom), 305 (top and bottom), 306 (top), 308, 309, 314, 316 (top and bottom), 319 (top and bottom), 320 (top and bottom), 321 (top), 323, 324 (top), 325 (top and bottom), 328, 329 (top, middle and bottom), 331 (top and bottom), 333 (top and bottom), 336 (top and bottom), 337 (top and bottom), 338 (top and bottom), 339, 340 (top and bottom), 342 (top and bottom), 343 (top and bottom), 344 (top left and top right), 345 (top and middle), 347 (top and bottom), 348 (top), 349 (top and bottom), 350 (top and bottom), 351 (top), 352 (top and bottom), 353 (top), 356 (top and bottom), 358 (top), 359 (top right), 360, 361 (top and bottom), 362, 364 (top and bottom), 366 (bottom), 367 (top), 371, 372 (top and bottom), 373, 375 (top), 376 (left), 377, 378 (left and right), 380 (top, middle and bottom), 381, 382 (top and bottom), 384, 385 (top), 386 (top and bottom), 387 (top), 389 (bottom), 391 (top and bottom), 393, 395 (top), 396 (top), 400, 401 (top), 402, 403 (top and bottom), 404 (top and bottom), 406, 407, 408 (top, middle and bottom), 409 (top and bottom), 411 (top and bottom), 412 (top and bottom), 414, 419 (top and bottom), 421 (top), 422 (top, middle and bottom), 423, 424, 425 (top), 426 (top), 427 (bottom), 428 (top), 429, 430, 432, 433 (top and bottom), 434, 442 (top and bottom), 443,
supplied by Military Archive and Research Services;

Pages 21 (bottom), 31 (bottom), 35 (middle), 36 (top), 46 (bottom), 49 (top), 49 (bottom), 50, 51 (top and bottom), 72 (bottom), 85 (top), 89 (bottom), 97 (bottom), 107 (bottom), 130 (top and bottom), 131 (top), 136 , 140 (bottom), 142, 152, 153, 160, 164 (top), 170 (top), 186 (bottom), 218, 222, 236 –237(bottom), 242, 244 (top), 246 (top), 247, 251 (bottom), 253 (bottom), 254, 255 (top right), 260 (top), 289 (top and bottom), 292, 301 (top right and bottom), 304, 307, 318, 334, 341, 358, 359 (top left), 365 (top and bottom), 385 (bottom), 397, 399, 413, 415, 420, 424 (bottom), 438 (top), 438 (bottom), 439, 440, 444(bottom),
supplied by © Bettmann/CORBIS

Pages 25 (top), 27 (top), 35 (bottom right), 37 (top), 38 (top and bottom), 39 (middle), 42 (bottom), 43 (top), 44 (top and bottom), 45 (bottom), 47 (top and bottom), 52 (top and bottom), 54 (top and bottom), 55, 56 (bottom), 60 (top and bottom), 63, 64 (top), 65 (top and bottom), 67 (top), 68 (top and bottom left), 69 (top), 72 (top), 74 (top), 75 (bottom), 77 (top), 78 (top and bottom), 80 (top left and top right), 82 (top), 83 (left and right), 84 (bottom), 85 (bottom), 86 (top left, top right and bottom), 89 (top), 91 (top and bottom), 92 (top and bottom), 93 (bottom), 94, 96 (bottom), 97 (top), 98, 99 (bottom), 100, 101 (top and bottom), 102 (top and bottom), 103 (top), 105 (top and bottom), 106, 107 (top), 109 (top and bottom), 110, 111 (top), 113 (bottom), 114 (top), 116 (top), 119 (top and bottom), 121 (top), 124 (top and bottom), 125, 128, 129 (top and bottom), 133 (bottom), 134 (top), 135 (top), 138 (top and bottom), 141 (bottom), 143, 149 (bottom), 154, 155 (top), 161, 163 (bottom), 169, 176 (bottom), 183 (top and bottom), 186 (top), 188 (top and bottom), 190 (top and bottom), 191,192 (bottom), 198 (bottom), 201, 202, 203, 213, 214 (bottom), 216 (top and bottom), 217 (top), 220, 228, 232 (bottom left), 234, 235, 236 –237 (top) 237 (top), 239, 243 (top and bottom), 250, 253, 255 (bottom), 257(bottom), 259 (top), 269 (top), 273 (top and bottom), 274 (top), 276 (bottom), 277 (top left), 278, 280, 281, 285 (top and bottom), 286, 287, 291 (bottom), 293, 295, 299 (top and bottom), 300, 302 (top and bottom), 303 (top and bottom), 306 (bottom), 307 (top), 310, 311 (top and bottom), 312, 313, 315, 317 (top, bottom left and bottom right), 321 (bottom), 324 (bottom), 326, 327, 330 (top, middle and bottom), 332, 334 (top right), 344 (bottom), 345 (bottom), 348 (bottom), 351 (bottom), 353 (bottom), 354 (bottom), 355 (bottom), 357, 363, 366 (top), 367 (bottom), 368 (top and bottom), 369 (top), 370 (top and bottom), 375 (bottom), 376 (right), 379, 387 (bottom), 388, 389 (top), 390, 392, 394, 398, 401 (bottom), 405, 410, 416 (top and bottom), 417, 418, 421, 425 (bottom), 426 (bottom), 427 (top), 431, 435, 436 (top), 437, 444 (top), 445, 446 (top and bottom),
supplied by Philip Gutzman;

Pages 30 (top and bottom), 31 (top), 32 (top), 35 (top), 37 bottom), 39 (top), 165 (top), 232-233 (main),
by © George Hall/CORBIS

Pages 32 (bottom), 39 (bottom), 58 (top), 248, 249, 269 (bottom),
supplied by © CORBIS

Pages 33 (top), 36 (middle), 301 (top right),
supplied by © Museum of Flight/CORBIS

Pages 36 (bottom), 369 (bottom),
supplied by © Leif Skoogfors/CORBIS

Pages 84 (top),
supplied by © Catherine Karnow/CORBIS

Pages 205, 234 (bottom), 255 (top right), 275,
supplied by © Wally McNamee/CORBIS

Pages 266 (bottom),
supplied by © Nik Wheeler/CORBIS

For jacket acknowledgements see page 4.